Frontiers in PRA and PLA: PRA & PLA in Applied Research

Dr. Amitava Mukherjee is currently the Senior Project Expert at the United Nations Economic & Social Commission for Asia and the Pacific (UNESCAP), Bangkok. Prior to which he was the Head of the United Nations Asian and Pacific Centre for Agricultural Engineering and Machinery, Beijing, China, and Regional Advisor on Poverty Reduction and Chief Techinal Advisor on Public Private Partnership, at UNESCAP, Bangkok. He has advised governments and/or its agencies and non-governmental organisations in Bangladesh, Cambodia, China, India, Indonesia, Lao PDR, Mongolia, Philippines, Pakistan, Timor-Leste, Sri Lanka and Central Asian countries (Azerbaijan, Kazakhstan, Kyrgyzstan, Tajikistan and Uzbekistan) and South Caucasian countries (Armenia and Georgia). Earlier he had worked extensively at the ground level in India and China and in the horn of Africa.

He has over 30 years of direct development experience especially in eliminating poverty and hunger; sustainable agriculture; community-based planning; participatory development. He has a large number of professional Reports, articles/papers and has over 35 books to his credit. He was the Team Leader of the Inter-divisional Task Force of UNESCAP which produced the *Sustainable Agriculture and Food Security in Asia and the Pacific, 2009* (Bangkok, United Nations) for the 65th Annual Commission Session of United Nations Economic & Social Commission for Asia and the Pacific.

Frontiers in PRA and PLA

PRA & PLA in Applied Research

Amitava Mukherjee

ACADEMIC FOUNDATION
NEW DELHI

First published in 2009
by

ACADEMIC FOUNDATION
4772-73 / 23 Bharat Ram Road, (23 Ansari Road),
Darya Ganj, New Delhi - 110 002 (India).
Phones : 23245001 / 02 / 03 / 04.
Fax : +91-11-23245005.
E-mail : books@academicfoundation.com
www. academicfoundation.com

Cataloging in Publication Data--DK
Courtesy: D.K. Agencies (P) Ltd. <docinfo@dkagencies.com>

Mukherjee, Amitava, 1950-
Frontiers in PRA and PLA : PRA & PLA in applied research/
Amitava Mukherjee.
p. cm.
With reference to India and Armenia.
Includes bibliographical references.
ISBN 13: 9788171887248
ISBN 10: 8171887244

1. Participatory rural appraisal--India. 2. Social learning--India. 3. Community development--India. 4. Participatory rural appraisal--Government policy--Armenia. I. Title. II. Title: Frontiers in participatory learning and action and participatory rural appraisal.

DDC 307.12120954 22

Typeset by Italics India, New Delhi.
Printed and bound in India.

To
Nanda Krairiksh
and
Yuenwah San

As a token of my unspoken
"Thank You"

Contents

List of Tables, Figures and Annexures..........9
Acknowledgments..........15
Introduction..........19

Part I

Organisation and Institutional Development

1. Application of PLA Methods in Human Resources Development: Assessing Knowledge and Attitude Gap of Rural Development Administrators in India..........27
2. Developing Mission, Vision and Values and Identity of a Development Organisation Through Participatory Learning and Action Methods..........55
3. Training Needs Assessment Through Participatory Methods..........73
4. Retreat of Ministers, Secretaries and Civil Society Actors on Capacity Building for Decentralised Administration..........143

Part II

Action Research

5. Inter-Sectoral Strategy: Need or Fad? An Investigation through Participatory Methods..........169
6. Micro-Level Hunger in Contemporary India: Perspectives of the Hungry..........195
7. Participatory Poverty Assessment..........239

8. Global Concerns: Loss in Biodiversity and its Impact on Agriculture Assessed Through Participatory Methods 273
9. Livelihoods, Eco-Tourism and Conflict in Sharing Natural Resources: The Case of Keoladeo Ghana National Park—An Analysis from the Stakeholders' Perspectives 309

Part III
Policy Analysis

10. Voices of the Poor for Review of Poverty Reduction Strategy Paper for Armenia 339
11. The Voice of the People: Enhanced Citizen Participation in Electoral Processes Through Participatory Learning and Action in Armenia 407
12. A Note on Concluding Remarks and Brief Policy Conclusions.......................................461

List of Tables, Figures and Annexures

Tables

1.1 Functions of DRDAs 32
1.2 Strengths, Weaknesses, Opportunities and Threats of DRDAs 36
1.3 Identification of 10 Best Problems by Scoring by Individual Voting 38
1.4 Ranking of the Best Problems of DRDAs 38
1.5 Pair-wise Ranking of 10 Best Problems 41
1.6 Ten Best Problems from Pair-wise Ranking 43
1.7 Solutions of Best Problems through Capacity Building: Group 1 44
1.8 Solutions of Best Problems through Capacity Building: Group 2 45
1.9 Matching Activities and Capacity Building 46
1.10 Knowledge, Skills and Attitudes Required at the District Level for Development Functionaries 50
4.1 Time Line Decentralisation and Local Governance in India 148
4.2 Remedial Actions: Leopard Group 154
4.3 Remedial Actions: Tiger Group 155
4.4 Remedial Actions: Lion Group 156
4.5 Remedial Actions: Cheetah Group 157
5.1 Styles of Development 170
5.2 Well Being: The Possibilities 175

5.3 Seasonal Food Calendar of Village Krishna Rakshit Chak, Medinipur, 1993 190

5.4 Seasonal Food Calendar of Village Krishna Rakshit Chak, 1995. 191

5.5 Food Calendar, 1998 of Village Krishna Rakshit Chak 192

5.6 West Bengal: Minimum Wages (As on 31/12/05) 193

6.1 Characteristics of Low, Middle and High Socio-Economic Status (SES) Village Tikri, Morya Basti 205

6.2A Food Calendar Prepared by the Women of Morya Hamlet, Tikri Village. 208

6.2B Seasonality Analysis by Women's Group in Bari Basti, Tikri Village 209

6.3 Monthly Income of Low SES Families in Morya Hamlet, Tikri. 210

6.4 Monthly Expenditure of Low SES Families in Morya Hamlet of Tikri 211

6.5 Food Calendar Prepared by the Women of Naipurwa Hamlet, Chandpur Village. 213

6.6 Food Calendar of Small and Marginal Farmers, Village Jangal Babban, Gorakhpur. 215

6.7 Scoring and Ranking of Causes of Hunger, Village Jangal Babban, Gorakhpur 216

6.8 Occupational Structure (Percentage of People in Each Category of Occupation) 217

6.9 Problem Ranking by Women in Two Hamlets of Sagarpur. 218

6.10 Historical Transect by Men's Group, Patayat Muhalla 218

6.11 Historical Transect by Men's Group in Hawelliwalle Muhalla 219

6.12 Historical Transect of Farming System and Crops (Male Group, Saini Muhalla) Uncha Gaon. 221

6.13 Seasonality Analysis of Agricultural Activities and Food Consumption (Men's Group Saini Muhalla). 224

6.14 Food Calendar by Men's Group of the Village, Netakundi 226

6.15 Seasonal Food Calendar of Women in the Village, Netakundi. 227

6.16 Seasonal Food Calendar of Men's Group in the Village, Dinasingh, Patna 230

6.17 Seasonal Food Calendar of Women's Group in the Village, Dinasingh, Patna 232

7.1 Social Groups in Village Gopalpur, Cooch Behar....258

7.2 Resources in Village Gopalpur, Cooch Behar....259

7.3 Problems in the Village and Suggested Solutions, Village Gopalpur, Cooch Behar....260

7.4 Institutions in Village Gopalpur, Cooch Behar 261

7.5 Schemes Implemented in Village Gopalpur, Cooch Behar....262

7.6 Problems (Women's Group) 263

7.7 History of Village Gopalpur, Cooch Behar....263

7.8 Seasonality of Poverty in Village Gopalpur, Cooch Behar....265

7.9 Decision Matrix: Men and Women....266

8.1 Decline in Diversity of Crops and Livestock in a Selection of Locations 278

8.2 Modernist Perspectives on Future Strategies for Agricultural Development....279

8.3 Comparison of Traditional and Modern Agriculture 280

8.4 Historical Transect of Main Crops and their Yield in Naipurwa Hamlet, Chandpur Village 282

8.5 Time Line: Historical Events as Recalled by the Senior Men of Naipurwa Hamlet of Chandpur Village....283

8.6 Time Line: Historical Events as Recalled by Men of Mahato Basti of Tikri Village 285

8.7 Historical Transect of Main Crops and their Yield (Maunds/Acre) in Tikri Village....286

8.8 Historical Transect by Men's Group in Aat Bisa, Khadhaoli....288

8.9 Changes in Agricultural Output by Men's Group, Aat Bisa, Khadaoli....289

8.10 Historical Transect of Farming System and Crops (Male Group, Saini Muhalla) Uncha Gaon....290

8.11 Historical Transect of Changes in Farm Produce (Male Group) Saini Muhalla, Uncha Gaon....291

8.12 Numbers of Rice Varieties and their Qualities Encountered in Three Non-irrigated Rice Regions of Myanmar............294
8.13 Use of Wild Plants for Food and Medicine by Farming Communities..........................295
8.14 Internal and External Resources for Agro-Ecosystems........297
8.15 Global Area of Transgenic Crop in 1996 and 1997 (By Trait)..............................298
8.16 Plot Number 1, Farmland in Panchgaon.........................301
8.17 Plot Number 2, Farmland by the Roadside in Panchgaon....302
8.18 Plot Number 3, Farmland by the Roadside in Delhi..........303
9.1 Time Line of Ghana Keoladeo National Park...................313
9.2 Historical Transect of Village Mallah, Bharatpur...............318
9.3 Problems Faced by Cycle-Rickshaw Pullers......................324
9.4 Comparative Table of Problems Faced by the Community and KNP..325
9.5 Schedule of Rates Charged by KNP (In Indian Rupees)......329
10.1 People's Concept of Poverty in Armenia.........................347

Figures

1.1 Force Field Analysis..51
1.2 Force Field Analysis by Group-1....................................53
1.3 Force Field Analysis by Group-2....................................53
4.1 The Empowerment Circle...147
4.2 Force Field Analysis by Leopard Group..........................150
4.3 Force Field Analysis by Cheetah Group..........................151
4.4 Forces Field Analysis by Tiger Group............................151
4.5 Force Field Analysis by Lion Group...............................152
4.6 Venn Diagramming by Group 1....................................158
4.7 Venn Diagramming by Group 2....................................159
4.8 Venn Diagramming by Group 3....................................160
4.9 Venn Diagramming by Group 4....................................161
5.1 Health Map, Krishna Rakshit Chak...............................182
5.2 Well-Being Grouping, Village Krishna Rakshit Chak..........185

5.3 Literacy Map, Krishna Rakshit Chak 186

7.1 Flow Diagram of Development Process in Ratherhat 270

7.2 Flow Diagram for Gopalpur 271

8.1 Polyculture (16th Century S.E. China) 306

8.2 Green Revolution, High-Tech Rice Manoculture (Contemporary Japan)..................................307

9.1 KNP: Bio-Diversity Map 315

9.2 The Cause and Effect Relationship of Closed Access Regime in KNP 322

Annexures

A-10.1 The Steps and Stages in People's Participation in PRSP Revision.......................................405

A-10.2 List of Villages and Communities Selected for Participatory Sessions 406

A-11.1 List of the Participatory Assessment Communities First Round: Pre-Election Period 427

A-11.2 List of the Participatory Assessment Communities Follow-up Round: Post-Election Period 428

A-11.3 Profile of the Selected Rural Communities 429

A-11.4 Motives and Reasons for Voting Identified by Participants of First Round and Follow-up Round Discussions by Community and Region 435

A-11.5 Reasons for Not Voting Identified by Participants of First Roundand Follow-up Round Discussions by Community and Region 441

A-11.6 Why Participation is Important (Reasons Identified by Participantsof Follow-up Round Discussions by Region and Community) 445

A-11.7 Factors Positively and Negatively Influencing Elections and Voters' Choices, by Region...................................448

A-11.8 Suggestions and Considerations for Improvement of Elections (Follow-up Round Results by Community and Region) 458

Acknowledgements

In the preparation of this work, I have received the support, help and assistance from a wide range of people. To all of them I am thankful. They are too numerous to be named here but to all of them many many thanks. I am especially grateful to the villagers in different countries who have given us in abundant measure their generosity, time and hospitality. However, I have to express my burden of debt to a few which are as follows.

Villagers and Community Members

India: Villagers of Chandpur, Varanasi (especially Rampati Devi, Dhandai Devi, Rita Devi); Villagers of Naipurwa Hamlet, Chandpur Village (especially Mohan Patel, Rajendra Prasad, Dhanilal, Shyamdayal Patel); Tikri, Varanasi, Uttar Pradesh (especially Indubala, Kamala, Urmila, Jali, Savita Devi, Rita Devi, Shanti Devi, Saraswati Devi, Urmila Devi, Shakuntala Devi, Dhanra Devi, Kumari Devi, Satti Devi, Sangeeta Devi, Phula Devi, Chnmna Devi, Bindo Devi, Chandrawati Devi, Sacho Devi, Rama Devi, Meena Devi, Arti Devi, Seema Devi, Prabha Devi, Kalawati and Amarnath Morya, Ashok Morya, Chatanki Morya and Panchan Morya) and villagers of Mahato Basti of Tikri Village, Varanasi, Uttar Pradesh (especially Pratap Narain, Hiralal, Radheysham, Ramesh Kumar Patel, Bahadur Patel, Munnalal, Ashok, Krishan); Villagers of Aat Bisa, Village Khadhaoli, Uttar Pradesh (especially Haji Karim Khan, Karim, Hamid, Jakir, Fajruddin, Rashi, Tyab Husain, Rati Khan, Yakub); Sagarpur, Uttar Pradesh (especially Suresh Gautam, Kamal, Nand Kishore Sharma, Shamevir, Puran Singh, Dhirendra, Shivchandi, Charanjit Lal, Ashok Gautam as also Harchandi, Mohan Singh, Balbir Singh, Ram Swaroop Singh, Rishal Singh, Nathu Ram, Dharamveer, Sant); Unchagaon, Faridabad, Haryana (especially Balbir, Bansi, Harish, Omprakash, Bhagawat, Krisen, Mahesh, Babloo); Krishna Rakshit Chak, Medinipur; Rickshaw Pullers and Guards of Ghana Keola Deo National Park, Bharatpur, Rajasthan; Villagers of Mallah Muhalla (especially Tulsi Ram Pandit, Vijan Pahelwan, Udai Singh Thakur, Nitra Pal Pahlwan, Bhim Singh (*Sarpanch*), Ratan Singh Rickshaw-*wallah* and others), Bharatpur, Rajasthan; Jangal Babban, Gorakhpur, (especially Vijay Kumar, Govind Yajav, Gania, Subhawati, Bhanwati, Gulabi, Kaushalya, Barfi and Indrani, Shubabati, Bhanmati, Indrabati, Gulabi, Gemia, Kaushalya, Girija, Brindabati and Barli, as also Jyotirmay Das), Neta Kundi, Orissa; Bolangir, Orissa; Dinasinghpatna, Orissa (especially Abhinayu Singh, Tajeshwar Singh, Sudhir Singh, Hemlata Singh, Sangita Singh, Brijbala Singh).

Indonesia: Villagers of Cinta Mekar, Western Java

Armenia: Berdashen, Chinar, Tavshut, Berd, Mets Mantash, Berdashen, Sarapat, Azatamut, Hoghmik, Khashtarak, Akhurik, Taghut, Sarakap, Verin, Artashat, Ttujur, Paruyr Sevak, Geghamasar, Urcadzor, Mets Masrik, Yeghegnavan, Aghpradzor, Mrgavan, Astghadzor, Nor Kyurin, Gegharkunik, Khnkoyan, Hajravank, Armanis, Tsovagyugh, Mghart, Khoznavar, Lorut, Bardzravan, Fioletovo, Lernadzor, Noramus, Nyuvadi, Arjut, Torunik, Fantan, Srashen, Geghashen, Tsghuk, Zovuni, Meghri, Charencavan, Zovasar, Buzhakan, Derek, Arzni, Ohanavan, Doghs, Nor Amanos, Metsamor, Nerkin, Sasnashen, Nalbandyan, Gyalto, Koghbavan, Tsaghkashen, Yeghegnut, Vernashen, Baghramyan, Artavan, Nor Nork, Zaritap, Davitashen, Rind, Hermon Araks, Jrarat, Lernagog, Lernamerdz, Dzoravank, Norashen, Tsaghkunk, Tsakkar, Aravus, Karahunj, Shaki, Vorotan, Achajur, Itsakar, Movsesgegh, Khachardzan, Dprevank, Sasunik, Hnaberd, Melikgyugh, Zedea, Gnishik/Mozrov, Vernashen, Artabuynk, Ani Avan, Jajur, Pokr Mantash, Lernut, Arevabuyr, Getapnya, Berdik, Urtsalanj, Lernapat, Sarahart, Halavar, Dzoragyugh, Arinj, Marmarik, Teghenik, Artavaz-Pyunik, Ajapnyak, Zeytun, Shengavit and Avan and the selected communities in Yerevan.

Individuals

Prof. Robert Chambers, Fellow, Institute of Development Studies, University of Sussex, UK; Dr. Ms. Neela Mukherjee, Chairperson, Development Tracks RTC, New Delhi; Dr. Jean Dreze, Social Activist, New Delhi; Prof. Kaushik Basu, C. Marks Professor of Economics, Cornell University, Ithaca, USA; Ms. Vasundhara Raje, Hon. Chief Minister of Rajasthan (then Hon. Minister of State for Personnel, Pensions and Public Grievances, Government of India); Mr. Digvijay Singh, Hon. Member of Parliament (then Hon. Minister of State for Railways, Government of India); Mr. Mani Shankar Aiyer, Hon. Minister for Panchayati Raj, Government of India (then Hon. Member of Parliament, Lok Sabha); Dr. Kim Hak-Su, Under Secretary General of United Nations and Executive Secretary, United Nations Economic and Social Commission for Asia and the Pacific, Bangkok; Mr. D. Bandopadhaya, IAS (Retd.), Former Secretary to Government of India, Ministry of Finance; Mr. S.R. Sankaran IAS (Retd.), Former Secretary to Government of India, Ministry of Rural Development; Mr. B.N. Yugandhar, Member, Planning Commission of India, New Delhi; Mr. K. Venugopal, Special Rapporteur, Human Rights Commission of India and Former Secretary to Prime Minister of India; Mr. Wajahat Habibullah IAS,

Chairman, Commission on Right to Information and the then Director, LBS National Academy of Administration, Mussoorie; Ms. Consuelo Vidal, United Nations Resident Representative and Resident Coordinator, UNDP, Yerevan; Mr. Govind Mohan, IAS; Sri Santosh Mathews, IAS; Mr. Pradeep Deb, IAS Advisor to the Executive Director, Asian Development Bank, Manila (then Joint Secretary, Ministry of Finance, Government of India); Mr. O.P. Agarwal, IAS (then Joint Secretary, Personnel, Pensions and Public Grievances, Government of India); Dr. George Mathews, Director, Institute of Social Studies, New Delhi; Dr. A.K. Singh, Professor of Economics, Giri Institute, Lucknow; Ms. Sudipta Ray, New Delhi; Dr. Meera Jayaswal, Head of the Department, Department of Psychology, Ranchi University, Ranchi; Dr. Ms. Batindri Jena, Bhubaneswar, India; Dr. Vandana Shiva, Director, Research Foundation for Science and Technology and Navdanya, New Delhi; Dr. Alak Narayan Sharma, Director, Insitute of Human Development, New Delhi; Mr. P. Raju, IAS, Principal Secretary, Rural Development, Government of Andhra Pradesh; Mr. Vijay Kumar, IAS, CEO, Society for Elimination of Rural Poverty Andhra Pradesh; Mr. Somesh Kumar, IAS, Regional Director South Asia , Aide et Action, Chennai (then District Magistrate, Anantapur); Dr. R.C. Chowdhury, Director General and Dr. R.R. Prasad, Professor and Head, Department of Social Development, National Institute of Rural Development, Hyderabad; Prof. K.V. Sundaram and Dr. R.P. Misra, New Delhi; Mr. A.R. Prusty, Director, CARE India and Mr. Depinder Kapoor, Director CARE India, New Delhi.

Mr. Suren Karayan, Deputy Minister, Ministry of Finance and Economy, Government of Armenia; Dr. Artsvik Minasyan, Deputy Minister, Ministry of Labour and Social Issues, Government of Armenia; Mr. Nerses Mkrtchyan, Head of International Economic Cooperation Department of Ministry of Foreign Affairs, Government of Armenia; Ms. Hranush Kharatyan, Head of Department of Ethnic Minorities and Religious Affairs, Office of the Prime Minister, Government of Armenia; Ms. Consuelo Vidal, UN Resident Coordinator and UNDP Resident Representative, Yerevan; Mr. Alexander Avanessov, Deputy Resident Representative, UNDP, Yerevan; Mr. Aghassi Mkrtchyan Country Economist, World Bank, Yerevan; Ms. Hripsime Manukyan, UNDP Office, Yerevan; Ms. Suzan Bagratuni, Perfromance Budget Project Coordinator, UNDP, Yerevan; Ms. Larisa Alaverdyan, Executive Director, Fund Against Violation of Law, Republic of Armenia and Former Ombud-person, Republic of Armenia; Varuzhan Hokanyan, Vice Chair, Center for Regional Development, Transparency International, Yerevan; Ms. Susanna Khalatyan, Advisor to the President, Union of Manufacturers and Businessmen of Armenia, Yerevan; Ms. Margarita Hakobyan, Programme Manager, Oxfam Great Britain, Yerevan; Mr. Arman V. Navasrdyan, Oxfam Great Britain, Yerevan; Mr. Hovhannes Azizyan, Project Local Coordinator, GTZ, German Technical Cooperation, Yerevan; Levon Barkhudaryan, Senior Advisor, DFID Armenain Regional Development

Programme, Yerevan; Mr. Melik Gasparyan, Senior Consultant, AVAG Solutions Ltd. and the animators who worked with me in Armenia, namely, Ms. Vahram Gharakhanyan, Ms. Hranush Tsaturyan, Ms. Arine Harutyunyan, Ms. Armine Avagyan, Ms. Hasmik Manucharyan, Vilen Hakobyan, Ms. Anahit Brutyan, Astghik Bakhalbashyan, Ms. Gayane Gevorgyan, Mr. Karen Badishyan, Ms.Karine Simonyan, Vehanush Hovhannisyan, Mr. Artur Nazaryan, Haik Grigoryan, Mr. Manuk Hakobyan, Marieta Mkhitaryan, Edgar Yengibaryan, Ms. Anna Zhamakochyan, Arusyak Gevorgyan, Mr. David Karmirshalyan, Ms. Gayane Asatryan, Mr. Gohar Nalbandyan, Ms. Hasmik Aslanyan, Ms. Meline Tovmasyan, Sargis Manukyan, Ms. Tamara Abrahamyan, Tigran Matosyan, Ms. Yelena Sahakyan, Ms. Anahit Aslanyan, Mr. Armen Minasyan, Mr. Davit Avetisyan, Ani Nazaryan.

Institutions

Government of India, New Delhi; Government of Andhra Pradesh, Hyderabad; United Nations Economic and Social Commission for Asia and the Pacific, Bangkok; Lal Bahadur Shastri National Academy of Administration, Mussoorie; Food and Agriculture Organisation, Rome; United Nations Development Programme, New Delhi; United Nations Development Programme, Yerevan, Armenia; United Nations Development Programme, Ulan Baatar, Mongolia; Society for Elimination of Rural Poverty, Andhra Pradesh; National Institute of Rural Development, Hyderabad; Planning Commission, Government of India, New Delhi; Institute of Human Development, New Delhi; Institute of Social Studies, New Delhi; Centre for Economic and Social Science, Hyderabad; Research Foundation for Science and Technology, Dehradun; Rajiv Gandhi Foundation, New Delhi.

The usual disclaimer applies. The errors both of commission and omission are solely mine.

Introduction

Go to the people,
Live with them, Serve them,
Respect them, Plan with them,
Start with what they know,
And build on what they have!

—Mass Educator, Jimmie Yen of China

This book is an exercise in exploration and synthesis.

Community participation or people's participation in the process of development has entered into development lexicon permanently in the past 50 years. New methods, tools and approaches to enlist community participation or people's participation, have been invented, improvised and developed by development practitioners and academic practitioners on an unprecedented scale, notably in the developing world. Variously called as Participatory Learning and Action (PLA), Participatory Rural Appraisal (PRA) or its earlier incarnation Rapid Rural Appraisal (RRA) Methods, these tools, methods and approaches have drawn from diverse disciplines such as geography, anthropology, sociology, management, economics and related disciplines.

These wider acceptances of participatory approaches to usher development has led to profound changes in the philosophy and conception of development and in the practice of the art of development. First, there is the transformation of the types of transfer. Power has shifted from the "Uppers"/"adults"[1] to the "children"/"lowers", especially the poor, marginalised, deprived, powerless and voiceless. Then the whole notion of "power over" people (a bureaucratic or colonial construct) has given way to "power over to" people, the power to change behaviour, the power to convene, facilitate, coach and support. All these "powers" are collectively the power to empower people. Not lord over them, not control them. Finally, in the ultimate analysis this transformation of power from "power over people" to "power to empower the people" has led to the alchemy of rekindling power within people and power to do things with people, which in turn has led to the now famous phrase: "They can do it", meaning people can analyse their situation, they can find solutions to their problems, they can plan, they can implement plans and programmes, they can monitor, they can evaluate and they can act. Reference is invited to Plate-1.

---

1 These in my terminology are the "Netas", "Babus", "Lalas", "Dadas" and "Jholas".

There have also been some positive changes in favour of the poor. Those in power (possession of information is also power!!) have started investing in developing relationships with people. There is an attempt to understand the context in which development is positioned, aid instruments are applied and investments in building relationships are made. And an interactive interrelationship between understanding the context, aid instruments and investing in relationships operates to make development more meaningful for those who need it most.

Granted the foregoing, it is not surprising that participatory tools, methods and approaches in development have been widely used in diagnosis and prognosis of both problems of development and poverty as well as of social issues. Though participatory methods, tools and approaches have received wider acceptance in both rural and urban planning, monitoring and evaluation, attempts have been made to use participatory tools and methods in research as a counter approach to traditional research and to influence larger macro-issues. Experiments have revealed that the participatory tools, methods and approaches admit of being grafted on to several other areas such as organisational development, capacity building and some areas of good governance. These experiments have been successful, but less well documented and even less applied. The literature that has grown around the "phenomenon of participation", as it were, is burgeoning.[2]

In this volume, an attempt has been made to present real life examples of the application of PLA and PRA methods to a wide range of circumstances and issues outlined above, and present, even if incomplete, scenarios of shifting "power over" people to "power over to" people, the power to change behaviour, the power to convene, facilitate, coach and support. The various chapters demonstrate that "They can do it". The intention here is to demonstrate that PLA and PRA methods are versatile and are capable of application in a wide array of fields.

Chapters 1 to 4 demonstrate the use of participatory methods in organisation and institutional development.

In Chapter 1, it is demonstrated that the application of PLA/PRA methods to diagnose the capability, poverty and ailments of rural development administrators in India, is efficient. The United Nations Development Fund in India was funding a Government of India project for building the capacity of development administrators in India who "play" with the social and economic lives of over 300 million people. As a prelude to implementing the project, it was decided to locate where the shoe pinches and what are the maladies.

2. There are several critics of these methods as well. Some even call these methods as mental metricism. Depending upon the which side of the fence one is sitting, the application of participatory methods and approaches to development has created a whole new range of possibilities and opened up new areas of work.

To do so a workshop of participants from different parts of India was held in Hyderabad, India. This chapter is the outcome of that exercise.

In Chapter 2, one can find the application of PLA/PRA methods in developing mission, vision, values and identity of an organisation. The Government was implementing a project in six districts, a Poverty Initiatives Project funded by the World Bank. Though this was a project implemented by the Government of Andhra Pradesh, funded by the World Bank, the arrangement was that the project will be implemented by an autonomous society called Society for Elimination of Rural Poverty (SERP). At the commencement of the functioning of the society, it was agreed that the society having personnel drawn from diverse disciplines and departments need to form a coherent group, if not a team. Towards that end, mission, vision, values and identity of SERP had to be decided upon. Chapter 2 is a documentation of how mission, vision, values and identity of SERP were developed using the PLA/PRA tools.

The SERP had several units in the six districts to implement the project at the cutting edge level. The personnel appointed at the district level were all new, some from the Government while others from NGOs or greenhorns from the market. There was a need to clarify the role of the different offices and officials so that there is clear understanding of the reporting relationships and division of work. In Chapter 3 how the use of PLA/PRA methods, in one of the districts, in role clarity exercise led to not only better understanding of the institutional arrangement for implementing development interventions at the ground level but also to better bonding and more cohesiveness in the team.

The Government of India in the Ministry of Personnel, Pensions and Public Grievances, New Delhi undertook in 2002 a series of measures to improve governance in the country. *Panchayats* (local level elected governments) are at the cutting edge of administration in many respects in all parts of the country. However, the standard of the *panchayats*' functioning was not uniform in all the states. For carrying out administrative reforms, it was deemed essential to locate the areas of reforms. Towards this end, a retreat of Ministers from the Government of India, Members of Parliament, Secretaries to Government of India, academicians, development experts and activities was held in July 2002. Chapter 4 provides the details of how PLA/PRA tools were ingeniously used to conduct the retreat, given that it was very difficult to elicit candid views on the subject without rancor and creating disaffection, from those in positions of power and authority.

Chapters 5 to 9, demonstrate the use of participatory methods in action research on the need to adopt an inter-sectoral approach to dealing with development issues, on the dimensions of hunger, participatory poverty assessment, biodiversity conservation and conflict over sharing of resources.

There has been a raging debate on whether poverty reduction requires an integrated approach or a sectoral approach. There are merits in both, and protagonists of each approach are strong in numbers and arguments. Chapter 5 investigates the issue of the appropriateness of an inter-sectoral strategy for reduction in poverty, both income and capability poverty, using PLA/PRA methods. Chapter 5 does not settle the issue but does indicate that within a set policy and political environment, an inter-sectoral approach may be a better of the two options.

The issue of hunger and deprivation in India has agitated many great minds and engaged numerous agencies including the UN,[3] often based on the perspectives of the experts (nutritionists, economist *et al.*). Chapter 6 tries to exhibit details often otherwise lost, through the application of PLA/PRA methods, the nuances of hunger from the perspective of those who matter most in the hunger debate: the hungry. These perspectives are from Haryana, Uttar Pradesh, Orissa and West Bengal (in India), each unique in its stage of economic development and political dispensation. Participatory approach to assessing hunger demonstrates that macro data on hunger masks important elements of hunger that a participatory approach brings out, including the fact that women often know better, than men, the real state of hunger at the household and community levels.

Chapter 7 demonstrates the use of participatory methods in analysis of poverty in planning for development. There have been many attempts to show how participatory methods have been used in planning at local level including a few by the author.[4] But this chapter has been included to show how women and men had used the participatory methods in West Bengal to identify the levels of poverty and isolate the causes thereof through the participatory methods and how it was an empowering process.

Chapters 8 and 9 are research on two outstanding issues of our time. Chapter 8 illustrates the use of PLA/PRA methods in understanding loss in biodiversity and its impact on agriculture in India. This chapter is an exercise in assimilation. It brings together and synthesises several pieces of work investigating different problems associated with loss of biodiversity in Indian agriculture, using PLA/PRA tools and brings out the rich tacit knowledge that people have in agricultural operations. The results have been impressive.

Chapter 9 relates to use of PLA/PRA tools to locate the sources of conflict over sharing of resources, notably water and forests, between the communities

3. The World Food Programme in India is one of the UN's major interventions in the arena of fighting poverty.
4. See his *Participatory Rural Appraisal: Application in Micro Level Planning*, (New Delhi: Vikas Publishing House) 1995 and "Participatory Rural Appraisal, Methods & Applications in Rural Planning" being *Essays in the Honour of Robert Chambers*, Second Edition, (New Delhi: Concept Publishing Co.) 2004.

living beside the famous Ghana Keoladeo Bird Sanctuary,[5] Bharatpur, Rajasthan, India and the flora and fauna (or more realistically conservation of flora and fauna) in the sanctuary. Many interesting features emerged as a part of the process including the fact that in the conservationists of flora and fauna in the sanctuary, the public sector, service providers and the private sector had all joined hands in different forms. But alas, the political process has prevailed and the flow of water to the sanctuary has since been reduced leading to an ecological disaster.

Chapters 10 and 11 demonstrate the use of participatory methods in review of policies at the macro level, both in the developmental and political sphere.

Chapter 10 demonstrates the use of PLA methods on a macro space. When the World Bank enjoined on Armenia in 2003, that it has to draw up its Poverty Reduction Strategy Paper (PRSP), a condition was added that the process should be a participatory approach. But participation as a concept was new to Armenia in 2003. There were numerous consultations held all over the country with civil society organisations, academia, international NGOs, donors and even the private sector through industry/trade associations. However, direct consultation with people was not possible. During the review of the PRSP in 2006, it was, therefore, decided that while wide ranging consultations with different stakeholders will be there, a track-II process of consultation with the general public on a sample basis throughout the country, was also to be initiated to run concurrently. This track-II consultation with the public was through the use of PLA methodology. Chapter 10 is a distilled output of the aforesaid track-II consultation. It shows how participatory methods have been used to review the Poverty Reduction Strategy Paper of Armenia.

In 2007, on the eve of Parliamentary Elections in Armenia, United Nations Development Programme (UNDP) initiated activities aimed at promoting citizen participation in the electoral processes under reference. Participatory sessions on election-related topics were organised and conducted with the representatives of various groups of the communities, particularly, representing all Marzes of Armenia, Yerevan city included. The participatory sessions were held in two rounds. The first round was held on the eve of the Parliamentary Elections (April-May 2007) in 44 communities of Armenia (4 communities in each Marz and Yerevan city). The participatory session of Phase 2 was held after the completion of the said Parliamentary Election (July-August 2007) in 50 per cent of communities covered by the first round—in 22 communities (2 communities in each Marz plus Yerevan city). Chapter 11 presents the summary of the outputs of the entire participatory process.

Chapter 12 is a note containing concluding remarks and brief policy conclusions.

---

5. It is an UNESCO World Heritage Site.

Part I

Organisation and Institutional Development

1

Application of PLA Methods in Human Resources Development

Assessing Knowledge and Attitude Gap of Rural Development Administrators in India

Give me the strength to make my love fruitful in service.
Give me the strength never to disown the poor or bend my knees before insolent might.
Give me the strength to raise my mind high above daily trifles!!!!

—Rabindranath Tagore

Introduction

Development and poverty alleviation have been major areas of concern of the governments, both at the central and state levels for the last 50 years. However, the results have not been encouraging. One of the reasons why development efforts by successive governments have not had the intended results has been the poor state of skills and knowledge the development administrators possess. There is a virtual unanimity amongst the observers of development administrators that the attitude and behaviour of development administrators is unhelpful in this regard. For example, the "we they syndrome", "we know they do not know", "poor are ignorant" etc., have been inimical to the people centred development processes initiated by the government.

Under the aegis of the UNDP a massive programme for "Capacity Building of the Rural Development functionaries", has been undertaken. To assess the knowledge and attitude gap, the NIRD organised a four-day meeting conducted in workshop-mode of development administrators, on "Capacity Building Rural Development Functionaries" from 28th November to 1st December 2000 at Hyderabad.

The objectives of the workshop were:

(a) To make an assessment of the areas of work and activities performed under each area of work by the DRDAs: *de jure* and *de facto*.

(b) To make an assessment of the areas of work and activities under each area of work performed by the project directors of DRDAs: *de jure* and *de facto*.

(c) To allow the PDs to make a self-assessment of the level and quality of the work and activities.

(d) To ascertain what are the causes that impede or hinder better performance of the PDs and the DRDAs.

(e) To ascertain which of these causes that impede or hinder better performance of the PDs and the DRDAs can be rectified through capacity building.
(f) To ascertain the nature and content of capacity building process that would best remove the causes that impede or hinder better performance of the PDs and the DRDAs.

The participants in the meeting were the selected project directors of the District Rural Development Authority (DRDAs) of the states, faculty members of the State Institute of Rural Development of Andhra Pradesh, Karnataka, Tamil Nadu, Maharashtra and Gujarat and development consultants, including the present writer.

Setting the Context

Day 1: Tuesday, 28.11.2000

The meeting began with a brief introduction to the UNDP Programme on capacity building. This was followed by introductions (participants and resource persons) and laying down the objectives of the workshop.

The workshop consultant started the process on a note that was followed throughout the workshop and ensured ownership and participation: "I am only a facilitator. This workshop is yours and the end product of this meeting will be your output. There will be a series of such meetings-cum-workshops (with participants drawn right from State Ministers of Rural Development, secretaries to the government and down to block development officers and village development officers). At each meeting, the outputs from all the earlier meeting-cum-workshops will be presented. The entire process will present both a worm's eye view and the bird's eye view on what should be the role of project directors of the DRDAs and what are the gaps that exist in their knowledge, skills and attitudes."

Following the introductions and setting of objectives, the participants were asked to make a 10-minute presentation on the functioning of DRDAs in the states that were represented by the participants.

Tamil Nadu

At the beginning of the year the DRDAs plan for the schemes funded by the centre—both for material management and financial management. The targets are determined and set. There is a strong Engineering Department in Tamil Nadu and, therefore, a lot of emphasis is placed on infrastructure development. The Collector is the convergence point of all activities. Besides, activities of the DRDAs in Tamil Nadu include:

- Monitoring and supervision of different agencies and Blocks.
- Generating reports/data that help the government in planning.

- Coordination with the line departments of the government at the district level.
- Linkages with the public, officials and people's representatives.
- Redressal of grievances of the public.
- Creating awareness about sanitation and drinking water amongst the rural masses.
- Mobilising other resources (from public, voluntary work/task etc.) for development.
- Meetings with line departments and others.
- Special schemes like the Model Township Scheme for scheduled castes (caste is an important issue in the state which prompted the Chief Minister to devise this scheme for providing housing to scheduled castes).
- Resources provided to MPs and MLAs for development are also routed through the DRDAs.
- Wasteland Development Programme and Drought Prone Area Programme (DPAP).

The Collector is the chairperson of the DRDA and the President of the *Zilla Parishad* (elected local level body primarily engaged in development functions) is the vice-chairperson.

Karnataka

In Karnataka since the Panchayati Raj Bodies are given a boost—the chief executive officer of the DRDA is the chairperson of the *Zilla Parishad*. The Collector is entrusted primarily with the revenue functions and maintenance of law and order.

Gujarat

The Collector is the CEO of the DRDA. The *Zilla Parishad* chairperson is a member of the committee. Some MLAs and *Sarpanches* (elected chief of village level elected body) are also on the committee. The DRDA mainly deals with development programmes sponsored by the Government of India. However, it also at times deals with special programmes of the State Government for example the Gokul Gram Yojna of the present government.

DRDAs have the services of chartered accountants for the audit of accounts. Social auditing of accounts is done by the *Gram Sabhas* at the *Panchayat* level.

Andhra Pradesh

In Andhra Pradesh the rural development work is handled by two commissionerates—the Commissionerate of Panchayati Raj and the Commisionerate of Rural Development. Implementation of all Central government funded development programmes is undertaken by the DRDAs.

The Self-Employment Programme and the National Services Assistance Schemes are managed by the DRDAs. The *Zilla Parishads* manage wage employment programmes. The programme officer, DPAP manages area development programmes. The District Manager, Housing Department, manages all housing programmes including the Indira Awas Yojana (IAY). However, the convergence of implementation of all these programmes takes place at the Collector's level, as he is the chairperson.

At the *Mandal* level (Block level) all programmes are implemented by the Block Development Officer or the Mandal Panchayat Development Officer.

In Andhra Pradesh, self help groups (SHGs) have an overwhelming importance in execution of development work. Hence, almost all the programmes are implemented through them and each government functionary has to concentrate on the capacity building of the SHGs and formation of new groups.

Functions of the DRDAs include:

- Undertaking survey for identifying people below the poverty line every five years.
- Project Proposal preparation for different development schemes.
- Formation of SHGs.
- Conducting trainings for the SHG members.
- Monitoring (and Evaluation) of implementation of development programmes.
- Development of critical infrastructure.
- Preparation of Credit Plans with the bankers.
- Coordination with the line departments.
- Arranging the DWACRA Bazaars (once in a year for 10 days).
- Building linkages with regulated and unregulated markets.

The Evolution of DRDAs

Following the brief introductory presentation on the functioning of DRDAs by the represented states, the participants were divided into two groups.

Task	Preparation of a timeline/historical transect of DRDAs.
Method	Discussion, use of the library, resource persons in NIRD or any other chosen by the participants.
Time	Since the task was given in the late evening hours, the participants were given the liberty of completing the task over night and presenting it the next morning.
Objective	To understand the history/growth of the DRDAs and the basic concept underlying their current operations.

Day 2: Wednesday, 29.11.2000

The day began with the participants asking extra time for finishing the task given in the previous evening. The presentations began at 10:30 a.m. Group 1 presented the timeline of the DRDAs growth to its present stage while Group 2 presented the shift in approaches to development and its reflection in the work of the DRDAs.

The participants had an interesting discussion on the special state government schemes that are being implemented by the DRDAs as well as the impact of the 73rd Constitutional Amendment (PRI Act). Some participants were of the view that the PRI Act has sounded the "death knell" of the DRDAs. Some saw it as a welcome happening as it would allow the DRDAs to "delegate" their too many responsibilities (it is important to note that the Panchayati Raj Institutions (PRIs) are viewed merely as implementers of the programmes). In Tamil Nadu a special scheme called Samthapuram is being implemented to promote communal and caste harmony. Under this scheme, model housing is provided for 100 families of mixed castes and religions. Poomalai scheme is currently the focus point of DRDAs in Tamil Nadu. This scheme is promoting rural products, and infrastructures for their promotions are being built at block, district and state level. In Tamil Nadu the current MLA fund allocation is Rs. 77 lakh.

In Andhra Pradesh, the Janamabhoomi movement occupies a lot of time of the DRDAs and its importance is emphasised. The emphasis is on *Gram Sabhas*, Micro level Plans and works. The SHGs have an over whelming importance and the Deepam Scheme (providing LPG stoves) is of great importance. The MP Local Area Development scheme in Andhra Pradesh has a realisation of only 77 per cent. This according to the participants is due to corruption and the fact that the MPs keep waiting for the "highest bidders" in terms of the cuts that they would receive.

One major point that was highlighted by all the participants repeatedly is the fact that "no evaluation of any DRDA implemented scheme has ever taken place." This therefore, is the single biggest reason for the failure of many schemes.

In 1999, some new guidelines for the restructuring of DRDAs were prepared but they are yet to be discussed or implemented.

After the presentations on the history of the DRDAs the facilitator gave another task to the two groups.

The Current State of the "Art"

Functions/Activities

Having understood the context in which the DRDAs were established and the basic philosophy guiding them, the participants were encouraged to look back on what they are currently engaged in. This was done through card sorting as under:

Task	List out all the activities done in the DRDAs.
Material	Flash cards, permanent markers.
Method	Discuss in the groups and write one activity on one flash card. Write all the activities that are done in the DRDAs.

The cards once written were sorted out through the Delphi method. The duplicate cards were clubbed and classified under functional heads. Once this was done the participants were asked to go through each list and add or delete anything that they thought was necessary. The result of the exercise was as follows:

Table 1.1

Functions of DRDAs

Accounts

- Maintenance of accounts
- Maintenance of various registers
- Reconciliation of accounts with implementing agencies, banks and treasury
- Sending the audit report to the government
- Computerisation of records
- Sending utilisation certificate
- Proposal for claiming of funds from Government of India and the state government
- Review of Audit reports
- Appointment of the auditor (once in 3 years)

Planning

- Collection of data and preparation of reports
- Assist block in preparation of the perspective plans
- Assist in annual credit plan preparation
- Preparation of the annual report
- Getting approval for the action plan from the *Zilla Parishad* and the governing body
- Getting and processing the proposals from implementing agencies
- Preparation of annual action plan of districts

Meetings

- Conducting various review meetings
- Conducting PRI meetings
- Conducting 20 point programme meetings
- Conducting district and block level SGSY meetings
- Conducting district level bankers meeting
- Arranging inaugural functions
- Arranging/conducting/governing/executive committee/sub-committee meetings
- Attending meetings of various government committees/video conferences
- Meetings with NGOs

contd....

...contd....

Capacity Building

- Identification of the training needs of *swarojgaries*
- Arranging training for field staff
- Conducting seminars/workshops
- Arranging training for SHGs
- Arranging camps and campaigns
- Plan and design training for SHGs
- Participating in seminars and workshops
- Arranging field visits and exposure visits

Office Administration

- Maintaining office discipline
- Writing confidential reports of office staff
- Conducting inquiries on public complaints
- Conducting departmental inquiries and disciplinary actions
- Sending periodical reports of various sections to the government
- Redressing public grievances
- Maintenance of various registers
- Computerisation

Monitoring

- Conducting annual physical verification of assets
- Field inspection of works
- Monitoring and supervision of works
- Interaction with beneficiaries
- Giving feedback to field functionaries
- Stock verification
- Monitoring through vigilance committees

Implementation

- Taking action on decisions of various committees
- According technical sanctions through technical wing (RD)
- Reallocation of resources to PRIs/implementing agencies
- Ensuring quality/timely execution
- Coordination of functions of DRDA/line departments/NGOs and other agencies
- Conducting interviews for selection of beneficiaries
- Promoting SHGs
- Giving administration sanctions for various schemes
- Conducting exhibitions at all levels
- Handing over of assets to local bodies
- Releasing funds to implementing agencies
- Arranging market linkages to SGSY products
- Monitoring the tender process
- Innovations in scheme works
- Enlisting people's participation
- Documentation

Evaluation

- Conducting evaluation studies for schemes
- Assisting evaluation teams
- Prevention of corruption

Once the classification was completed, the participants were given the following options:

- "If you want to change or add any card please do it freely.
- "Now take a post-it and after discussion write the number of times you do the listed activities (frequency of each activity).
- "If you don't do any activity write zero.
- "If you do an activity every day write continuous."

Once the exercise was complete, it was reviewed and analysed. The process was closed once the participants had agreed on the final output. A significant remark by a participant, endorsed without demur by all is worth your while to ponder over: Hark these words:

> There is nothing new and dynamic in the functions of DRDA in terms of development but the number of activities you do are far too many and of these the frequency of some activities is much too much, e.g. meetings and functions. We will undertake an appraisal of the functions and see what we do the most and what the least.
>
> In order to have a clearer picture of how the DRDAs utilise their "time" a scoring of the broad functions in terms of time spent on these functions, was attempted using the free scoring method.

An Appraisal of How DRDAs Utilise Their Time Using Free Scoring

Functions	*Scores*	*Rank*
Accounts	**************	5
Office Administration	*********************	3
Meetings	*******************	4
Capacity Building	*******	7
Planning	**********	6
Implementation	**	1
Monitoring	******************************	2
Evaluation	*	8

The results showed that the DRDAs spend most of their time on routine matters like maintenance of accounts, attending meetings, office administration and implementation of programmes, where implementation of programmes meant conveying sanctions, releasing funds, holding interviews, monitoring tender process, handing over assets to local bodies and so on. These, the participants felt, were routine functions, according to a well set pattern, requiring little application of the mind.

Innovations in scheme or development work, enlisting people's participation and documentation are only minor elements of what the DRDA functionaries do. Here, the participants remarked, documentation was implied for preparation of Completion Reports, Verification Certificates etc., and enlisting people's participation meant securing contribution from the poor people in cash or in the form of labour in development work. There was not much that the DRDAs do in terms of planning (in the true sense of the term), innovating new programmes or innovating new ways of implementing given programmes and evaluation of development projects implemented in the field. There was little emphasis on enlisting true people's participation in planning, implementing and evaluating development programmes.

SWOT

After the listing, classification and frequency determination of activities, it was important to know what were the strengths that DRDAs had which helped them to discharge the duties entrusted to their care and what were the weaknesses in their operations. The groups were asked to undertake the strength, weakness, opportunities and threats (SWOT) of DRDAs.

Task	SWOT of DRDAs
Material	Flash cards, markers
Method	Listing of the strengths, weaknesses, opportunities and threats by the two groups separately. Each strength, weakness, opportunity and threat was written down on one flash card. The cards from the two groups were then merged to make one set of cards. Laying down the cards on the floor. Classifying the strengths, weaknesses, opportunities and threats according to their similarities/likeness. Group discussion (2 groups). Clubbing of similar cards/eliminating duplicate cards. Re-grouping the cards under the four heads S, W, O & T.
Time	90 minutes

The process led to the generation of the output as in Table 1.2.

Once the SWOT was laid on the floor the participants entered into an animated discussion and soon realised that the weaknesses far outstripped the strengths. The weaknesses were related to institutional, structural and policy induced problems. The need to sort out the weaknesses was felt to be critical for any marked improvement in the development architecture at the district level in the country. But the participants felt that to deal with all the weaknesses will be too much and hence they felt that they needed to select the "10 best weaknesses".

To do so, the participants copied the weakness flash cards into two sets. These were then used for scoring and pair-wise ranking to arrive at the 10 best weaknesses or best problems. It was explained that currently in development the term "best problems" is used to emphasise that problems have solutions. And the term "good practices" is used in place of "best practice" as there cannot be any best practices (as different places and people have different realities). Something which may look best in situation "A" may not work in situation "B", such as the cases illustrated by the Sukhomajri experiment in

Haryana and the Chakriya Vikas Yojana in Daltanganj, Jharkhand: whatever worked wonders in Sukhomajri experiment failed in Daltanganj.

Table 1.2

Strengths, Weaknesses, Opportunities and Threats of DRDAs

Strengths

- Independent Society Status of the DRDAs
- Availability of financial resources
- DRDAs can do direct funding
- Autonomy in releasing funds and material management
- The Collector is the chairperson of the DRDA
- Scope available for developing the right attitude
- Coordination possible with the line departments dealing with development
- Computerisation
- Availability of data on people living below the Poverty Line
- Availability of various data
- Local bodies support to DRDAs
- Review and inspection done
- Conducting *Gram Sabhas* entrusted to it
- Explicit rules and guidelines are available

Opportunities

- Preparation of the Below Poverty Line List using transparent criteria
- Encouraging emergence of good local leadership
- Encouraging people's participation in all development programmes of the Government
- Greater use of Information Technology
- Increasing transparency in implementation
- Provide training to personnel
- Clarity roles between executive and policy makers
- Develop clear guidelines on transfer of staff
- Encouraging social audit
- Encouraging/nurturing NGOs
- Seeking alternative suppliers
- Evaluation of schemes
- Stock verification

Weaknesses

- Poor quality of services due to setting of targets
- Delay in sanctions, execution and release of funds
- Red tapism
- Lack of infrastructural facilities
- Dumping of more state programmes on the DRDAs
- Delayed release of funds from the state.
- Implementation of too many development schemes
- Diversion of funds by the state governments
- Lack of professionalism among the development functionaries.
- No field level functionaries

contd....

...contd....

- Absence of technical staff
- Lot of vacancies
- Understaffing in the DRDAs
- Frequent transfers of staff
- Too much political interference
- Lack of initiative and innovation
- Lack of training
- Poor quality of works
- Too many meetings
- Sycophancy towards superiors
- Rigidity in functioning
- Wrong reporting
- Lack of supervision
- Lack of transparency
- Corruption from within
- Reluctance to delegation

Threats

- Frequent change in government
- Frequent change in R&D policies
- Introduction of the MPLADS and MLALADS programmes
- Corruption
- Merging the DRDA with the *Zilla Parishad*
- Mushrooming growth of bogus NGOs
- Political interference in the preparation of the list of people living below Poverty Line
- Shortage of materials
- Political pressure

The pattern of scoring (by voting) generated the following picture:

Task	Scoring to arrive at 10 best problems.
Material	Flash cards (the weakness cards from SWOT exercise), seeds.
Method	All the 19 cards (weakness) were laid on the floor. Participants were asked to take 10 seeds each and place the seeds in front of the 10 problems which the relative participant thought was the best problem. Only one seed can be placed in front of one problem. Participants were free to abstain from placing any seed in front of any problem but they cannot place more than one seed against a particular problem.
Time	30 minutes

Table 1.3

Identification of 10 Best Problems by Scoring by Individual Voting

Problem	Score
Too much political interference	9
Poor quality of works	4
Delay in sanction, execution and release of funds	3
Lack of infrastructure	3
Dumping of state schemes	5
Diversion of funds by the state governments	0
Implementation of too many schemes	6
Reluctance in delegation	0
Lack of professionalism	7
Lack of training	7
Frequent transfers	3
Shortage of materials	1
Corruption from within	7
Lack of transparency	6
Lack of supervision	4
Wrong reporting	3
Too many meetings	9
Sycophancy towards superiors	4
Lack of initiative and innovation	9

Based on this the best problems were identified as in Table 1.4:

Table 1.4

Ranking of the Best Problems of DRDAs

Problems	Score	Rank
Too much political interference	9	1
Too many meetings	9	1
Lack of initiative and innovation	9	1
Lack of training	7	2
Lack of professionalism	7	2
Corruption from within	7	2
Lack of transparency	6	3
Implementation of too many schemes	6	3
Dumping of state schemes	4	4
Poor quality works	4	4
Sycophancy towards superiors	4	4
Delay in sanction, execution and release	3	5
Lack of infrastructure	3	5
Frequent transfers	3	5
Wrong reporting	3	5
Lack of infrastructure	3	5
	3	5
Shortage of materials	1	6
Diversion of development funds for other work	0	7
Reluctance to delegate	0	7

There are three interesting elements, which came out in the discussion that followed during the process of interviewing, scoring and ranking. First, that during scoring by voting there were participants who could not find more than 6 best problems. This was probed and it seemed that while some of the participants found six problems as being bad enough to leave the system stymied the DRDAs, others thought that it was necessary to have all the problems on the table and deal with them squarely. Second, there were at least two problems, which did not poll a single vote. This was explained by the participants in terms of the facts that these were problems when viewed in isolation but when viewed *vis-à-vis* the other problems, they slide down in the hierarchy of problems. These, the participants called the "secondary problems". Three, lack of training and lack of professionalism have been identified as being worthy of being given due focus.

It is interesting to note that during scoring, there were participants who could not find more than 6 best problems. Considerable discussions followed the ranking exercise in an attempt to come to a consensus about the 10 best problems. The consensus was that problems were in clusters and the participants were not able to further refine their view and separately rank the problems within the problem clusters. They nevertheless were keen that they should have no more than 10 problems to deal with. Both in order to triangulate the method and in order to see further if it was possible to make the ranking of the problems more discrete, resort was taken to pair-wise ranking.

The whole group was thus encouraged to get on with the pair-wise ranking.

Task	Pair-wise Ranking.
Material	Scored cards of 11 best problems from Table 1.4 above.
Method	Lay down the cards in the order of scoring (highest score first and thereafter in descending order). The cards should be laid down on X and Y axis. One person from the participants will facilitate while one will write the choice (of the group).
Time	90 minutes.

The pair-wise ranking shows that corruption is a major issue closely followed by too much political interference. Implementation of too many schemes and poor quality of works has the same rank and the two are closely linked as well (There is a cliché, "if you do too many things, the quality is bound to suffer").

The frequency of activities had shown that meetings occupy most of the time of DRDA officials and in pair-wise ranking it was ranked along with lack of training and transparency. It was noted that in spite of the numerous meetings, transparency was an issue, because the meetings mostly related to review of targets being set and achieved. Lack of professionalism and supervision were ranked sixth while initiative and innovation got two points and was ranked seventh. Last but not the least, sycophancy towards superiors has received zero points but it is still an issue, therefore, it has been ranked eight.

Seeking the Solutions

If indeed the problems enlisted in Table 1.6 were real problems, they need to be solved as well. And there has to be solutions of all the problems. The participants were, therefore, requested to explore ways and means to solve the problems in the light of the strengths, opportunities and threats that confront the DRDAs. Because the current mandate of the project was to seek solutions to problems of the DRDAs through capacity building exercises, the solutions it was clarified will have to focus on capacity building measures, though other elements can also be brought in. Since it was late in the evening, the participants decided that they would seek solutions after dinner sessions. The day, therefore, came to a close with the home task.

Task	Seek answers to the question: which of the best problems can be solved by capacity building?
Material	Chart papers, markers.
Time	Over night (presentations the next day).
Method	Work in the same 2 groups. Presentation the next morning.

Code	*Number of times Selected*	*Problem*	*Ranking*
A	20	Too much political interference	II
B	12	Too many meetings	IV
C	6	Lack of professionalism	VI
D	8	Lack of training	V
E	22	Corruption	I
F	16	Implementation of too many schemes	III
G	8	Lack of transparency	V
I	16	Poor quality works	III
J	6	Lack of supervision	VI
K	0	Sycophancy towards superiors	VIII
L	2	Lack of initiative and innovation	VII

Table 1.5

Pair-wise Ranking of 10 Best Problems

	Too much political interference	*Too many meetings*	*Lack of professionalism*	*Lack of training*	*Corruption*	*Implementation of too many schemes*	*Lack of transparency*	*Dumping of state schemes*	*Poor quality of works*	*Lack of supervision*	*Sycophancy towards superiors*	*Lack of initiative and innovation*
	A	B	C	D	E	F	G	H	I	J	K	L
Too much political interference A		A	A	A	E	A	A	A	A	A	A	A
Too many meetings B	A		B	B	E	B	B	H	I	B	B	B
Lack of professionalism C	A	B		D	E	F	G	H	I	C	C	C
Lack of training D	A	B	D		E	F	D	H	I	D	D	D
Corruption E	E	E	E	E		E	E	E	E	E	E	E
Implementation of too many schemes F	A	F	F	F	E		F	F	F	F	F	F
Lack of transparency G	A	B	G	G	E	F		H	I	G	G	G

contd...

...contd...

	Too much political interfer-ence	*Too many meetings*	*Lack of professi-onalism*	*Lack of training*	*Corru-ption*	*Implemen-tation of too many schemes*	*Lack of transpa-rency*	*Dumping of state schemes*	*Poor quality of works*	*Lack of super-vision*	*Sycoph-ancy towards superiors*	*Lack of invitative and innova-tion*
	A	B	C	D	E	F	G	H	I	J	K	L
Dumping of state schemes H	A	H	H	H	E	F	H		H	H	H	H
Poor quality of works I	A	I	I	I	E	I	I	I		I	I	I
Lack of supervision J	A	B	C	D	E	F	J	H	J		J	J
Sycophancy towards superiors K	A	B	C	D	E	F	G	H	I	J		L
Lack of initiative and innovation L	A	B	C	D	E	F	G	H	I	J	L	

Thus, if we reorganise the ranking, the situation looks like the following:

Table 1.6

Ten Best Problems from Pair-wise Ranking

Problems (read Weakness)	*Rank*
Corruption	I
Too much political interference	II
Implementation of too many schemes	III
Too many meetings	IV
Lack of training	V
Lack of transparency	V
Lack of supervision	VI
Lack of initiative and innovation	VII
Sycophancy towards superiors	VIII

The participants arrived at a definition of capacity building through facilitation by Dr. Amitava Mukherjee. Capacity building was defined as:

- Changes in attitudes and behaviour.
- Create ability to identify strengths and weaknesses.
- Acquisition of skills.
- Enhancement of knowledge.
- Establishment of systems to utilise resources.
- Setting up systems and procedures (limits of authority).
- Preparing usable manuals and procedures.

Day 3: Thursday, 30.11.2000

The two groups were ready with charts and presentation on how the best problems can be solved through capacity building. Though both were rich in content, the presentations revealed that there were some solutions to the problems identified by them. They were, however, not very sure if the results as expected from capacity building will ensue for three reasons. Firstly, capacity building is not taken very seriously by the powers that be. It is considered important but the priority accorded to capacity building, as an element in development administration, is significantly low in the order of priorities. Secondly, capacity building will not yield in enhancement of efficiency up to the warranted level, unless an enabling environment is created where the trainees are disappointed when they attempt to apply much of what they want to learn. Finally, there is little use in imparting training to pockets of functionaries. Islands of excellence often evaporate in real life situations. There is a need to build capacity both in quantitative and qualitative terms.

The presentation made by Group-1 is as in Table 1.7.

After the presentation a discussion followed. Clarifications were sought. Some of the major points from the discussions on presentations were:

- "Corruption can be reduced, it cannot be eliminated. It is an international phenomenon."
- "In Tamil Nadu there is a government order that no officer should be transferred before 3 years but it is flouted all the time."
- "Seeking solutions to the best problems in terms of capacity building was only a partial solution to a much larger problem. There was a need to build capacity of development functionaries in all aspects of development work."

The last issue led to considerable debate and the ultimate consensus was that since here was a chance to put forth their views, the participants wanted to emphasise and re-emphasise that capacity building should be across the board and across the functions. In order to do so the consensus was that the meeting-cum-workshop should indicate the capacity building need for each of the activities carried out by the development officials at the district levels, the focus being on the areas mentioned in Table 1.7 and Table 1.8.

Table 1.7

Solutions of Best Problems through Capacity Building: Group 1

Problem-1	Corruption	*Solutions:* Review of administration procedures and rules Clear cut policy on transfers Transparency and social audit Code of ethics in the organisations
Problem-2	Political interference	*Solutions:* Role clarity Training of non-officials
Problem-3	Too many schemes	*Solutions:* Review of all RD schemes Strategic planning
Problem-4	Poor quality of work	*Solutions:* Performance appraisal system Modify knowledge, skills and attitudes
Problem-5	Dumping of more state schemes	*Solutions:* Sufficient manpower to DRDA
Problem-6	Too many meetings	*Solutions:* Modernise office administration system Data based management system Improve the MIS
Problem-7	Lack of transparency	*Solutions:* Preparation of departmental manuals People's participation Social audit Citizen charter
Problem-8	Lack of training	*Solutions:* Knowledge, skills, attitudes
Problem-9	Lack of professionalism and lack of supervision	*Solutions:* Knowledge, skills, attitudes
Problem-10	Innovations and initiative	*Solutions:* Change of attitudes Knowledge and skills update

Once the presentation by Group-1 was completed, the participants decided to have the presentation by Group-2 and then have a discussion and question answer session. Presentation by Group-2 was as in Table 1.8.

The two Groups then jotted all the major functions of the development officials at the district levels and matched the same with capacity building measures. Since the number of activities of DRDAs, as covered in Table 1.1, was very large, the broad topics were divided amongst the two groups. While Group-1 dealt with accounts, planning and capacity building, Group-2 dealt with implementation, monitoring and evaluation. The results were as in Table 1.9.

Table 1.8

Solutions of Best Problems through Capacity Building: Group 2

Weaknesses	*Capacity building*
Corruption	Change in attitude and behaviour Systems and procedures Manuals and written procedures
Political interference	Change in attitude and behaviour Systems and procedures Manuals and written procedures
Too many schemes	System to utilise resource skills
Poor quality works	Change in attitude and behaviour Systems and procedures Manuals and written procedures Skills Knowledge
Dumping of state schemes	Skills System to utilise resources
Too many meetings	Skills Knowledge Ability to identify strength and weaknesses Systems and procedures
Lack of transparency	Change in attitude and behaviour Systems and procedures
Lack of training	Skills Knowledge Training
Lack of professionalism and training	Skills Systems and procedures Knowledge Ability to identify strengths and weaknesses Training
Lack of initiative and innovation	Change in attitude and behaviour Knowledge Training

Table 1.9

Matching Activities and Capacity Building

Group-1	
	Accounts
Maintenance of accounts	Financial code, T.C., A/cs. and PWD code. Book keeping (knowledge). A/cs system in the government (knowledge). Maintenance of various accounts and registers including cash book, preparation of monthly/ annual accounts (skills)
Reconciliation	Reconciliation of accounts with banks, treasuries and departments, arithmetic accuracy (skills)
Sending audit report	Details about the pro formas, periodicity and procedures (knowledge)
Review of audit report	Recognise the importance of review (attitude)
Settlement of audit objections	Drafting skills (skills)
Appointment of auditors	-
Sending utilisation certificates	Knowledge of pro formas
Proposals for claiming funds	Knowledge of pro formas
Preparation/Passing bills	Check lists (knowledge) Timely passing of bills and tightening the office administration (attitude)
Computerisation of records	Advantages of using computers and various computer programmes (knowledge) DOS, Windows, sending e-mails, internet, running the package programmes, updating the DBM towards better MIS, planning, monitoring and evaluation (skills)
	Planning
Identification of Below Poverty Line family	Concept of poverty, measurement of poverty, survey methods and procedures (knowledge). Collection of data, PRA methods, training to enumerators (skills). Positive approach towards below poverty line families (attitude)
Skill survey	Concept, assessment, data collection, PRA methods (knowledge and skills)
Assessment of requirements	Identification and prioritisation of needs (skills)
Assisting in ACP	District profile (knowledge). Coordination (skills)
Assisting the blocks in preparing perspective plans	Preparation of plans (knowledge)
Preparation of AAPs of districts	Techniques for preparation of plans
Getting proposals from implementing agencies/MLAs and MPs	Coordination skills
Getting approval of AAP by *Zilla Parishad*/BP	Coordination skills
Collection of data/generation of reports	Compilation and consolidation of reports (skills)
Preparation of annual reports	Compilation and consolidation of reports (skills)
People's participation and planning	Various tools and techniques to involve people (skills) Realise importance of participatory planning (attitude)

contd...

...contd...

Material management	Various material management systems (knowledge) Forecasting the requirements (skills). Identification of proper supply system (skills). Material control/periodical stock verification (skills)
Preparation of project report	Identification of financial, physical and human resources (knowledge) Project appraisal (skills)
	Capacity Building
Identification of training needs of *swarojgaries*/SHGs	Concept of SHGs, identification of problems (knowledge) Analysis of the problems (skill) Commitment to strengthen the groups (attitude)
Plan and design the trainings	About infrastructure, budget preparation, syllabus preparation, training materials (knowledge) Preparation of training modules/manuals (skills)
Arranging training of SHGs	Understanding the design (knowledge) Implement training programme by adopting various training methods/techniques (skill)
Arranging training for the field staff	Understanding the design (knowledge) Implement training programme by adopting various training methods/techniques (skill)
Conducting exposure visits	Understanding the design (knowledge) Implement training programme by adopting various training methods/techniques (skill)
Conducting seminars/workshops/ orientation programmes	Coordination skill
Arranging camps/campaigns	Campaign strategies (skills) Coordination skills
Participating in seminars and workshops	Willingness (attitude)

Group-2

	Implementation
Technical Skills	Time management and computers (skills) Guidelines, material, schedule rates, purpose (knowledge)
Resources	Priority, equity (knowledge and skills) Need assessment (knowledge) Availability (knowledge) Guidelines (knowledge, manuals and procedures)
Quality	Standardisation (skills and procedures) Supervision (skills) Technical know how (knowledge) Equipments, execution and testing (skills and procedures)
Timely Execution	Office management (A.S., T.S., Tender) (skills) Funds—availability and release (skills and procedures)
Coordination	Inter-personal relationships (skills, attitudes and behaviour); Management techniques (skills, attitudes and behaviour); Commitment (attitudes and behaviour)
Committee Decisions	Review and implementation (skills and procedures)

contd...

...contd...

Tender	Guidelines, conditions (knowledge) Time factor (skills and procedures) Transparency (attitudes, skills, behaviour and procedures) Procedures (skills and procedures)
Innovations	Initiative, Improvement (skills and knowledge) Needs assessment (knowledge) Technology, materials (knowledge) Exposure (attitudes and behaviour)
Release of funds	Time factor (skills and procedures) Availability (knowledge) Procedures (skills and procedures)
Selection by interview	Guidelines and procedures
Self Help Groups	Motivation (attitudes and behaviour) Homogeneity (skills, knowledge) Viability and feasibility (knowledge) Forward and backward linkages (systems to utilise resources) Technology, skill, value addition (knowledge and skills)
Exhibitions	Identification of place, time and products (knowledge) Coordination among agencies (skills) Entertainment (attitudes and behaviour) Competition, awards (attitudes and behaviour)
Administrative sanction	Guidelines (knowledge) Appropriate proposals, scrutiny (manual and procedures) Availability of resources (knowledge) Time factor (skills and procedures)
Documentation of schemes	Computerisation (skills) Photography of works before and after (skills and procedures)
People's participation	Transparency, motivation and popularisation (attitudes and behaviour)
Market linkages	Survey, tie ups (knowledge and skills) Infrastructure (knowledge, skills and works) Needs/trends (knowledge) Cost factors (knowledge)
Handing over assets	Procedures (skills and procedures) Purpose and utilisation (systems to utilise resources)
	Monitoring
Physical verification of assets	Data, registers (skills and procedures) Quality (systems to utilise resources)
Field inspection of works	Technical knowledge (knowledge) Plan (skills) Interaction with public (knowledge and skills) Quality (systems to utilise resources)
Feedback to field functionaries	Communication (skills, target, time frame) Procedures and specification (skills and procedures) Inspection reports (skills and procedures) Public opinion, press (ability to identify strengths and weaknesses)

contd...

...contd...

Monitoring and supervision	Reviews (skills and procedures) Delegation (attitudes and behaviours) Transparency (attitudes and behaviour) Quality (systems to utilise resources) Use of information technology (skills and knowledge)
Interaction with beneficiaries	Understanding problems and needs (skills, attitudes and behaviours) Inter-personal relationships (skills) Use of media (ability to identify strengths and weaknesses)
Stock verification	Surprise checks (skills) Computerisation (skills) Field verification visits Registers (skills) Periodical reports (skills and procedures)
Monitoring through vigilance committees	Regular meetings (skills and procedures) Transparency (attitudes and behaviours) Appraisal (skills) Follow-up actions (ability to identify strengths and weaknesses)
	Evaluation
Assisting evaluation teams	Purpose (knowledge) Data (knowledge)
Conducting evaluation studies	Collection of data (skills) Analysis of data (skills and knowledge) Inference (ability to identify strengths and weaknesses)

A presentation followed the results and some points that emerged from discussions were:

- "Our group feels that corruption is a systemic problem therefore, we are concentrating on policies and procedures."
- "There should be some morality in working in the government."
- "Role clarity of administrators and politicians does not exist."

However, capacity building was a broad term as defined by the participants themselves. It was necessary to know from the perspective of the project, what were the skills, knowledge and attitude required to be imparted while building the capacity of the development officials. Against the identified capacity building needs *vis-à-vis* the activities, shown in Table 1.9, the participants were asked to identify the knowledge, skills and attitudes that, in their view were required, for the personnel engaged in development at the district level. These are shown in Table 1.10.

Table 1.10

Knowledge, Skills and Attitudes Required at the District Level for Development Functionaries

Knowledge Required	*Skills Required*	*Attitudes Required*
	Group-1	
1. Financial accounts, treasury, PWD codes 2. Proper government accounting systems 3. Checklists for preparation and passing of various bills 4. Various computer training programmes 5. Various material management systems 6. Identification of financial/ physical/human resources for preparation of project reports	1. Drafting skills to settle audit objections 2. DOS, Windows, e-mail, internet, running package programmes, updating data base management system for better MIS 3. PRA methods 4. Identification and prioritisation of needs 5. Techniques for preparation of AAPs 6. Coordination skills 7. Various tools and techniques to involve people 8. Preparation of training modules	1. Timely reconciliation of accounts 2. Recognising the importance of audit reports 3. Timely passing of bills
	Group-2	
Upgradation of technology Adequate modern equipment And technique Library E-mail facilities Video conferencing	Time management Material management Managing politicians Financial management Office management Information technology Personnel management Evaluation studies	Transparency Delegation Commitment Involvement Participation Initiative Innovation Responsive administration

Field Force Analysis

Once the activities were matched with the capacity building needs, the exercise of dealing with elements within the development sector was treated as complete. The final step was to know what were the forces external to the development sector which impinged upon the developmental activities of the state. To do so, the two groups were asked to under attempt a Field Force Analysis first used by Kurt Lewin. The Field Force Analysis was explained as under:

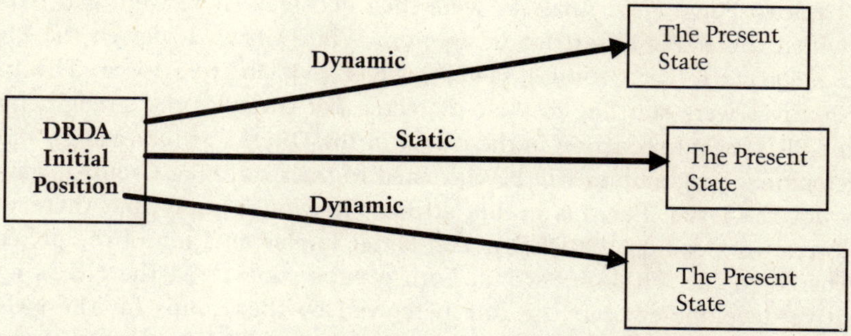

In any given situation there will be positive forces and negative forces operating on the economy or any system in society for that matter. The negative forces exert negative pressure and the positive forces exert positive pressure on the economy or any system in society on the economy or any system in society. These resultant effects of these forces will push towards change (for better or worse). The system is depicted in Figure 1.1.

Figure 1.1

Force Field Analysis

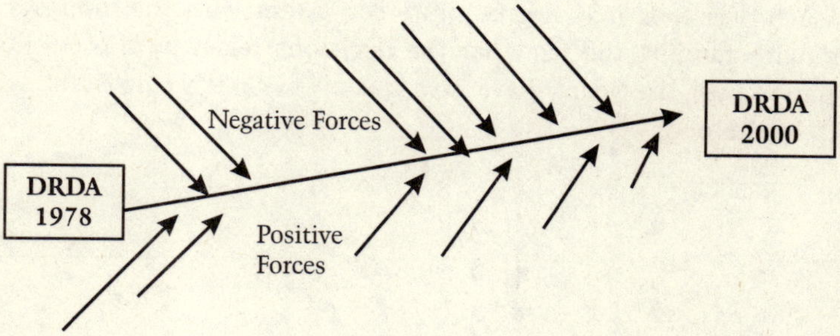

The DRDAs are no exception to this rule. Since their inception to this date how do the participants think the DRDAs have progressed and have they become better or worse or remained the same? What were the forces that operated upon the DRDAs?

The participants were unanimous in the decision that the DRDAs have grown over the years and they have changed for the better. If this is the case then perhaps it shows that the positive forces are stronger than the negative forces.

The participants were asked to divide into two groups and do the Force Field Analysis of the forces operating on the DRDAs. The time given for the exercise was one hour. The outputs were as in Figures 1.2 and 1.3.

The two Force Field Analyses were then debated. There were two issues on which there was difference of opinion. While Group-1 viewed the PRIs as a negative force, Group-2 saw the PRIs as a positive force. The two perspectives were startling in their character. For Group-1, the strengthening of the PRIs meant reduction in the power of the DRDAs as increasingly more development programmes will be entrusted to their care. For Group-2, power was not the issue. For this group, strong PRI would imply that there will be lower workload on the DRDAs and better implementation of the projects entrusted to the DRDAs. Second, both groups considered the NGOs as a positive development but the role perceived by the groups for the NGOs was very different. For Group-1, a larger number of NGOs meant that there will be more models of development that will be generated, for Group-2, more NGOs will help in organising the poor so that it would be easier to implement the programmes especially so where participation by contribution is enjoined as mandatory.

For both the groups, the current trends of privatisation and globalisation were wrong because, the underlying philosophy of these phenomena is survival of the fittest. The poor people being not the fittest, may be withered away in course of time. It is also a fact that decisions taken under a system of sweeping privatisation and globalisation are necessarily business decisions. Hence, such decisions may not be quite consistent with the interests of the poor, notwithstanding the fact that the decisions taken by the development functionaries over the years, have also not always been consistent with the interests of the poor.

Figure 1.2

Force Field Analysis by Group-1

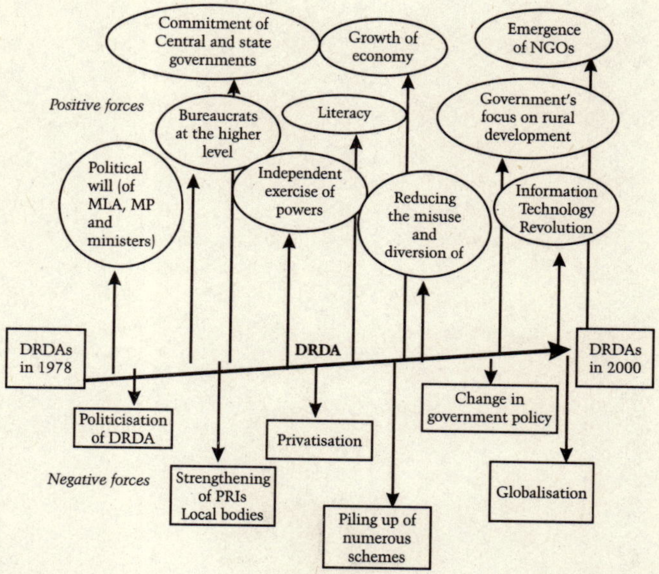

Figure 1.3

Force Field Analysis by Group-2

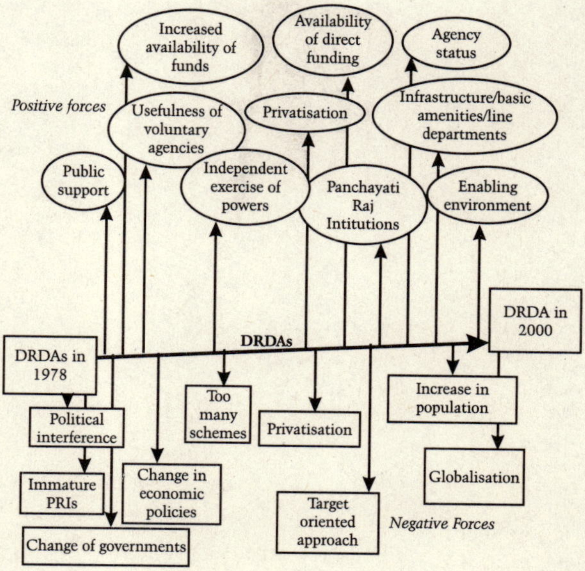

2

Developing Mission, Vision and Values and Identity of a Development Organisation through Participatory Learning and Action Methods

Let your crown be of humility, your freedom, the freedom of the soul.
Build God's throne daily upon the ample bareness of your poverty!!
And remember, huge is not great, pride is not everlasting.

—*Rabindranath Tagore*

Introduction

The Andhra Pradesh District Poverty Initiatives Project (DPIP) funded by the World Bank, covering six districts of Srikakulum, Vizianagaram, Adilabad, Mahabubnagar, Anantapur and Chittoor has been launched by the Government of Andhra Pradesh on 16th June 2000, under the name and style of VELUGU. The project was being implemented through the Society for Elimination of Rural Poverty (SERP), with the Chief Minister of Andhra Pradesh as the chairperson.

The goal of the DPIP is rural poverty reduction.

The main objective of the DPI project was to provide the rural poor (read poorest of the poor) and marginalised groups like the Dalits, women and people who are "differently abled", to meet their own social and economic development objectives.

Towards achieving the main objective, the project had four secondary objectives:

(i) creating self-managed grassroots institutions;
(ii) building the capacity of the established local institutions, especially PRIs and GOAP line departments, to operate in a more inclusive manner in addressing the needs of the poor;
(iii) supporting investments in sub-projects proposed by grassroots institutions of the poor to accelerate their entry and expand their involvement in social and economic activities (which term connotes investment in community owned assets and infrastructure and establishing linkages); and
(iv) improving access to education for girl children to reduce the incidence of child labour among the poor.

The structure of the implementing agency (SERP) consisted of the State Project Monitoring Unit (SPMU) and the District Project Monitoring Units

(DPMU), one in each of the six districts covered by the project. Each of the DPMUs will have several Mandal Community Support Cells.

The SPMU was headed by the CEO and has two State coordinators. The six SPMUs were headed by project directors. These functionaries constituted the key staff of the SERP. Since the incumbents had different backgrounds and different understanding of development and orientation to the DPIP, it was necessary to mould the incumbents into a team. As a first step towards that direction, it was felt important to develop a common vision, mission, core values and identity for SERP in the implementation of the DPIP. The development of the vision, mission, core values and identity for SERP, it seemed, was best done by the key functionaries of SERP themselves as described above. A two-day workshop was, therefore, organised to help the CEO, State coordinator and the PDs of the DPMUs, to develop the vision, mission, core values and identity for SERP in implementing the DPIP in Andhra Pradesh.

The Process: Introductory Session

The workshop began by an introduction to the workshop by CEO. He outlined the objectives and rationale for the workshop.

Since all of the participants had joined their posts a few days back, and since all of them had different perspectives and perceptions about DPIP, the CEO explained, they need to have a common vision, mission, core values and identity, in order to implement the project efficiently. These vision, mission, core values and identity could have been established and celebrated through a government order but it was decided not to adopt such a course because the ownership of such vision, mission, core values and identity, will rarely be beyond reproach and never internalised by those who mattered. Instead, in keeping with the participatory tenor of project implementation envisioned in the Project Appraisal Document (PAD), a participatory course was adopted where each of the key functionaries will fully and without fear or favour, contribute towards developing the vision, mission, core values and identity for DPIP.

The CEO, therefore, urged upon the participants to make their contribution to the fullest extent possible to develop the vision, mission, core values and identity for SERP in implementing DPIP.

Details of the Structure

An outline of the two days of the workshop was presented and the process to be followed was agreed upon.

At the outset, it was clarified that in this workshop, the attempt will be to develop vision, mission, core values and identity for SERP in implementing the DPIP. This workshop will not be attempting at developing vision, mission, core values and identity for SERP generally. This distinction was important and must inform the deliberations of the workshop at all times. It was also made clear that the workshop was a workshop of the functionaries themselves and that the facilitator was only facilitating the process, so that meaningful results could be obtained at the end of the two days, which will be owned and shared by all.

Rules of the Workshop

The participants agreed to enumerate a set of rules for the workshop for its orderly conduct and to ensure that all of the participants made best use of their time. The following rules were agreed upon:

Chart I

• Rules	• Punctuality	• Participation
• Speak our minds	• All participate as equals	• To speak one at a time
• Embrace errors	• Disagree	• Have fun

These rules were written down on a flip chart and prominently displayed in the workshop hall.

Two Groups were formed for working in the next session by count of numbers in cyclical order. Care was taken to ensure that the CEO and the State Project Coordinator were placed in different groups.

SWOT Analysis of DPIP

The first exercise was a SWOT analysis. It was explained by the facilitator that in order to develop vision, mission and core values, participants must have a full or fairly full understanding of the intricacies of the DPIP. Hence, recourse was taken to SWOT analysis of DPIP as articulated in the Project Appraisal Document (PAD). The participants broke into the two groups agreed to in the first session. The group with Mr. K. Raju (KR) was known as Group-1 and the group with Mr. Vijay Kumar (VK) was Group-2.

Each participant was given a copy of PAD and was requested to carry out a SWOT analysis of the project in their respective groups. They were provided with post-card sized cards on which to write the strengths, weakness, opportunities and threats. It was agreed that only one strength, one weakness etc., will be written on one card for better participation later. The participants agreed to assemble back in the plenary by 1.00 p.m.

The two groups followed different methods in their group work. In Group-1, KR took over the leadership, and pointed out to the group those portions of the PAD which were relevant and decided to concentrate on these portions alone. One member of the group was chosen to read out the relevant portions to the whole group. They then debated the strengths, weaknesses, opportunities and threats. Through a consensus building process they arrived at what the group thought were the points to be highlighted on the cards.

In Group-2, the participants adopted a different process. The group gave themselves some time to read the PAD individually. Once the reading was over, the members of the group came out with their own individual views on strengths, weaknesses, opportunities and threats. These were then debated amongst the group members and then a consensus was arrived at on the SWOT, which was reflected on the cards.

For the exercise, the participants needed more time than estimated and the assembly to the plenary was, therefore, deferred until after lunch time.

Presentation of Group Work

The two groups first placed the different cards with strengths, weaknesses, opportunities and threats written on them, under the separate headings of Strengths, Weaknesses, Opportunities and Threats on the floor of the workshop hall. The participants then made clusters of the cards bearing their views under each head, which were deemed related in their ideas and content. The following clusters were identified under strengths, weaknesses, opportunities and threats.

Chart II

Strengths

A. Staff and broad capabilities
B. Quality of programmes
C. Unique selling points
D. Management and financial structure
E. Others

Chart III

Weaknesses of the DPIP Project

A. Organisational level
B. Design of the project
C. At the level of resources
D. During implementation of child labour project

Chart IV

Opportunities

A. Opportunities for policy changes
B. Opportunities for behavioural changes
C. Organisational

Chart V

Threats

A. Technological related
B. Social threats
C. Economic threats
D. Political and administrative threats
E. Others

After clustering the cards under different heads was completed, the participants reflected on what each other have written. This helped them to identify duplications, which are inevitable in the process. The participants then separated the cards, which had the same or similar idea in order to eliminate duplication. This was done after clarifications were sought from the groups, to ensure that new ideas were not lost. Once the whole group agreed on the meaning of what was written on the cards and on their classification, the cards were removed from the floor and pasted on the walls under the same heads, as the entire lot of participants' understanding of SWOT of DPIP, for subsequent reference to the SWOT of DPIP and to keep the workshop discussions in perspective during the remaining two days.

The participants then as a whole reviewed the exercise on the wall and reconfirmed on the contents. The final picture looked like the following:

Chart VI

Strengths

A. Staff and broad capabilities

The service providers were all operating at the village level. They are both community owned and managed.

B. Quality of programmes

"Outsiders" would be facilitators. And the facilitation process will be sensitive to local realities and community choices.

Self-targeting by the poor themselves.

Flexibility in the selection of the poor.

Specific targeting of the poorest of the poor.

No financial target. Demand driven project of the poor.

By group targeting, the project provides primacy to community building.

Prioritisation of needs by the community will lead to efficiency of intervention.

Focus on sustainability by aiming at self-managed grassroots level institutions.

Human and environment aspects of poverty are focused.

C. Unique selling points

Outsiders are enablers; not "doers".

"Doer" becoming enabler through a process.

Creation of pro-poor environment among line departments and institutions.

Provides scope for the poor to identify and fill up critical gaps.

State Project Monitoring Unit—key stabilising factor for all the District Project Monitoring Units. It combines flexibility of NGOs and also credibility of the government.

Mandal Samakhyas (federation of SHGs at the sub-district level) can develop as pressure groups.

D. Management and financial structure

SPMU—can influence the government for pro-poor macro policies.

Strong Common Interest Groups (CIGs) will be in a position to challenge the vested interest.

Community Investment Fund (CIF) may build institutional approach to plan and implement social sector initiatives.

Village Organisation (VO) gives voice and visibility to the poor. They will have greater strength in terms of enabling the poor to address social issues apart from emerging as viable village financial intermediaries.

Mandal Support Cell (MSC) has flexibility in its composition in terms of skill mix.

E. Others

Focus on girl child education would have spin-off effect in population control and improvement of opportunities for girls.

Chart VII

Weaknesses

The weaknesses of the project are anticipated at four levels.

A. *Weaknesses at organisational level*

Frequent transfers of the district project managers may result in weakening the progress of the project.

Sustainability of CIGs/VOs/MSCs was doubtful once the project ends.

Number of resource persons planned at Mandal Support Cell for sustainable facilitation was inadequate.

Lack of adequate legal machinery at SERP/DPMU/MSCs to cope with conflicts arising out of facilitation.

VO/MS may hijack the CIGs in the name of leadership/facilitation.

Mandal Samakhyas may have some conflict with the existing administrative Mandal level set up.

Strong CIGs may lead to conflict against vested interests.

B. *Weaknesses in the design of the project*

No macro policies to expand the micro enterprises.

Focus was only on social mobilisation with lesser emphasis on expanding economic activities.

Ability to build the capabilities of *Gram Panchayats* and line departments was not an easy task for VO/MS.

Macroeconomic and fiscal management policies in Andhra Pradesh were not favourable to the process approach to development being adopted by the project.

The CIGs may disintegrate after receiving some benefit from CIF.

Amongst the key performance indicators, quantitative indicators were more numerous. This may compromise on measuring quality of performance.

A "time-framed project" cannot ensure the process approach especially in tribal areas.

C. *Weaknesses of resources*

In the utilisation of CIF, the issues relating to scale economics were not given a serious thought.

Per capita (household) availability of CIF as very small to eradicate poverty.

Arrangement or mechanisms to mobilise micro-credit, i.e., credit facilitation, was absent in the project design.

D. *Weaknesses in implementing child labour project*

The child labour component is not comprehensive and it does not include boys.

Number of institutions for girl child labour education provided for was not sufficient in relation to the numbers of child labour to be tackled.

Chart VIII

Opportunities

A. Policy changes

Building social capital for sustainability was clearly possible.

Results in pro-poor advocacy may be achieved.

Scope for influencing government policies for the poor existed.

Creating an enabling environment for pro-poor perspective may be possible.

B. Behavioural changes

Sensitisation of the department functionaries, may result in better delivery of government, services to the poor.

Learning and experiences from the project may lead to up project scaling eventually.

Village activists may emerge as leaders in the project villages.

An environment for social reforms may be built up in a small way.

C. Organisational aspects

Organisations of the poor after meeting their needs may question the structures, which have marginalised them.

Organisations of the poor will have more say in the decision making of PRIs.

Girl child labour intervention will act as a model for taking it to scale.

The outreach of other line departments through the Mandal Support Cell may be enhanced.

Success of Mandal Samakhyas may give opportunity for federation of the organisation of the poor above Mandal level. New project Mandal Samakhyas may emerge as a financial intermediary.

Chart IX

Threats

A. Technological aspects

Poor response from banks/financial institutions to CIGs may jeopardise the project.

Non-availability of quality facilitation to CIGs could render them dysfunctional.

Stereotyping of needs may harm the poor.

B. Social aspects

Multiplicity of SHGs at village level was a serious problem for convergence of SHGs.

Absence of focus on the destitute and the disabled (because they need special facilitation) could hamper poverty eradication.

Community may overestimate/underestimate their strengths/needs.

C. Economic aspects

Existing supply driven programmes may waken DPIP initiatives.

D. Political and administrative

Politicisation of VOs and MSs could damage the DPIP intervention

Government may withdraw its investments because of CIF in the DPIP project area.

Other government agencies may not recognise CIGs

Line departments and PRIs may not positively change to support DPIP initiatives.

Insufficient facilities could lead to failures.

Implementing NGOs may create dependency without creating capacity for self-help.

Linkage between CIGs/VOs with PRIs may give rise to local conflicts.

E. Others

Ways and means position of the government may divert DPIP funds.

Target (numbers) approach could defeat DPIP's objectives.

The fear of enablers becoming doers, could make the target community suspicious.

Vision

In Plenary

The facilitator explained the need for vision. He began by quoting the famous line "I have a Dream", of Martin Luther King Jr., which heralded the Civil Rights Movement in the US and explained how that changed the way a nation works. No Olympic athlete ever got to win the Olympic gold medal by mistake. A compelling vision of his/her stellar performance inevitably guides all the "tear and sweat" for many years.

What is vision, was then spelt out. It was the "ideal". It was a mental picture of where an organisation wants to go or where we want the stakeholders ideally to reach. Vision could be a temporal vision or it could be a spatial vision.

> If you don't know where you're going, it doesn't matter which way we go.
>
> —Chesire Cat in *Alice in Wonderland*

How do we get a vision? We get a vision through attempting at a description in words that conjures up a similar picture for each member of the group of the final destination of the group's work together.

In working out a vision, it was pointed out, one should bear in mind that one will never be greater than the vision that guides her/him.

The facilitator explained that the vision statement should require the organisation's members to stretch their expectations, aspirations and performance. And the vision statement should be realistic and credible, well articulated and easily understood, appropriate, ambitious and responsive to change.

In Groups

After clarifications and discussions on the conceptual inputs, the participants broke into two new groups, with KR and VK in different groups. (KR's Group was called Group-1 and VK's Group was called Group-2.)

The "Group Work" moved along similar lines in both the groups. The groups brainstormed on what they would like to accomplish in future. That different ideas do not have to be a problem, was clearly understood. The two groups debated amongst themselves, *inter alia*, on the following questions:

> How do we want our community to be different?
>
> What role do we think or want SERP to play in the context of DPIP in the community?
>
> What will success look like?

The two groups, came out with two separate statements each. The participants wrote these statements down on flip charts. These flip charts were then pasted on the wall and the two groups jointly examined the vision statements generated by each other.

Chart X

Group-1

(KR's Group)

The disadvantaged communities will be empowered, through capacity building and establishment of common interest groups. The poor in the districts will overcome all economic and cultural barriers. The marginalised groups will fight social exclusion and overcome psychological barriers to their self-development.

Chart XI

Group-2

(KR's Group)

The poor marginalised groups will have improved their household asset base. The marginalised profile in the DPIP districts will be enabled to increase their productivity through capacity building, through better utilisation of available resources. At the end of the project, the target communities will have full access to services through their organisation.

In Plenary

All the participants then met in plenary.

The two groups debated on the merits and demerits of the statements generated in the groups. Clarifications were sought by one group from the other on the vision statements. It was then agreed that the vision statement of Group-2, was more powerful, but it did not emphasise the "people centered nature of the development", envisioned by the structure of DPIP, an element that was significant in Group-1's statement. It was also agreed that there were other elements in Group-1's vision statement, which were fit for being included in the vision statement. After considerable confabulation and redrafting of the vision statements by both the groups together, the following vision statements were finally agreed upon.

Chart XII

Vision

The disadvantaged communities shall be empowered to overcome all social, economic cultural and psychological barriers through self-managed organisations. They will have increased productivity with improved skills, and asset-base; they will be able to utilise the available resources to full potential and have full access to services.

The final vision statements were written up on flip charts and pasted on the wall for future reference.

Mission

Having agreed on the vision statement, the few sessions were dedicated to develop the "Mission" for SERP in implementing the DPIP.

The facilitator explained that a Mission Statement usually consists of a few sentences through which the essence of the organisation to the stakeholders and to the public is communicated. Some examples were given. It was also indicated that alternatively an organisation can say more about who they are, what they are doing and why they are doing so, through the mission statement.

It was recognised that neither approach was necessarily the right one for SERP in implementing DPIP. What was more important was that the key functionaries of DPIP arrive at a mission statement such that it articulates one guiding set of ideas which is articulated, understood and supported by the stakeholders, executive committee members, staff, volunteers, donors and collaborators of DPIP.

> By the end of the decade we will put a man on the moon", said John F. Kennedy. That night, when the moon came out, all Americans could look out of the window and imagine... And when the time came to appropriate the enormous funds necessary to accomplish this vision, the American Congress did not hesitate. Why? Because this vision spoke powerfully to values Americans held dear. "America as a pioneer and America as world leader.
>
> Adopted from "Frenquently Asked Questions on Strategic Planning". *spfac/faq.htm*

Experts believe that four primary characteristics of successful "development organisations", were:

A clear agreed-upon mission statement.
A strong competent executive director.
A dynamic board of directors (read members of the EC).
An organisation-wide commitment to fund raising.

SERP at that point in time was concerned with only the first of these primary characteristics. Against the foregoing backdrop, the facilitator then laid out the probable contents of the mission statement. There should be a purpose statement and the business statement.

The purpose statement usually includes two phrases:

- An "infinitive" that indicates a change in status such as "to increase", "to decrease", "to prevent", "to eliminate", and
- An identification of the problem or condition to be changed.

An example is "to eliminate homelessness", where "to eliminate" is the infinitive and "homelessness" is the condition to be changed.

The business statement usually outlines the "business(es)" (that is, activities or programmes) the organisation (read SERP in implementing DPIP) chooses to pursue for its purposes. Specifically the business statement should answer, "What activities are we going to do to accomplish our purpose?" Examples were given to elaborate on the concepts. The business statement often include the verb "to provide", or link a purpose statement with the words "by" or "through". For example, let us take the purpose statement to be "to eliminate homelessness". The business statement could be: "To eliminate homelessness by providing job training to homeless individuals and by giving them loans to construct housing for the homeless."

In Groups

Having clarified the conceptual issues, the participants formed the same two groups which had framed the vision statement, so that there is continuity in the process. The groups were encouraged in addition to the above discussion, to consider the following three questions:

What is the problem or need the organisation (SERP) is trying to address?
What makes the organisation (SERP) unique?
Who are the target communities of the organisations work?

The groups followed the same process they followed in developing the vision statement. The two groups then produced the mission statements separately, which were recorded on flip charts by Group-2, while Group-1 had them written on the white and green boards provided in the workshop venue.

In Plenary

The flip charts of Group-2 was pasted beside the mission statements of Group-1 on the boards. Both the mission statements had elements, which the participants as a whole thought must find a mention in their final mission statement. After an extended debate the following formulations were agreed upon and accepted:

Chart XIII

Mission

Our mission is to enable the disadvantaged communities perceive possibilities for change and bring about change by exercising informed choices on equal footing. As a sensitive support mechanism we will foster self-reliant and vibrant organisations of poor through social mobilisation and community empowerment process.

We will focus on optimum utilisation of resources, expanding skill and asset base of the poor with full access to services.

The final mission statement was also pasted on the wall.

Values

The group then took up the issue of values. The session began with a brainstorming on what are values. Several meanings of the term came from the participants. One of them correctly said that values are beliefs. Elaborating on this, the facilitator extended the concept to interpret values as beliefs which an organisation's members hold in common and endeavour to put in practice. The values guide an organisation's members in performing their work. In developing values, the participants ask themselves the question: "What are the basic beliefs that we share as an organisation and which are inviolable?"

Values could be both spoken/written and unspoken/unwritten. Ideally an individual's personal values will align with the spoken and unspoken values of the organisation. On being asked what happens if there is divergence between individual's values and the values of the organisation, it was explained that the only course would be to affect a "divorce" as it were, between the individual and the organisation. If there are too many people in the organisation with the values that are not aligned to the organisation's values, there may be a demise of the organisation itself in essence, unless the system is able to auto eliminate those individuals who do not share the organisation's values.

The Game

Unlike the vision and mission the participants worked in the plenary as a "group of the whole" and developed the values by playing the "Shipwrecked Sailors' Game."

Each participant imagined they were on a long voyage on a ship and each of them were allowed six pieces of luggage. These six pieces of luggage were values that they held dear to their hearts. Participants were, of course, allowed the liberty of having less than six pieces of luggage, if they chose to. They were asked to write these values on "postit slips" of papers, taking care that they write only one value on one postit slip. Fifteen minutes were allowed for the activity.

Once they had these six values jotted down on their slips, they were asked to imagine that the ship they were traveling was shipwrecked. They will have to abandon the ship and huddle on to lifeboats, but they are allowed to carry only five pieces of luggage. That is, they have to abandon one luggage (value), if they had six values, in order to get into the lifeboats. Only three of thirteen participants had six values and so in the first instance only three participants dropped one value each, which included "hard work" and "sincerity". These values which were abandoned in the first round were pasted on one side of the wall.

They were taken to an island in the lifeboats from where they were to be flown out to their destination, but the problem was that they were allowed only four pieces of luggage on board the aircraft. And hence those who had five pieces of luggage (values) had to abandon one more value of their choice. Five participants dropped one value each, which included honesty and empathy for the poor. That is, participants were left with no more than four values each now. These values which were abandoned in the second round were pasted alongside the values dropped in the first round, on one side of the wall.

The game was half way through. After the aircraft was airborne and cruising at an altitude of 32,000 feet, all of a sudden it developed a snag and had to force land at a place away from the final destination. No alternative aircraft was available with the Airliner to fly the participants out. But the Airliner arranged for helicopter services so that the participants could reach their final destination without much delay. However, the problem was that the participants could carry only three pieces of luggage in the helicopter though they all had four. Hence, they had to abandon another luggage (value) now and all participants, eager as they were to get back home, abandoned one luggage (value) each. These values which were abandoned in the third round were also pasted on one side of the wall along with the earlier abandoned values.

The helicopter took the participants safely to their destination. Hence, they were off-loaded with three values in three pieces of luggage each and they proceeded to cross over the customs area. Disappointment was in store for them here too: they were told they could take inside the country only two pieces of luggage. One piece of luggage they had to surrender. There was no option. The participants did so and ended up with two pieces of luggage with two values. These values which were abandoned in the fourth round were once again pasted on one side of the wall beside the ones which were abandoned earlier.

The two values that each participant had were then pasted on the wall on the side adjoining the abandoned values. All the participants examined the set of values and sought clarifications from the respective authors who had written the values, in case the meaning was not clear to them. Once this was done, values which were duplicates were separated out.

The remaining values were then transcribed on post-card sized boards. These cards were placed on the floor in one vertical column. All the participants again examined this column of values and looked for possible duplication that might have crept in. Once this was done, values which were duplicates were once again separated out. In all, the group was now left with 13 values. However, 13 was considered too large a number of values to be included in the core and put to practice. Hence, the group decided to score these values individually and see if they wanted all of them in any case.

Blank cards were placed along the right side of the 13 values. Each of the participants was allowed in turn to assign a score to each of the values from 0 to 10. Once the participants marked their individual markings, the scores were aggregated. The group decided that they would only take cognisance of values, which have scored more than 50 per cent of the total marks achievable, namely, 65. Thus, the following values remained.

The group then went back to the abandoned values and applied their minds on whether they had abandoned any value in haste, which was critical to the success of DPIP. They found a few, of which honesty and being religious, were considered very important, for they bring in compassion, truthfulness and integrity. There was considerable debate on the issue. Though it was generally agreed that being religious was important but it was agreed that inclusion of such a value in the core values may be misconstrued in the current socio-political context. More importantly, compassion, empathy and truthfulness were already explicitly stated. It was, therefore decided that the values identified above were the set of values that the group will stick to, own and have as their core values. These values were then pasted on the wall under the heading of core values.

Chart XIV

Values Scored

Integrity	127
Truthfulness	107
Commitment to work	124
Compassion for the poor	80
Gender justice	60
Social equity	59
Selflessness	50
Service to the poor	61
Strong moral character	50
Service above self	40
People centered development	58
Faith in the power of the people to bring change	62

Chart XV

Core Values

Compassion for the poor.
Empathy for the disadvantaged.
Integrity.
Truthfulness.
Commitment to work—vision and mission

Chart XVI

Lower Order Values

(a)	Honesty	(b)	Being religious
(c)	Hard work	(d)	Sincerity
(e)	Empathy for the poor	(f)	Gender sensitivity
(g)	Compassion	(h)	Charitable disposition
(i)	Love for the people	(j)	Patriotism
(k)	Ability to change	(l)	Adaptable
(m)	Good behaviour	(n)	Helping attitude

The values, which were abandoned, were placed on the wall under the heading of Lower Order Values.

Identity

In Plenary

The participants were asked to come up with their idea of identity. A wealth of ideas came and two significant responses were that "identity was what we were perceived as by others" and that "identity was our image". The facilitator explained what is identity: Our identity is what we are perceived to be by significant others. He explained that identity could be made. Identity can be changed.

AM clarified the difference between identity and image. This was done by showing transparencies of: a cartoon of *Deccan Chronicle* dated 17th June 2000, about VELUGU; of news item in *Eenadu* dated 17th June 2000; of what he was told by some functionaries in Mehbubnagar: "A bunch of officers being outside the system, trying to operate the same system"; "Old wine in a new bottle,"; or what a section of the Press mentioned: "Another government programme" of what the MP implicitly said at the public function to mark the launch of VELUGU: "Goodies once again" of what the Chief Minister's description of VELUGO.

The facilitator explained the need for an identity and what contributes to making an identity. The name, logo/symbol, rituals, motto, USP and the face of the organisation (which includes office décor, vehicles, entourage, body language, and verbalisation) were important in making identity and image.

In Groups

The participants broke into two groups to work out a logo, a motto and a USP to develop an identity for SERP in implementing DPIP. They were told that the logo has to be within the framework outlined by the Janmabhoomi Programme's Logo.

The processes followed in both the groups were similar. Individuals were first encouraged to make their own logo and then they were discussed and a consensus arrived at. The two groups also came up with their own unique selling points. Both the Groups thought that the Song adopted for VELUGU was appropriate and since the name has already been adopted from above, *viz.*, VELUGU, they need not tinker with the name.

In Plenary

The participants discussed the different logos and the different unique selling points. The issue of logo was sorted out by amalgamating the logo adopted for the Janmabhoomi Programme and of the different logos presented by the two groups. The USP took a long time to be resolved, and ultimately the USP agreed upon was "People Centered Development".

The Response

After the group had finished their work the entire final output as also the working sheets were displayed on the walls, nearly session-wise. The workshop venue had a colourful look.

Mr. S.R. Sankaran had kindly agreed to respond and react to the vision, mission, values and identity developed by the participants, as part of the process of triangulation. Mr. B.N. Yugandhar, President of the EC of SERP had also agreed to be the other discussant.

The participants, especially Rajshekhar, took Mr. S.R. Sankaran and Mr. B.N. Yugandhar around the workshop hall explaining to them the process through which these were arrived at and drawing their attention to the display where appropriate. Both Mr. Sankaran and Mr. Yugandhar had several questions to ask and displayed great interest in the work done. KR explained to Mr. Sankaran that he along with Mr. Yugandhar could have issued a fiat outlining the vision, mission, values and identity, but such a move would have been anathema to the tenor and principles underpinning the project. Hence, all the efforts have been made to develop the vision, mission, values and identity for SERP in implementation of DPIP, along with all the key functionaries.

The facilitator then gave his impressions of the workshop. He was pleased at the level of participation and the interest taken by all the participants, despite one of them being slightly indisposed and two of them having family commitments. He also felt that the process would help the participants forge into one team, though much more work has to be done. He then analysed the session-wise feedback, wherein most sessions, the feedback was almost 90 per cent, for the first session it was about 80 per cent. The usual trend of the second session being less favourably viewed did not happen here. One reason why the first session had a lower feedback was that the participants needed more time to read the document thoroughly. He thanked the participants. He thanked KR for his support.

Jayaesh, one of the participants, then made a brief presentation of the vision, mission, values and identity.

The participants were provided with an opportunity to express their individual views and provide feedback. All of them felt that the workshop was very useful and that they have learnt a lot. They were confident of owning up the vision, mission, core values and identity, and will be able to carry their staff along with them. KR, however, opted to be modest and said that this was only the beginning of the learning process and that the workshop should be seen as starting point only.

Mr. Sankaran, in his reaction, said he was yet to fully internalise the entire output of the workshop, but he was on the whole pleased to see the output. He was intrigued by the fact that the workshop on vision, mission, core values and identity was being held after the PAD was finalised. (The team was in place only after the PAD was approved and hence it was not possible to have workshop on vision, mission, core values and identity before the finalisation of the project.) He exhorted the participants to pursue the people centred approach. What he considered critical in the scheme of things was the set of core values arrived at the workshop, which almost partook the nature of the Ten Commandments. Nevertheless, if the participants can hold on to the one value of truthfulness, Mr. Sankaran felt, they will succeed in their attempts at circumventing many of the evils that affects public servants and delivery of public services today. He wished them well.

Mr. Yugandhar said he was pleased to see the process and the involvement of the key staff. He hoped that the staff of SERP will be able to develop a different way of functioning where decisions will not be imposed from above and where flexibility and innovations will be at a high premium. He urged upon the participants in their key role to usher in a demand driven people centred development. He, therefore, expressed in so many words his disappointment at the core values not having an explicit mention of faith in the people's ability to bring about their betterment. He exhorted the participants to bear in mind what the great development practitioner of our time Akhter Hamid Khan Sahab told him once on the secret of his success in the Orangi project, namely, "Training, training and more training". That is, for success one needs to renew oneself, unload past dead baggage and move forward.

Revisiting Vision, Mission, Values and Identity

After Mr. Sankran and Mr. Yugandhar left, the participants revisited the vision, mission, core values and identity. In the light of the remarks made, they thought that "faith in the power of the people to bring change" which was implicit in the mission and vision statements needs to be brought into the core values. After discussion, it was reconsidered that "compassion for the poor" and "empathy for the disadvantaged" are related, though not exactly the same thing and because the group believed in the power of the people, compassion may not be as strong a value as they thought it to be at first. Hence, it was decided to drop from the core values "Compassion for the poor" and include "Faith in the power of the poor people to bring change" as one of the core values. Thus, the final set of core values was arrived at as under:

- Empathy for the disadvantaged.
- Integrity.
- Truthfulness.
- Commitment to work-visions mission
- Faith in the power to the people to bring change.

3

Training Needs Assessment Through Participatory Methods

Thousands of candles can be lit from a single candle,
And the life of the candle will not be shortened.

—*Gautama Buddha*

Introduction

The Society for Elimination of Rural Poverty (SERP) started functioning from June 2000. The Society had commenced the process of recruitment of staff, and almost all the key functionaries were in position at the state level and at the district and *mandal* levels, barring Srikakulum, where most of the DPMU staff were yet to be positioned. The Society had in place a training strategy, which enjoined that there shall be a Training Needs Assessment (TNA). This exercise was in partial fulfilment of that strategy.

Objectives of this TNA

Since the SERP had just started and it had drawn staff from different departments and sources, through alternative modes of recruitment, this TNA was not directed towards correcting any inefficiency in the functioning of SERP. The TNA was designed to ascertain what skills, knowledge and attitudes that the staff in position should ideally have and what are the gaps that need to be filled in.

Thus, the TNA was designed to be a participatory process involving the following:

- Deciding the target population.
- Defining and identifying needs for skill, knowledge and attitudes of the target population.
- Ascertaining the gap in skill, knowledge and attitudes of the target population.
- Prioritising them.
- And setting objectives in the light of the assessment findings.

In broad terms, therefore, it was attempted to:

- Find out the type and extent of training needed.
- Class of individuals in need of training.

The Needs Assessment

What was attempted to do here is to conceive a gap between an existing situation ("what is") and another, under (ideal) or desirable conditions ("what should be"), as shown below:

The Need Gap
What Ought to be—Desirable Situation
Gap Need = Difference, Shortfall, Deficiency
What is—Actual Situation

Applied to the needs of individuals, for instance, this translated itself into an "ability gap". That is, the deficiency in knowledge, skills and attitudes which are likely to impede the attainment of job performance at the desired level. This may be shown by the following figure:

Training Needs as Ability Gap

What knowledge, skills and attitudes are required?
What knowledge, skills and attitudes does s/he have?

↓

The Ability Gap (Training Need)

This approach was adopted to distinguish between two alternative courses of action that is possible once the process of TNA is completed. These are:

- Fitting the employee to the job by provision of suitable training.
- Fitting the jobs to the employees by limited amount of job redesigning and/or providing job aids.

Typically TNA could be at the macro-level or at the micro level. In the macro approach the broad areas of training required are spelt out usually by function/occupation and quantifying their importance at the aggregate level. In the micro approach attempt is at identifying the type of training required as also those in need down to the level of the individual units or individual.

In the current exercise the 'micro approach' was taken because of two reasons. One, the CEO, SERP at the time of presentation of the training strategy had specified that training at the individual levels have to be worked out, notwithstanding the time and resources required. Two, since to the best of our knowledge and belief and on the basis of information provided, recruitment in SERP had proceeded on the rationale of past experience and applying the rule of thumb. Thus the techniques usually applied for adopting the macro-approach, *viz.*, person power planning and labour market signalling techniques would have been inoperative.

In the micro-level approach adopted here the attempt here was to address the concerns at two levels:

1. *Occupational level* needs involving identifying the skills, knowledge, attitude and behaviour requirement for carrying out different jobs and functions.
2. *Individual level* needs involving on deciding the organisational and occupational needs leading to who or which individuals are in need of what type of training.

Though the difference between the two levels is best not over-emphasised, but it is important to note that we bore in mind the fact that the first level of needs assessment was done in abstraction from the individuals who require training. Thus, there are clear overlaps between the two but we have adopted both as each represents a particular perspective from which identification of needs was done.

The Methods

We have used the following methods:

- We had formal and informal interviews of key staff such as the CEO (holding charge of personnel and recruitment at the SERP level), Line Managers, Training Co-ordinators/Managers, Heads of DPMU etc.
- We had direct observation of employees at work both at the SPMU and DPMU levels such as in Anantapur.
- We had a participatory "Job description, Job and Task Analysis" workshop, in which we assessed staff attitudes and feelings about their work. This was done with MCSC Staff and Staff of DPMUs in Srikakulum and Mahabubnagar, and to a limited extent at Vizianagaram.
- We also had brainstorming to find out from a cross section of opinion within SERP on attitudes towards training and training needs.

For individual level Training Needs Assessment, we additionally used

- a simple questionnaire (which is at Appendix A-3.5);
- had key consultations such as with the Collectors (in Anantapur, Srikakulum, Mehbubnagar and Vijaynagram), PDs, DRDAs (such as in Srikakulum, Adilabad, Anantapur and Vijaynagram), Lead Bank Managers, and development professionals (such as Prakash, Veena Mazumdar, Kamala Bhasin, Shashi Rajgopalan, Vijay Mahajan, Jimmy Mascarenhas) who are outside the system;
- conducted interviews and had group discussions such as the one we had in Adilabad and Anantapur;
- and examined work samples in all the districts.

Though we have in SERP several people who have come from government departments, NGOs, UNDP and other organisations (on secondment in some cases), we had not accessed their past records and reports as also their Performance Appraisal Reports. We had asked the CEO for these records and reports but we were advised to satisfy ourselves without these.

Occupational Level Needs

Occupational level needs assessments were directed toward identifying the particular knowledge, skills, attitudes and behaviour required for the satisfactory performance of a given job or function. In order to identify such needs:

- We first attempted to define the nature and scope of the tasks and operations covered by the job.
- And then we attempted at trying to find out which job should be given priority in the training programmes.

The Process

As a first step the State Project Monitoring Unit, through the State Project Co-ordinator, was requested to draw up a job-description of all the key functionaries at the SPMU, DPMU and Mandal Community Support Cells. This was done and the protem job descriptions are placed as Appendix A-3.1. This was studied at length and an idea was formed of the job descriptions of the following functionaries:

Monitoring and Evaluation Specialist (Monitoring and Evaluation Component). Project Executive Officer. Finance Manager. Documentation (sic). Training Co-ordinator. Institution Building (sic).	At the State Project Management Unit
Training (sic). Monitoring and Evaluation (DPMU) (sic). Gender (DPMU). (Sic). Documentation (DPMU). (sic).	At the District Project Management Unit
Social Organiser. Community Organiser	At the Mandal Community Support Cells

There was no job description of the CEO, State Project Co-ordinator and the PDs of the DPMUs.

Since we were assigned to visit DPIP in three districts, *viz.*, Vizianagaram, Srikakulum and Mahabubnagar, we decided to carry out the above functions in respect of different occupations in different districts, as under:

In Vizianagaram, the following process was followed: Firstly, we attempted to define the nature and scope of the tasks and operations covered by the job of the Community Organisers (COs) and Community Coordinators (CCs) in one group. This was done through PRA. The intention was to define the nature and scope of the tasks and operations of the CCs and COs as perceived by the CCs themselves. Secondly, we then ascertained through PRA techniques, the knowledge and skills that the group as a whole possessed.

Thirdly, the data from the exercise was shared and then triangulated with other key players with whom DPIP will interface intensely, like the Collector and District magistrate, the Project Directors of the DRDAs and the PO of the ITDP Programme, DRO and the PD, DPIP. The outputs from the exercises at Vizianagaram are given as Appendix A-3.1.

In Srikakulum, we followed a different scheme, still focusing on the CCs and COs. First, we attempted to define the nature and the scope of the tasks and operations of the CCs, through PRA with the CCs and COs (jointly) as they perceived it. Second, we went further down the road to identify the activities under each tasks and operations. Third, we found out from the group what they thought were the skills, knowledge and attitudes necessary/required to carry out the tasks and operations and what were the skills and knowledge available with them. Fourth, we made an attempt at finding out through participatory methods what values they have and then went on to work out with the groups to catalogue out the attitudes and behaviour necessary to uphold those values in the discharge of the tasks and operations.

We shared and triangulated the data and information generated by the foregoing process with the key players with whom DPIP will interact such as the Collector, the Lead Bank Manager, the PD of the DRDA, Project Officer of ITDA, the chief of a leading NGO working in Srikakulum, chief of CMEY etc.

The outputs from the exercises at Srikakulum are at Appendix A-3.2.

In Mahabubnagar, we had a different focus, *viz.*, on DPMU staff, and we attempted at understanding the nature and scope of the tasks and operations of the CCs and COs from them but separately. On the first day we worked out the nature and scope of the tasks and operations of the Project Director, the Training Co-ordinator, the Gender Specialist, the M&E Co-ordinator and the Joint Director. This was done with them jointly, along with the Project Executive (Gender) at the SPMU (Ms. Amitha) and the Joint Project Director (JPD), Mahabubnagar, through a largely participatory mode. The role of the Joint Project Director was to be decided between the PD and JPD and communicated to us over the next three days. This was necessary as it required working out a working mechanism to share the tasks and operations of the PD between the PD and the JPD, without truncating either of the two roles and without disturbing the accountability mechanism. On the second day we had a role clarity exercise about the tasks and operations of the CCs and COs, from them but separately along with the key staff of the DPMU. The information was shared and triangulated with the Collector, Mehbubnagar and with the protem job chart drawn by the state co-ordinator.

The outputs from the exercises in Mahabubnagar are at Appendix A-3.3.

In Anantapur, all these were shared and reactions were obtained from the Collector, with special reference to issues of participation and social mobilisation.

Training Needs at the Occupational Level

Vizianagaram

From the above process, the COs and the CCs were asked to identify their functions and then break each of their functions into tasks. This was done to ensure that they have role clarity in what they are suppose to do and then examine in the light of these their skills and knowledge as also the skills and knowledge they would need additionally to carry out their tasks. In order to do so the instruments bearing number Proforma-I and Proforma-II of Appedix A-3.1 were used.

In course of the exercise it transpired that they were not aware of the details of some the DPIP programme components. This was a decision of the DPMU not to inform the COs and the CCs about the "Community Investment Fund" for the time being so that they do not begin by sending proposals for CIF, without first facilitating creation of platforms of the poor. It was, therefore, decided that in the given circumstances it would be best not to attempt at working out a "job description" of the COs and CCs, but concentrate on their key functions and then carry out a "gap analysis" with the help of Proforma-II and Proforma-III.

In order to understand the knowledge base of the participants we carried out a problem ranking exercise followed by Pair-wise Ranking. Then the groups were urged to do a Force Field Analysis of the state of rural poverty as they understood it in two groups. The outputs are in Appendix A-3.1.

As a consequence of the foregoing, following needs were identified for COs and CCs for DPIP, Vizianagaram.

Skills

- Social mobilisation skills.
- Skills for participatory planning at the community level.
- Training people (training of trainers).
- Identification and locating resources.
- Advocacy, lobbying, networking and influencing.
- Conflict resolution.
- Project identification and preparation in off-farm employment projects.
- Micro-credit.

Knowledge

If one were to review the problem identification and prioritisation, it seems that they have picked up a good deal of information about the many faces of poverty being in the development field and from their own experience of poverty itself. The force field analysis and the pair-wise ranking of problems indicate that most of the time they assess poverty from institutional and behavioural angles only. That there are structures, policies and processes, which also cause poverty is missing. The knowledge that need to be imparted to them relate to a few aspects.

- Causes of poverty.
- Alternative models of development, such as watershed approach.
- Knowledge of DPIP.
- Contextual ideas.
- Gender and development.

In terms of attitudes, the group dynamics during the workshop and during their individual interaction are indicative of the need to deal with the following attitudes and behaviour:

- Dominance and arrogance.
- We-They syndrome.
- Unlearning.
- Self awareness and self critical.
- Complementarity of different wings of the organisation.

Srikakulum

The training needs that came out in Srikakulum confirmed the findings of Vizianagaram but had the advantage of refining what was arrived at in Vijaynagram. The training needs for Community Organisers (COs) and the Community Co-ordinators (CCs) was preceded by an exercise of arriving at a job description of CO and CC. In Srikakulum the DPMU has decided that the CC will be CO but will be "more among equals". That is, the basic functions and tasks of the CCs and COs, will remain the same but the CCs will have some additional responsibilities.

Thus the final job description for the CCs and COs of Srikakulum, arrived at together with the PD, DPIP Srikakulum and the joint PD of Mahabubnagar is the following:

- Facilitating: facilitate the poorest of the poor to realise their full potential.
- Mobilising: to form SHGs and help form groups of poor on other issues.
- Building of people's capacities.
- Advocating, lobbying and campaigning for the poorest of the poor.
- Working with and co-ordinating with people's institutions, government, private and financial institutions and PRIs.
- Monitoring and reporting.

Based on the above, after a process the following needs were identified:

- Social mobilisation skills.
- Participatory rural appraisal methods and techniques.

- Skills for analysing and participatory planning at the community level.
- Training people (training of trainers).
- Identification and locating the poorest of the poor.
- Locating and mobilisation of resources.
- General management skills including communication skills.
- Advocacy, lobbying, networking and influencing.
- Conflict resolution.
- Project identification and preparation in off-farm employment projects. Micro-credit.

The process followed in identifying the functions and tasks of the CCs and the COs to arrive at the job description is in Appendix A-3.2.

In order to understand their knowledge base a detailed workshop was carried out on poverty. The result of the process is included in Appendix A-3.2. Based on this exercise read with the process followed for arriving at the job description of the CCs and COs mentioned in the foregoing paragraph, the assessment of knowledge required for the CCs and COs include the following:

- Knowledge about Acts and Laws affecting the poor.
- Gender justice and issues.
- Government development programmes.
- Local language (particularly those working in the Hill *Mandals*).
- Culture, customs, traditions, food habits of the people.
- Agriculture.
- Local health and sanitation issues.
- Functioning and management of CBOs.

A very detailed exercise was carried out to ascertain the values that the group would consider "core values". The end result was that the core values of DPIP Sirkakulum was agreed as:

- Dedication.
- Honesty.
- Truthfulness.
- Helpfulness.
- Faith in poor people's potential.
- Empathy for the poor.

Based on the above, a non-exhaustive but comprehensive exercise was carried out to determine what attitudes and behaviour people should have to uphold the values, which DPIP Srikakulum have adopted as core values. From the behaviour and attitudes identified and the behaviour during the interaction that we had during the three days, it is important to deal with the following:

- Dominance and arrogance.
- We-They syndrome.

- Unlearning.
- Self-awareness and self-critical.
- Gender sensitivity.
- We know; they don't know attitudes.

Mahabubnagar

The DPMU in Mahabubnagar is the most complete set of staff in place. Hence, the focus of the training needs assessment was on the staff of the DPMU. The details of the process are outlined in Appendix A-3.3. Suffice it is to say here that the DPMU staff first had a detailed analysis of their respective roles having regard to the protem job description provided by SPMU. They then debated amongst themselves the Job description and then worked out the skills, knowledge and attitudes that the different functionaries need to have.

The skills required by the PD, DPMU are as follows:

For the PDs

Skills

- Setting up and administration of a performance appraisal system.
- Managing change: inter-personal counselling, group problem solving, motivational skills.
- Conflict resolution.
- Social mobilisation.
- Project appraisal and monitoring of community investment projects.
- Time management.
- Participatory micro-level planning.

Knowledge

- Gender justice and gender equity.
- Computerised financial management.
- Best practices in HRD.
- Discovering the self (MBTI and the like).
- Best practices in development.
- Management practices in non-governmental organisations.

For the Training Co-ordinator

Skills

- Direct trainers skills.
- Facilitation skills.
- Training in participatory methods.
- Training andragogy for barefoot professionals/para-professionals.
- Training technology (TNA, TSP, etc.)

- Development of training material and aids.
- Developing a resource centre for capacity building.

Knowledge

- Specialised training institutions and individuals.
- Customised training courses.
- Manuals on subject matter.
- Gender justice and gender equity.
- Best practices in HRD.
- Best practices in development.
- Management practices in non-governmental organisations.

For Monitoring and Evaluation Manager

Skills

- Developing monitoring and evaluation indicators.
- Participatory M&E.
- MIS.
- Project appraisal, monitoring and evaluation.
- Documentation skills.

Knowledge

- Changes in development.
- Best practices in M&E.
- Community investment projects.

For Gender Specialist

Skills

- Training of trainers.
- Participatory skills.
- Social mobilisation.
- Communication including documentation, report writing.
- Value-based advocacy, lobbying and campaigning.
- Negotiation.
- Conflict resolution.

Knowledge

- Development and gender dimensions.
- National policies on women and gender.
- Laws relating to gender justice and equity.
- International forces having a bearing on gender justice and equity.

Appendix A-3.1

Vizianagaram

Day-1

The sessions at Vizianagaram were primarily with the COs and CCs, with some staff from DPMU. Most of the key staff in DPMU have been recruited but have not joined.

On the first day the attempt was to make an assessment of the level of skills they have and the knowledge and understanding of poverty and development they possess in general.

To begin with we used Proforma-I for the participants to write down what they think their functions are and which of these they can perform well and what villagers can do better. This was for their own reflection and to make them think about their new role and the most important stakeholder. After they had written these on their own exercise books and papers, they were encouraged to come to the board and write down their tasks making sure that they do not repeat what others have already written. There was considerable debate and discussion, showing that their understanding of their role was in its formative weeks.

At the end of it the group identified the following as their Tasks:

Tasks

- Needs of group understanding.
- Establish linkages.
- Identify local resources.
- Identify the skills of the poor.
- Formation of CIG.
- Training of women/youth.
- Micro level planning/sub project preparation.
- Awareness building on gender etc.
- Prioritisation of credit.
- Inspiring poor of the poor.
- Help people overcome—barriers.
- Arrest wasteful expenditure.
- Identify the poorest of the poor & girl child labour.
- Identify community activists.
- Identify CBO.
- Strengthening primary education/adult education.
- Motivating men.
- Mapping.
- Bridge school support to girl children.
- Strengthening defunct groups.
- Primary health care.
- Awareness to solve our problems.

Having examined their tasks, the participants were now divided into groups to discuss what skills they have and to come out with a common list of skills that majority of them have. The groups were asked to reflect on their skills in the light of the tasks they have identified. The groups wrote their skills on separate charts, which were displayed on the walls of the workshop venue. After eliminating the duplication, one consolidated list was arrived at. The skills that the participants have are as under:

Skills

- Motor driving.
- Cooking.
- Computer.
- Smiling, acting.

- Gardening.
- Playing with children.
- Listening.
- Learning.
- Facilitation.
- Motivation skills.
- Accounting.
- Public speaking.
- Training—income generating.
- Previous experience.
- Singing, dancing and painting.
- Tailoring.
- Report writing.
- Poetry.
- Social skills.
- Participatory skills.
- Organising demonstration.
- Rendering medical advice on Ayurveda.
- Activities.
- Field experience.

Once the tasks were identified and the skills were located, it was thrown open to the participants to introspect and tell to themselves through self-criticism, what or which of the tasks they have enumerated, which they cannot do well. The participants were broken into two groups and asked to make a careful judgement of what they can and what they cannot do and write down only things that they cannot do well. The list that came out are as under:

List of Things We Cannot Do Well

- Building linkages.
- How to release child labour.
- How to identify resources.
- How to analyse.
- How to deal with political interference.
- Training people.
- Identification of school drop-outs.
- How to influence people.
- How to influence.
- Stay in village.

The day ended with an interview with the Press.

Day-2

Having had a fairly good account of the skills that the participants had, we administered a small questionnaire which is Proforma-III of this Appendix to ascertain some personal details having bearing on the tasks at hand.

It was also felt necessary that some approximation of the knowledge base was important. This was done through Delphi Methods, Pair-wise Ranking and Force Field Analysis.

Problems

As a next stage they were asked to write down on flash cards what they thought were the problems which would confront them in working for the poor. Participants were encouraged to have a "non-holds barred" approach in exposing the problems. One flash card was to have one problem written out on it. Once this was done, these flash cards were then laid out on the floor and clusters formed. Problems, which appeared more than once, were taken as one problem. The problems were then classified into groups and one set of problems came to be identified.

The participants then spent some time on debating whether these problems occurred only once in a while or were persistent and caused major problems for the community. Those problems, which were encountered on a one-off basis, were then eliminated. The final list of problems identified in development of the target area and target communities emerged but it did not have finer distinctions between immediate, proximate and basic causes of poverty and underdevelopment. Most of these problems were felt and/or experienced by the participants either in their own lives or in the course of their working experience. The list of problems that emerged reads as follows:

Problems

- Negative attitudes of bank.
- Interference of corrupt politicians and the rich (vested interests).
- Superstitions.
- Leadership domination.
- Lack of participation in development.
- Absence of two wheeler vehicle.
- Parents' attitudes about girl child labour.
- Absence of teaching aids.
- Attitude, behaviour and inefficiency of the M.D.O.
- Lack of training.
- Cannot stay in villages.
- Tribal language problem.
- Touts (middlemen).
- Caste and class discrimination.
- Remuneration problem of activists.
- Corruption amongst government employees.
- Lack of awareness amongst men about women's problems.
- Defunct groups.
- Government policies.
- Existing NGOs.
- Lack of local knowledge on the part of the COs and CCs.

In the problems identified, the participants included the problems likely to be encountered in developmental efforts which were exogenous to the functioning of the DPMU, Vizianagaram as also the problems relating to their functioning as COs and CCs, which were endogenous to DPMU, Vizianagaram.

Two Stage Ranking

We then asked the participants to rank these problems. First they were encouraged to score these problems in ascending order of their severity. The method they used was that the participants were asked to place a "tick mark" against the five problems, which they considered most important from the long list of problems. Once this was done, the number of ticks that each problem got was counted and aggregated. Then five of these problems which got the highest number of ticks were categorised as Class-I problems.

Class-I Problems

(A) Government policies.

(B) Corruption amongst government employees.

(C) Corrupt politicians and the rich (vested interests).

(D) Caste and class discrimination.

(E) Touts (middlemen and vested interests).

Box 3.1

Pair-wise Ranked

A = 1
B = 0
C = 2
D = 3
E = 2

These Class-I problems were considered the best problems and each was assigned symbol starting from "A" to "E". Then they were again ranked to find out which of them were considered the best among the best problems through Pair-wise Ranking. The result is shown in Box 3.1. Those problems, which were considered, Class-II problems were also ranked in a similar fashion and the results are in Box 3.2.

Class-II Problems

(A) Bank.

(B) Superstitions.

(C) Lack of training.

(D) Leadership domination.

(E) Defunct groups.

(F) Lack of participation in development.

(G) Absence of two wheeler vehicle.

Box 3.2

Pair-wise Ranking of Class-II Problems

A = 1
B = 4
C = 5
D = 3
E = 5
F = 3
G = 0

If we look at Boxes, it is apparent that the participants thought that amongst the class-I problems, caste and class discrimination was the biggest problem followed by corrupt politicians and the rich and the touts (middlemen). Thus, the biggest problems are processes of social injustice/inequity and exploitative intermediation. The personal problems, which the participants first identified as barriers to development were erased. The process helped the participants to eschew the tendency to present personal problems as problems of development.

Appendix A-3.2

Srikakulum

The foundation course for selected CCs/COs of Srikakulam DPIP began with a session on introductions and expectations on the eve of 17.10.2000. The basic purpose of the three week foundation course is to induct the new team members into the DPIP philosophy. The TNA was built into the course so that they could see their roles and identify their skills and knowledge, through a process of cumulative learning.

The participants were asked to give an idea of what their expectations are. They did so and the range of expectations as given below was exhaustive.

Expectations

- Getting new ideas and teaching of social development process.
- Want to get an idea and PRA training.
- How to eradicate poverty and develop the poor people.
- Eradication of child labour and mother and child welfare.
- How to form rural people into organisation.
- Knowing and developing various skills by interacting with various kinds of people.
- Creating and cultivating the manner of interacting with people.

- Interaction and living with team.
- Obey with smile.
- Skills—communication techniques.
- Sustainable process.
- How to uplift poor people from the rural area, we will give some financial assistance from Velugu project.
- Building up an idea as to how one can do social work and develop the underdeveloped people.
- How to organise the poor to reach our vision.
- How to motivate the poor people to take on development activities.
- Communication skills.
- In what way can we bring change in the people (any technique).
- Learn the proper way of approaching.
- Develop "no wrong attitude towards other human beings".
- How to develop a plan of action.
- DPIP (Velugu) objectives—how to make an action plan.
- How to make an action plan.
- How to make a work plan.
- Identification of the poor.
- Basic skill development (related to Velugu in specific if any).
- Want to get an idea about the conditions in the district from the field visit.
- Share the experiences and ideas with others regarding social development.
- Get a good vast field experience.
- Listen to the experiences of field workers to know the actual conditions.
- Experience.
- SHG formation.
- What is DPIP.
- Guidance for helping the poor.
- Our role for uplifting the poor.
- How to coordinate with the people.
- What is the role of a volunteer who works for the upliftment of the poor.
- How to communicate with the people in the village.
- How to mingle with them and make them feel that they can do this work.
- How to motivate people.
- To make Velugu run impartially without yielding to the political persons.
- Want to approach poor and educate them on health matters.
- What are the economic issues related to poverty eradication.
- How to form groups for poverty eradication.
- Mobilisation of local resources for upliftment of the poor.
- What is the advantage of savings for the society and for us.

- To go to people, live with them, educate them and learn from them as well.
- To know about the principles, methods required for poverty elimination.
- How to take the programme to the remote villages.
- How does the education of women help family and society.
- What should I do as a social activist for poverty eradication.
- What is the role of CC for the upliftment of the poor.
- Discussion on the developmental activities to be taken up by the CBOs.
- Inform the poor about Velugu programme.
- How to help the poor in their development.
- Will Velugu solve all the problems in the village.
- Will Velugu help all the people in the *Mandal.*
- What to do to make people apolitical.
- What are the aims and objectives of the Velugu problems and methods to make it successful.
- Provide the basic services in the rural area and improve the employment opportunities.
- How to conduct *Gram Sabha.*
- How to identify the poorest of the poor.
- How to identify the people below the poverty line.
- Where do the problems of the people lie.
- How to identify the poor.
- How to improve the skills for working as a social activist.

Evolution of the Workshop Over the Specified 4 Days—18.10.2000-21.10.2000

17.10.2000	Introductions (participants, resource persons and
7 p.m.	organisers) Use of pairing game.
8:30 p.m.	Participants Expectations from the workshop. Delphi method (sorting of cards).
18.10.2000	
9:00 a.m.	Group contract, laying the ground rules for effective participation and learning (large group discussion). Game to enthuse and energise the participants. Formal beginning of the workshop with the Collector's arrival and speech, speeches by some other district officers as well (lecture). Presentation on the DPIP project (lecture with the aid of transparencies).
1:00–2:00 p.m.	LUNCH
2 p.m.	Songs by the participants.

	Role of Community Co-ordinators/Social Organisers in DPIP (small group discussion and presentations). The tasks under each role. The skills and knowledge required to discharge the roles.
4.00p.m.	TEA
4:30 p.m.	Fruit Salad Game to form groups, and to energise the participants. Small groups were asked to discuss the activities as per the roles specified by them in the earlier exercise.
19.10.2000	
9:00 a.m.	Previous evening's homework charts pasted on the walls and visited by the participants. Assessment of Skills and Knowledge Available: What skills you have and what skills are required? What knowledge you have and what is required? (small group discussions and presentations)
1:00-2:00 p.m.	LUNCH
2:00 p.m.	Values (game, card sorting, comparing, prioritising).
4:00 p.m.	TEA
4:30 p.m.	Continuation of the values exercise.
7:00 p.m.	Unscheduled session by DRDA official.
20.10.2000	
9:00 a.m.	Poverty. Definition of poverty in small groups and finalisation in the large group. Who causes poverty? (small groups) What causes poverty? (small groups)
1:00–2:00 p.m.	LUNCH
2:00 p.m.	Attitudes and behaviour. role-plays, use of transparencies, lecture.
4:00 p.m.	TEA
4:30 p.m.	Group exercise on value, attitude and behaviour, presentation and summation. home-work—participants asked to individually write on a piece of paper the appropriate attitudes and behaviour for the value "faith in people's potential".
21.10.2000	
9:00 a.m.	Large group discussion—follow up on the home work. Open group discussion on field trip.

	Role-play based on a real life experience (during the study phase of DPIP).
	Session on Dos and Don'ts in the village—role-play, transparencies.
	Discussion on fears and apprehensions during the field visit.
1:30 p.m.	LUNCH
	Individuals asked to give their preferences of the Mandals where they would like to work.
	Groups for the field visit formed and asked to choose the villages they would like to visit.
	Feedback on the workshop—content, methodology, resource persons and any other.
	Summation of the 3 day input and recap of each session as per the inputs, learnings and methods.

Notes on Arriving at the Job Description and TNA of Community Co-ordinators and Social Organisers (18.10.2000–19.10.2000)

On the evening of 17.10.2000 approximately 35 CCs/COs gathered at the DRDA training centre at Srikakulam. The expectations (from the workshop) session led to the realisation that the group was very keen on knowing its role in DPIP. Therefore, the next morning half a day was spent on the subject. Once the roles were determined and understood the Training Needs Assessment was undertaken.

Large group was divided into 3 small groups and was asked to list down the roles of a CC as per their understanding (at least 10).

Team 1

1. Facilitator
2. Motivator
3. Build good rapport with people
4. Act like a catalyst
5. Identify some social and economic aspects and train people on those aspects
6. Mobilise and form groups
7. Identification and strengthening of
8. Support the related organisations
9. Good observation
10. Know about government facilities

Team 2

1. Stay in the village
2. Develop rapport
3. Find out the poor
4. Facilitate identification of problems and solutions
5. Find out how CBOs are functioning and enable people to know about it
6. Create awareness about local resources and help people to utilise them
7. Exposure visits groups, skills
8. Have coordination with other institutions
9. Development not only in economic but also in health, education, child labour, environment
10. Use local language and policies

The charts were pasted on the wall and the groups were asked to visit each chart and strike off the common roles identified by them. The large group then discussed the roles that were left and arrived at a list of 10 possible roles for a CC:

Roles of a Community Coordinator

Facilitator
Motivator
Coordinator
Catalyst
Trainer
Mobiliser
Educator
Advocate
Observer
Organiser

These roles were then clubbed into six roles by merging similar roles together as (1) Facilitator, (2) Trainer, (3) Organiser, (4) Catalyst, (5) Observer and (6) Educator.

The large group was then divided into five groups and given a home task—each group was asked to pick up two roles and write the activities that they would entail and make presentations on the same the next day, i.e, 19.10.2000. The groups came out with the following outputs:

Group: Banana

Activities of a Facilitator

1. Analyse poor people's problems in a village; they be mobilised and made to think.
2. People of common interest be made into groups and provided necessary information.
3. Facilitate preparation of plans by the poor people themselves.
4. Through PRA, local problems, issues, resources be identified and mobilised.
5. Build rapport for expression of problems and analysis.
6. Identify and utilise local human resources and skills of the people.
7. Suggest proper legal procedures and legal methods.
8. Facilitate group formation by duly informing the people of the utility of CIG/SHG for poverty eradication.
9. Educate people about the importance of income generation in lean season.
10. Depending on the necessity and context, provide support in connecting with other agencies.

Group: Mango

Activities of the Educator

1. Tell people why they are poor.
2. Enable people to overcome poverty.
3. Educate people about government programmes.
4. Tell people about group formation.
5. Tell people about the importance of education.
6. Educate people on the need for and utility of people's participation.
7. Tell people about the advantage of health and family planning.
8. Educate on environment.
9. Educate of merits and demerits of social practices.
10. Tell them about their rights.
11. Use audio-visual means.

Group: Pineapple

Activities of the Organiser

1. Formation of poor people's Societies.
2. Formation of People's Interest Groups based on the particular problems in their village.
3. Utilising locally available resources to meet their basic needs.
4. Making possible 100% participation of the people.
5. Arrange meetings with villagers.
6. Training, exposure visit, exhibition for problem solving.
7. Help eliminate middlemen between government and people.
8. Conduct vocational training for their skills and abilities.
9. Arrange meetings with the help of CBOs.

Group: Banana

Trainer

1. Train people in government programmes.
2. Literacy health agriculture trainings through role play films, audio visual equipments.
3. Exposure visits.
4. Group discussions, sharing experience and opinions.
5. Group level trainings.
6. Leadership.
7. Book keeping.
8. Financial management.
9. Gender sensitisation.
10. Executive committee members.
11. Asset management training.

Group: Grapes

Catalyst

1. Enable poor to identify their own problems and solutions.
2. Inform people about government programmes and the methods and means of accessing them.
3. Facilitate group formation among the poor.
4. Teach book keeping and finance management.
5. Educate people about their socio-economic and political rights.
6. Enable people to identify their own resources and means to utilise them.
7. Identify skills and develop them.
8. Help people to develop a plan for themselves.
9. Help people to become self reliant by instilling human attitude.
10. Help poor to quickly solve their problems.

Group: Grapes

Observer

1. Observe geographic, social, political and economic situation.
2. Observe health, education, religious and psychological situations.
3. Observe the behaviour and practices of the poor.
4. Observe SHGs.
5. Observe government institutions in a village and people's participation in those institutions.
6. Observe local issues and solutions for those.
7. Observe utilisation of local resources.
8. Observe local traditions, practices, cultural, social evils.
9. Interpersonal relations of the poor.

Group: Apples

Strengthening (Part of the Role of CC)

1. Enable people to form groups and identify their problems and enhance their unity.
2. Identify the skills as a group and as individuals.
3. Train the people to strengthen their skills.
4. Improve the expression skills of the individuals so as to dispel fear and insecurity.
5. Provide minimum education.
6. Help people utilise the available local resources.
7. PRA.
8. Create social awareness.
9. Direct rapport with the government departments.
10. Help women for equal participation.

Skills required

Apple group: Mobiliser

1. Techniques to be used to identify the poor.
2. Formation of SHGs, working, utility etc.
3. How to prepare plans with poor people's participation.
4. How to communicate the government programmes.
5. Knowledge about acts, rights etc.
6. Capability of using the local resources.
7. PRI act.
8. Gender sensitisation.
9. Right expressiveness and confidence.

Skills we have

Grapes group: Observer and catalyst

1. Data collection.
2. Communication.
3. Coordination.
4. Society observation.
5. Mobilisation.
6. Group formation.
7. Strengthening.
8. Managerial skills.
9. Problem identification and analysis.
10. Development and planning.

Skills we need

Grapes group

1. Identification of poorest of the poor.
2. PRA techniques.
3. Utilisation of government programmes.
4. Cultural activities.
5. Effective communication.
6. Management skills.
7. Resource mobilisation.
8. Psychological strength.

Skills required

Banana group: Facilitator

1. Communication skills.
2. Charisma.
3. Organising skill—leadership qualities.
4. Proper understanding and knowledge in different aspects.
5. Initiative skills.
6. Able to strengthen the skills.
7. Proper identification, preference ranking.
8. Friendly nature.
9. Logical mind and scientific thinking.
10. Presence of mind.
11. Analysing and planning skills.

Skills we have

Banana group

1. Friendly nature.
2. Proper identification.
3. Preference ranking.
4. Skills to motivate and encourage people.
5. Communication skills.
6. Ability to conduct exposure visits.

Skills required

Pineapple group: Organiser

1. Effective communication skills.
2. Skills about group formation.
3. Skills in participatory method.
4. Skills in economic activities.
5. Group management skills.
6. Techniques in identifying the poor people.
7. Proper plan to achieve targets.

Skills we have

Mango group

1. Capacity to under society.
2. Capacity to observe.
3. Capacity to explain and talk.
4. Sufficient education.
5. Some ideas.
6. Practical skills.
7. Some technical skills.
8. Some communication skills.

Skills we have

Apple group

1. Develop rapport with any kind of person.
2. To tell about the basic rights.
3. To identify the problems of society.
4. To identify the skills of poor.

Knowledge required

Grapes group

1. Local cultural issues.
2. Resource utilisation.
3. Rights and acts related to them.
4. Identifying the poorest of the poor.
5. Expression in the simplest form.
6. Total information about government programmes and institutions.

Knowledge required

Pineapple Group

1. Dealing with villagers.
2. Media knowledge.
3. Observation knowledge.
4. Understanding the poor people.
5. Customs and traditions.
6. Government policies and programmes.
7. Thrift system.
8. Motivating people for health and sanitation.
9. Knowledge for specific aspects.

Knowledge we have

Grapes group

1. Identifying the poor (some extent).
2. Caste and its importance.
3. Identifying the problems and some solutions.
4. Resources identification.
5. Can tell people about social, political, economic, psychological, educational and health issues.
6. Government programmes and institutions.
7. Formation of SHGs.
8. Identification of skills amongst the poor.

Knowledge we have

Mango group

1. Local language.
2. Social problems.
3. Communication.
4. About Velugu programme.

Knowledge we have

Banana group

1. Aware of the rural atmosphere.
2. Factors for poverty.
3. Local diseases.
4. Local traditions and customs.
5. SHG formation and maintenance.
6. Agriculture patterns.
7. Biodiversity.
8. Local caste system.
9. Local food habits.
10. Social evils.

Knowledge we need

Pineapple group

Need knowledge in all the aspects.

Knowledge we need

Apple group

1. Government policies and programmes.
2. Traditions and customs.
3. Poor people's problems and
4. Rights and acts.

Notes on how Values were Arrived at in Srikakulum

Values form the basis of our attitudes and behaviour and in any institution, group or individual they become the guiding force. The touchstones of a long an arduous journey. In this instance the journey is "eradicating poverty". DPIP has been conceived with great pains and a vision of poverty-free Andhra Pradesh. But as is often the case many great visions bite the dust and fall on the wayside because of lack of values to guide the way. DPIP, therefore, taking no chances and values are of as much importance as the activities and the infrastructure of the programmes.

Keeping this in mind the session on values was undertaken with patience and care. The concept was introduced with a game:

Game	Crash landing
Materials needed	"Post-its" or pieces of paper and pen/pencils
Time needed	two hours
Purpose	To arrive at the core values for a programme or for self or for an institution etc.
Method	Ask the participants to sit in a semi circle. Give each participant six leaves of post-its or six leaves of paper. Present a scenario—you are all travelling to a far off land and you are going by air, and the airline rules say that you cannot carry more than six pieces of luggage. Now on the six leaves write down the six most important pieces of luggage that you would like to carry. Imagine that the six pieces are the six most important values and write them down. Once the participants have written the values, tell them that the plane had to crash land on an island due to some technical snag. The pilot asks the passengers to give away one least important piece of luggage. Collect the "thrown luggage" in a tray or a bowl. Ask the passengers if they would like to retrieve something and

give away something else. Paste the "thrown luggage" on the wall.

Now the passengers board the ship which has come to rescue them. The captain asks them to throw away one more piece of luggage (least important but more important than the first piece that you threw). Collect the piece and paste it on the wall.

The ship begins to sink and the only option is to board the small life-boats. Ask the passengers to give away one more piece of luggage. Collect and paste on the wall.

The small boats reach an island where the passengers are asked to board a helicopter. The pilot asks them to throw away one more piece of luggage. Ask the passengers to get up and paste their respective pieces on the wall.

The helicopter takes off but is unable to land because of too much weight. The pilot asks the passengers to throw away one more piece of luggage.

Since at the end of the last round all the participants are left with one piece of luggage each, ask each one to take a flash card and write down the remaining value in bold writing.

Ask them to place the cards on the floor in a straight line. If the group is large, the list will be very long. So to arrive at a minimum manageable number of values have a discussion in the large group and ask them to prioritise. Then club the ones that mean similar things.

Agree on a minimum number of values that the group would like to keep. In this instance the group agreed to six values.

Since the list was really long the group had to resort to many methods so as to reduce the items in the "List of Values" to the agreed six values, with the least amount of friction. In the final round, the participants were asked to place a blank card in front of each value and place ticks against only six values that they would like to keep. In the end the list was reduced to the following values:

Core Values of DPIP

1. Dedication.
2. Honesty.
3. Truthfulness.
4. Helpfulness.
5. Faith in poor people's potential.
6. Empathy for the poor.

Notes on How Understanding of What is Poverty was Facilitated in Srikakulum

The participants were divided into four groups and asked to come up with a definition of poverty. After a discussion of about 30 minutes the groups came up with a definition of "Poverty". This was then put up on the walls and the groups were to explain their definitions. The discussions generated a lot of heated debate as to what can and cannot be included in the definition. The argument centered around whether to include "psychological needs" as part of poverty or not.

The definitions displayed by the groups were as follows:

Group
Chapati

A situation in which a person is unable to meet the minimum needs (food, shelter, clothes) through his income is said to be a situation of poverty.

Group
Idli with Sambhar

Those who are not able to meet their social, economic and psychological needs and have a backward position in society are said to be in a position of poverty.

Group
Idli with Chutni

Those persons who are not able to meet their social, economic, psychological and political needs and have a backward position in society are said to be in a situation of poverty.

Group
Pesarattu

When people are dependent on others and cannot meet their social, economic and minimum needs; such a situation is called a position of poverty.

After the definitions were discussed the participants were asked to return to their groups and see if they wished to change the definitions. One group changed their definitions of poverty:

Group
Chapati

The state in which the people do not possess the social, basic need, economical, health and psychological security is said to be poverty.

The facilitator enabled the participants to come up with a common definition of poverty in the large group. It was clarified that the debate on what is or isn't poverty is an unending one and that opinions on it are divided the world over. However, the

Indian reality is that poverty is pegged at a certain income level and those below it are considered below the poverty level. The participants were absolutely clear about the difference in the term "poverty" and "poor". This was reflected amply in the definitions given by them since no one gave the definition of "poor". They all emphasised that the state or situation of being poor is poverty. The common definition of poverty as arrived at by the large group is as follows:

> A state in which the people are not able to meet their basic minimum needs (food, clothes, shelter) and do not possess social, economic, health and psychological security is said to be the state of poverty.

Once the participants had described poverty they were asked to list down "who are poor." This exercise was done in the large group—one person wrote on the board while the rest of the group called out. The list that emerged is as follows:

- Scavenger
- Coolie
- Child labourer
- Disabled
- Aged
- Schedule castes and schedule tribes
- Rickshaw puller
- Bonded labourer
- Orphans
- Women (most)
- Destitute
- Nomads

Once they had exhausted the list, the facilitator took them to the list prepared by the facilitator:

Who are functionally poor?

- Small and marginal farmers
- Herdsmen and pastoralists
- Artisans and artisanal fisherfolk
- Refugees
- Other artisans
- Landless
- Tribal people
- Displaced persons
- Women
- Informal sector daily wage earners

Thereafter, the participants were asked to get back into their groups and prepare a list of who causes poverty? The following lists emerged:

The large group went over each list and discussed the reasons for putting down each category. It was realised that no category is absolute and that there will always be some people in any category that will be honest and sensitive to the poor people.

Thereafter, the participants were asked to get back into their groups and discuss what causes poverty. The groups were asked to list down the processes that cause poverty.

Group: Idly Chutni

- Middlemen
- Landlords
- Moneylenders
- Exploiters (businessmen)
- Corrupt and government employees
- Lazy people

Group: Pesarattu

- Vested interests
- Middlemen
- Moneylenders
- Selfish political leaders
- Corrupt officials
- Companies
- Astrologers
- Quacks

Group: Idli Sambhar

- Landlords
- Political leaders
- Administrators (corrupt)
- Casteism (upper caste people)
- Dominant male
- Poor people
- Moneylender
- Middlemen
- Psychological factors

Group: Chapati

- Landlords
- Middlemen
- Upper caste people
- Male dominant (aristocrats)
- Selfish political leaders
- Moneylenders
- Corrupt officials
- Bad habits
- Priests (some)

The groups came up with long lists of processes that cause poverty. However, it may be noted that some of the processes listed are not really processes but symptoms of poverty:

Group: Chapati

- Natural calamities
- Deforestation
- Pollution
- Political disorder
- Environmental (land) degradation
- No utilisation of resources
- Superstition
- Lack of awareness of welfare programmes
- Vices
- Unemployment
- Urbanisation and industrialisation
- Population growth
- Lack of grass-roots level planning
- Lack of knowledge on nutrition
- Lack of education
- No access to health facilities

Group: Idli and Sambhar

- Natural calamities
- Illiteracy and ignorance
- Social traditions and customs
- Unequal distribution of land
- Joint family system (leads to fragmentation of land)
- Over population
- Lack of utilisation of resources
- Low savings
- Excessive expenditure
- Demonstration of effect
- Policies
- Unproductive investment
- Lack of awareness on government policies
- Higher level policies, not at the base
- Not able to select correct beneficiaries
- Lack of people's participation

Group: Pesarattu

- Natural calamities
- Displacement
- Price hike
- Casteism
- Superstitions
- Male domination
- Illiteracy
- Population
- Underutilisation of resources
- No unity
- Low wages
- Accessibility to credit
- Less rural industrialisation
- Improper policies

Group Idly and Sambhar

- Policies
- Unproductive investment
- Lack of awareness on government policies
- Higher level policies, not at the base
- Not able to select correct beneficiaries
- Lack of people's participation

Group: Idli and Chutni

- Natural calamities
- Lack of resources
- Depletion of resources
- Inability to use resources properly
- Faulty identification of beneficiaries
- Price rise
- Wages not commensurate to the labour put in
- Population growth
- Illiteracy
- Superstition
- Social evils

The groups were then encouraged to look at the charts put up by the facilitator as per his experience and understanding and compare their charts.

Proximate Causes of Poverty
(Prepared by the Facilitator)

- Isolation
- Material deprivation
- Alienation
- Dependence
- Lack of decision making power
- Vulnerability
- Assetlessness
- Insecurity

Basic Causes of Poverty
(Prepared by the Facilitator)

- Dualism
- Domestic policies
- Degradation of natural resources
- Natural cycles and disasters
- General biases
- Cultural and ethnic biases
- General biases
- Exploitative intermediation
- Political conflict and civil strife
- International forces

In the post lunch session the flow of the workshop was a little disturbed by the entry of the ITDA Chief. He had come with the express purpose of meeting Dr. Amitava Mukherjee and stayed on to address the workshop and remarked, *inter alia*, that "there were two kinds of poverty: One, poverty because of the system and two, poverty out of choice".

Notes on Session on Attitudes and Behaviour Commenced

A transparency on the subject was shown and discussion initiated.

Move Away from Domination

Role-play was done on landlords and bonded labourers, moneylenders and borrowers, husbands and wives (in pairs with reversals).

The purpose was to enable an understanding of behaviour that is dominating.

Most of the participants depicted the behaviour as violence. There was a lot of laughter and physical pushing and hitting. On being asked how they felt as the dominated and then the dominator, most said that they felt bad and humiliated as the oppressed. However, nobody was really forth coming on how they felt as the oppressor. It was noticed that some women were trying to depict a more subtle form of domination—humiliation, crying, begging, helplessness. Specially in the role of wife they were trying to depict oppression and domination through monotony, husbands sitting and laughing with friends while they are asked to bring tea, cook food and keep out of the way.

The facilitator asked the participants:

1. Why was there so much laughter in doing something that shows domination?
2. Why did most participants show domination as aggression?
3. What did the women feel and what were they trying to show?

The point is that domination is not always physical and apparent. It is very rarely that one finds a moneylender misbehaving with the borrower and yet there is oppression, domination and exploitation in the relationship. The same is applicable to the landlord and bonded labour relationship. The domination is subtle, crippling and psychological in that it destroys the spirit and dignity of a person. Therefore, one must always be aware of the subtle forms of domination.

Arrogance Must be Avoided

All behaviour that shows arrogance e.g. wagging the finger, not allowing others to talk, body language must be avoided.

Abandon Holding the Stick

The poor people in village are the best judge of their situation and need. They must be the ones from whom we learn. It is not our purpose to go and lecture; years of "holding the stick" syndrome has made development a top down process. For years bureaucrats sitting in planning commission have decided what the poor need and how they should get it, but now there is a realisation that the government programmes and view of the poor have been faulty. Therefore, DPIP is an opportunity to reverse the top down model of development. Learning from the people, planning with the people, implementation by the people and monitoring and assessment by the people have to be the touch stones of our work.

Be Self-Aware and Self-Critical

We must at all times be aware of our body language, spoken words, clothes and action in the field. It is important to remember that 70 per cent of our communication is non verbal. Our behaviour must be inclusive, sensitive and open. It is important to reflect on our work and analyse it critically so as to keep alert and creative.

Do Not Lecture

For example the session on arriving at the job description could have been through a lecture but instead we took time and involved the people in describing their own roles. It was more effective and will be remembered by the participants. In the same vein it may be remembered that poor people also appreciate creativity. When possible, use inclusive methods of learning and involve in developing new methods of doing things. Learning is a mutual process.

Abandon the Search for a Blue Print

There is no one way of doing a thing therefore, it may be remembered that constant search is the only answer, a search for newer creative ways, better methods and prgrammes.

Embrace Errors

It is only human to err but the mistake must be accepted and lesson learnt. If we do anything wrong it is always to say so and move on rather than keep making mistakes to hide one mistake.

Respect Diversity

No community or group of people is homogenous. For years in our country it was assumed that all poor people are the same therefore, one type of programme will yield similar results everywhere. Most of our government programmes, like JRY, IAY and now SGRY etc., have been designed on this premise with the result that they have failed miserably. Even among the poor there are people who are poorer. Men and women have different needs, children have different needs, different tribes in differing localities have differing needs. Therefore, diversity must be respected. Respect not only diversity of problems but as much diversity of solutions, diversity of views, diversity of opinion. The desire to homogenise and have "fit-all" free size attitude should be abandoned.

Listen and Observe

Instead of just hearing, the emphasis should always be on hearing with an objective and seeing with an objective.

Notes on Exercise Linking Values Attitudes and Behaviour Carried out in Srikakulum

Values, attitudes and behaviour are thus linked with each other. Values and attitudes are the invisible parts of our personality while behaviour is the visible part of our personality such as the way we talk, the way we dress, the way we act and the way in which we communicate.

An exercise was done to distinguish between the three:

Values	*Attitudes*	*Behaviour*
Are beliefs on which we practise	Are an approach, a way of seeing things	Is the way we act in doing our job; what is visible through action, body language dress and speech

The participants were asked to divide into 5 groups based on the values the group had arrived at for DPIP the previous day. They were asked to then work in groups and come up with some examples and behaviour related with each value. Thereafter presentations were made on the subject. At the end of the exercise the difference between the three was fairly clear to the participants.

Helpfulness

Attitude	**Behaviour**
To react immediately.	Be responsive.
Be available to all.	Be generous.
Help to the fullest.	Be with people.
Think responsibly.	Help to extent possible.
Identify the needy people.	Enlighten people to know the reality.

Faith in poor people's potential

Attitude	Behaviour
Understand local language.	Stay in the village and develop rapport.
Respect opinions and problems of the poor.	Give patient hearing.
Mobilise the poor.	Encourage people.
Participatory attitude.	Should be encouraged through skill development/training.
	Involve the poor in everything.

Honesty

Attitude	Behaviour
Poor should decide.	Involve all.
Don't yield to pressure.	Faith in work.
Bravery.	Work together.
Develop rapport.	Respect the poor.
Poor have potential.	Have affection.
Have faith.	Never impose our ideas.
Respect people's opinions.	

Truthfulness

Attitude	Behaviour
Don't wilfully commit mistakes.	Admit mistakes.
Right attitude.	Discharge duties properly.
Have faith.	Work daringly.
Have right perception.	Follow the right behaviour.
Unselfish.	Work honestly.
Not to cheat.	Don't cheat.
Value good things.	Follow good things.

Empathy

Attitude	Behaviour
Listen patiently.	Behave patiently.
Respond.	Consider the poor as we do ourselves and help.
Feeling of equality.	At all times behave respectfully.

It may be noted that the above charts do not distinguish between attitudes and behaviour very clearly. It was explained that it is not necessary that every attitude will have a different list of behaviour. Many attitudes can be reflected in one action or vice a versa. Basically, the important thing to remember is that behaviour is the visible part of us while attitudes and values are invisible. Behaviour constitutes of what we say, how we say it, what we do, how we do it and the way we dress.

Appendix A-3.3

Mehbubnagar

Day-1

The Project Director, the Joint Project Director, the Gender Specialist (DPMU), the Gender Specialist (SPMU), Programme Manager, Social Discrimination Project; and the Monitoring and Evaluation Manager, and Manager Administration, all of DPIP Mahabubnagar, worked out the following Job Descriptions.

Project Director

1. Co-ordinate DPMU Activities
2. HRD and Personnel management is the responsibility of the PD. This includes recruitment of staff for DPMU, MCSC, consultants, experts and determining their terms of reference and terms and conditions of recruitment; and nurturing staff under his/her charge.
3. Establish and administer a system of Performance Appraisal of the staff in DPMU and MCSC, with appropriate follow up mechanism to improve performance as may be warranted.
4. Defining boundary conditions for all functionaries in DPMU/MCSC including setting out limits of authority, delegation of powers.
5. Interface with SPMU, SERP, IPE and other DPMU.
6. Interface with and co-ordinate with other line departments, NGOs, civil society actors, CBOs and other institutions.
7. Be responsible for financial management including appraisal and sanction of sub-project proposals.
8. Convene the District Poverty Mission/District Advisory Board Meetings.
9. Such other tasks as may be assigned by the chief executive officer, SERP and SPMU from time to time.

Manager Administration

1. Overall management of the office-establishment and general administration.
2. Correspondence to SPMU/DPMU/line departments/MCSC and reports relating to establishment and general administration.
3. Logistic arrangements for DPMU activities.
4. Maintenance of equipment/vehicles/buildings etc.
5. Link between DPMU/MCSC/Samakyas.
6. Other tasks that may be assigned by the project director from time to time.

Monitoring and Evaluation Manager

1. Facilitate and develop Baseline Data and develop MIS at all levels of the project (SHG/CIGs/MMS/DPMU).
2. Facilitate Participatory Monitoring, Evaluation and Impact Assessment of the project and develop indicators for M&E and IA at all levels.
3. Capacity building of CBOs/COs/CCs/on M&E in co-ordination with the Training Co-ordinator.
4. Develop and operationalise a feedback mechanism on project activities/processes to improve performance and disseminate learning.
5. Monitor the performance of the project activities and initiate remedial action.
6. Documentation of "good practices" and "best problems" for information dissemination.
7. Responsible for input/output monitoring of the project at all levels through a computerised MIS.
8. Other tasks that may be assigned to him by the project director from time to time.

Gender Specialist

1. Sensitise and build capacity of all stakeholders on gender issues where stakeholders include DPMU/CO/CC/CBOs/line departments/families/community.
2. Incorporate gender dimension in all project interventions with particular focus on adolescent girls/girl children/single women.
3. Be responsible for advocacy and networking with institutions having relevant experience on gender issues.
4. Identification of resource persons for capacity building of the stakeholders on gender issues.
5. Documenting and facilitating the development of information centre at the district resource centre on gender.
6. Any other task that may be assigned by the project director from time to time.

Training Co-ordinator

1. Identifying the training needs of the stakeholders at periodic intervals.
2. Develop training modules and training materials relevant to local context and for local cadre of "bare-foot professionals".
3. Identification and capacity building of resource persons within or outside and network with training institutions/individuals.
4. Conduct and co-ordinate training programmes in project area at all levels.
5. Co-ordinate with the training co-ordinator, SPMU to develop training plans for DPMU.

6. Carry out training audit and evaluation of training programmes except those conducted by the training co-ordinator herself/himself, for which the PD will carry out training audit and evaluation.
7. Help the project director in assessing the effectiveness of the training/workshops etc.
8. Sensitise line departments and other institutions on relevant issues.
9. Coordinate with line departments to train local cadre in relevant areas.
10. Carry out training needs assessments and co-ordinate the trainings for personnel employed by the CBOs.
11. Other tasks that may be assigned by the project director from time to time.

Finance Manager

1. Be responsible for developing and implementing computerised financial management system in collaboration with the financial manager SPMU.
2. Maintenance of manual financial management till such time as a computerised FMS is not in place.
3. Undertake regular financial monitoring of the DPMU/CBOs—MMS, VOs, SHGs, CIGs, which include field visits.
4. Co-ordinate training to accounts staff at DPMU and CBOs on financial management system.
5. Liaison with banks and micro-credit institutions in the district.
6. Documentation
7. Prepare periodical financial statements of DPMU for social audit.
8. Any other task that may be assigned by the PD from time to time.

Company Associate

1. Maintenance of computerised financial management software.
2. Maintenance of all computer hardware and software in the DPMU.
3. Management of database and systems administration.
4. Computerisation of all office correspondence, reports, MIS etc.
5. Other tasks that may be assigned by the project director from time to time.

Day-2

On Day-2 all the Social Organisers (COs) and the Community Co-ordinators (CCs) along with the PD and other Key Staff of DPMU met at a place outside Mehbubnagar.

Step-1:

Each of the participants was allowed 15 minutes to contemplate and discuss with their neighbours the role that they have to play as Social Organisers.

Step-2:

They were requested to write down their thoughts on a piece of paper.

Step-3:

Once this was completed, a volunteer was asked for who would write on the white board the proceedings of the meeting.

Step-4:

The participants were then asked in the clockwise direction to tell us what they have perceived as the functions of the CO. As they read out their views, the volunteer recorded the same on the white board. While in the beginning each participants had a lot to say as we progressed, they became more frugal as their previous speakers would already have had said what they intended to say.

Step-5:

When all the participants had their say, they were encouraged to identify the ones which were repetitions and delete them. There were several repetitions, which were deleted.

Step-6:

Participants were requested to revisit what have been recorded on the White Board and see if they can club them, taking care not to confuse between functions, behaviour, methods and values.

Step-7:

Once the job description was worked out they were displayed on the wall of the main hall of the workshop venue and all the participants were encouraged to reflect on them and make changes if they so desired. Some changes were made. Thereafter the job description was finalised.

The final job description of the COs was worked out, which is as under:

Social Organiser

1. Facilitate preparation of plans for *Mandals*: Annual Work Plan and Financial Plan.
2. Co-ordinate with community co-ordinators and community volunteers in implementing project activities.
3. Monitor activities, assess the progress of the activities and follow up at the *Mandal* level.
4. Facilitate CBOs to develop and implement their own programmes.
5. Be responsible for MIS at the *Mandal* level.
6. Build linkages with Government institutions/NGOs/banks/other financial institutions at the *Mandal* level.
7. Link between DPMU and Mandal and other DPIP *Mandals*.
8. Identify training needs/capacity building needs at the *Mandal* level for staff/community members and communicate the same to training co-ordinator, DPMU.
9. Co-ordinate and conduct training programmes at the *Mandal* level in developing capacity of NGOs.

10. Facilitate community based organisations to resolve conflicts.
11. Identify the weaknesses in the management of CBOs and working out ways and means along with them to deal with the weaknesses.
12. Focus the project interventions on social issues like unsociability, child marriage, child labour etc.
13. Document all activities and initiatives at the *Mandal* level—"good practices" and "best problems".
14. Identify opportunities and linkages at the *Mandal* level—small industries, marketing opportunities etc.

A process similar to the one followed for the social organisers was followed for determining the job description of the community co-ordinators, except that the COs were not part of the exercise whereas the CCs were part of the exercise for setting up the job description of the COs.

The job description for the CCs arrived at looks like the following:

Community Co-ordinators

1. Identify the poorest of the poor and form new groups.
2. Build capacity of the existing groups and train them on various aspects including on local resources development, skill development etc.
3. Work for the sustainability of the CBOs—SHGs, VOs and MSS and build awareness on various issues like rights and entitlements.
4. Assess the extent of discrimination based on gender and castes.
5. Promote sustainable (low external input) agriculture and facilitate the use of indigenous technology.
6. Linkages of government programmes and the line departments.
7. Facilitate the community activists, volunteers and help them through book keeping and auditing.
8. Facilitate in developing use of participatory methods in identifying local resources and managing and implementing programmes by CBOs.
9. Focus on child labour, health, women, SCs, STs and education.
10. Facilitate groups to deal with/manage conflicts.
11. Facilitate the process whereby the community is able to identify the problems to initiate actions.
12. Advocacy, lobbying and campaigning for the poor.

Once this was completed, these were written on chart papers and pasted on the walls of the main hall of the workshop venue, where all the participants (COs, CCs and the DPMU Staff) were invited and encouraged to critically look at the functions of the CCs and comment upon. Clarifications were sought and then these were taken as final in so far as the groups were concerned.

Appendix A-3.4

Adilabad

Role-clarity and TNA workshop in Adilabad on 12th and 13th November 2000.

The brief outline of the Workshop is as follows:

Day-1

Introduction of resource person and participants.

Expectations of the participants from the workshop.

Group formation.

Clarification of the roles and activities concepts.

Role of the community co-ordinator—small groups.

Activities for each role—small group.

Expected role of the project director (through the eyes of the community co-ordinators).

Day-2

Identification of skills and knowledge for the activities—small groups and presentations.

Skills and knowledge that exists within the group—small groups and presentations.

Filling up the individual questionnaires.

Panel for responses to the roles of the PD identified by the community co-ordinators.

Arriving at the DPIP core values—Game.

Values, attitudes and behaviours—an initiation.

Day-1: 12.11.2000

The day began with the introduction of resource persons and participants. The participants and the resource persons sat in circle and introduced themselves along with an action to describe the way they were feeling at that point in time. Sometimes this can be used to gauge the mood of the group and the sessions can be adjusted accordingly.

Once the introductions were done, the participants were asked to play a game:

Game	**Fruit salad**
Time needed	25 minutes or less depending on the number of participants
Purpose	Group formation
Process	• The facilitator writes down names of as many fruits on the board as the groups to be formed (in this instance five groups were to be formed named as mangoes, grapes, oranges, papaya and banana). • The participants are asked to sit in a circle on chairs. • The facilitator stands in the centre of the circle and calls out at random one of the names of the said fruits. • Participants of that particular fruit group are then to run and exchange seats, the one left out then takes on the centre stage and calls. • If the facilitator at any point yells "fruit salad" the entire group is supposed to run and exchange seats. • The game produces laughter and physical activity thus energising and relaxing the participants.

Once the participants were divided into groups, they were asked to sit in small circles. In order to bring about an understanding on the issue of "role" and "activity", the participants were asked to give the Telugu and Hindi translation of the terms. Thereafter the participants were asked to discuss within the group and decide a role that a man or woman plays in the society. Each group was then asked to present the role and its corresponding activities. Through the activity it was possible to distinguish the difference in the two concepts and the groups could move on to discussing their role/s as community coordinator. The groups came up with the following:

Grapes

- Observer
- Motivator
- Councellor
- Educator
- Organiser
- Supervisor
- Participator

The rest of the participants then asked the group for clarifications:

What do you mean by participator? Don't you think in order to do the roles specified one has to anyway participate?

What is the difference between educator and motivator?

Motivator has an element of "*chaitanya*" which the educator may not have.

What is the difference between supervisor and counsellor?

Bananas

- Organise them and establish their own identity
- Strengthen them, local management and self rule with support of main stream institutions
- Developing agenda
- Social organiser
- Learner
- Educator
- Observer
- Synergise
- Developer
- Teacher
- Learner
- Evaluation manager

The facilitator asked the second group to cross out what had been written by the first group. This was seen as "losing out" by some members. The following questions were clarified:

What is the difference between educator and teacher?

What do you mean by interpreter?

Views and ideas of people differ from village to village, therefore someone will have to put them together and interpret them.

"Interpreter is not a translator. He/she adds to what is being said—gives meaning".

"Organise them but how can one establish his own identity. People have an identity...one is making them aware of their identity. A correction therefore, needs to be made.

What is the difference between a learner and an observer? One learns from observing?

Mangoes

- Observer
- Motivator
- Mother
- Teacher
- Organiser
- Councellor
- Catalyst
- Coordination

The following clarifications were sought and given:

The facilitator once again asked the group to cut out what ever had been written in the earlier charts. He explained that "cutting does not mean that it is unimportant, it simply means that we all are thinking in the same lines. And that it has been said earlier".

Explain "mother".

What do you mean by catalyst? "The word comes from chemistry, it's a chemical that helps in the reactions but does not change its own properties.

Coordinator is a "*samanayak*".

Papaya

- Mingling with the people: integrator
- To utilise natural and human resources—trainer
- Social change—motivator
- Educator
- Group builder
- Coordinator
- Organiser

Oranges

The following issues were clarified:

What is the difference between trainer and educator? "We need to spend some time on the advocacy role".

Some of the things listed in this chart are qualities and qualities are not a role.

• Motivator	• Patience
• Coordinator	• Enthusiasm
• Trainer	• Encouragement
• Mobiliser	• Brave
• Educator	• Motivation
• Advocate	• Advocacy
• Observer	• Coordination
• Love, Sympathy, Kindness	• Observation

In the post lunch session, the groups were asked to write down the remaining (those that were not crossed out) roles on flash cards. These were then laid on the floor in a straight vertical line:

1. Mother
2. Catalyst
3. Coordinator
4. Trainer
5. Group builder
6. Integrator
7. Advocacy
8. Supervisor
9. Organiser
10. Educator
11. Counsellor
12. Motivator
13. Observer and learner
14. Participator
15. Interpreter
16. Synergiser
17. Developing agenda

18. Strengthen them, local management self role with support of main stream institutions
19. Evaluation manager

The long list of 19 roles was reduced to 14 through debate and clarifications and clubbing together similar roles. Then a further consensus was built among the group to decide on a smaller list of core roles for the community co-ordinators. Once the group agreed to bring the number to seven the procedure of voting was adopted to arrive at the decision.

The participants were asked to place a blank flash card against each of the remaining 14 roles. Then they were given a "kitty of seven ticks" and asked to place ticks against any seven roles of their choice. The participants had the option of marking less than seven ticks, if they did not find seven roles but they can neither put more than one tick against any role nor put more than seven ticks. An "honour system" was accepted. The result was as follows:

Roles	*Number of Ticks*
Mother	15
Catalyst	9
Co-ordinator	28
Trainer	18
Group builder	7
Integrator	1
Advocate	22
Organiser	28
Educator	27
Counsellor	15
Motivator	33
Observer	27
Learner	13
Supervisor	

The maximum score that any one role could receive was 40 (no. of participants). The process of placing the ticks and then counting them was explained as "scoring". Then the seven roles which secured the highest scores were decided on as the roles of a Co-ordinator:

1.	Motivator	33
2.	Organiser	28
3.	Coordinator	28
4.	Educator	27
5.	Observer/learner	27
6.	Advocacy	22

Once the roles were agreed on, the participants were re-divided into three groups through a game. The three groups that emerged were as follows:

1. Latha group dealing with Organiser, Motivator
2. Ganesh group dealing with Advocacy, Observer and Learner
3. Rajeshwar group dealing with Educator, Co-ordinator.

The groups were then given the task of discussing the activities against each role (as ascribed to the groups). Once this was done the charts were rotated among all the three groups and the members were asked to add any activity/ies that they felt had been left out.

Concept of Advocacy was explained briefly in order to facilitate the determination of activities:

Advocacy is to:

1. Create pressure and pressure points to change policies, laws, programmes, activities etc., that are anti poor.
2. Pressurise and create pressure points for implementation of pro poor laws, policies, programmes etc.

The groups made the following presentations on the activities appertaining to each role:

Latha Group: Motivator

- Identification of talent, encourage them e.g., human resources.
- Encourage in their interested field for example agriculture.
- Motivate to eradicate poverty, e.g., successful stories in their localities means to overcome poverty and also motivate them to overcome social psychological barriers.
- Motivate to adopt new agricultural practices e.g. demonstrate progress.
- Encourage people to participate in PRI meetings.
- Motivate people to establish adult education.
- Motivate people to adopt family welfare schemes—facilitate to discuss in group meetings, appreciate people who have adopted family welfare methods, facilitate group meetings to discuss health and hygiene issues.
- Motivate parents to send their children to school.
- Sensitise people on social evils like untouchability, drinking liquor, child labour, bonded labour.
- Creating awareness on development schemes.

Latha Group: Organiser

- Identify the poorest of the poor.
- Identify existing groups.
- Help in solving problems of groups.
- Strengthening of organisations.
- Facilitate to access required funds.
- Observe the working process of the groups.
- Facilitate the activities of the groups.
- Giving importance.
- Organise people for a common cause.
- Facilitate members to participate in group activities.

Ganesh Group: Observer and Learner

- Observe geographical conditions (natural resources, population, poverty).
- Observe living conditions—social, economic, political, cultural and services.
- Observe income, expenditure and savings.
- Observe literacy rates (primary, secondary, high school, drop outs, employment).
- Observe wages (work, men and women).
- Observe women and child problems—child labour, dowry etc.
- Observe when they are free—getting up to sleeping.
- Observe all government policies—implementation.
- Observe their lifestyle.

Ganesh Group: Advocacy

- Guide the poorest of the poor to protect forest conservation.
- Encourage poor people to pressurise the government to implement land reforms.
- Guide the very poor people to abolish bonded labour.
- Organise poorest of the poor to reduce child labour.
- Encourage the people to dispense with child marriages and dowry.
- To bring awareness about human rights.
- Sensitise the poorest communities about gender inequality and fight for it.
- Motivate the poorest people to oppose SC/ST atrocities.

Rajeshwar Group: Coordinator

- Creating coordination among the poorest.
- Linkages between government institutions and people (line departments).
- Linkages between existing village institutions (AWWL, COMM, VTDA).
- Linkages between resource persons (ANM, AW etc.).
- Linkages with NGO networks.
- Linkages with Velugu team in other *Mandals*.
- Having common understanding.

Rajeshwar Group: Educator

- Undertaking literacy programmes—educating women about the need for literacy by conducting interaction sessions, group discussions, educating villagers about effects of drop outs, encouraging people to have adult education.
- Health education—conducting seminars, film shows and health camps.
- Skill development—conducting awareness camps, exposure visits and exchange visits, conducting training programmes for transfer of technology.
- Social activities—conducting cultural programmes, film shows, seminars, causes and means to overcome poverty, encouraging optimism and individuality.
- Economic activities—interaction with people, exchange visits to successful groups, DWCRA and thrift camps, exposure to expert views by workshops, identifying internal potential.

Responses to the presentations and clarifications given on the following:

- Communication is very important—one must be sure that what he/she is presenting is what he/she really wants to communicate.
- The group that presented on advocacy just identified issues for advocacy and did not concentrate on activities, requested to rewrite the charts.
- Co-ordination role also did not reflect any activities. As a matter of fact, the group members used the words co-ordination and forming linkages or networking interchangeably.
- Will we as organisers identify the poor or the poorest of the poor?
- Will you form groups or facilitate group formation?
- In motivation one needs to think—how can people get motivated, how they get motivated and then frame the activities.

After the presentation on activities, the participants were divided into two groups. They were given the handout on velugu project and asked to read it. Thereafter, they were asked to come up with their expectations of the role of a PD.

The groups came up with the following after a lot of discussion and hesitation:

Role	**Responses of the Facilitator**
• Designer	Please contemplate on designer of what?
• Guide	Please specify guide to whom, for what?
• Inspirational leader	
• Advice team member in implementation	
• Coordinate the CCs and COs and other subordinates.	
• Facilitate his team	Specify which team and to what end?
• Decision maker	Specify what the PD is supposed to do?
• He is responsible for HRD	
• He is responsible for personnel and hiring, recruiting etc.	
• Evaluation	Give details of what, whom, why?
• Educator	Be more categorical "who will he educate?
• Monitoring and review	monitor whom and what?
• Linkages with the line departments	
• Coordinate with various DPMUs	
• Mobiliser of resources	

The groups were asked to work late and rewrite the charts on activities as well as clarify the roles of PD.

13.11.2000

The participants had worked the previous night and made appropriate corrections to the charts on activities related to the roles of the community coordinator. The expected roles of the project director were also written on flash cards and put up on the wall.

The day's proceedings began with the division of participants into five groups. The groups were asked to work on identifying the knowledge and skills that they will need in order to be effective in the roles identified by them. The groups came up with the following:

Group 1

Knowledge and Skills Needed for the Role as Coordinator

KNOWLEDGE

1. Who are the poorest of the poor.
2. Where are the poorest.
3. Knowledge about the line departments.
4. What is the Velugu programme/activities.
5. Identification of active needs.
6. Rehabilitation of the alcoholic poorest of the poor.
7. Knowledge about local institutions and sphere of their activities.
8. Knowledge of SC/ST communities.

SKILLS

1. Communication skills.
2. Networking skills.
3. Skills to identify the poorest of the poor.
4. Helping them and taking help.
5. Skill of listening patiently to their problems.
6. Discovery and alleviation of rural poverty.
7. Determination of the effect of the poorest of the poor responsibilities.
8. How to develop groups and individuals.
9. Interpersonal skills.

Group 2

Knowledge and Skills Needed for the Role as Educator

KNOWLEDGE

1. About social problems like child marriages, dowry system, untouchability, child labour etc.
2. About causes of diseases, control and prevention.
3. About economic problems like—savings and expenditure, income generation and development activities.
4. About education—school dropouts, men and women.
5. About leadership qualities.
6. Modern technology—agricultural methods etc.
7. Knowledge of gender equality.
8. Knowledge of SC/STs and weaker sections.

SKILLS

1. Action—mono action
2. Songs, dance, drama—*kalajatha* for health and education awareness.
3. Demonstration—field shows.
4. Exhibition—charts, films, photographs.
5. Training—participatory approaches.
6. Expressions—teaching, lecturing, conducting public meetings.

Group 3

Knowledge and Skills Needed for the Role of Organiser

KNOWLEDGE

1. Who is the poorest of the poor.
2. What is poverty.
3. What are the causes of poverty.
4. Where are the poorest of the poor.
5. Group formation.
6. Qualities of good groups.
7. Knowledge about minimum needs requirements.
8. Welfare programmes.
9. Gender equality and SC/ST problems.

SKILLS

1. Observing skills—living conditions.
2. Facilitation skills.
3. Skill to conduct meetings.
4. Communication skills.
5. Ability to learn from the poor.
6. Skill of unlearning.
7. Listening skill.
8. Analysing skill.
9. Skill to bring gender equality.
10. Skill to involve SC/ST.

Group 4

Knowledge and Skills Needed for the Role of Observer and Learner

KNOWLEDGE

1. About MRO and other departments.
2. Local language.
3. Preparation of questionnaire.
4. Poorest of the poor.
5. About dropout working as child labour in various fields.
6. Know about their life style.
7. Know whether the government policies are implemented or not.

SKILLS

1. Data collection from MRO, MDO, PHC, schools and other government offices.
2. Interaction with people.
3. Questionnaire, interview and discussion skills.
4. Data collection from ANM, *anganwadi* worker etc.
5. Survey skills.
6. Communication skills.
7. Living among the people skill.
8. Interaction with groups—DWACRA, CMEY, VTDA.
9. Discussions with the beneficiaries.

Group 5

Knowledge and skills needed for the role of Motivator

KNOWLEDGE

1. About people who have talents.
2. Knowledge of talents relevant to the poor.
3. About areas in which poor people are interested.
4. About their dislikes.
5. What is poverty.
6. Causes of poverty.
7. Where poverty is prevalent in the society.
8. Current agriculture methods.
9. Demonstration of agricultural plots.
10. Exchange and exposure visits.
11. What is illiteracy.
12. Methods of family planning.
13. Causes for drop outs.

SKILLS

1. Interaction and rapport building.
2. Communication skills.
3. Listening ability.
4. Skill to observe.
5. Skill to read body language.
6. Organise group meetings.
7. Organise debates.
8. Organise film shows.
9. Sing motivation songs.
10. Skill to implement participatory methods.
11. Identify existing agricultural practices.
12. Identification of illiteracy problem.
13. Bring gender equality.

Once the presentations were over the facilitator made the following comments/ observations:

- Do you find any gaps in the presentations? He pointed out three major gaps:
- There is no mention of gender in any of the presentations (in the above charts it seems like gender has been mentioned but it was only added by the participants after being pointed out).
- No one has spoken about *dalits* and tribals though they are the focus of the DPIP project (in the above shown charts this has been added after being pointed out)
- Then there is whole issue of people centered development. Not participation but people centered development because participation is possible even without it being people focused.

It was agreed that these issues will be crosscutting issues and should be taken as integral to all the activities and not dealt with as separate issues.

Once this was done, the participants were asked to get back to the small groups and write down the knowledge and skills that they already possess have. The participants came up with the following:

Presentation 1

Communication skills i.e. local and tribal languages
Networking skills
Identification of the poorest of the poor
Formation of groups
Identifying active needs
Organising the poorest of the poor
Conducting meetings
Driving licence
Knowledge about line departments
Gender equality
Knowledge about dropouts and child labour
Demonstration
Living among the poorest of the poor
Skills to involve the depressed and disadvantaged communities
Drama, dance, singing, body language

Presentation 2

Group formation skill
Motivation skill
Living among the poor
Approach and interaction skill
Identification of the weaker section of the society
Identify the poorest of the poor
Observation skill
Communication skill
Organisation skill
To encourage the women to participate in awareness and development
Group book keeping skill
Local language skill
Analysis skill
Knowledge of the living conditions of the poor
Knowledge of the minimum needs
Knowledge
Of socio-economic problems
Knowledge on groups

Knowledge on natural resources
SC/ST lifestyle knowledge
Knowledge of gender equality
Knowledge about dropout and child labour

Presentation 3

Communication skills
Observation
Participation skills
Local language skill
Actions skill
Singing and dancing
Exhibition
Forming women and self help groups
Counselling skills
Knowledge about government programmes
Knowledge about child and women problems
Knowledge about SC/STs problem
Knowledge about conducting surveys
Knowledge about group formation

Presentation 4

Motivation skill
Communication skill
Observation skill
Analysis skill
Skill of participation
Skill of acting
Identification of the poorest of the poor
Knowledge about tribal ladies and their problems

Presentation 5

Knowledge of defining poverty
Knowledge of causes of poverty
Knowledge of "Velugu" programme
Knowledge of SC/ST community
Knowledge of women problems
Child labour, IMR, dropouts
Interaction skills with the poor people
Communication skills
Interpersonal skills

Observation and learning skills

Skill to involve the poorest of the poor in development

Networking skills

Listening skills

Observations by the facilitator:

This methodology of arriving at what we do and do not know is called a gap analysis. Nobody has mentioned the skills (required or existing) of project formulation. It is the most critical skill needed in this project, as the emphasis is on building the capacities of the community to prepare projects for their own development.

The post-lunch session started with the responses of the PDs to the roles expected of them by the Community Co-ordinators.

Expected role of the PD, APD, JPD

1. Coordinator
2. Monitoring the implementation and progress of the project
3. HRD
4. Mobilise resources
5. Facilitator
6. Guide
7. Advice
8. Designer—capacity builder

Venugopal Sought Clarifications on the Following Counts

Please clarify: advice to whom and what?

What is the difference between guide and advice? "Do we mean giving ideas about the project? Modalities and project guidelines is what you mean?"

Is Guide and Advice the same thing?

The term Coordinator needs to be elaborated.

The participants responded to the issues raised by Venugopal, except guide and advice.

The facilitator then resolved the difference between guide and advice. Guiding the CCs is tantamount to showing them the path. Advising is responding to the path indicated or chosen by the CCs. In some cases, advice so given is binding (advice amounts to an order) but in case of guidance there is no element of compulsion.

After the reading and discussion on the Velugu project, the following roles were added: "Finance and budgeting".

Responses by Sivakotti Prasad

Capacity building role implies that one has to build capacities of the community but I want to ask whose responsibility is it? Is it the project director's responsibility or the trainer at DPMU or the CC and SO at the *Mandal* level? He thought it was the responsibility of the CCs and COs at the *Mandal* level. The participants thought "it was a joint responsibility".

What activities are you expecting from the PD under HRD? How can the PD organise exposure visits for 30 groups? This work will have to be done by the CCs.

PD will be responsible for building the capacities of the staff and for the community he will guide and advise.

Is mobilising the resources, the sole responsibility of the PD? Who will do it at the *Mandal* level? He did not see it in the role chart or the activity charts of the CC. It should be added.

Is monitoring the sole responsibility of the PD? He thought it was also the responsibility of the CO at the *Mandal* level.

Do you accept that all the mentioned roles of the PD are also the roles of the CCs and COs at the *Mandal* level?

The CCs agreed that the roles of the PD were also the roles of the CCs and COs at the *Mandal* level and at the Community level respectively.

Responses of Navin Mittal

Who will motivate the CCs and COs? He thought that perhaps the roles of guide and advice can be subsumed under the wider role of the facilitator.

He pointed out that there are two aspects—HRD and Thinking. Who will do the thinking? Nobody has said anything about that. Planning and looking ahead are important functions. According to him facilitation should be emphasised and not advice and guide. Facilitating is to bring out the best in people through a process. What Dr. Mukherjee has been doing here is facilitation, being a catalyst.

We have been educating and lecturing for years and it has not led us anywhere. Now we need to change and instead of telling people we need to ask and facilitate.

HRD is related to the staff of DPMU and Capacity Building is for the communities.

The Facilitator then mentioned that we have to consider—who will do the visioning, thinking and conceptualising? For innovations and initiatives someone has to think. The PD has to think ahead, in fact the facilitator thought he would say he has to dream.

The Facilitator requested the Group to consider: Who will set the limits of authority? Who will decide as to who will do what? It was agreed by all that this should be the role of the PD.

The Third Session of the day was given to Values.

Values

Q What are values?

After questioning and debating, it was agreed that Values are beliefs that are put into practice.

In order to arrive at the core values a game was played. The process of it is as follows:

Game	**Sinking of the Titanic**
Materials	Post-its or flash cards or just pieces of paper (usually six pieces per participant but in this instance we used only four), pen/pencil
Time	Two hours
Purpose	Arriving at the core values
Process	Ask the participants to sit in a semi-circle, pass the post-its and ask them to take four leaves each (in this instant we also asked the participants to pair up and decide on the values).

Ask the participants to write down one value on each leaf.

Draw a picture of a ship on the board – "imagine you are in the Titanic on your way from England to New York and the unsinkable ship begins to sink. The captain announces that the passengers can only take 3 pieces of luggage and therefore must discard one".

Collect the discarded values and paste them on the wall/board.

Ask the passengers to imagine that they are now on life boats and have reached an island. On the island a helicopter awaits them. The pilot asks the passengers to discard one more baggage as it cannot take the weight.

Now the participants discard another value, this is collected and pasted on the wall/board.

Ask the passengers to imagine that they have reached safely and are passing through customs but the customs people ask them to deposit one baggage as duty clearance.

Now the participants give away another value, this is collected and pasted on the wall, board.

At the end all participants are left with just one value.

Ask the participants now to write the remaining value on a flash card and place on the floor in a vertical line.

Ask the participants to take a look at the cards and if the list has repetitions ask them to club them. In this instance the line after clubbing looked somewhat as follows:

Empathy
Obedience
Faith
Belief
Truthfulness
Confidence
Honesty
Discipline
Loyalty

Seek clarifications and make sure that all the words before you are values, clearly specified. On clarifications in this instant the values finally looked as follows:

Empathy (for the poor)
Faith (in poor people's capacities)
Belief (in God)
Loyalty (to boss)
Obedience was replaced by Dutifulness
Truthfulness
Honesty
Discipline

Once the group has reached this stage and the list seems too long, ask them to decide on the number of core values that they would like to practise and then go in for voting (in this instant the group decided on five core values)

Ask the participants to place one blank card in front of each value and put a maximum of five ticks each (on the blank cards), then count the ticks and put the numbers against each value:

Value	*Score*	*Rank*
Empathy (for the poor)	10	
Faith (in poor people's capacities)	13	V
Belief (in God)	12	
Loyalty (to boss)	12	
Dutifulness	18	IV
Truthfulness	34	II
Honesty	36	I
Discipline	24	III

The top five scorers in this case were agreed on as the core values for DPIP project in Adilabad.

Once the group had agreed on the core values, the process was further enhanced so as to bring about an understanding on the difference between value, attitude and behaviour. The participants were asked to divide into five groups and take up one value each. Have a short discussion and come up with corresponding attitudes and behaviours.

Attitude	is an approach, an outlook
Behaviour	is the way one acts, behaves. It is what is visible to others – actions, speech, dress etc.

Once the groups had discussed the subject the following presentations were made:

Value	**Attitude**	**Behaviour**
Dutifulness	Dedication Determination Strictness Humbleness Compassionate Daring	We enjoy the work Determination to complete the assigned work We will perform the duties as if we are doing it for ourselves We will not be influenced by temptations To do the assigned jobs in the absence of the superiors also Ignoring the hurdles while carrying out the assigned job
Discipline	Morality Sincerity Self confident approach Friendly approach Truthfulness Transparency Responsibility Accountability	Punctuality Respect poorest of the poor people Respect as colleagues Respecting others rights Respect to law Respect for people's ideas Respect the culture Respect elders Self control Respect to means and goals
Faith in poor people's capacity	Confidence in poor people Empathy with the poor Respect to the poor Sharing everything (views, beliefs, feelings etc.	We facilitate them to utilise their resources Planning, improve their capability Try to create opportunities Mobilise them Coordinate Dream Learn from people

Honesty	Sincere Punctual Truthful Commitment	Working sincerely Being punctual No corruption Loyalty to principles Never telling lies Being truthful No cheating Being with commitment
Truthful	Accountable Accepting mistakes Should not be selfish Not yielding to temptation Not telling lies We must approach existing conditions	Transparent Rectification Treat all as equals Should not cheat Committed to the principles

The concept of faith in people's capacities was very difficult to understand and the participants were very hesitant in owning it, in fact initially when the groups were formed no one was willing to join the group on the said value.

There is an overwhelming need "to control" seems high on the agenda of the participants, and accepting others views is often viewed as a loss.

Obedience to the boss, loyalty to the boss is a concept that seems to be most important to the participants.

In a project where the emphasis is on the people and building their capacities such an attitude is of concern and needs to be worked on. It is important to build a culture of participation and not dominance and control.

The group by and large is very enthusiastic and can be groomed and built.

Most of the group members fell in the 20-25 age groups thus it's a sign of hope.

Attitude of dominance is very strong and needs to be taken away while belief in a command structure seems to be of importance.

One of the participants said that the same person should not present over and over as every one's capacities need to be built. This is a wonderful sign and shows that we are aware of ourselves.

A lot of people have shown an understanding of the concept of poverty but the understanding on gender is very weak and that is a matter of concern.

People centred development does not seem to be a concern, the emphasis is once again on government run programme, delivery, control and this is also a matter of concern.

Appendix A-3.5

Anathapur

Day-1 (15th November 2000)

Pre-Lunch Session: Session I

The workshop began with an introduction of the participants and of the facilitators. There were in all 34 participants. Some of the participants were from SAPAP and nearly all the participants had experience in development.

The participants were first asked to put forth their expectations on flash cards, noting one expectation on one card. The cards were then displayed and discussed with the participants. Expectations that were beyond the scope of the workshop were separated out.

The participants were then divided into groups. The group formation was through a game. Once the groups were formed they were assigned of the responsibility of listing out the roles/functions that they anticipate they would be expected to play in Ananthapur, as Social Organisers and Community Co-ordinators. They were allowed one hour and thirty minutes to do so. And the lists were to be written down on chart papers and displayed on the walls of the workshop venue. The groups did not find the assignment as easy at it sounded in the beginning. They nevertheless made their best effort and completed the task as assigned with some hesitation.

On completion of the task, each group was encouraged to put up their charts on one of the walls and make oral presentations. All the groups made their presentations and discussed the outputs. It was soon discovered that almost all the groups had listed functions, activities, values and behaviour expected of the CCs and COs, all bundled in the same charts. Thus it was difficult to cull out the functions/roles of their CCs and COs from the output. And, thus, it was not worthwhile going into the process any further. An alternative route was to be adopted.

First the concepts of values and behaviour were explained. It was then decided that the groups would list out the activities now, eschewing values and behaviour out from the list. The groups went back to work on it, and were requested to write the activities flash cards. Each flash card can have only one activity written on it. The groups were allowed one hour to do so. The groups started working on it and now found the going easier. They finished the task well ahead of time.

Once the groups finished recording their activities, the flashcards were laid out on the floor. As a next step, the groups were then encouraged to make clusters of cards. These flashcards were categorised into eight clusters.

Post-Lunch Session: Session II

The participants examined all the clusters of flash cards. They did two exercises:

One, they eliminated the duplicate cards.

Two, they then shuffled cards from one cluster to another, in order to make sure that the grouping of the activities recorded on the flash cards were appropriate and compatible. Once this was done clear clusters of activities could be easily identified by the participants.

The eight clusters, each signifying a role and the activities thereunder that emerged are as follows:

Function 1

Identifier

Activities:
Identification of the poorest of the poor
Identification of the physically handicapped groups
Collection of the baseline information about the poor families
Collection of the secondary data
Identification of felt needs
Using PRA techniques and identification of the poor
Identification of the poor households
Plan for eradication for untouchability
Plan for important human resource
Plan for village development
Plan for individual house hold development
Plan for preparation of community investment plans
Plan for accessing various government programmes for the poor peoples
Plan for sensitisation of poor on poverty conditions

Function 2

Planner

Activities:
Planning
Field of observation planning
Plan for mobilising the people for income
Generation activities
Plan for saving mobilisation from the people

Function 3

Capacity Builder

Activities:
Formation of groups
Training for groups
Formation of village organisation
Training for village organisation
Training for book-keeping
Training for preparation of investment plans
Training on linkages
Training on asset management

Function 4

Awareness Builder

Activities:
Creating awareness on gender sensitisation
Creating awareness on building of local institutions
Creating awareness on social and economic issues
Creating awareness on common problems
Creating awareness on poverty influencing factors
Creating awareness on social securities
Creating awareness on community investments
Creating awareness on community participation sanitation and environment
Creating awareness on child labour, dowry system and super system
Creating awareness on utilisation of local resources
Creating awareness on self development
Creating awareness on self-confidence and self-development
Creating awareness on resource management

Function 5

Social Mobiliser

Activities:
Building confidence among the poor
Formation of the groups
Conducting of the health camps
Conducting of veterinary camps
Sensitising on nutrition and food
Preparing the poor people for self employment
Building peoples institutions
Sensitising the women on participation in development activities

Function 6

Educator

Activities:
Educating the poor people about the government programmes
Educating the poor people on child labour and child marriages
Educating the destitute on their self confidence
Educating the poor people on bad habits
Educating the poor people on group meetings
Educating the poor people on problem of bonded labour
Educating the poor people on gender issue
Educating the poor people on physically handicapped
Educating the poor people on importance of education

Function 7

Facilitator

Activities:
Mingling with people as one among them
Rapport building
Building of individual relationship in the community
Singing and dancing with the community
Listening the community problems
Participating in the *Shramadan*
Building the confidence among the destitute
Building the unity among the poor people
Facilitating the people discuss their issues in the *Gram Sabha*
Building the group concept
Attending the group meetings
Encouraging the women for groups
Facilitating the people on child labour and bonded labour
Build the community organisation
Facilitating the poor people on active partitions
Interaction with the community
Developing the unit and integrity

Function 8

Guide

Activities:
Individual interaction
Counselling
Suggestions on special issues
Preparing and individual to overcome his individual problems

Post-Tea Session: Session III

Having decided upon the roles/function of the CCs and COs, the participants were divided into eight groups and each group was then encouraged to locate what they perceive to be knowledge and skill requirement of the jobs. Each Group was allowed one and a half hour to do so.

After one and a half hour, the groups re-assembled, and put up their outputs on flip charts. The each group made presentations of its output and there were questions raised and clarifications sought. Necessary corrections, additions and alterations were made. The final results for each of the functions on skills and knowledge, function-wise are as under:

Group 1

Identifier

Skills

Skills in rapport building
Enlisting community participation
Sharing skills
Participatory techniques
Facilitation skills
Communication skills
Listening skills
Household survey skills

Knowledge

Planning
Interact
Understanding of poor and poorest
Identification and the poorest of the poor
Causes of poverty
Prospects of the poor
Dominant features of the poverty

Group 2

Planner

Knowledge

The community needs
Time schedule and seasonality
Source of financial assistance
Local material and community assets
Awareness of needs of the poorest

Skills

Rapport building
PRA methods
Communication skills
Capacity building skills
Facilitation and monitoring skills
Skills to conduct review
Evaluation skills
Personality development skills

Group 3

Awareness Builder

Skills

Communication skills
Cultural activities skills—songs, games, jokes
Skills in using local language
Documentation skills
PRA techniques (matrix ranking and pair-wise ranking)

Knowledge

Knowledge of the human psychology
Understanding and knowledge of local language
Knowledge about PRA training methods
Knowledge in documentation
Specific subject knowledge such as child labour, bonded labour, agriculture, environment

Group 4

Capacity Builder

Knowledge

About poverty and poorest of the poor and potentials of the poor
Various methods of trainings
Various cultural activities
About social issues and other social problems
About opportunities available to the poorest of the poor

Skills

Mingling with people—social skills
Effective communication skills
Skills in identifying the capacities and potentialities of the poor
Trained trainer—direct trainers skills
Good facilitators' skills

Group 5

Social Mobiliser

Knowledge

Comprehension about social problems
Exposure to social issues
Knowledge of appropriate and behaviour
Sharing experiences
Knowledge of successful stories in social mobilisation
Knowledge about the government programmes and officers
Knowledge about the resources (physical, financial and human) and environment
Knowledge about the steps in social mobilisation

Skills

Communication skills
Listening skills
Observation skills
Leadership skills
Management skills
PRA techniques
Skills in problem solving and conflict resolution
Cultural activities, songs, games: rapport building skills Social skills
Planning, monitoring and evaluation skills

Group 6

Educator

Knowledge

Government programmes
Government institutions
Poverty, its causes and dimensions
Financial resource and institutions
Aims and objectives of DPIP and different poverty Alleviation programmes
Project management and preparation
Social mobilisation
Knowledge on special subjects

Skills

Communication skills
Language skills
Understanding
Observation skills
Listening skills
Must have patience
Project designing skills
Must be culturally sensitive

Group 7

Facilitator

Knowledge

Poverty, its causes and dimensions
Aims and objectives of the project
Project structure and how to ensure proper functioning
Available resources—human, environmental and physical
Geographical conditions of the areas
Available financial institutions and their schemes
Linkages—transport, marketing, government and non-government that are available
Social problems
Subject matter knowledge
Language

Skills

PRA tools
Decision making
Understanding
Communication skills
Listening skills
Skills to be culturally sensitive

Group 8

Guide

Knowledge

Human attitude and behaviour
Group/individual/community dynamics
Methods of effective communication
Information about common problems
Scope and limitations of a facilitator
Local situations and traditions

Skills

Effective communication skills
Analytical skills (how to analyse various problems)
Skills for analysis of human behaviour
Listening skills

Day-2 (16th November 2000)

Pre-Lunch Session: Session IV: Knowledge & Skills Possessed

The participants were then asked to reflect on their roles. They were encouraged to examine the activities under each role and then ask two questions:

What knowledge do we have?

What skills do we have?

After 15 minutes, the Fruit Salad Game was played and based on that the participants were divided into 6 Groups, named as Banana Group, Apple Group, Guava Group, Mango Group, Grapes Group, and Pineapple Group.

The groups were allowed 90 minutes to complete the task and put up on their chart papers what they think are the knowledge and skills that they have.

The groups were more comfortable in expressing what knowledge they have, but were less inclined to spell out what they have as skills. The only group, i.e., pineapple group spelt out separately the knowledge and skills they have. The other groups were content with setting up on chart papers an idea of their knowledge base. The outputs put up on chart papers are as follows:

1. Banana Group

Knowledge Possessed

Planning
Interact
Knowledge about the failures
Reading successful stories
Government programmes
Resource and environment
Knowing government financial institutions
Social problems
Linkages

Opportunities on the rural poor
Criteria for selection of the poorest of the poor
Causes, features and dominating issues of poverty
Comprehension
Good practices
Communication skill
Listening skill
Rapport building
Observation skill
Teaching skill
Facilitation skill
Training skill
Cultural skills

2. Apple Group

Knowledge Possessed

Identification of the poor
Good practices
Causes, features and dominating issues of the poverty
Successful stories
Government programmes
Knowledge about government institutions
Social problems
Common needs of the poor
Time schedule and seasonality
Various cultural activities
Scope & limitations of facilitation

3. Grapes Group

Knowledge Possessed

Communication skills
Analytical
Listening
Rapport building
Project designing
Observation
Leadership
Teaching skill
Conflict resolution
Planning, monitoring and evaluation
Criteria for identification of poorest
Causes, features and domination issues of the poverty
Reading about the best practices
Knowledge about resources/environment
Knowing the government programmes
Knowing the financial institutions
Aims and project objectives
Linkages available
Opportunities available to the poorest local situations and traditions
Social problems and language

4. Guava Group

Knowledge Possessed

5. Mango Group

Knowledge Possessed

Planning
Interact
Identification of the poorest of the poor
Causes, features, dominating issues of the poverty
Knowing financial institutions
Aims and objectives of the project
Social problems
Common needs identification
Information and material collection
Various cultural activities
Opportunities available to the poorest of the poor

6. Pineapple Group

Knowledge Possessed

Listening skills
Rapport building
Teaching skills
Leadership
Conflict resolution
Capacity building
Facilitation
Planning
Interaction
Criteria for identification of poorest of the poor
Causes of poverty, symptoms, and dominant systems of poverty
Knowledge about failures—best problems
Knowledge about government programme
Knowledge about resources and environment
Knowledge about government institutions
Financial institutions
Aims and objectives of the project
Geographical conditions
Social problems
Common needs
Language
Opportunities available to the poorest of the poor
Local situations and traditions

Skills Required

Effective communication skills
Analytical skills
Listening skills
Rapport buildings

PRA method
Designing skills
Observation skills
Teaching skills
Leadership skills
Management skills
Conflict resolution
Planning, monitoring and evaluation skills
Capacity building
Facilitation skills
Documentation skills
Training skills
Analysis of human behaviour
Cultural activities
Gender sensitising skills

The participants visited the output of each group and the question-answer session was lively. It was apparent from the discussion that the terms skills and knowledge were used interchangeably.

Post-Lunch Session: Session: V: Core Values

The last session was on core values. The concept of values was explained and the core values of DPIP as a whole were spelt out. These were empathy for the disadvantaged, Faith in the power of the poor, commitment to work, integrity and truthfulness. The participants were then given the option of either accepting the core values of DPIP as their own or of developing their own set of core values. After a brief discussion the participants thought that the core values of DPIP could be accepted as core values for DPIP Ananthapur and there was no need to have a separate set of core values.

Having arrived at this decision, the participants then spent some time understanding the meaning and implications of the values accepted as core values by DPIP.

The participants then broke into five groups by count of numbers. The groups were named as groups A to E. Each group took up one value and was assigned the responsibility of spelling out the "Attitude and Behaviour" the staff of DPMU Ananthapur should have in order to adhere to the value, chosen by the group. Time allotted was 95 minutes to complete the assignment.

The groups at first were not comfortable with the terms attitudes and behaviour. These were therefore explained in each group. The groups then worked out a process by which they would carry out the exercise. Each member of the groups wrote down what they thought were the appropriate attitude and behaviour of the value they were dealing with and then aggregate their thoughts, eliminating the duplications which were bound to be there.

They then wrote their thought on flip charts and put up their presentations and each group made an oral presentation as well. Clarifications were sought. In several cases changes were suggested and carried out in the charts. The final outcome is as under:

Group-A

Core Value: Empathy for the Disadvantaged

Group Discussion

Mingle as one among the disadvantaged section of people
Have pro poor nature/attitude
React or help in time (positively)/build confidence in the disadvantaged
Don't wound/hurt the feelings of others
Allow the poor people to ventilate their emotions and feelings
Respect the self dignity of the disadvantaged people
Advocate the cause of the disadvantaged

Group-B

Core Value: Faith in the Power of the Poor

Group discussion

Belief that they have rich potential to solve their problems
Belief that they know everything
Belief they have awareness of local resources
Respect the intelligence and understanding capacity of the poor
Believe in their self-confidence
Recognise their competitive spirit
Accept their leadership qualities

Group-C

Core Value: Commitment to Work

Group Discussion

Be dynamic
Have self confidence
Be honest
Respect others
Listen to the poor
Have best time management: complete the work in time
Extend co-operation—co-ordination
Be sincere
Giving/give helping hand to people
Have enthusiasm to carry out your work
Curiosity or inclination to lead
Gain knowledge from poor
Planning
Mingle with people
Concentrate on work
Have role clarity
Communicate well

Group-D

Core Value: Integrity

Group Discussion

Time maintenance
Have punctuality
Practice accountability
Ensure proper utilisation of funds
Act with responsibility
Shoulder your responsibility
Show your respect to the poor
Try for economical utilisation of funds and resources
Be impartial and judicious use of funds
Build linkages
Utilise the opportunities to the rural poor

Group-E

Core Value: Truthfulness

Work together
Work collectively according to the decision taken collectively
Work for achieving the target
Impartial distribution of resources
Every part of work should be useful to the people
We should not create false hopes and we should not give any false promises.
In every movement community should be encouraged to participate actively.
Be transparent in words as well as deeds
Have self-evaluation
Work within the rules and regulations of the project

Post Tea Session: Session VI: Wrapping Up

The PD DPIP reviewed the work done and sought clarifications from the participants. He said he was very satisfied with the output and agreed to what the group as a whole had to say about their needs and about their role clarity. He hoped that the participants would be able to better discharge their responsibilities now, as they knew what was expected of them. The facilitator was thanked by the PD, and the participants.

Knowledge Required

Consolidated

Planning
Interact
Criteria for identification of the poorest of the poor
Causes, features and dominating issues of the poverty
Comprehension
Good practice
Knowledge about the failures
Reading successful stories
Knowing the government programme
Knowledge about the resource and environment
Steps in social mobilisation

Knowing government institutions
Aims and objectives of the project
Geographical conditions
Linkages—transport, marketing and government and non-government
Social problems
Common needs identification
Language
Time schedule
Information and material collection
Human psychology
Documentation
Training methods
Various cultural activities
Opportunities available to the poorest of the poor
Group—individual/common dynamics
Human attitude and behaviour
Scope of limitations of the facilitations
Local stations and traditions
Appropriate information about common problems

Skills Required

Consolidated

Effective communication skills
Analytical skills
Listening skills
Rapport building
PRA methods
Designing skills
Observation skills
Teaching skills
Management skills
Conflict resolution
Planning monitoring
Evaluation skills
Capacity building
Facilitation skills
Documentation skills
Training skills
Analysis of human behaviour
Cultural activities

4

Retreat of Ministers, Secretaries and Civil Society Actors on Capacity Building for Decentralised Administration

Where the mind is without fear and the head is held high;
Where knowledge is free;
Where the world has not been broken up into fragments by narrow domestic walls;
Where words come out from the depth of truth;
Where tireless striving stretches its arms towards perfection;
Where the clear stream of reason has not lost its way into the dreary desert sand of dead habit;
Where the mind is led forward by Thee into ever-widening thought and action;
Into that heaven of freedom, my Father, let my country awake.

—*Rabindranath Tagore*

Introduction

The Retreat[1] at the Lal Bahadur Shastri National Academy of Administration, Mussoorie, from 5th to 7th July 2005, was part of an overall effort by the Government of India to improve governance. This retreat was the second in the series, the first being held in Pune. The theme chosen for this retreat was Capacity Building for Decentralised Administration. The participants in the retreat comprised of Union Ministers, Member of the Parliament, Secretaries to Government (both at the Centre and States), academicians, activists, experts in rural development and NGOs. The total strength varied from 22 to 28 during the three days of the retreat.

To set the broad framework of the retreat, as starting point a paper was presented, in the plenary, on the experience of Kerala in restoring power to the people through participatory planning at the micro-level and investing the *Panchayats* with earmarked resources to execute the plans. The participants then moved on to an informal setting shorn of chairs, formality and hierarchy.

Rules of the Workshop

The facilitator explained to the group that the retreat was a workshop of the participants and not of the facilitator/organiser. The role of the facilitator was only to see that the flow of information and exchange of experience, data and knowledge were smooth and the analysis of such exchange of experience, data and knowledge was objective and unhindered. It was, therefore, considered necessary

1 Held under the auspices of the Department of Training, Ministry of Personnel, Pensions and Public Grievances, Government of India, New Delhi.

for the participants to agree upon a set of rules, which will guide the workshop. The rules that the participants agreed upon to follow were as under:

- We will not personalise issues/observations/remarks/analysis
- We will have lot of fun
- We shall be brief
- There will be only one meeting at a time
- We will be futuristic
- We will be punctual

The facilitator then pointed out to the participants certain forms of behaviour which are best avoided/adopted as the case may be, in a retreat of this kind. The pattern of behaviour agreed upon had the follow components:

- *Avoiding dominance:* this was important to ensure that those who were less vocal, shy and reflective, were not bullied down and hierarchy did not operate.
- *Avoid arrogance:* this was necessary to let everyone express their data, experience and knowledge freely and fully and allow others to learn from them.
- *Embrace error:* this was necessary to learn from mistakes and move forward instead of trying to defend the indefensible.
- *Avoiding biases* (particularly gender biases, institutional biases, political biases, professional biases, people bias): this was essential for an honest analysis of experience, data, information and knowledge and learn from such analysis as also arrive at objective actionable outputs.
- *Respecting diversity:* this was necessary to ensure free flow of ideas and learn from others' views (even the dull and the mundane has something to offer!)

It was agreed that the retreat was deficient in two respects. First, that there was no representation from *Panchayat* functionaries from any level though the retreat was by design directed towards their capacity building. Hence it suffered from "people" bias. Secondly, the number of men participants far outnumbered the women and hence the retreat also suffered from the infirmity of "gender bias". The deliberations in the retreat will be cognisant of these two deficiencies.

The participants then surrendered their badges (with their names and designations) to the facilitator, as a token of their willingness to operate in the retreat without boundaries of official satraps and as equals, adhering as far as possible to the "democracy of the ground".

Johari's Window

It was explained to the retreat participants that the andragogy to be followed in the retreat will be based on the principal of moving from the "known to unknown". In the context of the retreat, the term "we" is supposed to mean the "Government" and the word "they" connote the participants of the retreat. All data, information and knowledge can be boxed into four boxes of the Johari's Window. In Box-1 of Johari's Window we have data, information and knowledge which both the government as well as the participants have, which includes the provision of Article 243 of the Constitution, the formation of *Panchayats* in different states, the anti-poverty programmes of the government and the poor quality of their implementation etc. Box-2 of Johari's Window contains data, information and knowledge, which the participants posses, but the government does not have. Such information/data includes the reasons for which the provisions of Article 243 of the Constitution have not been given effect to despite the formation of *Panchayats* in different states, a differentiated picture of the level of competencies available in the Panchayati Raj Institutions in the different states etc., and why available institutional arrangement for capacity building in the country does not "deliver the goods". In Box-3 of Johari's Window, one could incorporate data, information and knowledge to which the government is privy to, but the participants can neither have any access nor knowledge of it. Such information/data may include reasons why the states which violate the provisions of Article 243 of the Constitution have not been taken to task, if a differentiated picture of the level of devolution of powers to the Panchayati Raj Institutions is contemplated by the government and so on. And Box-4 of Johari's Window, comprises data, information and knowledge which neither the participants nor the government has or has access to.

The attempt in the retreat was to fill up Box-2 of Johari's Window.

Johari's Window

	They know	*They Don't Know*
We know	Box-1	Box-3
We don't know	Box-2	Box-4

The Conceptual Specifications and the Perspective

The expression "decentralised administration", was taken, for the purposes of the retreat, to mean institutions created under Article 243 of Constitution of India, generally referred to as Panchayati Raj Institutions (PRIs). The terms "decentralised administration" and "decentralised governance" were used interchangeably.

The participants attempted a definition of what is meant by capacity building in the context of Panchayati Raj Institutions. There was considerable debate on whether it was appropriate for the retreat to discuss capacity building of PRI functionaries. According to one school of thought the PRI functionaries had the required skills and knowledge to transact their business and usher in their own development, while the other school maintained that there was a need to build their capacities. The difference of opinion was resolved upon realising that knowledge was of two kinds: implicit knowledge and explicit knowledge. The PRI functionaries had implicit knowledge (such as knowledge of the appropriate technology for cultivating their fields, medicinal properties of certain plants/herbs available in their neighborhood, sky-signs to forecast rainfall, availability and usability of local resources, local constraints etc.) but they may not always have explicit knowledge (which includes technical skills on how to prepare micro-level plans for economic and social development, details of resources available from the state etc.). Thus, while the PRI functionaries may have implicit knowledge, there was need to supplement the same with explicit knowledge as defined above.

Granted that, the participants identified the crucial elements, which would constitute capacity building of Panchayati Raj Institution functionaries. It was agreed that capacity of PRI functionaries would be deemed to have been built if:

i. The PRIs have the required skill.
ii. If they have functions, functionaries and funds (FFF) transferred to them (presumably in accordance with the spirit and letter of the Constitution).
iii. PRIs have the knowledge and skill to take action.
iv. They have the capacity to lobby for FFF.
v. They have the capacity to discharge their responsibilities in a just manner.
vi. Imbibe the capacity to evolve endogenously.
vii. There exists external stimuli to support them to evolve into strong institutions.

An assessment of the current state of the capacity of the PRIs, in respect of the elements identified, was made through a construction of the Empowerment Circle. The process followed closely approximated the following process. A circle was drawn with seven radii. Each radii represented one element of the components of capacity building. Each participant was given seven pieces of post-it slips, with the option of pasting one such post-it slip on each of the seven radii depicting the elements of capacity building in the *Panchayats*. If a participant perceived that at the present time, *Panchayats* generally had 100 per cent of a particular element, she/he would paste a post-it slips at the centre of the circle from where the radius emanates. If on the contrary she/he thought that the *Panchayats* had none of it, she/he would paste a post-it slip at the on the circumference of the circle instead, where the respective radius meets it. If she/he thought that the *Panchayats* had 50 per cent of an element, she/he would paste the post-it slip at the centre of the respective radius and so on. Each participant was encouraged to write down his/her name on all the post-it slips, to enable them to arrive at a self-assessment of how far their individual perceptions were aligned to the group perceptions. The picture that emerged is at Figure 4.1. In Figure 4.1, there are very few slips at the centre of the circle. Indeed there is none and most of them are clustered at levels near or below the 50 per cent mark. A fleeting glimpse of the empowerment circle, therefore, is indicative of the utter chaos that prevails in the competency levels of the PRIs (generally) in the country and the need to bring some semblance of order in contemporary capacity building efforts for PRIs.

Having decided upon the concept of capacity building and having carried out the assessment of the state of capacity building of the PRIs, the participants were taken through a timeline of the evolution of the PRIs in independent India. This put the discussion in perspective and gave some sense of the direction in which the PRIs have moved over the years, especially after the passage of the 73rd and 74th Constitution Amendment Acts in the early nineties. The time line is at Table 4.1.

Figure 4.1

The Empowerment Circle

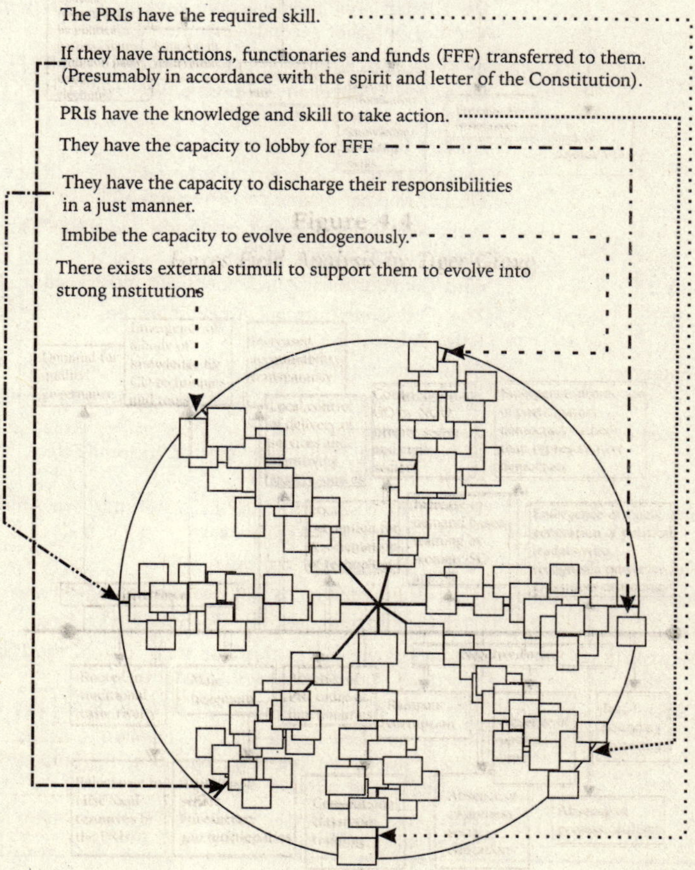

Table 4.1

Time Line Decentralisation and Local Governance in India

YEAR	*MAJOR EVENTS*
1952	Community development and Sahakari Samaj
1957	Balwantrai Mehta Committee
1958 - 1959	State government enacting *panchayat* Acts.
1959	Jawaharlal Nehru inaugurating the first generation *Panchayats* in Rajasthan (Nagaur)
1962	ZP Act of UP
1964 - 1977	Decline of First Generation of PR
1966 - 1967	Ministry of Community Development became a department under Ministry of Food & Agriculture
1977	Tribal sub-plan in Tribal Area commenced
1977	Asoka Mehta Committee
1978	Asoka Mehta Committee Report submitted
1978	West Bengal *Panchayat* elections on political party lines. The beginning of second generation PR
1978	Zinabhai Darj Committee on Social Justice/ Orient elections
1983	Karnataka government following West Bengal Panchayat Act, ushers in PR
1985	Andhra Pradesh followed suit
1980s	Idea of District Government especially the writings of Nirmal Mukharji came to be recognised
1988	Parliament Consultative Committee under P.K. Thungan made its recommendations
1989 May 15	63rd Constitutional Amendment Bill introduced in Parliament
1989 October 15	The 63rd Constitutional Amendment Bill was defeated in Rajya Sabha
1990 September 7	64th Constitutional Amendment Bill introduced in Parliament
1990	*Panchayats* were brought under administrators in Karnataka
1991 September	72nd (*Panchayats*) and 73rd (*Nagarpalika*) Amendments introduced in Parliament referred to Joint Select Committee of Parliament
1992 December 22	Lok Sabha passed the Bills (as 73rd and 74th Amendments) on *Panchayats* and *Nagarpalikas*
1992 December 23	Rajya Sabha passed the Bills
1993 April 24	The 73rd Amendment Act was brought into force
May 30	The 74th Amendment Act was brought in force
1994 May 30	Madhya Pradesh was the first state to hold the *Panchayat* Elections under the new dispensation
1996 December	The 73rd Amendment was extended to Scheduled Areas
1996	Kerala launched People's Plan Campaign, a unique experiment under the new Panchayati Raj lauded nationally and internationally
2001	Bihar was the last state to hold the first election (after 23 years) under the new system

Clearly, in terms of the timeline, some states have progressed while others have been laggards. The response of the states to usher in the new PRIs has, *prima facie*, varied in direct proportion to their development, barring a few exceptions. The relatively more developed (either politically or economically) states like West Bengal, Andhra Pradesh, Karnataka and Kerala have made significant progress, while other states like Bihar have fallen behind. Indeed West Bengal had enjoined holding elections at regular intervals well before the Constitutional safeguard for compulsory election to PRIs was put in place and Kerala had introduced people centered planning irrespective of whether it was mandated to do so or not.

Judged from that perspective, it would seem that states, which have empowered the PRIs, are also the states where the capacity of the PRIs to discharge their constitutional obligations was larger. States which have withheld delegation and decentralisation of functions, functionaries and finances, are the states where the capacity of the PRIs to discharge the Constitutional and legal responsibilities entrusted to their care, are the least evolved. However, the participants were unanimous in their view that the contemporary state of the PRIs in terms of their capacity and capability, was a monument to the failure of the respective State Governments, cutting across party lines, to decentralise governance and make these institutions effective units of self-governance. There is a lot that is left to be desired.

The Diagnosis

Having looked at the evolution of the PRIs and their current state, the participants were divided into four groups through the Jungle Game, named as Leopard, Tiger, Cheetah and Lion. The four groups were asked to work out a Force Field Analysis of the state of PRIs, where force was taken to mean energy that can change the position of an object (in this case the PRIs). The force field analyses as presented by the participants are at Figures 4.2, 4.3, 4.4 and 4.5. The four groups worked out the force field analyses on flip charts with the help of flash cards and pasted them on the workshop room hall. These were then presented as a "Poster Session" where different groups examined what other groups have done and sought clarifications.

While the different groups came out with a wide array of forces that keep the PRIs trapped in a low level equilibrium trap, they also could name several forces that sustain the PRIs, at whatever level they currently operate. What strikes one is the fact that of the basket of negative forces that hinder the progression of PRIs, lack of political will, transgression by the legislators (both at the Central level and the state levels) into the domain of the PRIs, the resistance to empowering the PRIs from the political executive and the hostility of the bureaucracy towards the PRIs have been the common refrains.

The last two negative forces have been instrumental in generating subsidiary negative forces in the guise of non-transfer of functions, functionaries and finances (FFF) to the *panchayats,* support to the plethora of parallel bodies entrusted with developmental functions that legitimately belong to the PRIs and lack of funds for the PRIs. In consequence, the PRIs could neither build their own capacities endogenously nor were there external stimuli to upgrade their knowledge, skill and technology base. On the social front, casteism, illiteracy and lack of access to information and knowledge (as also skills) have been major drags on the PRIs.

Figure 4.2

Force Field Analysis by Leopard Group

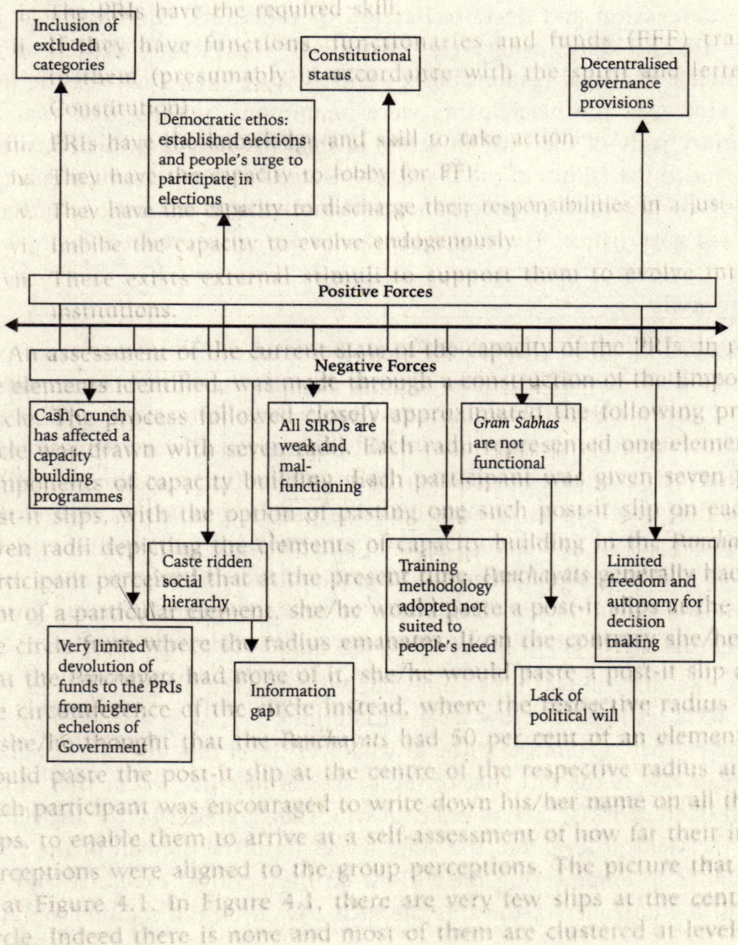

Figure 4.3

Force Field Analysis by Cheetah Group

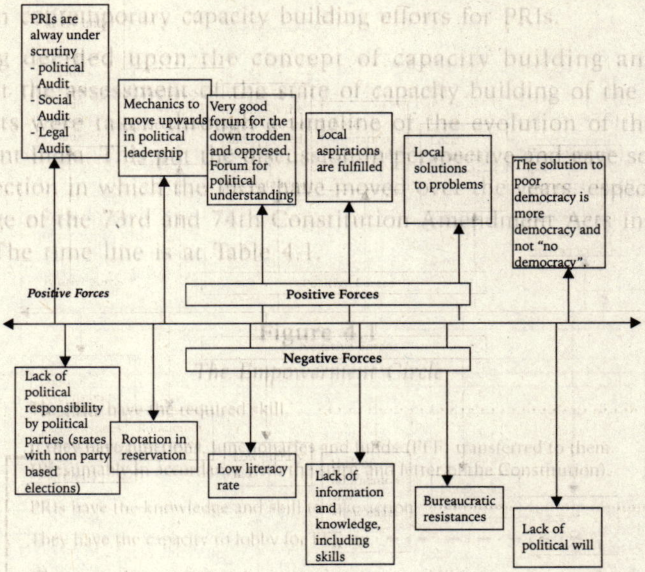

Figure 4.4

Forces Field Analysis by Tiger Group

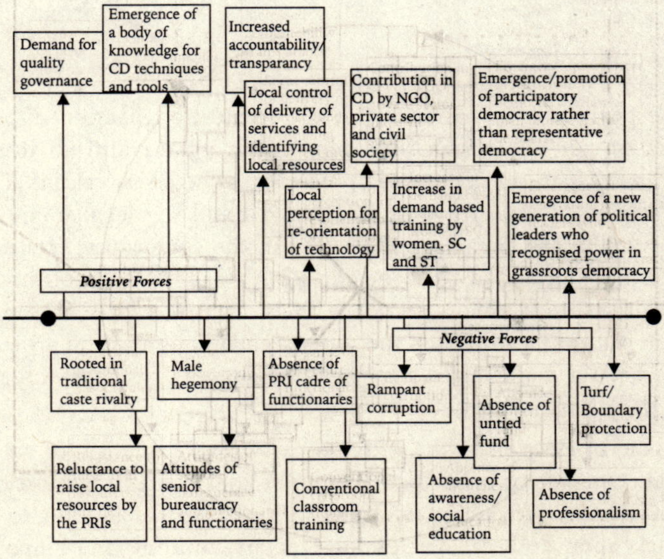

Figure 4.5

Force Field Analysis by Lion Group

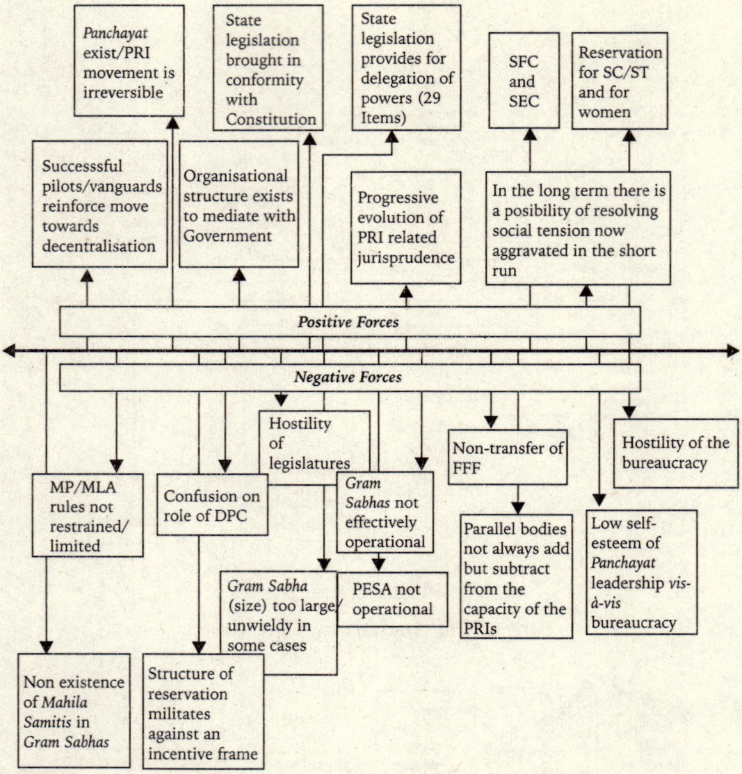

Of the positive forces that favour the institutionalisation of *panchayats*, the depth of our democracy and democratic norms and an urge by the people to participate in democratic processes emerged as crucial. The public scrutiny system of the PRIs that has evolved and the legal framework that the provisions in the Constitution as also in the conformity Acts enacted by the states, have provided to make the PRIs a fact of our political life, are strong positive forces that sustain the PRIs. That the PRIs have provided a democratic platform to the poor and the marginalised groups to articulate their voice has been a major force that sustains support for these organisations amongst the masses in general.

The issue of election to the PRIs on party lines came up for an animated discussion. One set of participants thought that contesting elections along party lines would provide an option to those who get elected to the PRIs to fall back upon political parties for capacity building and empowerment. Others, however, thought that such a course would prevent those who had no party affiliation from participating in *Panchayat* elections. Such a system would also put to disadvantage those who wanted to be neutral. After much debate it was agreed that there is no final answer to this vexed question, and indeed it has been debated and baffled political *pundits* since the days of the Balwant Rai Mehta Committee.

On the whole, the participants agreed on an incredible number of negative forces that operate on the PRIs, but the dominant ones seem to be non-transfer of functions, functionaries and finances to the PRIs, which in the last analysis can be traced back to lack of political will to empower them, hostility of the bureaucracy towards PRIs and the proclivity of the legislators to usurp the role that legitimately belong to the *panchayats*.

And the Prognosis

Once the Force Field Analyses were examined, the groups reassembled to work out a course of remedial actions to convert the negative forces into positive forces and/or circumventing the negative forces. The outcome of the exercise is at Tables 4.2, 4.3, 4.4 and 4.5. These were presented on the wall and a formal presentation made by each group. Then the issues raised were debated. Though there was consensus on most issues, on the issue of reservation, there were two views. One point of view disfavoured the policy of reservations because it provided negative incentive to those who will be rotated from taking long term development measures and had too short a time at her/his disposal to bring about long lasting changes. The other view, however, thought that rotation was a good policy for it provided a chance to those who would have been otherwise eliminated from the race.

The key to finding solutions to the vexed issue of building capacity of the PRIs as it emerged from the exercise of finding ways and means to convert the negative forces into positive ones, revolves around four sets of issues. One, bringing about effective decentralisation, through transfer of resources, functions and functionaries to the PRIs is critical. Capacity of powerless, functionless and emaciated institutions can neither be built, nor can they be expected to develop themselves autonomously. Two, revitalising the entire architecture set up for capacity building of developmental functionaries was a necessary precursor to capacity building of panchayati raj functionaries. Three, the technology of building capacity needs to be made consistent with the ethos, attitudes and mental make up of the Panchayat functionaries. Imagination and innovation in delivery of inputs (including developing easy to use manuals, user-friendly guidelines/handbooks etc.) for building capacity would pay rich dividends. Use of participatory methods using visuals more than verbal symbols for communication in the courses were at the heart of the matter. Four, there is need to build a national consensus that the responsibility of building capacity of the PRIs rests with a wide range of actors, including political parties, the government, the NGOs, training institutions and other civil society organisations. There was a need to develop a coalition of these actors.

Table 4.2

Remedial Actions: Leopard Group

Negative Forces	*Possible response to convert them into positive forces*
Very limited devolution of funds from Centre to state to PR	Economically viable *panchayat* units
Cash crunch has affected capacity building programmes	- Control over local resources - 1-2% of devolved funds, earmark for *panchayats*—now divertable
All SIRDs are weak, neglected and malfunctional and marginalised Lack of Information Training methodology is not adapted to people's needs	- Senior officer or professional to head SIRD - District level training-cum-information—research centres (Involvement of NGOs, academician, professionals etc.) IT—be made a focus area - Training methodology should suit illiterate people also film and video, pear group meetings, not lectures should be medium - Second level of training - Basic training material - Sharing of experiences - Documentation of good experiences - For *Sarpanches* etc. - NGOs local resource persons should be used for training - Issue based training - Area planning - Financial matters - Training should be joint—for public representatives and officials - Officials should include all line departments
Gram Sabhas are not functional	*Gram Sabhas* 1. Nodal officers made responsible for holding *Gram Sabhas* 2. Work in Campaign mode to make *Gram Sabhas* vibrant 3. Village level committees with NGOs be involved 4. Elected representatives at village level should commit themselves to hold *Gram Sabhas*.
Limited freedom/ autonomy for decision making, Lack of political will Caste ridden social hierarchy is a hindrance in functioning of PR	- Regular, free and fair elections to PR bodies and - Regular holding of *Gram Sabhas* will breakdown caste barriers - Political parties through their political outfits should express political will for decentralisation - Every political party should have a *panchayat raj* Cell to train their own workers.

Table 4.3

Remedial Actions: Tiger Group

Negative Forces	*Possible response to convert them into positive forces*
Rooted in tradition caste rivalry	Education and social awareness through formal and informal modes for a transformation
Reluctance to raise local resources	Inventory of local resources. Incentives by government e.g., priority in poverty schemes, untied funds, recognition, as development agency to raise own resources
Rampant corruption	Anti corruption raising determents, simple procedures for trial and punishment, confiscation of ill gotten gains (focussed on PRI)
Absence of education and social awareness	- Education and social awareness through *Gram Sabhas*, ward meetings, and SHGs, NGOs, mobilised to campaign - Time bound elementary education to be implemented
Male hegemony SHGs/	- Empower female groups with training, recognition resources - 50 per cent female participation in all PRI (from MM) Committees (standing) - women's education
Absence of untied funds	Untied funds proportional to funds received by PRI from central/state schemes
Attitude of senior bureaucrats and functionaries	Continue building awareness, new management methods, mindset changes
Absence of professionalism	- Marshalling local knowledge/expertise for creating professionals needed at local level with experts from outside - Post training forums for exchange, dialogue, information and learning
Absence of PRI, Cadre of functionaries	Transfer of line departments under control supervision and discipline of PRI (with transferable) stop state level recruitment
Turf boundary protection	Local mechanisms to settle inter and intra PRI disputes
Conventional class room training	Conventional training replaced with participatory training

Institutional Analysis

Having decided upon the prognosis for building capacity, the participants were divided into a set of new groups, to examine the efficiency and efficacy of institutional arrangement for building capacity of PRIs. The institutional analysis was carried out in terms of Venn Diagramming. These diagrams are at Figures 4.6, 4.7, 4.8 and 4.9. The groups were also asked to suggest ways and means to improve one amongst the institutions engaged in capacity building of PRIs, chosen by them for the exercise. The Venn Diagrams were prepared with paper cut out, flip charts and gums. These were pasted on the walls and a Poster Session followed.

Table 4.4

Remedial Actions: Lion Group

Negative Forces	*Possible response to convert them into positive forces*
Hostility of state legislators	- Conscientisation/Mobilisation of *panchayat* members to struggle for rights - Political sensitisation
Hostility of Bureaucracy	- Effects of HHF - Subordinate functionaries to PR institution to DF - Clarity of Roles - Progressively using a pre set series
Non transfer of HHF	- simultaneous deviation of F/F/F
Gram Sabhas ineffective	- Identification/Endowment approval to 3 mode mandatory - Devise state specific strategies
Non constitution of DPC/ confusion of role of DPC	- Legal enforcement - CSP/State sponsored programme should give way to block government - Total revamps of planning programmes towards general decentralisation
Parallel bodies not always add but subtract	- State/Central government should refrain from foisting parallel bodies
Low self esteem of PR representatives *vis-à-vis* bureaucracy	- Training of *Panchayat* Representatives - Assertion of leading role of PR Representatives
Inadequate powers to raise resources	SFC should be more effective
Non existence of *Mahila Samiti* in *Gram Sabha*	- Special *Mahila Gram Sabha* - Special *Gram Sabha* for disadvantaged groups
Structure of reservation/rotation militates against incentive frame	- Can we do something in law?
PESA not operational	Central representative was first representative/ renewed act defeat spirit of PESA
Gram Sabha size unwieldy	State specific representative
MP/MLAs role unrestrained	- Political Conscientisation of PR representatives - State of *panchayat* reports by PR representatives - State governments to restrict role of MP/MLA to consultative function

Group-1, whose Venn Diagram is at Figure 4.6, had taken two variables to show the position of the institutions. The size of circle indicated the relative potential of the different training institutions to build capacity of the PRIs on paper, that is, in theory. The distance of the circles representing the institutions from the PRIs, indicates the actual delivery on the ground. Larger the circle in the Venn Diagram, greater is the potential of the institution to build capacity of the institutions under reference. Further the circle representing an institution is placed from the circle representing the PRI, lower is its actual delivery in building capacity of the PRIs. According to Figure 4.6, those institutions, which have larger potential to deliver the goods are the ones that are not doing so at their full potential. Only local

NGOs have been rated as having a large potential to build capacity and they are actually doing so in reality. This group felt that Regional Institutes for Rural Development (RIRDs) were the most important institutions but were far away in terms of their actual delivery of inputs. SIRDs and NIRD, the principal training outfits of the Ministry of Rural Development are both seen as having a very low potential for building capacity of PRI functionaries. This group made detailed suggestions on how to improve the SIRDs so that they achieve their full potential.

Table 4.5

Remedial Actions: Cheetah Group

Negative Forces	*Possible response to convert them into positive forces*
Lack of political will	Caste-based development model to be changed to normative development planning model
Lack of political responsibility	Amendment in state laws to conduct elections on party lines
Low rate of literacy and awareness	- Tailor made training methods to low literacy levels - Incentive to *panchayats* to achieve literacy to a higher level - Role of NGOs—should play major role - Use of Multimedia has to be enhanced
Bureaucratic Resistance	Strong government can reduce bureaucratic resistance and bureaucracy can be used as a tool for development
Rotation in Reservation	Constitutional amendment of A-243-D for reservation based on population criterion and not on rotation. Review after every delimitation.
Lack of technical knowledge and technical skills	- Develop technical rules - Develop technical manuals - Training camps and workshops in a coordinated manner - *Panchayats* should participate and decide about capacity building needs

Group 2, whose Venn Diagram is at Figure 4.7, had also taken two variables to show the position of the institutions. The size of circle in Figure 4.7, indicates the importance of the different training institutions to build capacity of the PRIs on paper. The distance of the circles representing the institutions from the PRIs, indicates the relative efficiency of the institutions to build capacity of the PRIs. Larger the circle, more important is the institution. Further the circle representing an institution, from the circle depicting the PRI, more inefficient it is in building capacity. The picture that Group 2 showed gives no cause for cheer. Most of the institutions, which are important players, are inefficient in building capacity, notably ATIs, ETCs, SIRDs and to a lesser extent NIRD. There was considerable discussion on the role of the Ministry of Rural Development, which was shown as being important and efficient in building capacity of the *Panchayat* functionaries. The group clarified that the Ministry had a very important, though indirect, role in building capacity of the

PRIs by providing the requisite funds and articulating the political backing of the government for building the capacity of the Panchayati Raj Institutions. ETCs were the institutions, which Group-3 chose for improvement, because the group thought that these institutions were best placed in terms of reach and spread and are mandated to improve the skill and knowledge base of people in areas which are covered by the 29 subjects of the Eleventh Schedule of the Constitutions.

Figure 4.6

Venn Diagramming by Group 1

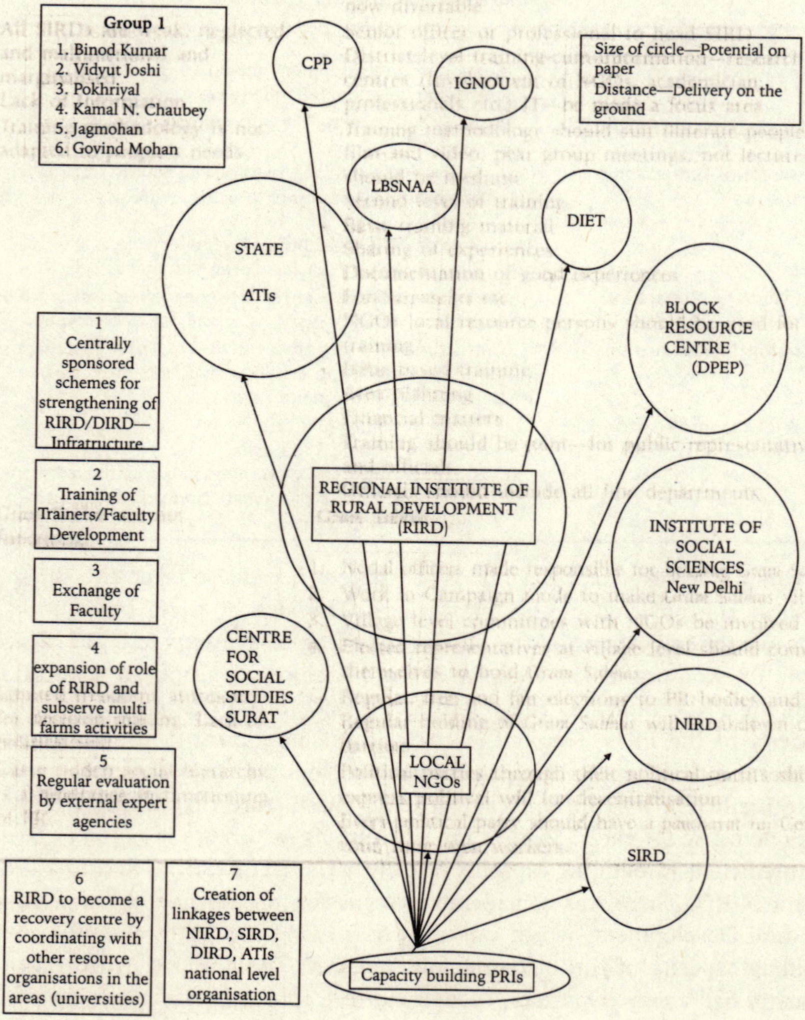

Figure 4.7

Venn Diagramming by Group 2

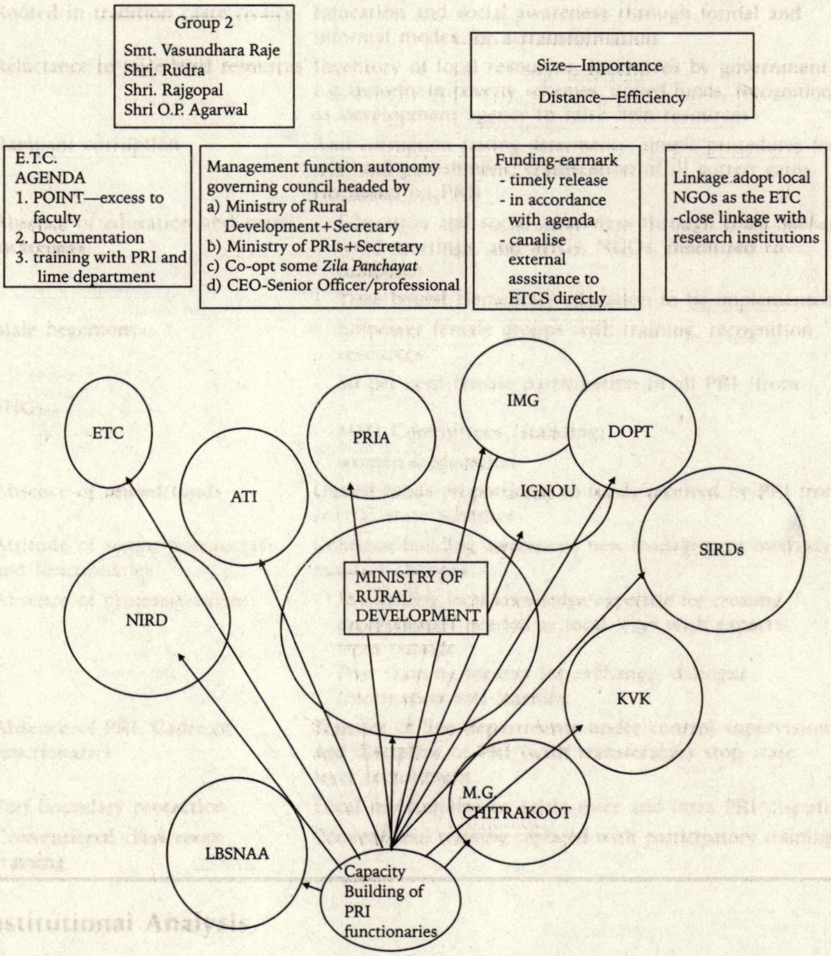

Group 3, whose Venn Diagram is at Figure 4.8, had taken two new variables to show the position of the institutions. The size of circle in Figure 4.8 indicates the importance and capacity of the different training institutions to build capacity of the PRIs. The distance of the circles representing the institutions from the PRIs, indicates the relative efficiency of the institutions to build capacity of the PRIs. Larger the circle, more important is the institution and greater is its capacity to be of service to the PRIs. Further the circle representing an institution, from the PRI, more inefficient it is in building capacity. This Group considered specific institutions more than classes of institutions. Their finding is also similar to those of Group 7. SIRDs were the institutions, which Group 3 chose for improvement, because these were the most important institutions in their perception for capacity building of PRIs.

Figure 4.8

Venn Diagramming by Group 3

A.K. Singh, George Mathew, A.R. Bandopadhya,
Ms. Saroj Arora, Anwar Jafri

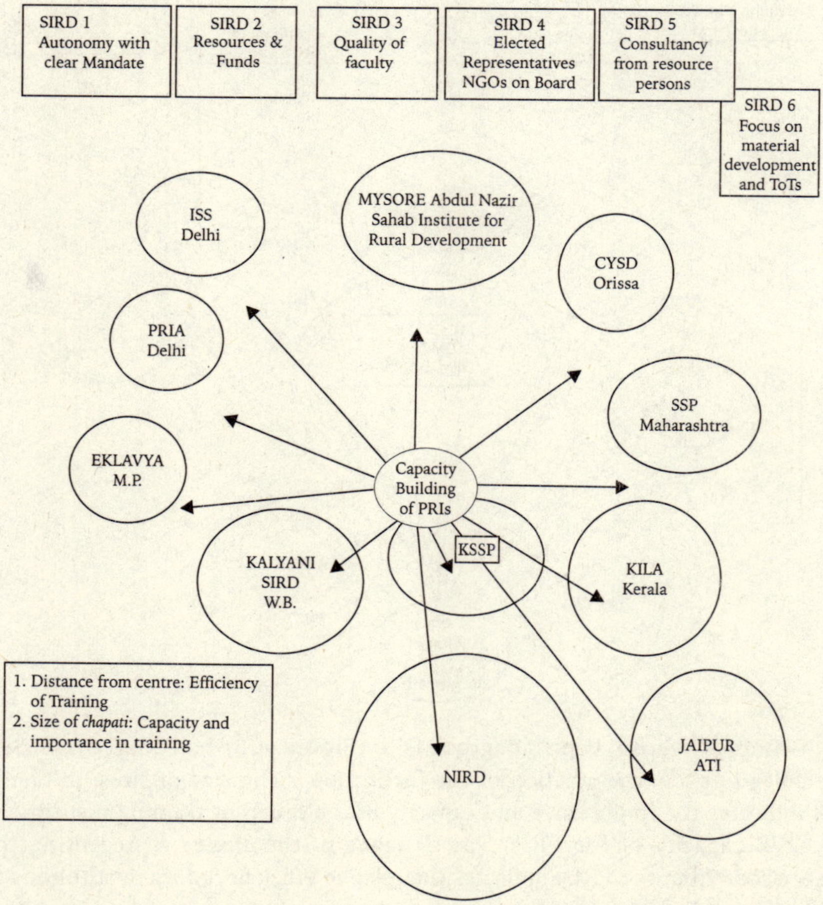

Figure 4.9

Venn Diagramming by Group 4

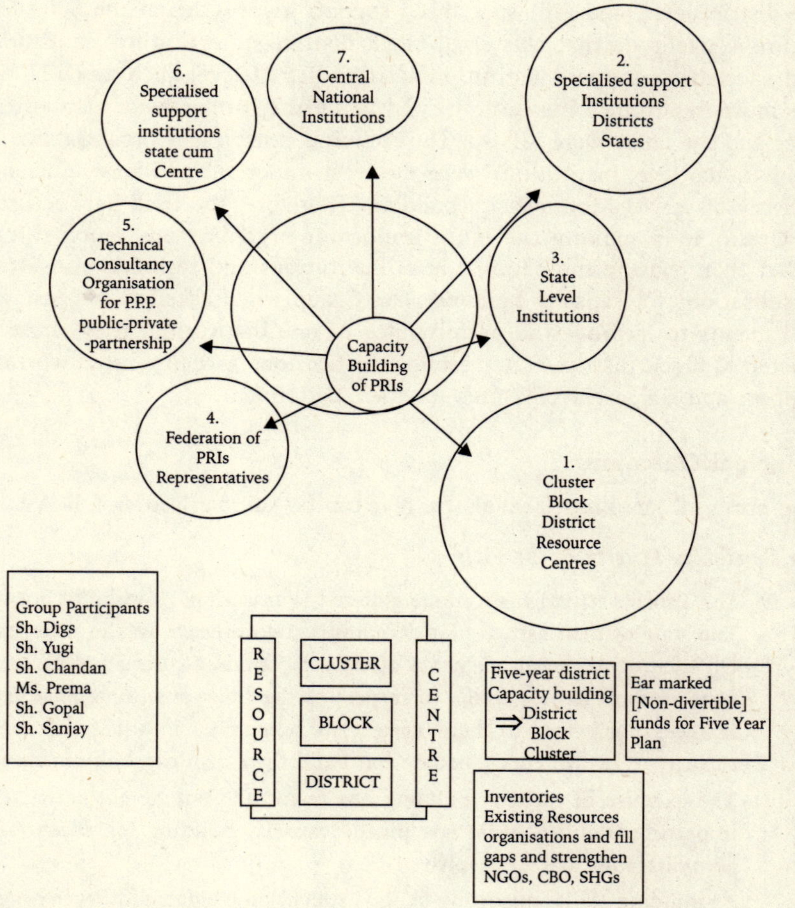

Group 4, whose Venn Diagramming is at Figure 4.9, adopted a novel approach. They considered kinds of institutions rather than specific classes of institutions. The size of circle in Figure 4.9, like in Figure 4.7, indicates the importance of different kinds of training institutions to build capacity of the PRIs. The distance of the circles representing the institutions, from the PRIs, indicates the relative efficiency of the institutions to build capacity of the PRIs. Larger the circle, more important is the institution. Further the circle representing an institution, from the PRI, more inefficient it is in building capacity. They considered six kinds of institutions that are or could potentially be involved in capacity building of Panchayati Raj Institutions. These were (i)

national level institutions, (ii) state level training institutions, (iii) cluster of block, district and state level institutions, (iv) federation of PRI representatives, (v) technical consultancy organisations, (vi) specialised support institutions at the district level, and (vii) specialised support institutions at the State level. Figure 4.8 tells us that cluster of block/district/state resource institutions and specialised support institutions at the district level such as DIET were the most importance institutions, and while the former were also efficient ones and the latter were less so. The technical consultancy organisations and the national level institutions were the least important and least efficient in delivery of services for capacity building. Therefore, the trick lies, according to Group 4, in making the more important organisations more efficient rather than chasing the national level institutions and technical consultancy organisations for capacity building. The Group when asked to suggest ways and means to improve the performance of one institution, they chose the cluster of block/district/state resource institutions as being most worthy of support and suggested measures for their betterment.

Principal Outcomes

The principal learnings from the retreat can be summarised as follows:

On Capability Poverty of the PRIs

(i) The Panchayati Raj Institutions suffered from serious “capability poverty”. The state of their capacity for decentralised governance was in utter chaos. On each of the seven elements of capacity building considered above, the state of the PRIs especially in respect of the functions, functionaries and finances transferred to them, capacity to administer in a just manner and capacity to evolve endogenously and build their own capability is abysmal.

(ii) The exercise of capacity building has to include but be not restricted to imparting training. More specifically capacity building for decentralised administration has to involve:
- Building skills, imparting skills, explicit knowledge and developing the right attitudes.
- Working out institutional arrangements (both within and outside of government) for imparting such skills, explicit knowledge and developing the right attitudes.
- Developing operating systems, manuals and guidelines on aspects covered under Article 243 of the Constitution.
- Allowing PRIs to function as mandated by the Constitution, which involves transferring functions, functionaries and finances to the PRIs.
- Creating space for, and eliminating intrusion into the domain of the PRIs to operate and evolve into empowered institutions.

Capacity building efforts for PRIs must be cognisant of and be informed by these components of capacity building.

On Institutional Arrangements for Dealing with Capability Poverty of the PRIs

(iii) The institutional arrangement for training of PRIs is utterly chaotic and confused. The institutions which are most efficient in delivery of the inputs are the ones that are unimportant and the institutions which are important (or has the potential and/or the capacity to impart training) are either inefficient or too far removed from the place where the action lies. In revamping the institutional arrangement for training of PRIs, it emerged that the centrality of the district and sub-district level training institutions cannot be overemphasised.

(iv) While the centrality of the district and sub-district level training institutions, in building capacity of the PRIs came out in bold relief, their abject weakness to deliver the goods also came out in equally bold relief. If inputs for capacity building of PRIs are to be delivered efficiently, attention of the powers that has to be refocused on extricating the district and sub-district level training institutions, from the cesspool of backwardness of both their hardware and software.

(v) The chaos in the institutional arrangement for training of PRIs and the abject weaknesses of the district and sub-district level training institutions were worse confounded by the absence of any training policy, training strategy and training plan to build the PRIs. The states must forthwith develop training policy and training strategy together with a five-year training plan in respect of PRIs.

(vi) Absence of finances for revamping institutional arrangement for training of PRIs and build their training software, is a major gap in building capacity of the PRIs. It is imperative that a proportion of the funds (say 5 per cent) for development channeled through the PRIs and a proportion (say 1-2 per cent) of the resources raised by them has to be earmarked for capacity building of these institutions.

Impact of Devolution of Functions, Functionaries and Finances in the Context of Capacity Building of the PRIs

(vii) A critical hurdle towards building capability of the PRIs has been the niggardly devolution of functions, functionaries and finances to these bodies. Imparting skills, knowledge and attitudes, howsoever robust, to PRIs will be singularly infructuous unless they have the scope to apply such skills, knowledge and attitudes within their functional domain, as enjoined in the Eleventh Schedule to the Constitution of India. Any meaningful exercise of capacity building of the PRIs must be preceded by concrete (not virtual) devolution of functions, functionaries and finances to these bodies.

(viii) Only with devolution of functions, functionaries and finances to the PRIs, these institutions can evolve endogenously and build their own capability, by *inter alia* harmonising the external stimuli available to them.

(ix) For capacity building of the PRIs, the *Gram Sabhas* must be made vibrant and useful, so as to attract members of the *Gram Sabha* to their meetings. To do so, the *Gram Sabhas* have to be endowed with mandatory functions akin to what has been provided for *Gram Sabhas* in the five Schedule Areas, like selection of beneficiaries for Government Programmes etc.

On Contents of Capacity Building Exercises for the PRIs

(x) The capacity building exercise of the PRIs must include a sustained effort at bridging the information gap that exists.

(xi) The capacity building exercise of the PRIs must include:

- the technology for developing village plans, integrating them and aggregating them for block plans, integrating and aggregating block plans into district plans and finally integrating and aggregating district plans into state plans and
- ways and means to deal and build new alliances with new institutions such as community based organisations and participatory platforms (created either by the government or by agencies outside of government) that interface with the PRIs.

(xii) Strengthening community based organisations, such as Women's Groups, which have been autonomously fostered by the communities themselves as support organisations and their integration with the standing committees of the PRIs, has to be made an integral part of exercises directed at building the capacity of the PRIs.

On Creating an Enabling Environment through Constitutional Administrative/Legal Measures for Capacity Building of the PRIs

(xiii) A major impediment to capacity building of PRIs is the system of rotation of certain functionaries enjoined in the Constitution. The incumbents who occupy positions which are subject to rotation on a term by term basis has no incentive to develop either their capacities or of their peers and subordinates. Additionally, resources invested in building capacity of such functionaries are largely dissipated once she/he is eliminated from the PRIs architecture through the system of rotation. A Constitutional Amendment is warranted to ensure that frequency of such rotation is reduced (except in case of reservation of seats for SC/ST constituencies). However, there can be stipulation that each functionary is not eligible to seek the same office for more than two/three terms.

(xiv) The proliferation of parallel institutions, often as creatures of state action, to discharge functions entrusted to the PRIs, has intruded into the jurisdiction of the PRIs. To create space for the PRIs and allow them to build their capacities and evolve as efficient institutions of decentralised governance, creation of such parallel bodies must be dispensed with.

(xv) The role of the MPs and MLAs, have to be redefined and rationalised *vis-à-vis* the PRIs and the attitude and behaviour of the bureaucracy towards the PRIs has to be changed from being adversarial and even confrontational, to one of partnership.

Part II

Action Research

5

Inter-Sectoral Strategy: Need or Fad?

An Investigation Through Participatory Methods

It is not because things are difficult that we do not dare;
It is because we do not dare that things are difficult.

—Seneca

Introduction

The discourse on development and poverty alleviation (read eradication) has taken many streams and prattling, in some cases ending in blind alleys and dry ravines; in others leading to fields of rich harvest. One debate on which the stream has always been full and swift is the discourse on the efficacy for a uni-sectoral *versus* the inter-sectoral approach (some have rechristened it as integrated) to poverty eradication. No one has said the last word and the debate continues. This paper is an attempt at looking at the issue through a participatory approach.

The Theory

The debate on uni-sectoral *versus* inter-sectoral approach to poverty eradication has developed under the shadow of a historical debate on the choice of the best economic systems, articulated as parts of Western history. The first system is grounded on the concept that economic growth spearheaded by an entrepreneurial class unfettered by state control or initiative guided solely by the system of markets and prices, is best suited to eliminate poverty. In the second system, a reaction to the first, economic growth controlled and initiated by a burgeoning state bureaucracy, spearheaded by labour movements, codified in a Plan, is capable of eradicating poverty. As a reaction to both these systems, a third system urges that growth is best ensured by enhancing local level autonomy and the presumed beauty of the smaller economic cycles, and supported by social (people's movements). "Think globally, act locally", is the crux of the third system. We will call these the Alpha, Beta and Gamma economic systems. Galtung calls these the "blue", "red" and "green" approaches.[1] In the real world, economies pursuing the Beta economic systems are turning to Alpha economic systems such as the states of the erstwhile USSR, China, and East European countries, for example. And

1. See Galtung, Johan (1994). *Human Rights in Another Key.* Cambridge, UK: Polity Press. p.104.

economies pursuing the Alpha system are trying to be even more intensely Alpha, (the United States, Japan and Germany, are examples in point) with more "gigantisms", under the cover of "globalisation", with more gigantic problems, inviting Gamma opposition all over the world.

This brings us to two sets of questions for development theory and practice: one relating to the issue of level, and the other relating to the issue of aspect.

On the issue of level, we need to ask: Is it predominantly macro-oriented approach, building strong economies, with strong entrepreneurial and/or bureaucratic elites and an international order accommodating the power and privileges of these interest elites best designed to eradicate poverty? Or is it predominantly micro-oriented approach, building strong human beings and strong local communities, in which human beings can unfold themselves a *l'hauteur de l'homme*, the better option?

On the issue of aspect, we need to decide: is it predominantly one dimensional strategy, and in that case does it focus on economic dimensions, on social structure, on cultural aspects, or what have you, the best way forward? Or is any attempt to have a multi-dimensional strategy, even a holistic strategy, taking the "totality" as the focus of development, encompassing a number of dimensions, the better way?

If we work out the permutation and combination of the two issues of aspects and levels, there can be four styles of development. This is shown in a tabular form below.

So far in real world situations we have mainly seen the "Macro-Oriented One-Dimensional" and the "Micro-Oriented Multi-Dimensional" styles, that is, the first and the last of the four styles. The other two styles may also be found empirically, but with the prevalence of the two mentioned.

Table 5.1

Styles of Development

SL. NO.	ASPECT	LEVEL
1	Micro-Oriented	Multi-Dimensional
2	Micro-Oriented	One-Dimensional
3	Macro-Oriented	Multi-Dimensional
4	Macro-Oriented	One-Dimensional

"Macro-Oriented One-Dimensional" style came to us in the garb of either the liberal-capitalists and the Marxist-socialists, both concentrating attention on the economic dimension of development: the former following the Alpha variety and the latter the Beta version. The former has led to growth without much control over the critical variables, the latter to control without much growth. The American Block typified the Alpha variety; and the erstwhile Communist Block typified the Beta variety. The 'crisis' that these two models cause when exported, with variations at the margin (in some cases), to the developing countries, is the "development crisis".

This situation has been exacerbated by the fact that the leaders of these blocks demanded of their "client states", that they adhere to the Alpha and Beta varieties respectively, or else they faced the risk of being dubbed as security risks. This has drastically changed today. The Beta variety champions have vanished. The American Block, championing the cause of Alpha variety now demands that all countries follow the Alpha variety and has no compunctions to use the leverages it has with the IMF, WB and the WTO in its pursuit of arm-twisting countries to fall in line.

We have at the other extreme the "Micro-Oriented Multi-Dimensional" style called "human development" or "community development", as the relatively minor style. Characteristic of this style in theory, and to a more limited extent in practice, is a high level of local self reliance, short economic cycles, informal and Gamma economics, direct democracy, participation and emphasis on human growth and individual development through provisioning of health services and education. Many communities, however, tend to focus on only one such aspect and become imbalanced, while many others focus on issues that go beyond pure economic variables and acquire a more balanced track of development.

At the current point in history, some argue, since the current styles are so overwhelmingly macro-oriented one-dimensional, a strong emphasis on micro-oriented multi-dimensional style commends itself. Even if a totally Gama variety is not possible, at least a 'more Gamma variety' should be a convenient point of departure. Real improvement in the quality of life is best experienced at the micro-level.

However, two caveats are in order here. One, macro-level variables are a strong reality and are capable of both facilitating and impeding quality of life at the micro-level. They cannot be ignored and has to be factored in any development scheme. Second, though a holistic approach has much to commend itself, nevertheless thinking in totality and putting those thoughts into practice in totality, are germane to paralysis. Everything becomes too complicated to kick-start the system. And then a holistic approach may lead to totalitarianism since all the variables have to be changed at once. This as a blue-print for all communities can become very dangerous. The best course is, therefore, to opt for starting at one corner, with one aspect, even introducing contradictions between the "old" and the "new" and set the process rolling, with a much larger agenda in mind to follow. Imbalance can also catalyse forward momentum. Satisfaction of the needs of the people should in this scheme of things remain at the centre stage.

The developmentalists of the Alpha and Beta varieties did try to pay lip service to bringing people centre stage. But they tried to do so by co-opting the human needs elements by making them one dimensional, focusing on the material needs most clearly related to their economic growth and institution building. This is unacceptable. Because in placing people at the centre, a development strategy has to be cognisant of both the material and non-material needs, not any one of them. If some day the Gamma movement with its anarchist overtones of "small is beautiful", is really successful (notwithstanding the fact that "some big is necessary"), there would then be the need for a movement in favour of a more macro-oriented approaches. Today, the macro movements are more than successful and very deeply entrenched and we need to go whole hog for Gamma development.

Thus, poverty eradication for development can be viewed as a complex dialectic between the micro and macro levels and between the one-dimensional and the more holistic (multi-dimensional) approaches. In this complex dialectic where shall we place the rights approach to development?

Human rights and human needs approaches do not discriminate between the needs and rights of different classes of people in society as its concern is universal, which explains why the rights of the needy and the marginalised, should get priority. In principle, these approaches from the bottom up, an indispensable corrective to the top-heaviness and the self-serving nature of so much of what elites put forward as "development". But human rights differ from human needs in being institutionalised in a particular way, linking a norm-sender (in our case the Constitution of India), norm-receivers (the State enjoined upon to implement the rights), the norm-objects (individuals), and then there is the norm-content (the substantive content of the norm). Thus, by its very structure the four tier human rights tradition is more consonant with the top heavy, Alpha-Beta development models, protected, facilitated or initiated by the State. It is less consistent with development based on small, basic and autonomous units where the primordial human, decentralised and horizontal, female/rational rights tradition, would fit better. Thus, there is the implicit stand point that human rights tradition is a "centralised vertical male/abstract, macro approach coming to the rescue of the micro level and in so doing increasing the legitimacy of the norm setter and the governments at the expense of making the micro-level more dependent.

Be that as it may, so long as rights approach to poverty eradication works for development of the poor, it should be pursued, irrespective of whether there are inherent limits to poverty eradication for development and there are dangers lurking round the corner. What we need to seek is consistent translation of human rights thinking into local normative culture, at once emphasising the basic needs entitlement. Particular human rights, made specific to local culture and historical context, may be as significant as universal human rights. Fortunately enough, none of the approaches are excluding mechanisms. The situation is not, an "either or situation".

Development process can be either dependent on structure or on institution. The question is whether rights based approach to poverty eradication for development is institution dependent or structure oriented. This distinction is crucial. The meaning of this crucial distinction can be best clarified through a few examples. Let us take the cases of food, energy and participation.

In the field of food:

Is the focus on being fed, or on living in a structure that is able to produce sufficient food through appropriate structural arrangements?

In the field of energy:

Is the focus is on access to institutions for somatic and mental health services or on living in a structure that produces maximum somatic and mental health?

In the field of participation:

Is the focus on access to ballot box or on life in a participatory structure?

If the focus is on being fed, then all that is needed is to organise humanitarian assistance, distributing food to hungry masses, a scene reminiscent of the famines in Africa or of India in the 40s. It is based on the institution of the donors and their willingness. It will relieve current hunger, but what about the pangs of hunger tomorrow. It does not address either the proximate or the fundamental causes of hunger. On the contrary, if the focus is on producing sufficient food through structural arrangements, then the structure of production has to be changed, which would include in the Indian case, change in landholding pattern, change in technology and distribution.

In the structural approach the basic idea is that the desired goods and services are made available almost automatically and that certain "bads" and "disservices" (such as hunger, famines, disease, illiteracy, filth, pollution and erosion of natural resources) are eliminated as well nearly automatically. Examples are pollution and control of erosion of natural resource base. Pollution and control of natural resources depletion, such as land erosion, in a farming system is built into the structure. When a farmer growing food grains for subsistence, she/he is eco-conscious, for she/he knows that she/he and her/his offspring(s) will be the victims of the consequences of eco-imbalances, if she/he does not participate in management of natural resources use. Contrast this with a MNC in agro-business. The MNC in agro-business, does not take into account the consequences of eco-imbalances caused by its action (and there are examples galore) because the consequences of such of its action on natural resources will be far away from where it is located.

"And when they become too disastrous, the MNC will, like nomads but less softly, move to other areas on which to prey".

In the structural approach certain obstacles are removed by changing the structure. The structural approach is preventive rather than curative when the focus is on bads and disservices. In our example, the farmer does not squander away environmental and ecological resources, and then tries to restore the balance. She takes care that she uses environmental resources in a sustainable way.

This in one sense answers the question revolving around the relationship between development and human rights. It is a relationship of both compatibility and contradiction: of compatibility with Gamma approach; of contradiction with Alpha and Beta approaches. However, it does not automatically follow that the only valid approach is micro-level, holistic development, protected by building adequate structures that define mutual rights and obligations, for this would pre-suppose a world where all societies are in the same historical situation, and that the good society is contradiction free. Having said that, we hasten to add that there is little doubt that much more emphasis should be placed on local level approaches for development and human rights, and on the structural approaches for achieving both of them.

The Theory on Food and Right

This general view on rights approach to poverty eradication for development, leads us to a theory of how to relate right to food with development. We need a clear image of goals of food we are seeking, so that we know what right to protect or promote. In doing this we would emphasise structure and automaticity. We would also bear in mind that the right to food is also related to human needs comprising the broad classes of needs for survival, well-being, identity and freedom[2], bearing in mind that production and distribution to satisfy needs are necessary but not sufficient conditions to satisfy needs. Respect for nature, structure and cultures are also matters of deep significance.

When we are looking at right to food, right to food cannot be considered in isolation because food is not a sector of development but an essential aspect of the entire discourse on development. This warrants that we run through the entire gamut of goals of development to identify the dimension of right to food in each one of them. These goals of development could be clubbed into nine aspects, *viz.*, survival, well-being, identity, freedom, production, distribution, nature, structure and culture. Let us examine these goals as goals in right to development in the next few paragraphs.

2. See Mukherjee, Amitava (1999). "Out of the Abyss of Underdevelopment: The Challenge Confronting Civil Society Actors", Paper for the *82nd Conference of the Indian Economic Association*, Amritsar, December 27-29, Guru Nanak Dev University.

Survival: Survival as an aspect of the goal of the right to food means the probability of anyone dying of starvation will be ruled out. Such starvation could be due to either misguided production, or mal-distribution of food produced, or ecological imbalances, or lack of self-reliance, including dependency on those who can make use of food as a weapon, or some combination of these. Basically this is tantamount to having sustainability of people over time, such as over seasonal variations in food supply, as a goal of right to food.

Well-Being: Well-being as an aspect of the goal of the right to food means that there will be adequate food consumption, both quantitatively and qualitatively, at the individual level. There is a subjective approach, the individual's own judgement, and an objective approach, a scientific approach which in turn would split into western ethno-sciences. Table 5.2 suggests the possibilities. Nothing less than the complete set of these possibilities should be considered as the goal of right to food. To disregard the individual's own judgement is professional arrogance and to disregard non-western approaches is western arrogance and parochialism. Both are widespread.

Table 5.2

Well Being: The Possibilities

Approaches	*Quantitative*	*Qualitative*
Subjective	Feeling of a full stomach; no hunger, no pain.	Eating food that tastes good.
Objective (Western)	Adequate amount of calories, proteins, vitamins.	Adequate balance, harmony.
Objective (Non-Western)	Adequate amount of food relative to need.	Adequate balance, cold/hot, yin/yang etc.

Identity: Identity as an aspect of the goal of right to food means that production and consumption of food will engender contact with self, society, culture and nature. Production and consumption of food is not something remote and external, carried out in total alienation between producers, distributors and consumers.

Freedom: Freedom as an aspect of the goal of right to food implies that individuals will be free to exercise their choice, both with regard to production and consumption of the food, including the possibility of choosing of their own free will, *status quo* in food production and consumption. Within it, will be embodied the fact that the people exercising this choice will have the consciousness about the consequences of the choice they would be making.

Production: Production as an aspect of the goal of right to food means that factor-inputs is necessary and sufficient quantity will be available for producing food to bring about survival, well-being, identity and freedom.

Distribution: Distribution as an aspect of the goal of right to food means ensuring that the level of satisfaction from participation in consumption and production of food for those at the bottom of society, in terms of survival, well-being, identity and freedom will be increased, particularly ensuring that discrepancies in levels of satisfaction for the total population and between groups will be decreased. Particular attention will be paid in ensuring equality and gender justice in food production and consumption, and in ensuring child survival.

Nature: Nature as an aspect of the goal of right to food means ensuring that, as a result of food production and consumption, the level of maturity of the eco-system will be increased or at least not decreased, both in terms of diversity and symbiosis. This has also to be viewed as a necessary condition for guaranteeing inter-generational food security. Bio-organic approaches are one response to this demand.

Structure: Structure as an aspect of the goal of right to food means making sure that food-related needs will be satisfied to a large extent on a local basis; that there will be a potential for local adequacy, in times of crises (even food autarchy when necessary!), including seasonal variations. That is, there will be self-sufficiency in food at the local level, a necessary imperative condition for dealing with any eventuality arising out of use of food as a "weapon", by those who have control over food.

Culture: Culture as an aspect of the goal of right to food enjoins that the food system will strengthen the viable cultural patterns and imposes no unwanted alien culture. This is particularly so, because an alien culture thrusts other values and tastes, and engenders unwanted relationships to others and to nature, which are not desirable, except in cases where this happens to be the outcome of a deliberate, voluntary, and participatory (read democratic) choice.

The totality of this then should be the deeper goal of right to food. However, the ultimate unit of development in this perspective will remain the individual human beings, as only individuals can sense the pain of deprivation and enjoy satisfaction.

The Reality

It is the story of village Krishna Rakshit Chak.[3] The study essentially began in an attempt to decipher the menace of hunger in the village, through a food calendar and turned out to be a longitudinal study of great insights. Since assessment of hunger was the point of departure, we would begin this paper by a very brief summary of the food security situation in the village. We would then see how the hunger situation could be remedied. This would provide the basis for conceptualising the need for an integrated approach.

3. This is essentially a micro-study. Its setting is in an unknown village in rural Bengal, in the tribal district of Medinipur. For details see Mukherjee, Amitava and Neela Mukherjee (1994). "Rural Women and Food Insecurity: What a Food Calendar Reveals", *Economic and Political Weekly* 11, March. The food calendars in this Chapter were facilitated by Dr. Neela Mukherjee.

The Hunger Situation

In Krishna Rakshit Chak, the people being landless tribals, their access to food is through exchange based entitlements. Food is procured by either exchanging back breaking labour with those who have land and other productive resources, for food grains and money to buy food, or by exchanging labour with nature to gather, hunt, catch and collect food from common property resources and micro-environments. The dependence on both, the primary source of food (food produced by the application of land, labour, capital and enterprise) and on the secondary source of food (food produced in forests, rivers, streams, ponds, micro-environments etc.) is remarkable.[4] The poor villagers access food from the primary food system by working as agricultural labourers on daily wages, and they access food from the secondary food system by gathering, collecting and hunting. Despite there being the two sources of food, the poor in the village suffer hunger for extended periods of time. And distressingly, over the period of study from the first half of 1993 to 1999, the hunger periods have been enlarged, and probably deepened as well.

For instance, the villagers go to bed hungry everyday, there being no way they can consume 2100 calories of food recommended for a normal life. The people of the village additionally suffered severe hunger during the three months of *Chaitra, Baisakh* and *Jyestha* and again in *Ashwin* and *Kartick*. Reference is invited to Table 5.3. In 1995 and thereafter (refer to Tables 5.4 and 5.5, for the 1995 and 1998 Food Calendars), the villagers suffered severe hunger for seven months, from *Chaitra* right up to *Kartick*, the period which encompasses the cultivation and significant portions of the harvesting/post harvesting season, when the work load.

Significantly, therefore, the severity of hunger is highest in the months when the people have to work the hardest. It is also interesting that the major source of protein for the villagers remain the secondary food system, particularly water sources. But the sad part of it all is that dependence for protein is not only overwhelmingly from the secondary food system but that it is increasing over the years, while, the absolute quantities of protein, fibre and vitamins content in the food basket of the poor are on the decline. It is significant that the fall in food consumed from the secondary food system has also made the food basket of the villagers less palatable and robbed it of its variety. The hunger faced by the villagers is not undifferentiated: the women and the girl children consume less and often the "left-overs". And therefore, women and girl children suffer greater hunger than men and the male children, a phenomenon symptomatic of the rural situation throughout India.

The primary lesson is that notwithstanding the absence of a "systemic" shortage of food, reflected in rising food production, a burgeoning buffer stock of

---

4. See Mukherjee, Amitava (1995). *Structural Adjustment Programme and Food Security*. Aldershot, Hongkong, Sydney etc.: Avebury.

food with the government and a functioning PDS, hunger is a common feature, year after year. And the relative intensity of hunger is also on the rise. That is, food security at the household level is fundamentally different from food security at the macro-level. Second that the intensity of hunger varies with the availability of food in the local market (the supply factor) which regulates local prices of food and the availability of employment, or what is termed as the power to access the available food (the demand factor), though the supply factor is the dominant one. This leads to the third lesson: the "state of hunger", in the short run, is regulated both by the vagaries of nature and the vagaries of those who own resources. Not by the acts of the government alone.

The crucial lesson is that most of the food from the secondary food system is collected by women, particularly the younger women and the girls. The reason is that within the family there is an intra-familial distribution of power, and the eldest woman's decision is final and binding. The eldest woman in the family distributes intra-familial work according to the energy required to be expended. Since the energy requirement for collecting, gathering and hunting food from the secondary food system is very high, often requiring long miles of walk, these tasks are entrusted to the care of the younger women, and the girl children in the family. And finally the women who not only collect, gather and access for, they are the ones who process food as well. An unusually large part of their waking time is used up in fulfilling these functions.

Strikingly, the villagers regretted that the cabbage, pumpkin, spinach, "*pui saag*" (*palak* or spinach), leaves, herbs, green banana, mango, wild plants etc., which they consumed in 1993 were all gone. They explained that, the total output of food from the secondary food system is falling as the area under "commons" is shrinking with their diversion for alternative usage. Moreover, the relatively well-off farmers who earlier allowed the poorer people free access to sizeable amounts of these kinds of food from their fields, ponds etc., as these were considered "inferior food", are not any longer prepared to allow such indulgence. They are now themselves selling them at Charabani, Khemasuli, Tangra, Golbazar and Kalai Kunda Gate No. 2 markets. The reason being that the inflationary spiral has eaten into the capacity of the relatively well off farmers to make both ends meet.[5]

Why Such Hunger?

Persistent hunger stalks Krishna Rakshit Chak and it seems to be growing. The consensus that either more food production (to increase supply) or more employment generation programmes (EAS) or a massive rise in self employment programme such as IRDP, or some combination of the three, seems to be a false God. Even a comfortable food stock and a functioning public distribution system fails to do the trick. That all these have been in

5. For more details see Mukherjee and Mukherjee (1994).

operation in Krishna Rakshit Chak and indeed the country for many many years, need not detain us any longer. A lasting solution has to seek remedy for the underpinning factors perpetuating and worsening hunger.

Ending hunger needs an acceptance that the deprivation of food takes many forms and have disparate causes. And hence a differentiated view has to be adopted and shedding piece meal approaches, which abound in plenty. Increased food availability and higher purchasing power goes a long way to eliminate hunger, but much more needs to be done: (i) enhancement of general economic growth; (ii) expansion of employment and fair wages; (iii) diversification of production; (iv) enhancement of medical and health care; (v) arrangement for providing food to vulnerable groups; (vi) spread of basic education and literacy; (vii) strengthening of democracy and the news media; and (viii) reduction in gender-based inequalities.[6]

What Happened in Krishna Rakshit Chak?

It warrants an investigation of Krishna Rakshit Chak against this backdrop, to which we would presently turn. We would examine the landscape in Krishna Rakshit Chak through the villager's eyes by using participatory methods.

Enhancement of General Economic Growth

Let us examine the well-being grouping whose analysis tells us about general economic growth. Table 5.6 exhibits the well-being grouping. The inhabitants belong to Lodha Tribe and are landless.[7] The villagers prepared a village map at Table 5.6. With the village map the villagers ranked the households on the basis of annual food availability, for hunger stalked them to no ends. Annual availability of food was directly linked to the capacity of adjoining forests and water bodies to provide food support, apart from agriculture and hence their concept of well being was described in terms of linkages with agriculture, the forest, common property resources, the ponds, governmental interventions and 'others'. There is no other economic activity.

The desperate situation is manifested by the fact that out of 50 households, there were 30 households which received assistance under the Integrated Rural Development Programme (IRDP) of the Government of India (households with a circle round them in Table 5.6) and 13 households (households with a black dot) who received special assistance under the Integrated Tribal Development Plan of the government. And there is only one household employed in the services sector. That is, 86 per cent of the households are surviving on poverty alleviation programme (and are therefore, admittedly below the poverty line).

6. Sen, Amartya (1997). "Hunger in the Contemporary World". London: Suntroy Toyota International Centre for Economic and Related Disciplines. No. 8, November.
7. We are treating them as landless, though surplus land has been distributed to them under the West Bengal's aggressive land reforms agenda, in the sense that they have no land on which economic activity was possible.

This is an unusually large number. Indeed there are only two households (households with a multiplication sign) who were ranked above "poorest of the poor", and even they were surviving on the strength of IRDP. Given the informal taxation in place and the leakages, the fact that 86 per cent of the people received assistance under the poverty alleviation programme is itself very strong evidence that the people are indeed poor.

The situation has remained virtually unchanged over several years. There is neither the services sector nor the industrial sector, not even village and cottage industries. There has been an all round development in agricultural growth in West Bengal, but since Krishna Rakshit Chak has mostly landless inhabitants, the benefit of increased growth in agriculture has bypassed them. There has been virtually no general economic growth and therefore, the first condition necessary for hunger elimination is missing.

Expansion of Employment and Fair Wages

What about expansion of employment and fair wages? From the fact that there has been no general expansion of economic growth, expansion of employment is *ipso facto* not possible. Employment being restricted to cultivation and harvesting in lands belonging to others, there is no change. Not only has agriculture remained mono-cropping once during *Rabi*, there has been no change in technology of production which is employment generating as well. Traditional methods of cultivation with moderate use of chemical fertilisers are all that is to write home about.

As to fair wages Krishna Rakshit Chak being in a state run by a leftist government, fair wages for labour should be a given fact of life. The ground reality is otherwise. The labourers in the village being agricultural labourers, they are not organised and hence the advantages of collective bargaining is not be available to them. Nevertheless, enforcement of the Minimum Wages Act is within the remit of office of the District Administration. Minimum wages for the state is shown in Table 5.6. Inter-state variation in minimum wages exists but not within a state. Reference is now invited to Table 5.6. At a time when the Central government's issue price of rice for distribution in the Public Distribution System is Rs. 5.65 and Rs. 8.30 per kg[8] for below poverty line and above poverty line families respectively. A daily wage of Rs. 69 for agricultural labourers (most people in the village are agricultural labourers) is clearly unfair. It is not even a living wage, far less than the minimum prescribed wage.

Diversification of Production

We need not labour the point that there has been no diversification of production. As the villagers pointed out that the area depended, despite

8. Government of India (1999). *Economic Survey.* New-Delhi: Ministry of Finance, Government of India. February.

advances made in the agricultural sector in the state, on rains for cultivation and hence their well-being is intricately linked with rain gods, the agricultural sector remains traditional. The crops grown are still paddy of the traditional varieties with some rare farmers using improved variety of seeds. Being all agricultural labourers, not even pure tenant or concealed tenants, use of improved variety of seeds or otherwise, has no impact on the lives of the poor. Agriculture has remained a seasonal mono-cropping exercise.

A weak food base lessened the capacity of the households to support experimental labour migration by members of the poor households trying to find employment to diversify the household's income base as well. They have no traditional crafts. There are no artisans in the village.

Enhancement of Medical and Health Care

Understanding health in village Krishna Rakshit Chak was a different experience. When a return visit was made to the village to learn about their health status, the villagers were more than happy. "They brought some coloured sketch pens from their primary school and were looking for papers when we were actually offering them some sheets of paper."[9] The health map was prepared concurrently with the food calendar discussed above. It was facilitated by the primary school teachers from the village.

The Health Map (Figure 5.1), identifies diseases like polio, tuberculosis, leprosy, asthma and piles, as the preponderant ones. Details in matters of family planning are astonishing: households actually practising/adopted family planning, number of pregnant women in the community, lactating mothers and households with cases of miscarriage, are clearly marked. Old age as an aspect of health, often neglected in general health descriptions and households with aged people are explicitly mentioned.

Family planning is practised in 22 households, which is 44 per cent of the total households living in the village. If we were to look at the social structure, it is obvious that a little less than 50 per cent of those identified as 'poorest of the poor' are left out of the family planning net. This limited utilisation of family planning methods can have serious implication. It is nobody's case that there ought to shivers down our spines as population will outstrip food production, but "if the general impact of a higher population growth is curtailment of the well-being and freedom of women and men in society, then there are real problems to consider."[10]

9. Mukherjee, Neela (1998). *Participatory Rural Appraisal, Methodology and Applications*. New-Delhi: Concept Publishing Co.
10. Sen, Amartya (1994). "Population and Reasoned Agency: Population Growth and Food Security", *Development* No. 3. Particularly in relation to hunger.

Figure 5.1

Health Map, Krishna Rakshit Chak

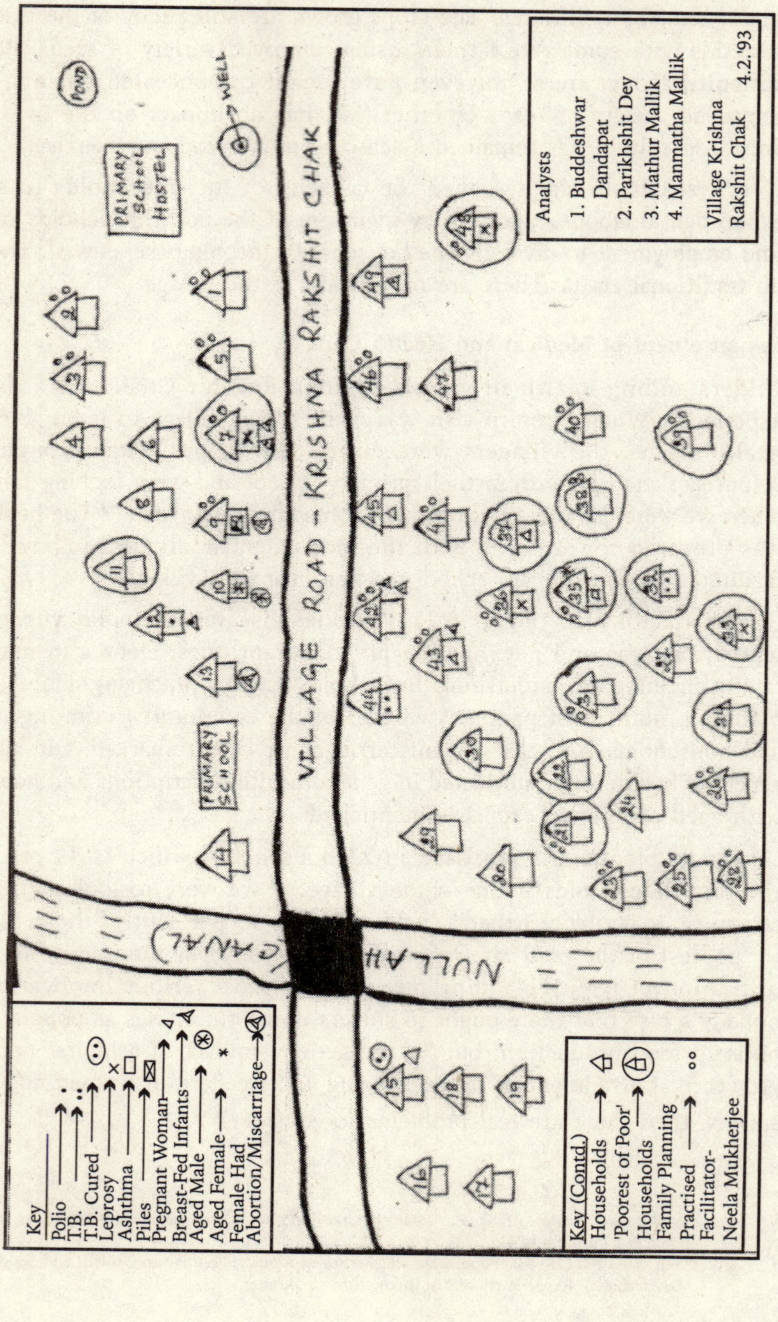

The leprosy cases affects almost 25 per cent of the 'poorest of the poor'. This seems to be in line with the all-India picture where the incidence of Leprosy is 200 per cent higher in less developed villages than in the developed ones.[11] The incidence of tuberculosis, asthma and old-age all afflict the 'poorest of the poor' households.[12] This is not surprising given that the 'poorest of the poor' for one, have lower capacity to buy health services, and for the other, they are more under nourished than the rest of the community, making them more vulnerable to diseases.

The Well-Being Map (Figure 5.2) of Krishna Rakshit Chak discussed earlier, to no one's surprise indicates the existence of temples, drinking water wells, primary school and even school hostel for the tribal children, but makes no mention of any health facility; not even a Maternity and Child Health Sub-Centre.[13] The nearest health facility is seven kilometers away. Apart from the problems of carrying the sick and the old over long distances, the social stigma and ostracisation that follows on detection of diseases like leprosy and tuberculosis makes it even more difficult for them to access basic health care facilities, even if distance is not a constraining factor. If we add to the general standard of health, the element of malnutrition reflected by the food calendars (Tables 5.3 to 5.5), the status of health in Krishna Rakshit Chak provides no cause for cheer.

Spread of Basic Education and Literacy

The Social Map (Figure 5.3) is a literacy map of Krishna Rakshit Chak. Taking adult literacy as an indicator of the spread of basic education, we looked at female literacy. Only 44 per cent of the households have literate females, or if the percentage is calculated on the total female population, out of a total of 59 female adults, only 22 are literate, that is, literacy rate for women is 37 per cent. Of the adult males only 3 are illiterate out of a total of 78 adult males, that is, the literacy rate among men is 96 per cent. The total literacy rate is about 67 per cent. Against the backdrop of total literacy rate of 60 per cent in the country, this *prima facie* looks satisfactory. Such satisfaction, however, has to be sobered by the fact that Midnapore was covered under the Total Literacy Campaign (TLC), where the district is claimed to be 100 per cent literate. Either there is something amiss about claim of the TLC or that

11. Philipose, Pamela (1999). "Rhythm of the Countryside", *The Express Magazine*. New Delhi, 8th November, p.4.
12. There is a recent study which shows that the incidence of tuberculosis is 32 per cent higher in poorer villages than in the better-off ones. See Shariff Abusaleh (1999). *Human Development Report: A Profile of Indian States in the 1990s*. New Delhi: NCAER and Oxford University Press.
13. The health infrastructure is organised in several tiers. The district has a referral hospital. A block, a development unit at the sub-district level with a population of approximately 1,00,000 to 1,50,000, has a Public Health Centre (PHC) and in some cases a second unit called Additional PHC. MCH sub-centres at the sub-block level is to serve a population of 5000 people.

without sufficient post literacy campaign, literate people have slid back into illiteracy. In any event, a literacy level of 67 per cent in a village of a district declared to be 100 per cent literate and after 45 years of continuous efforts at providing elementary education to all, looks rather disappointing. If we factor in the cultural factor, that in Bengal, education is highly regarded and sought after[14], and if we further factor in the political elements of the state, that its citizens are politically conscious which places a high premium on demands for good education, the disappointment is all the more. We are not getting into the lively debate on the quality of elementary education, which has been the subject matter of a great debate in recent years.[15] What is precisely more disturbing is the huge gap between female literacy rate, of 37 per cent, which is well below the national literacy rate for women, and the male literacy rate of 96 per cent, which is way above the average literacy rate for men nationally.

It is significant that the female literacy is only 22/57 while male literacy is 75/78. That is, there is a gender bias in the practice of imparting and accepting basic education. This is, further reinforced by the intra-familial distribution of power. We mentioned earlier, that the arduous task of accessing food from the secondary food system falls on the younger women and girls in the family, which prevents them from attending schools. This is more so during the hunger months when they work harder as accessing food flowing from the primary food system becomes dearer and difficult. Because accessing food from the secondary food system is the responsibility of the women and the girls, they have either no time to attend school or have such low energy levels that reading is not possible.

Reduction in Gender Biased Inequalities

Reduction in gender biased inequalities implies that literacy and education not only help to combat gender biased inequalities in distribution but also tend to moderate fertility rates.[16] Fertility rate is seen to come down sharply as a result of greater power of young women within the family.

Let us consider the gender issue from three objective criteria. One, access to health; two, the state of elementary education and discrimination in access to food.

Last things first: discrimination in accessing food. We have mentioned that there is asymmetry in access to food. While men and the male children are

14. In Satyajit Ray's famous movie, *Pather Panchali,* when the wife of the poor teacher complains to him that the grocers have all the creature comforts while their children suffer from malnutrition, the teacher replies, which is symptomatic of a typically Bengali ethos, "after all I am a teacher", meaning that "even if we suffer, I am in an exalted vocation, teaching and not trading."
15. See Probe Report (1998). on the *State of Elementary Education in India.* New Delhi: Oxford University Press.
16. Murthi, Mamta *et al.* (1995). "Mortality, Fertility and Gender Bias in India: A District Level Analysis", *Population and Development Review,* December.

Figure 5.2

Well-Being Grouping, Village Krishna Rakshit Chak

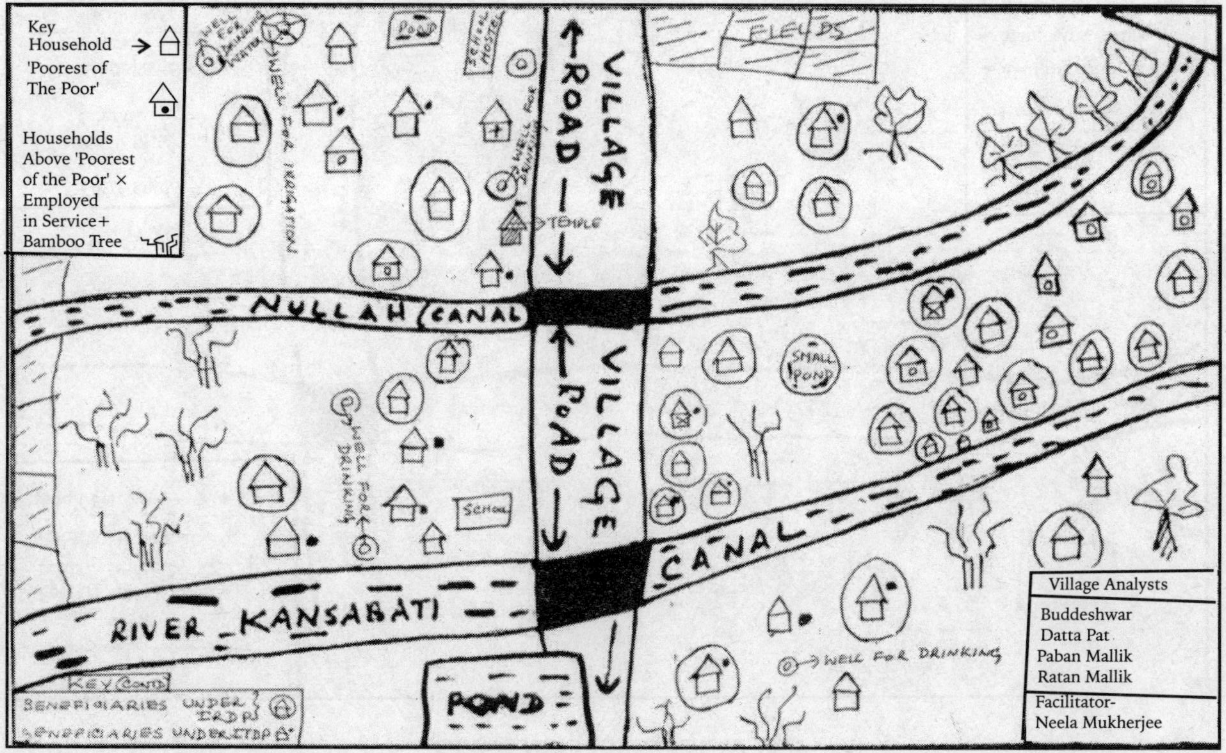

Figure 5.3

Literacy Map, Krishna Rakshit Chak

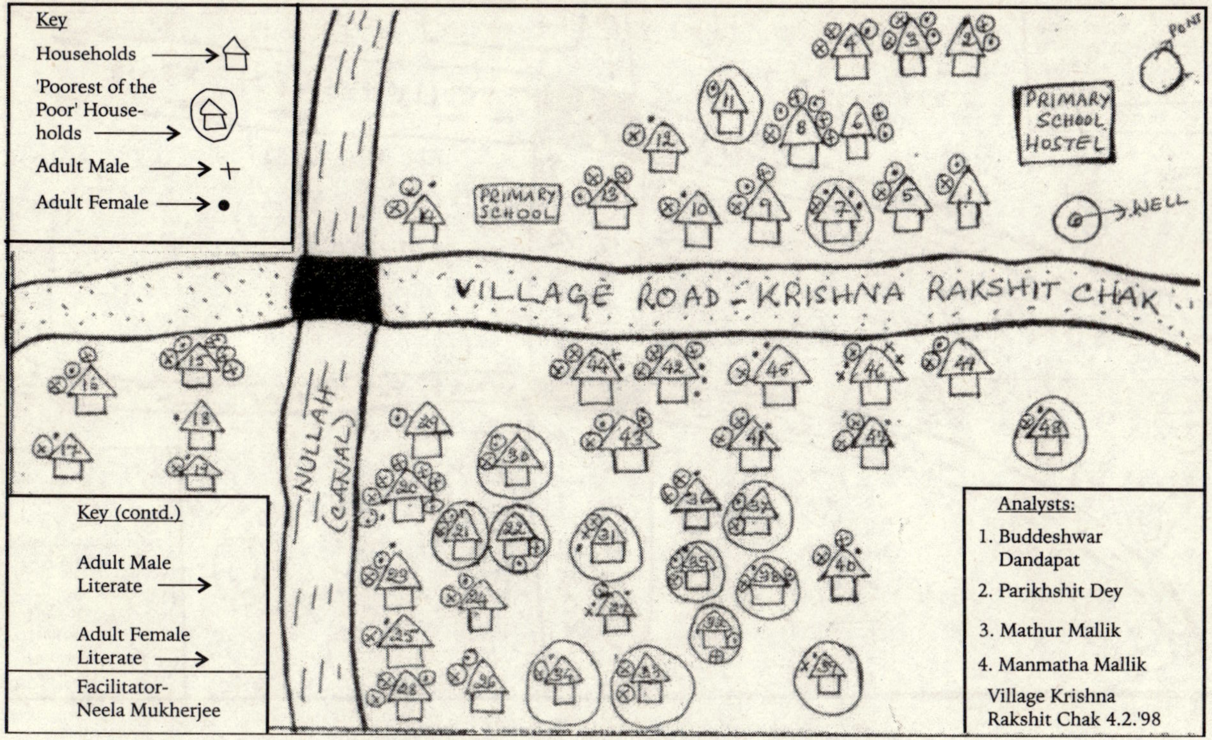

better fed, the women and the girls eat less and poorer food. It is sad that in the history of Bengal this phenomenon has persisted for decades. A noted observer of the Great Bengal Famine of 1943 has remarked: "The patriarchal values of Bengali Hindu society required priority to be given to the feeding of the male members of the household so as to ensure the continuance of the male line".[17] This is more often the case where the male members of the households are the bread winners.[18] Despite all the empowerment and politicisation of local level governance, including reservation of seats in local level elected institutions (*Panchayats*), things have not changed dramatically for the better. Even those parts of Bengal which have gone through several rounds of fire, show significantly same behaviour.

The discrimination in terms of education is brought forth both by the lower female literacy rates and the time that the women spend to access food by re-appropriating their time for school to collect and gather food from the common property resources and micro-environments and indeed process such food as well. Not surprisingly, the level of female literacy of 37 per cent when pitched against the male literacy of 96 per cent, tells us the whole story. The fact that women and the female children, spend more time in making food available to the household can only explain part of this huge gap in literacy rates. There are other causal factors including the social belief that girls would be married off to other households and that they do not require education for after all they will be, in the last analysis, only managing the kitchen and the children at home.

With regard to health, there is nothing apparent in the health map indicating discrimination in accessing health facilities. But that the women additionally suffer from mental disease. There is enormous pressure on the women who cannot get married for want of dowry. The paying capacity of the poor households, who cannot afford two square meals a day and the much needed primary health care, is unable to sustain the demands of paying handsome dowry to buy the eligible girls their husbands. The result is that those who remain spinster and those households which have spinsters are subjected to social and familial pressures, bordering on torture.[19] Lacking any asset, including carts and animals to pull them, the poor women often already in poor health trek long distances, carrying their children, to get minimal health care and fetch potable water, often transported as head-loads. This is no less arduous than collecting, gathering and fetching food from the secondary food system and processing food within the household.

17. Greenough, Paul (1982). *Prosperity and Misery in Modern Bengal, the Famine of 1943-44*. Oxford: Oxford University Press.
18. Arnold, David (1988) *Famines, Social Crisis and Historical Change*. Oxford: Basil Blackwell.
19. There was in Bengal a social norm that wherever a family failed to have its girl(s) married, the family would have such girls married to a Banyan Tree. This demonstrates a very strong bias against unmarried women. This may have been one of the sociological reasons for which very young girls, often minors, were married off to old men (not infrequently with several wives).

Lessons: Approaches to the Problem

When we broaden the analysis of the problem of food security from producing more food in the primary food system and from enhancing the capacity (read purchasing power) of the poor to access food, we have to be cognisant of the effects of the state of health, state of elementary education, reduction in gender based inequalities, the diversification in production, employment and fair compensation for labour sold and of course general economic expansion. There is often the bogey of resource constraint raised. The state government and indeed the Central government face financial situations that are difficult and therefore, hard choices are made and the resources for catalysing increased production, better basic/elementary education, primary health care, employment and stricter enforcement of laws relating to fair wages, are cut off. Acceptance of this argument is made difficult by the fact that "the divergence between private and social benefits, and also between private and social costs".[20]

One can use here the 'minimal threshold' concept introduced by the human rights activists.[21] A minimum (read core) set of four rights as also their levels are conceived as a platform of effective self-provision, which put the poor on the threshold of further progressive steps of development (with other sorts of feasible development aid as necessary) toward assurance of the higher standards. The key feature of these core rights and the core portion of each right is the interdependence of these as essential minimal components for self-provision contribution.

What then are these four rights? They are right to food, right to employment, right to health, and right to education. In respect of the right to food, production and access to food staples is the core. In the health sector, pre-requisites for promotive health care, such as potable water and avoidance of malnutrition-related weakness and health threats (which can prevent getting to an available health facility) and access to family planning facilities are central. For the employment right reliable food-productive employment is the most important and in education, immediate food and health productive education would have priority.

Failures of achieving minimal levels in these portions of the four rights areas are interrelated and interdependent, as can be seen in the example of the rural poor. Lack of reliable minimal food access weakens health of women, men and children, owing to debilitating malnutrition related diseases. This in turn weakens their capacity to produce food in their rural subsistence

20. Sen, 1994.
21. See for instance Andreasssen Bard-Anders, Tor Skalnes, Alan G. Smith, and Hugo Stokke (1985). "Rights and Needs in a Third World Context: A Model for Disaggregating Economic and Social Rights", Paper read at the *World Congress of the International Political Science Association*. Paris, France, 15th-20th July.

agriculture, and weakens the capacity for meaningful employment for food translatable income. Poor health and malnutrition make it difficult for the poor villagers, many of whom live in remote areas, to access clean water and health care facilities, in further weakening their health. Distance is also a problem suffered by the rural poor for getting education in nutrition, health, farming techniques and other food productive kinds of knowledge. Scant employment during the lean season in the rural areas and other slack times (and general unemployment), in urban areas, has a direct impact on the food and nutrition and health of households. Lack of a morning meal hinders the learning of the children, reinforcing the impact of commonly bad educational quality in the remote areas where the poor live. A weak food base lessen the capacity of the households to support experimental labour migration by members of the poor household trying to find employment to diversify the household's income base. Reliable access to minimalist levels in any one of these core portions of the key right values, in particular access to food, tends to be linked with the reliability in the others.

This makes a strong case for an integrated approach. There is no need to labour the standard textbook loop exhibiting inter-connectivity of the social sectors, *inter se*, on the one part and the economic sectors, *inter se*, on the other part.

If one was to advocate a uni-sectoral approach, the residual gaps (inevitably large in poorer communities) could make serious inroads into efforts at eradicating poverty. This in no way distracts the invaluable contribution that uni-sectoral strategy can make to poverty eradication. It is only to remind ourselves that such strategies stand a far better chance of success, if the complementary strategies are to be present. For instance, excellent work in basic education is invaluable in itself but it can make a much more serious dent on poverty, if primary health care, sources of livelihood and gender justice are present as well. There is considerable evidence to the effect that excellent health intervention improves health status in poor communities but the general state of poverty stays frozen in time, unless supported by complementary developments like improved education.[22]

The case for cross-sectoral strategy for eradication of poverty is very strong.

---

22. See for instance Kale Memorial Lecture by B.S. Minhas on "How lack of basic education for the girl children could be a spoiler for development".

Table 5.3

Seasonal Food Calendar of Village Krishna Rakshit Chak, Medinipur, 1993

Month	*Rice*	*Potatoes*	*Pulses*	*Vegetables@@*	*Fruits@*	*Food@@ from Water Sources*	*Others from Wild*
1	2	3	4	5	6	7	8
Magh	****** ****** ***	******* ******	***	Cabbage	-	-	Wild boars and wild rabbits
Phalgun	****** ***	******* ****	**	Spinach	-	-	*Neem* leaves
Chaitra	****	****	**	Pumpkin	-	Fish and wild water plants	-
Baisakh	****	***	*	*Pui* leaves and herbs	Mango Jackfruit	Fish, snails and wild water plants	-
Jyestha	****	****	**	*Lota,* leaves and herbs	Mango Jackfruit	Fish, wild water plants	-
Asardh	****	***	***	*Jhinge* (nearer to Sukini), Green Papaya	-	-	-
Srabon	****	****	*****	Green Papaya	-	-	-
Bhadra	****	***	***	Green Banana	-	Fish and snails	-
Ashwin	****	***	**	-	-	-	-
Kartick	**	***	**	Radish, leaves	-	-	-
Aghrayan	****	****	*****	Tomatoes	-	-	-
Poush	*****	******* **	***** *	Brinjals	-	--	Wild rabbits

Notes: (i) The number of "star" marks under column heads rice, potatoes, pulses represent the number of stones used by the villagers to show the consumption of the relative item of food.

(ii) @Fruits from some trees growing near ponds and elsewhere in the village.

(iii) @@ From CPR and Forests.

(iv) Prepared by Women's Group, Krishna Rakshit Chak, Medinipur, West Bengal. 4.2.93.

Legend:

Magh: Mid-January to Mid-February
Phalgun: Mid-February to Mid-March
Chaitra: Mid-March to Mid-April
Baisakh: Mid-April to Mid-May
Jyestha: Mid-May to Mid-June
Asardh: Mid-June to Mid-July
Srabon: Mid-July to Mid-August
Bhadra: Mid-August to Mid-September
Ashwin: Mid-September to Mid-October
Kartick: Mid-October to Mid-November
Aghrayan: Mid-November to Mid-December
Poush: Mid-December to Mid-January

Table 5.4

Seasonal Food Calendar of Village Krishna Rakshit Chak, 1995.

Month	*Rice*	*Potatoes*	*Pulses*	*Vegetables$*	*Fruits#*	*Fish$*	*Snails$*	*Others from Wild$*
1	2	3	4	5	6	7	8	9
Magh	****** ****** ***	****** ****** *	***	-	-	-	-	-
Phalgun	****** ***	****** *****	**	-	-	-	-	Neem leaves
Chaitra	*****	***	-	-	-	-	-	-
Baisakh@	****	***	-	-	-	-	-	-
Jyestha	****	***	-	-	-	-	-	-
Asardh	****	**	-	-	-	-	-	-
Srabon	****	***	-	-	-	-	-	-
Bhadra	**	-	-	-	-	***** *****	-	-
Ashwin	****	***	**	-	-	***** *****	*****	
Kartick	**	***	***	Leaves	-	***** *****	******	
Aghrayan	****	****	*****		-		-	-
Poush	*****	****** ***	******		-		--	-

Note: (i) The number of "star" marks under column heads rice, potatoes, pulses represent the number of stones used by the villagers to show the consumption of the relative item of food.

(ii) @ This is the first month of the Bengali Calendar.

(iii) # Fruits from some trees growing near ponds and elsewhere in the village.

(iv) $ From CPR and Forests.

(v) Prepared by Women's Group, Krishna Rakshit Chak, Medinipur, West Bengal.

Legend:

Magh: Mid-January to Mid-February
Chaitra: Mid-March to Mid-April
Jyestha: Mid-May to Mid-June
Srabon: Mid-July to Mid-August
Ashwin: Mid-September to Mid-October
Aghrayan: Mid-November to Mid-December
Phalgun: Mid-February to Mid-March
Baisakh: Mid-April to Mid-May
Asardh: Mid-June to Mid-July
Bhadra: Mid-August to Mid-September
Kartick: Mid-October to Mid-November
Poush: Mid-December to Mid-January

Table 5.5

Food Calendar, 1998 of Village Krishna Rakshit Chak

Month	*Rice*	*Potatoes*	*Pulses*	*Vegetables from CPR*	*Fruit from CPR*	*Fish from CPR*	*Snails from CPR*	*Others from Wild*
1	2	3	4	5	6	7	8	9
Magh	***** *****	*****		-	-	Some fish	-	-
Phalgun	***** ***	****		Yes	-	Fish *Jhinuk*	-	Neem leaves
Chaitra	*****	****	-	-	-	-	Yes	Rabbits
*Baisakh***	***	***	-	Brinjals	-	-	Snails,	*Jhinge*
Jyestha	***	***	-	*Kalmi Sag, Susmi Sag, Gim Sag,*	-	Fish	-	-
Asardh	***	*	-	Wild potatoes, Mushroom	-	-	-	-
Srabon	****	*	-	-	-	Weeds,	Yes	-
Bhadra	***	-	-	-	-	*Laatha, Chang, Fusati, Magur*	Snails (*Samuk*)	-
Ashwin	***	-	-	Jhinge Borbotee Snake Gourd	-	*Punti, Magur, Chang*	-	
Kartick	***	-	-	*Sag,* Seem, *Pui Sag*	-	Fish	-	
Aghrayan	***** ***** **	**	-		-	Fish	-	-
Poush	***** ***** **	**	-	*Sag,* Radish	-	-	--	-

Note: The number of "star" mark under column heads rice, potatoes, pulses represent the number of stones used by the villagers to show the consumption of the relative item of food. "Yes" means occasionally consumed in insignificant amounts, not worth quantifying. Prepared by Women of Krishna Rakshit Chak, Medinipur, West Bengal.

Legend:

Magh: Mid-January to Mid-February

Phalgun: Mid-February to Mid-March

Chaitra: Mid-March to Mid-April

Baisakh: Mid-April to Mid-May

Jyestha: Mid-May to Mid-June

Asardh: Mid-June to Mid-July

Srabon: Mid-July to Mid-August

Bhadra: Mid-August to Mid-September

Ashwin: Mid-September to Mid-October

Kartick: Mid-October to Mid-November

Aghrayan: Mid-November to Mid-December

Poush: Mid-December to Mid-January

Table 5.6

West Bengal: Minimum Wages (As on 31/12/05)

Name of Scheduled Employment	*Child Daily Minimum Wages (In Rs.)*	*Adult Daily Minimum Wages (In Rs.)*	*Skilled Daily Minimum Wages (In Rs.)*	*Semi-Skilled Daily Minimum Wages (In Rs.)*	*Unskilled Daily Minimum Wages (In Rs.)*
Agriculture worker	52.53	69.43			
Bakery		108.4			
Brick manufacturing			119.88	112.19	108.35
Ceramic industry			109.12	107.00	105.77
Printing press			79.64	78.87	65.90
Bone meal			97.39	96.39	95.97
Stone breaking & stone crushing			96.07	95.69	95.38
Silk printing			109.12	106.96	106.00
Tailoring			107.65	106.65	106.23
Powerloom men <10			108.92	108.15	107.77
Rubber and rubber products manufacturing			107.77	106.77	106.35
Clinical nursing home			103.69	101.23	100.38
Plastic industry			109.12	106.85	105.77
Saw mill			111.46	109.19	106.88
Public motor transport					
Glass industry			115.34	113.12	112.35
Forestry or timbering operations	56.16	73.92			
Salt manufacturing industry			83.69	81.69	79.23
Shops					
Flour mills			110.50	109.54	108.58
Beedi making		107.98			
Construction & maintenance of roads or building operations			116.39	102.69	99.75
Oil mills			122.04	121.78	120.12
Tanneries and leather Manufactories			121.73	115.96	112.12
Iron foundry			116.88	113.81	112.65
Handloom					72.50
Paints and chemical Factories			114.46	112.46	109.50
Fishery		72.12			
Rice mill				54.64	53.49
Dal mill			114.58	112.65	110.73

Source: Department of Labour, West Bengal.

6

Micro-Level Hunger in Contemporary India

Perspectives of the Hungry

Dadaswa Annam, Dadaswa Annam, Dadaswa Annam
(O'King Provide Food, Provide Food, Provide Food)

—Lord Krishna's first commandment to Yudhistir at the closure of Battle of Kurukshetra

Introduction

The issues revolving around hunger have afflicted us throughout recorded history. We are at a peculiar crossroad when the nation is confronted with a painful disjuncture: we have the highest production of food ever and we, at once, have the largest number of people who go hungry to bed everyday and many even die of starvation. It seems that though there is apparently food security and absence of hunger at the national level, food security at the micro-level is in jeopardy and hunger haunts millions of people. This Chapter is an attempt to examine the face of hunger at the micro level, from the perspective of those who suffer from the pangs of hunger. It focuses on the temporal dimension of hunger, in terms of seasonality and inter-month variations in food consumed and in the variety, palate and nutritional content of the people's diet. There are few studies which have focused on these aspects of hunger in contemporary India. To put the debate in perspective, the Chapter will also briefly look at some of the macro-variables to indicate the state of hunger at the macro-level as well. The analysis here is based on secondary and primary data, but principally on "participatory" primary data.

Section 2 is a brief description of the methodology and techniques used in the study. It also gives a brief idea of the villages covered. Section 3 provides a definition of food security and hunger and the logic for including the different elements in the definition of food security and hunger. Section 4 is a brief description of the different elements of India's food production and distribution. Section 5 very briefly describes the reality of food security and hunger, from the macro perspective. Section 6 contains the micro-picture of food security from the eight villages of four states from the perspective of those who suffer hunger. It is in this section that attention is drawn to the temporal dimension of hunger, in terms of seasonality and inter-month variations in consumption, variety, palate and nutrition in food consumed by the people in the villages. Section 7 is a summary of conclusions. The concluding section has some elements of policy recommendations.

The Methodology

In this chapter the macro-picture is described in terms of available secondary data which is in abundance. The micro-picture will be based on Participatory Learning and Action (PLA) techniques, successor to what used to be earlier called PRA or RRA methods. The methods used have been, primarily, historical transects, seasonality analysis, food calendars and semi-structured interviews (see Mukherjee, 1994 and Mukherjee, 2001 for a description of these methods). The micro-study was carried out in the villages in two villages from Haryana, three from Uttar Pradesh, one from West Bengal and two from Orissa.

The villages have been so chosen that they reflect different socio-economic realities. There is one Haryana village which is from the Green Revolution heartland producing primarily food crops, *viz.*, wheat, while the other is also from the Green Revolution heartland but producing primarily cash crops, *viz.*, vegetables. Of the three villages studied in eastern Uttar Pradesh, the poverty heartland of India, one is a village marked by 'concealed tenancy', the other is a village which is highly stratified along caste lines while the third is a village of small and marginal farmers. The village in West Bengal is a tribal village, in a state ruled by the left parties for decades, registering high growth in agricultural production. The two villages studied in Orissa, relate to villages frequently visited by natural calamities, the latest being the super cyclone that hit them in October 1999.

The Concept of Hunger

Hunger has been variously defined. For our purposes, a nation or a community or a household is considered to be free from hunger if six conditions are met:

a) Food is available at all times. That is, there is enough food in the system. In the absence of enough food in the system at all times, people cannot access food and must, therefore, go hungry.

b) Food that is systemically available is also culturally acceptable. People will not eat food, which is not acceptable culturally (in the broad sense). A Hindu may not eat beef, even when it is available. A Muslim may not eat pork, even if pork goes abegging.

c) People have economic access to food. That is, people have the purchasing power to buy food. Even if culturally acceptable food is available in the system, people will go hungry if they have no purchasing power to buy that food, or what is called economic access. In the great Bengal famine of the early 1940s, people were dying outside granaries full of food grains, because, *inter alia*, they had no purchasing power to buy the food (Sen, 1986).

d) People have physical access to food. That is, people can buy food if they have the purchasing power. There must be a place where people can buy food, which is culturally acceptable and if they had the purchasing power to do so.

e) Food that people consume has the requisite nutritional value for a healthy life. Food that people can access must have nutritional value. Consumption of food, which has no nutritional value will leave people without energy for a healthy life and hence hungry.

f) People have access to potable water, for absorption of food by the body. Unsafe drinking water will prevent absorption of nutrition from food into the body, because unsafe drinking water leads to diseases and other forms of attrition.

Whenever any of these conditions or some combination thereof are violated, food security is jeopardised, and hunger sets in. Symptomatically when none is undernourished and no one faces absence of access to food, we have absence of hunger. There is a subtle distinction between hunger and starvation, which is of fundamental importance.

In official parlance hunger is often defined in terms of calorie intake. The "subjacent hungry comprise those consuming between 1800-2200 calories per day; medial hungry are those who with calorie intake between 1600-1800 a day; and the ultra-hungry have the lowest calorie intake (less than 1600 calories per day)" (Gaiha and Kulkarni, 2008).

Elements of India's Food Economy

Food Production

It is often said India is today self sufficient in food production. India's food output in recent years has been around 205 million tonnes per year. In 2000 it was 209 million tonnes and even in 2006, it was 208 million tonnes. The annual compound growth in food grains production during the last decade at around 3.6 per cent had generally outstripped the growth in population, which stood at about 2 per cent per annum. And the buffer stock of food held by the Government of India is in excess of 18 million tonnes of food, according to the *Economy Survey 2006-2007*.

Food and Public Action

For long the government believed that the food produced in the country did not reach certain sections of the population. The Government of India, therefore, made two interventions. One, it set up the public distribution system (PDS) and two, it established the system of price incentives to farmers, to grow more food and sell them to the government for feeding into the PDS. Started in the early 1960s, the PDS entails supplying to the vulnerable sections of society essential commodities, notably food grains, at subsidised prices, to shield the poor from the volatility of prices and fluctuations in the supply of essential commodities. In the macro-micro terminology, the PDS in India is intended to translate the macro level self-sufficiency in foodgrain production to micro level food security by ensuring access to food and other essential commodities, to poor families. The PDS in India has a network of over 4,00,000 fair price shops (FPS) and is supposed to serve about 220 million families (*Hindustan Times*, First Editorial, 3 January 2008) who live below the poverty line) and is probably the largest such distribution system in the world. Many noted commentators, including Sen (1998) maintains that India could avoid large scale famines and save millions of lives because of the PDS, something that other countries which did not have such a system, such as China, failed to prevent.

Incentives to Farmers to Grow more Food

To sell food grains through the PDS, the government procures food grains, mostly rice and wheat, at a declared procurement price and provides a minimum support price to farmers. The prices are designed to promote farming and encourage surplus farmers to continue to grow more food in response to price incentives. For good or bad, the minimum support prices for wheat and rice declared by the government from time to time, have pitched the domestic prices of wheat and rice above their current international market prices. In consequence the government is able to build up a food stock of millions of tonnes which was likely to shoot up to 20 million tonnes this year.

The high level of food production and the extensive network of PDS outlets, taken one with the other, have succeeded in creating an impression that people in India is food secure and hunger is a thing of the past. The bureaucracy and the political executive have particularly endorsed this view.

The PDS That Does Not Work

The PDS failed to reach the poor effectively, urban bias and lack of transparency and accountability. Although the PDS is a centrally sponsored programme, its implementation is dependent on the state government. In states with appropriate political and administrative and infrastructural facilities, the public distribution system has worked; in most it has floundered.

Due to poor targeting, the system is being used (misused) by all irrespective of the standard of living. Of the food provided through the PDS, 36 per cent of wheat, 31 per cent of rice and 23 per cent of sugar are diverted away from the PDS. Diversion of rice is 64 per cent in Bihar and Assam. Diversion in wheat is 69 per cent in Punjab and 100 per cent in Nagaland. Excepting for sugar, *jowar* and standard cloth, there is virtually no variation in the utilisation of items supplied according to levels of living. The objective of resources transfer has not been achieved.

The leakage from the system and other wastes associated with PDS is proverbial. The inefficiency of the entire bureaucracy of food is questioned. Studies by the National Council for Applied Economic Research (NCAER) and ORG-Marg in 2007 confirm what many suspected that India's "targeted" public distribution system (TPDS) does not reach out to the poor. A decade ago, India moved from a system of universal coverage to one of providing subsidised grain to the poor and non-poor at different prices. This kind of targeting was seen as a way to address the food and nutritional needs of the 220 million below the poverty line. But that has not happened.

The NCAER study estimates that 40 per cent of the ration cards meant for the people living below the poverty line are held by those who are non poor. The diversion of subsidised grain meant for those above the poverty line into the open market is just as rampant. The NCAER study further found the existence of about 23 million fake ration cards, including 11 million in Uttar Pradesh alone, some of which are perhaps used to siphon off APL grain. TPDS has helped neither BPL nor APL card holders. It is one of the biggest rent-seeking programmes of the government.

A not insignificant number of observers believe that the PDS has served the interest of the big farmers only, who had surplus to sell to the state (NCAER, 2000). Consequently, no attempt has been made to extend the coverage to PDS to other crops and the required back up R&D have not come about.

In fine, states with appropriate political, administrative and infrastructural facilities, the public distribution system has worked but in most others it has floundered. Due to poor targeting, the system has being misused extensively. The inefficiency of the entire bureaucracy of food has come out in harsh relief.

The Reality at the Macro-Level

However, the harsh reality is that despite this huge food production, a huge buffer stock and an extensive network of the PDS, millions of people are hungry and many even die of starvation. Hunger and tragedy hit different parts of the country every year. Happenings in Kashipur, Orissa where thousands of villagers in the summer of 2000 were at the brink of starvation death, because they had only mango kernels to eat, had shaken the conscience of the people of the country. Kashipur is not unique. The cruel starvation deaths, sale of children and post-harvest migration in other parts of Orissa have attracted international attention. Meena Menon (1999) wrote: "In the impoverished, drought stricken area of Kalahandi, a man sold his daughter for 30 kg. of rice. These are not isolated cases." Small wonder then, that as on date around 320 million people are hungry, a fact which has galvanised even the Supreme Court of India to hand down a directive to the Central and State governments, "to devise a scheme where no person goes hungry when the granaries are full and lots being wasted due to non-availability of storage space" (Sharma, 2001).

The Average Indian is Hungry

Indeed it is an even harsher reality that the average Indian is hungry. Despite the impressive output of food grain, our current availability of cereals per capita is only 390 gms per day. Indeed the per capita availability of cereals and pulses has declined over the last 15 years. The per capita net availability of pulses is about 31.5 gms per day and the per capita net total food availability is 422.4. gms per day (*Economic Survey, 2006-2007*). Even allowing for errors in calculations, the sad fact remains that hundreds of million of Indians have much less than 422 gms per day, for that is only the average. Nutritionally for a healthy life per capita availability of cereals and pulses per day should be at least 510 gms per day. The per capita availability of cereals and pulses for the Indians is, therefore, below the acceptable level for a healthy life. And hence, the average Indian is hungry because she or he does not have food which gives her or him the required nutrition.

The picture becomes worse, if we take a differentiated look. On an average, daily food consumption should provide us about 2400 K. cals per person. But for the poorest 30 per cent of the people, their food intake provides them with only about 1600 K. cals. About 60 per cent of India's children suffer from malnutrition. Over 74 per cent of all children under 3 years of age suffer from anemia, with the percentage going as high as 84 per cent in Haryana. As much as 53 per cent of India's children under the age of five are malnourished, as compared to 32 per cent in sub-Saharan Africa. The recently released results of the third (2005-06) National Family Health Survey (NFHS-3) show that almost half (46 per cent) of all children under three are underweight and almost 80 per cent of children in the age group of 6-35 months are anaemic. (Strategies for Children under Six by Working Group on Children Under Six, *Economic and Political Weekly*, 29 December 2007). Nearly 52 per cent of married women in India between the age of 15-45 are anaemic, as compared to only 20 per cent in sub-Saharan Africa (The Hunger Project, 2001).

Calculations of general undernourishment—what is sometimes called "protein-energy malnutrition"—is nearly twice as high in India as is in Sub-Saharan Africa on an average. Judged in terms of usual standards of retardation in weight for age, the proportion of undernourished children in Africa is 20 to 40 per cent, whereas the percentage of undernourished Indian children is a gigantic 40-60 per cent. (Scrimshaw, 1998). While Indians, therefore, live longer than Africans, nevertheless there are many more undernourished children in India, in both absolute terms and as proportion of all children, than in Africa. Thus, Sen (1995) pointed out, these stark figures confront us with the fact that the forces of normal mortality—unprevented by good nutrition and health care—kill more people every four or five years in India, than the death toll of the world's largest recorded famines.

The future looks dim. Just as the per capita availability of cereals and pulses has declined over the last 15 years, by reversing the trend cereals availability will have to increase by about 70 million tones, which is not easy because over the last 15 years, cereals output increased by just 30 million tonnes. Given the food price volatility in the global market, dependence on imports for more than 10-15 per cent of our needs, will be courting disaster. Some experts believe the remaining increase will have to come through higher output of vegetables, poultry and milk.

The Reality at the Micro-Level

Looking at the macro-picture tells us a sad story but it still does not tell us the full story. The pictures of hunger at the micro-level are even more compelling, to which we may now turn.

Hunger in West Bengal

Hunger in a Tribal Village: Village Krishna Rakshit Chak

Krishna Rakshit Chak is a tribal village in Midnapore district in West Bengal. The villagers are landless and all belong to Lodha tribe. Hunger in the village was studied in 1993, 1995 and in 1998, through Food Calendars. In the three repeated exercises, the women were encouraged to prepare the Food Calendars. At the beginning, in 1993, women were hesitant and shy, but once prodded, they soon were able to engross into intricate details of food consumption, procurement and intra-household distribution of food. It is important to lay down the process followed in the successive iteration of producing food calendars in Krishan Rakshit Chak as also in other villages covered in this study.

Using various locally available material like stones, pebbles, leaves etc., and traditional knowledge of time and space, women first wrote down on the ground the 12 months (according to the Bengali Calendar) and identified various parameters related to food consumption. The months were written down as the first column and the parameters relating to food consumption were written down as the first row. Once the first row and column were written down, the villagers used stones to indicate the relative amounts of each item of food consumed in the different months. For instance in column 2 of Table 5.3, against the month of *Magh*, the consumption of rice was shown by placing 15 stones under the column head rice. Then against the month of *Phalgun*, the consumption of rice was shown by placing 9 stones under the column head rice. This means that the consumption of rice had declined in *Phalgun vis-à-vis Magh*. And so on for each month and each item.

In effect there was ordinal ranking of consumption levels of each item of food in different months.

It should be noted that across different months and between different items in the food basket, women of Krishna Rakshit Chak have only indicated relative changes in consumption and not absolute quantities of food consumed during the different months of the year. Each column in the food calendars is to be read as "stand alones", indicating the relative amount of the particular food item (named as the column head) consumed. In Table 5.3, Column 1, for instance, the women depicted the pattern of rice consumption through the twelve months of the year. And so on. It is reiterated that these numbers do not indicate the absolute quantities of rice consumed during these months, such as 15 kg in *Magh*, 9 kg in *Phalgun* and 2 kg in *Poush*.

Additionally, numbers across the columns are non-additive and non-comparable. Thus, the number 15 under rice against *Magh* and the number 13 under potatoes against *Magh*, do not indicate that the consumption of rice was higher that the consumption of potatoes in *Magh*. The reason is that the ordinal rankings down each column are non-additive. This is the schema followed in all the Tables (Table 5.3, 5.4 and 5.5) showing the Food Calendars.

The three Food Calendars (Tables 5.3, 5.4 and 5.5) show two food systems. People consume rice, potatoes etc., which are produced by the application of technology in the economic sense. This is called food derived from the "primary food system". People also access fish, fruits, honey, gums, small animals, birds, tubers, snails, leaves, leafy vegetables etc., from the common property resources (CPRs), micro-environment (Chambers, 1992) and forests, and from gleaning and collecting food from lands belonging to richer, relatively well-off farmers, in neighbouring villages. This is called food from the "secondary food system" (Mukherjee, 1994a).

The poor villagers of KRC, therefore, not only collect, gather and hunt food from the CPRs, forests and micro-environments, but also glean food from the land of richer farmers. The cabbage, pumpkins, ridge gourd (*jhinge*), papaya, green banana, radish, tomato and brinjals etc., (that the poor villagers collect from other farmers' lands and gardens) as part of the produce of CPRs are the crops which the well-off farmers do not harvest from their lands, because they are damaged by pests or insects, frost bitten, hit by hailstorm, or disease. Both systems of food play critical roles in providing food to the villagers of Krishna Rakshit Chak.

Seasonal Variations from Primary Food System

The Food Calendars also reveal that there are seasonal variations in availability of food from both the systems. Rice consumption reaches its peak in Magh (mid-January to mid-February) after which it declines until *Chaitra*, (mid-March to mid-April) to remains stationary through to *Ashwin* (mid-September to mid-October). After *Ashwin* it further declines of the earlier period in *Kartick* (mid-October to mid-November). Rice consumption generally picks up in *Aghrayan* (mid-November to mid-December). Thus, consumption of rice, the principal staple food in Krishna Rakshit Chak, reaches the lowest level of consumption during the hot summer months of *Chaitra, Baisakh* and *Jyestha*, (mid-March to mid-June). It then continues to be low throughout the monsoon season of *Asard, Srabon* and *Bhadra*, (mid-June to mid-September). Consumption of rice is thus the lowest when the work-load is the highest. Levels of consumption of potatoes and pulses similarly show significant variations and they reach the lowest during summer and monsoon months.

Seasonal Variation from the Secondary Food System

Some vegetable from the CPRs and forests, and food of one kind or the other from the secondary system, are consumed by the villagers of Krishna Rakshit Chak almost all through the year except in *Aswin*. Unlike the primary food system, the secondary food system cannot be analysed in terms of variations in individual items, because most of the food from the secondary system are seasonal. For instance, fruits such as mangoes and jackfruit, from CPRs are available only in *Baisakh* and *Jyestha* (mid-April to mid-June). Fish, snails and wild water-plants are consumed in *Chaitra, Baisakh, Jyestha* (mid-March to mid-June) and *Bhadra* (mid-August to mid-September) only.

There are, however, certain notable features of the secondary food system, which warrants a few comments. First, the secondary food system provides fibre, animal protein and nutrition in the diet of the villagers of Krishna Rakshit Chak. In the absence of the secondary food system, it would have left the quality of the food consumed by the villagers so much more deficient in nutrients and vitamins. Second, the number of foods that the villagers access from the CPRs and forests, are more and higher when the basket of food from the primary food system is the lightest, *viz.*, the months of *Chaitra* to *Bhadra* (mid-March to mid-September).

The Two Hunger Periods

The Food Calendars also reveal that people suffered differentiated hunger. They are hungry throughout the year but they are more so during some months. Let us look at columns 2, 3 and 4 of 1993 food calendar. There are two "hunger periods" for the villagers of Krishna Rakshit Chak in 1993. The first hunger period occurs in the summer months of *Chaitra, Baisakh* and *Jyestha* (mid-March to mid-June) taken together. The second hunger period occurs during the months of *Aswin* and *Kartick* (mid-September to mid-November) when again apart from lowest levels of consumption of food from the primary food system, food consumption from the secondary system also falls. This is also the period when employment availability is dismal. The power to access food is, therefore, also very low. During the first hunger period, the bounties of nature, through the common property resources, forests etc, come to the rescue of the villagers. Unlike the first hunger period, there is no "safety net" for the poor villagers during second hunger period, from the secondary food system.

In 1995 Food Calendar, the two "hunger periods" became one long hunger period from *Baisakh* through *Kartick* (mid-April to mid-October). The two hunger periods of five months duration was converted to one long hunger period of seven months duration.

The 1998 Food Calendar indicates that hunger continues and there are now four phases of hunger. Phase One, runs from *Aghrayan* to *Magh*, when people eat the most. Phase Two covers *Phalgun* and *Chaitra* (mid-February to mid-April), when people eat less and hunger sets in. Phase Three, runs from *Baisakh* to *Bhadra* (mid-April to mid-September) when the consumption is at a very low level. And Phase Four between *Ashwin* and *Kartick* (mid-September to mid-November) when a typical diet of the poor households consists primarily of only rice.

One redeeming feature of the state of hunger emerging from the 1998 Food Calendar is that the quantum of food available from the water bodies has increased significantly. And this remarkably enough came about because a huge tank (called Rajbandh) which usually auctioned by the *Panchayat*, is under dispute now and it could not be auctioned. As a result, the villagers access the produce of the tank. The quantity of food accessed from the secondary food system, therefore, is back to its 1993 level.

Hunger in Contemporary Uttar Pradesh

Hunger in a Village of "Landlords" and Tenants: Tikri

Tikri is a village in Varanasi, Uttar Pradesh. In Tikri, people use leased-out and leased-in land for cultivation. The village is stratified along class lines. The villagers of Morya *Basti*, Village Tikri use five criteria to classify people as falling in three classes *Garib* (low socio-economic status), *Kamate-Khate* (middle socio-economic status) and *Amir* (high socio-economic status). The criteria are size of landholding; condition of house and its physical facilities; economic status; facilities provided to their children and capacity to meet the expenses for "social function". The characteristics of the three classes of people are in Table 6.1.

Clearly the issue of hunger would, by the definition given by the people, concern those belonging to Lower SES. Hunger will neither bother people belonging to Middle SES nor to Higher SES. The issue of hunger is, therefore, examined in the context of people belonging to Lower SES only. This does not, however, mean that all those who belong to Middle and Higher SES, are free from hunger. Because of disparity in intra-familial distribution of power and because of traditions and customs, in many households categorised as falling in Middle SES and Higher SES, there are women and girl children suffering from hunger of different degrees. We are not pursuing that line of inquiry.

Table 6.1

Characteristics of Low, Middle and High Socio-Economic Status (SES) Village Tikri, Morya Basti

Criteria	*Low SES*	*Middle SES*	*High SES*
Landholding	Less than 5 *Biswa*	5 *Biswa* to 1 Acre	More than 1 Acre
Condition of the House	Clay built. Single storied. No toilet, no latrine and bathroom. Only one room for one family. No source of drinking water.	Cemented. Single storied with latrine and source of water: well. Separate guestroom (*Baithak*) and *Chauki* (Wooden Cot).	Cemented. Well maintained, double-storied or more, house with hand-pump, well etc., for drinking water, toilets, latrine, bathroom and *Baithak*.
Economic Status	100 per cent dependent on daily wages to arrange for food	Do not have to strain resources for meeting daily needs.	Economically very sound. Moneylenders for Middle SES and Low SES people.
Employment	Daily wage earners.		
Agricultural Labourers	Cultivators, daily wage earners and milk vendors.	In service and/or in business	
Facilities for Children	Cannot afford to send children to school. Children start working at an early age and help parents in their work.	Children are enrolled in local school.	Children are enrolled in "good" schools.
Capacity To Bear Expenses To Meet Social Obligations	Cannot afford to bear expenses to meet social obligations associated with birth, marriage, death etc.		
Survive on borrowings and charity during emergency such as illness, death etc.	Can partially bear expenses to meet social obligations out of own resources and partly out of borrowings	Spend ostentatiously during social occasions.	

Given our concept of hunger, food production is an important variable (though not overwhelming) in eliminating hunger. Take the case of Morya Hamlet. Wheat produced in the hamlet, meets the needs of the inhabitants for 4-5 months in a year. Paddy harvested meets the needs of the villagers for 3-4 months. Maize and *Bajra* produced are enough to meet food needs of the community for only a few days. And all the villagers do not grow all the crops. Thus, food produced in the village meets only a part of the total quantity of food necessary for securing food for all the villagers. For the rest of their food-needs, people buy food from the open market.

Food produced in the village is culturally acceptable and given the employment opportunities outside of agriculture, available in and around Tikri, people did have the requisite purchasing power to access food. Apparently people did not suffer starvation but existence of differentiated hunger is discernible.

The facts revealed by the Food Calendar produced by the Women of Morya Hamlet as in Table 6.2 are instructive. Significantly the group of women starts the Food Calendar from the month of May-June (*Jeth*), because May-June is the month when cultivation season (*Kharif*) starts and it is associated in the psyche of the people as the beginning of the process of food production. If we look at column 2, it is manifest that the women and men of Morya Hamlet, Village Tikri, suffer from various degrees of hunger for a considerable part of the year. But their hunger is at its peak during the three very hot summer and humid monsoon months of *Jeth* (May-June), *Asarh* (June-July) and *Sawan* (July-August). That is the period when women, men and children survive on just one unwholesome meal for 3 months. As *Bhado* (August-September) comes, the nutritional value of food intake of the villagers increases due to inclusion of vegetables harvested from their own fields. With the advent of *Bhado* (August-September), harvesting of some pulses also starts. This enables people to include some pulses as well in their diet, which further increases the nutritional content and palate of their food basket. The pattern of food intake in *Kuar* (mid-September to mid-October) was generally a continuation of the pattern obtaining in *Bhado* (mid-August to mid-September). For the four months from *Kartik* to *Magh* (mid-October to mid-February) people earned handsomely, as this was the principal farming season. They used their earning in good measure to buy food. Thus, daily intake of vegetables, bi-weekly or tri-weekly intake of pulses and some amount of milk, poultry, meat and fish, at least once a month, makes the diet best during this period of the year. During *Fagun* and *Chait* (mid-February to mid-April) though people still manages to get two meals, the nutritional content of the food and their palate are considerably diminished. This is because the quantity of pulses, vegetables and milk steadily become scarce in their diet, until they vanish by the end of *Baisakh* (mid-April to mid-May). *Jeth, Asarh* and *Sawan* are the

real "hunger months" for the villagers of Morya Hamlet. Table 6.2A read with Table 6.2B, indicate that food intake is at its worst during the months when people had to work the hardest and the weather the harshest, the summer and monsoon months. For these are the months when the villagers get to work in their own fields, find wage employment in others' fields and work hard at home to deal with disease and sickness that visit the people during this part of the year.

The villagers of Bari Basti (Bari Hamlet) of Village Tikri also give us their Food Calendar as at Table 6.2B.

These villagers divide the year in terms of farming seasons, *viz.*, summer, rainy and winter. During summer months, a typical food basket of the villagers in Bari Basti contains pulses, *chapattis* and rice. They have vegetables included in their diet every alternative day. During the rainy season, their food basket improves and includes pulses, rice, and *chapatti*, vegetables every alternate day, and meat, fish or poultry once in two months. Every household has two meals a day. When winter sets in, rice, pulses, vegetables and sometimes *Khichri* (a kind of heavy porridge) make their meals. Though the Food Calendars of Morya and Bari Bastis are not comparable because different time frames are used, nevertheless the general trends from both the Food Calendars have considerable congruence. The "hunger months" are about the same and the hunger months correspond with the period when the women work the hardest.

Interestingly, there is a high degree of correlation between income and food intake. Let us look at Tables 6.3 and 6.4 detailing income and expenditure of people in Morya Hamlet. Starting from *Jeth* (mid-May to mid-June) when their income is at the lowest. Villagers' income starts rising from *Asarh* (mid-June to mid-July), when cultivation starts and employment opportunities expands. It peaks in *Magh*, and then it starts falling again to reach a fairly low level in *Baisakh* (mid-April to mid-May). A typical villager's income comprises income from agriculture, sale of milk, daily wages earned by men and women separately and artificial pearl garland making by women, of which income from agriculture is the smallest component and daily wage is the largest constituent. While daily wages earned by women remain virtually constant throughout the year at Rs. 200 per month, daily wages earned by men vary from month to month. It remains at Rs. 400 per month for 6 months from *Jeth* (mid-May to mid-June) to *Kartik* (mid-October to mid-November) and then jumps up to Rs. 600 per month in *Aghan*. The wage rate for men remains at that figure till summer sets in, in *Baisakh* (mid-April to mid-May) when it falls back to Rs. 400 per month. Income villagers (read women) earn from garland making out of artificial pearl remains constant at a low ebb from Jeth (mid-May to mid-June) till *Bhado* (mid-August to mid-September) at Rs. 120 per month, and then picks up to reach Rs. 180 per month in *Kuar* and stays at that level till *Baisakh* (mid-April to mid-May).

Table 6.2A

Food Calendar Prepared by the Women of Morya Hamlet, Tikri Village

Months	*Food Intake*	*Serial Number*
Asarh (June-July)	One meal of few *chapattis* and salt or chilli paste.	1
Sawan (July-August)	One meal of few *chapattis* and salt or chilli paste. Towards the end of the month, two meals are possible.	2
Bhado (August-Sept.)	One stomach filling meal of *chapattis*, vegetables and rice. Pulses very rarely.	3
Kuar (Sept.-Oct.)	The same diet as in *Bhado*.	4
Kartick (Oct.-Nov.)	Stomach filling meal of *chapattis*, vegetables and rice. Two meals.	5
Aghan (Nov.-Dec.)	Stomach filling meal of *chapattis*, vegetables and rice. Two meals.	6
Poosh (Dec.-Jan.)	Same as in *Aghan*.	7
Magh (Jan.-February)	Same as in *Poosh*.	8
Fagun (Feb.-March)	Same as in *Magh* but intake of pulses and costly items get reduced. Two meals.	9
Chait (March-April)	Same as in the month of *Fagun* but the intake of pulses gets further reduced.	10
Baisakh (April-May)	Same as *Chait*.	11
Jeth (May-June)	One meal of *chapattis* and salt or chili paste.	12

Village Analysts: Indubala, Kamala, Urmila, and Jali.
Facilitated by: Meera Jayaswal. Date: 11.11.98.

Reference is now invited to Table 6.4. Aggregate expenditure of the people basically pertains to expenditure on three items: food, miscellaneous items and social obligations. Of these, expenditure on food is by far the largest chunk of the expenditure. It is about 66 per cent for *Jeth* (mid-May to mid-June) and *Asarh*; 80 per cent for *Sawan, Bhado* and *Kuar* (mid-July to mid-October); 96 per cent for *Kartik* (mid-October to mid-November); above 80 per cent from *Aghan* (mid-November to mid-December) to *Chait* (mid-March to mid-May); and above 76 per cent in *Baisakh* (mid-April to mid-May). Expenditure on food increases in absolute terms also from Rs. 600 per month in *Jeth* (mid-May to mid-June) to Rs. 1300 per month in *Poosh* (mid-December to mid-January) and only marginally declines in *Chait* and *Baisakh* (mid-March to mid-May). Thus, the pattern of expenditure exhibits a copybook case of an under-developed economy, where expenditure on food consumption is unusually high. The rise in expenditure on food has a high degree of correlation with the incremental variations in income. Compare columns 7 and 1 of Table 6.3 with columns 1 and 5 of Table 6.4 and the picture will be clear. If we also compare last column of Table 6.3 with column 5 of Table 6.4, an excess of expenditure over income during the summer months of *Baisakh* and *Jeth* (mid-April to mid-June) and the wet month of *Asardh* (mid-June to mid-July) is discernible. This is the time people got into debt.

Table 6.2B

Seasonality Analysis by Women's Group in Bari Basti, Tikri Village

Season	*Livelihood*	*Constraints to Livelihood*	*Consumption Pattern*
Summer (*Cheth, Baisakh, Jeth*)	Work as agricultural labourers during harvesting of wheat and planting of onion seedlings	Work under scorching sun leads to heat stroke("loo"), fever, boils and malaria.	One meal of pulses, rice, *chapatti*, and vegetable every alternate day.
Rainy (*Asarh, Sawan, Bhado*)	Some women work as agricultural labourers during paddy sowing. Women also work for 8 days in deweeding. They get employment for about 10 days in paddy transplantation. Some crops are also harvested which help women get jobs for 15-20 days	Swelling of hands and feet due to work in paddy fields, in rain. Suffer from cold. These are the worst months as only females earn, while men sit at home as they find no employment in the towns.	Pulses, rice, *chapatti*, and vegetables every alternate day. Meat/fish/eggs once in two months. Two meals a day.
Winter (*Kuar, Kartick, Aghan, Poos, Magh* and *Fagun*)	Men get more work in Towns during early *Kuar* to end *Kartick*, which are considered as the best months of the year. In the beginning of winter, employment is available in harvesting paddy and *bajra*. Women go out to sell vegetables in the village and in the neighbouring villages.	In *Magh*, men do not work due to a social custom called *Bhenv*. Expenditure increases due to use of warm clothes and detergent. Cold and cough are major health problems. Difficult to work in the fields for weeding in cold as the body starts aching.	*Bajra chapatti*, rice, pulses and vegetables every day. Sometimes eat *khichri* (a kind of porridge) made of *Bajra*.

Village Analysts: Savita Devi, Rita Devi, Shanti Devi, Saraswati Devi, Urmila Devi, Shakuntala Devi, Dhanra devi, Kumari Devi, Satti Devi, Sangeeta Devi, Phula Devi, Chnmna devi, Bindo Devi, Chandrawati Devi, Sacho Devi, Rama devi, Meena Devi, Arti Devi, Seema Devi, Prabha Devi, Kalawati.

Facilitator: Sudipta Roy.

Date: 31.1.99.

On the whole then, people were not food secure throughout the year, though they did not suffer from chronic hunger. Undernutrition and malnutrition of women was clearly made out. Incidentally, in case of Tikri there was none of the food from the secondary food system. Because the guava orchard and the mango orchard in the village had been cleared to raise crops etc., because apparently yield from these trees had declined so sharply that retaining them was of little value (Mukherjee, 2001).

Table 6.3

Monthly Income of Low SES Families in Morya Hamlet, Tikri

Months	*Daily Labour (Men)*	*Daily Labour (Women)*	*Garland Making*	*Selling Milk*	*Agriculture*	*Total*
Jeth	400	100	120	100	-	720
Asarh	400	100	120	200	-	820
Sawan	400	200	120	300	50	1070
Bhado	200	200	120	300	100	920
Kuar	400	200	180	500	250	1530
Kartick	400	200	180	500	250	1530
Aghan	600	200	180	500	250	1730
Poos	600	200	180	400	250	1630
Magh	600	200	180	400	250	1630
Fagun	600	200	180	400	100	1480
Chait	600	200	180	300	100	1380
Baisakh	400	-	180	300	-	880
Total	5600	2000	1920	4200	1600	15320

Village Analysts: Amarnath Morya, Ashok Morya, Chatanki Morya, and Panchan Morya.
Facilitator: Ms. Meera Jayaswal.
Date: 5.11.98

Hunger in a Socially Stratified Village: Village Chandpur

Chandpur is also a village in Varanasi, UP. It is in the same Block as Tikri.

The state of food security in Chandpur was about the same as in Tikri. Take the case of Patel *Basti* (Hamlet) of Chandpur. The wheat produced in the hamlet meets the requirement of the villagers for 4-5 months in a year. Paddy harvested meets the needs the villagers in the hamlet for 3-4 months. Maize and *bajra* produced is enough to meet the needs of the villagers for 8-10 days and 1-2 months respectively. The food produced in the village meets about half the quantity of food necessary. For the rest of the food needs people have to buy food from the open market in exchange for goods, labour or money.

Table 6.4

Monthly Expenditure of Low SES Families in Morya Hamlet of Tikri

Months	*Expenditure*				*Loan*
	Food	*Miscellaneous*	*Social Visit*	*Total*	
Jeth	600	200	100	900	500
Asarh	600	200	100	900	200
Sawan	1000	100	100	1200	200-
Bhado	1000	100	100	1200	-
Kuar	1000	100	100	1200	-
Kartick	1200	100	150	1450	-
Aghan	1200	100	200	1500	-
Poos	1300	100	200	1600	-
Magh	1300	100	200	1600	-
Fagun	1300	100	200	1600	-
Chait	1200	100	100	1400	-
Baisakh	1000	150	150	1300	-
Total	12700	1500	1700	15900	900

Village Analysts: As in Table 6.3.

Apparently people do not suffer starvation but existence of relative hunger is visible. Take the case of Naipurwa Hamlet of the village. Women reveal their state of hunger through the Food Calendar. The Food Calendar prepared by Rampati Devi, Dhandai Devi and Rita Devi and others, is reproduced in Table 6.5. Significantly women in this hamlet, like women in Tikri have started the Food Calendar from the month of *Asarh* (June-July) and ended it in *Jeth* (May-June). And for the same reason.

It is manifest from column 3, Table 6.5, that the women suffer from various degrees of hunger throughout the year. During the months of *Baisakh* (April-May), *Jeth* (May-June), *Asarh* (June-July), *Sawan* (July-August) and *Bhado* (August-September), that is, from mid-April to mid September, for five months women survive on just one meal of *chapattis* and chilli paste and some inexpensive vegetables. Their hunger is at its peak during the very hot summer and wet monsoon months. Once harvesting of some pulses starts and the poor earn some wages from *Kuar* (mid-September to mid-October) that the villagers' diet improves. They have some nutrition and palate in the food intake by way of pulses and vegetables, which lasts for the five months from *Kuar* to *Magh* (mid-September to mid-February). During *Fagun* and *Chait* (mid-February to mid-April) pulses become rarer in the diet of the poor, until it vanishes in *Baisakh* (mid-April to mid-May).

Table 6.5

Food Calendar Prepared by the Women of Naipurwa Hamlet, Chandpur Village

Months	*Financial Condition*	*Food Intake*	*Serial Number*
Asarh (June-July)	Loan for purchasing seeds, from the village headman or the moneylender	One meal of few *chapattis* and salt or chilly paste or some inexpensive vegetables	1
Sawan (July-August)	Take loan for purchasing food	One meal of few *chapattis* and salt or chilly paste or some inexpensive vegetables	2
Bhado (August-Sept.)	Take loan for purchasing food	One meal of few *chapattis* and salt or chilly paste or some inexpensive vegetables	3
Kuar (Sept.-Oct.)	Income starts from sale of vegetables and from working as agricultural labourers	The same diet as in *Bhado* but intake of pulses and vegetables start.	4
Kartick (Oct.-Nov.)	Income from vegetable sale and *Birdi/Rudrax* garland making	The same diet as in *Kuar*.	5
Aghan (Nov.-Dec.)	Income from vegetable sale and *Birdi/Rudrax* garland making	Milk supplement is added to diet	6
Poos (Dec.-Jan.)	Income from vegetable sale, work in fields and *Birdi/Rudrax* garland making	Same as in *Aghan*	7
Magh (Jan.-February)	Income from vegetable sale and *Birdi/Rudrax* garland making	Same as in *Poos*	8
Fagun (Feb..-March)	Reduction in Income from vegetable sale. Income from *Birdi/Rudrax* garland making is sustained	Same as in *Magh* but intake of pulses get reduced.	9
Chait (March-April)	Income from non-agricultural work. Income from wages earned in harvesting wheat	Same as in the month of *fagun* but the intake of pulses gets further reduced	10
Baisakh (April-May)	Income from non-agricultural work. Income from wages earned in harvesting wheat	One meal of *chapattis* and salt or chilly paste or inexpensive vegetables.	11
Jeth (May-June)	Take loan for food at 10 per cent per month	One meal of *chapattis* and salt or chilly paste or inexpensive vegetables.	12

Village Analysts: Rampati Devi, Dhandai Devi, Rita Devi.
Facilitator: Ms. Meera Jayaswal.
Date: 12.11.98.

A total view of the hunger in Chandpur indicate that women suffer acute hunger for five months—*Baisakh* to *Bhado* (mid-April to mid-September), a relatively less acute hunger for two months in *Fagun* and *Chaith* (mid-February to mid-April) and some hunger for five months of *Kuar* to *Magh* (mid-September to mid-February). Practically at no period during the year, are the women totally free from hunger. And the women of Chandpur also told us, like the villagers of Tikri, that their food intake is at its worst, during the summer and monsoon months *Baisakh* (mid-April to mid-May) and *Bhado* (mid-August to mid-September) when they work the hardest. Columns 2 and 3 of Table 6.5, also reveal a high degree of correlation between income and food. During the months of *Jeth*, *Asarh*, *Sawan* and *Bhado* (mid-May to mid-September) women in the village depend on loans for defraying expenditure on food. Only when their income from sale of vegetables and wage earnings improves, do they include pulses and even milk in their diet.

On the whole then, women suffer hunger all through the year, though there is variation in inter-month intensity of hunger. Undernutrition and malnutrition of women are clearly made out. Given the wage rates, the employment rates and yield from agriculture in the area, it is unlikely that men would have food security throughout the year either, though they would probably be better-off than women.

The expenditure pattern of the village as shown by the following *Chapatti* Diagram is interesting. The whole *chapatti* is equivalent to 16 Annas (the old currency denomination).

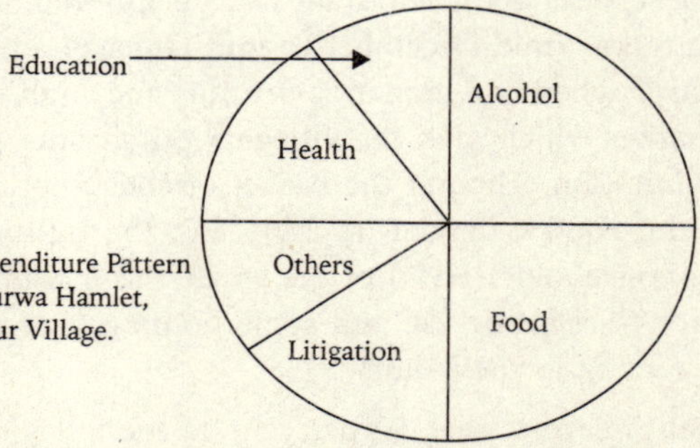

The Expenditure Pattern of Naipurwa Hamlet, Chandpur Village.

The expenditure pattern looks astonishing. Only 4 Annas (approximately 25 per cent) are spent on food, another 4 Annas (approximately 25 per cent) on consumption of liquor, 2 Annas (approximately 12 per cent) on health, 2 Annas (approximately 12 per cent) on education; 3 Annas (approximately 15 per cent) on litigation and rest on others. This pattern of expenditure has serious implications for the village in terms of its impact upon the social capital, condition of health, literacy and food security of the villagers. This is particularly so when about 25 per cent of total village income is expended on consumption of liquor.

The unusually high appropriation of household income for liquor and litigation makes serious inroads into the accessibility of the poor households to food. The unusually high proportion household income allocated to liquor and litigation, has apparently been done by cutting back expenditure on buying food, providing basic education to children and accessing primary health care. Elimination of hunger depends a great deal upon not only food production, distribution and access to food but also on nutrition of food, general access that people had to basic education and primary health care (Sen, 1995) and availability of potable water.

Hunger in a Village of Small and Marginal Farmers: Jangal Babban, Gorakhpur

Jangal Babban is a village of small and marginal farmers in Campierganj Block, District Gorakhpur, UP, India. The farmers grew both food crops and cash crops, in the nature of vegetables.

Table 6.6 depicts the food consumption pattern of 50 per cent of the villagers, comprising about 170 households, especially those who are not poor. Apparently because the households under reference are small and marginal farmers they do not face starvation. But they face hardship during the months of *Chait* (mid-March to mid-April), *Baisakh* (mid-April to mid-May) and *Jeth* (mid-May to mid-June), as the consumption level of every item in their food basket declines perceptibly. Though the items in the food basket remains the same over different months in a year, the content become more 'watery', as the villagers best described their state of consumption. The best months for the villagers are *Poos* (mid-December to mid-January) and *Magh* (mid-January to mid-February) when the granaries are full and high value vegetables are sold in the market which give the villagers purchasing power to buy 'other items' of consumption. Though the basket of consumption looks impressive, as shown by the Food Calendar at Table 6.6, the bulk of the consumption basket for the households (HHs) of the small and marginal farmers (SMF) is made up of rice or *chapattis*, *dal* and some home grown vegetables. Milk and fish/meat were rarer in their diet.

The general picture is that 50 per cent of the villagers of Jangal Babban, where small and marginal farmers, do get enough food to eat, though inter-month variations in the levels of consumption are considerable, for at least nine months in a year. For the remaining three months, these villagers remain hungry. It is notable that the villagers consider a family as hungry if it manages no more than one meal during these months. And since rice and *roti* dominates their food basket, it does, *prima facie*, indicate "hungry months", as it were for them. The nutritional content in terms of vitamins, fibre and protein remains deficient.

This brings us to the other 50 per cent of the households who are not small and marginal farmers. The 'Other' 50 per cent of the villagers (belonging to the "non-agricultural households") remains hungry for six months, *viz.*, in the months of *Poos, Magh, Falgun, Chait* (mid-December to mid-March) and then again *Sawan* and *Bhado* (mid-July to mid-September).

Table 6.6

Food Calendar of Small and Marginal Farmers, Village Jangal Babban, Gorakhpur

Months	*Items of Food Consumed*						
	Rice	*Roti*	*Dal*	*Vegetables*	*Milk*	*Meat/ Fish*	*Remarks*
Magh (mid-Jan. to mid-Feb.)	*****	****	*	*	**	***	
Fagun (mid-Feb. to mid-March)	***		*	*	**	***	
Chait (mid-March to mid-April)	*	*	*	*	*	*	
Baisakh (mid-April to mid-May)	*	*	*	*	*	*	
Jeth (mid-May to mid-June)	*	*	*	*	*	*	
Asarh (mid-June to mid-July)	**	*	*	*	*	**	
Sawan (mid-July to mid-August)	**	**	*	*	**	**	
Bhado (mid-August to mid-Sept.)	**	**	*	*	**	**	
Kuar (mid-Sept. to mid-Oct.)	***	**	*	*	**	**	
Kartick (mid-Oct. to Mid-Nov.)	***	**	*	*	**	**	
Aghan (mid-Nov to Mid-Dec.)	***	**	*	*	**	***	
Poos (mid-Dec. to mid-Jan.)	***	****	*	*	**	***	

Note: The ranking is ordinal from top to bottom column-wise. The columns are non additive and non-comparable. The dots represent the number of onions placed to indicate the quantity of the food consumed.

Village Analysts: Vijay Kumar, Govind Yajav, Gania, Subhawati, Bhanwati, Gulabi, Kaushalya, Barfi and others.

Date: 08/8/2001.

Facilitated by: Amitava Mukherjee.

Table 6.7

Scoring and Ranking of Causes of Hunger, Village Jangal Babban, Gorakhpur

Sl. No	*Causes of Hunger & Poverty*	*Scoring*	*Ranking*	*Remarks*
1.	Alcoholism	ooooooo oo	II	People used whatever they earned by working on daily wages on alcoholism.
2.	Laziness	oooooo	IV	They were not willing to put in labour. There are 10 per cent such families.
3.	Anger	ooooooooo	III	Some of the households were not willing to listen to advice and work.
4.	Large families	ooo	VII	
5.	Landlessness	ooooo	V	
6.	Resourcelessness	oooo	VI	
7.	Illiteracy	oooooo ooooo	I	Villagers considered this as the biggest bane of poverty.

Note: Free scoring was used with seeds.

Date: 9/08/2001.

Village Analysts: Indrani, Shubabati, Bhanmati, Indrabati, Gulabi, Gemia, Kaushalya, Girija, Brindabati and Barli.

Facilitated by: Amitava Mukherjee.

For the 50 per cent of the 170 households who have limited access to food half the year round, the situation is difficult. A scoring and ranking was done of the causes of poverty and hence hunger for this 50 per cent of the households (the "non-agricultural households") in Jangal Babban. The story is like what is shown in Table 6.7. It seems that to deal with food security for half the households in the village, the answer may lie outside the domain of food production, distribution and nutrition. Indeed, the villagers were emphatic through Table 6.7 that 50 per cent of the households are suffering from classical poverty caused by assetlessness, resourcelessness, illiteracy, pressure of large families and non-economic factors (such as laziness, alcoholism and intemperate attitude).

Hunger in Contemporary Haryana

Hunger in a Green Revolution Belt Village: Village Sagarpur

Sagarpur is a village in Faridabad District of Haryana. Sagarpur not only lies in the heartland of Green Revolution, in Haryana, but also in one of the most industrialised districts of the country.

Sagarpur has six hamlets or *muhallas*. In each of the six *muhallas* of the village, baring the *Harijan Basti,* about 90-95 per cent of the people depended on agriculture. It was, not only a source of income, it is also a source of employment, food and fodder. As in many other similar villages in Faridabad, people pursue alternative livelihoods within the village and outside.

Table 6.8 has percentage of people in each category of occupation. Because some people are in two or more occupations concurrently, they figure in all the occupations in which they are engaged. The table does not distribute the total population (in the relevant age group) into different occupations, which is why the percentages in each column do not add up to 100.

Table 6.8

Occupational Structure (Percentage of People in Each Category of Occupation)

Occupation/Source of Income	*Patayat Muhalla*	*Hawelliwalle Muhalla*
People with more than 1 source	21	25
HH with more than I source	29	30
People highly dependent on agriculture	21	27
People highly dependent on industry	15	10
In government service	28	25
In business related jobs	06	05
Labourers	10	08
Selling milk	50	70
Unemployed	20	25
Total adult males	60	75

Agriculture remains at the heart of the livelihood system in Sagarpur, though a fairly large section of the population has more than one source of livelihood. Within the farming system, the inhabitants rely partly on livestock system and more fully in cropping system, involved in the field and the crop.

The occupational structure of the village shown by Table 6.8, *ipso facto,* indicates that a village of agriculturists as also of people who pursue multiple occupations, cannot be hungry. The data in terms of the Problem Prioritisation in Table 6.9 nowhere indicate non-availability of food as a problem. Even the Historical Transects (at Tables 6.10 and 6.11) drawn up by the village in Sagarpur, do not indicate that insufficient food or hunger ever visited the community. However, food security in Sagarpur has to be seen from a disaggregated perspective: one from the perspective of different classes of villagers and two, from the perspective of women.

Table 6.9

Problem Ranking by Women in Two Hamlets of Sagarpur

Ranking by Women of Baghail			*Ranking by Women in Hawelliwalle*		
Problems	*Scoring*	*Rank*	*Problems*	*Scoring*	*Rank*
Drinking habit of men	********** 10	1	Unemployment	******** 8	1
Illiteracy of women	******** 8	2	Land acquisition by HUDA	******** 8	1
Shortage of money	******** 8	2	Corruption	****** 6	2
No hospital in village	****** 6	3	Shortage of money	****** 6	2
Small Land -holding	***** 5	4	Drinking habit of men	****** 6	2
Insufficient electric supply	**** 4	5	Low electric supply	***** 5	3

Table 6.10

Historical Transect by Men's Group, Patayat Muhalla

Decade	*Livelihood*	*Industry*	*Farming System*	*Cropping Pattern*
1940-1950	99.5% in agriculture and rest in Azad Hind Fauz or caste based occupation	None	Irrigation by *Rehant*; organic manure; ploughing with bullocks; harvesting with sickle; own seeds, rains for water	*Jowar*, Gram, Sugarcane, Wheat (less), *Bajra*, barley
1950-1960	97% in agriculture and rest in caste based occupation or Army	Escort and Bata	Same as in 1940-1950	Same as in 1940-1950
1960-1970	92% in agriculture; 20% in milk vending; 1% in military service; 1% in industry and rest in caste based occupation. 2% unemployed	Gadore Company	Tubewell and canal irrigation; country seeds; tractor for ploughing; organic manure	Same as in 1950-1960, but sugarcane and paddy introduced
1970-1980	Agriculture: 85%; industry: 2%; labourers: 4%; government service: 2%; milk selling 30%; unemployed 4%; traditional caste-based occupation: 1%		Tubewell and canal irrigation; HYV wheat seeds; tractor for ploughing and harvesting; chemical fertilisers, pesticides, pesticides	Main *Rabi* Crop: Wheat. Main *Kharif* Crop: *Bajra*. Gram stopped

contd...

contd...

Decade	*Livelihood*	*Industry*	*Farming System*	*Cropping Pattern*
1980-1990	Agriculture: 75%; industry: 5%; govt. service: 2%; milk: 30%; unemployed: 10%; labourer ^%; business: 2% and milk: 35%	Pyala's LPG Bottling Plant		
Same as in 1970-1980	Same as in 1970-1980, but sugarcane declined. Mustard introduced.			
1990-1999	Agriculture: 60%; milk: 40%; govt. service: 2%; labourer: 10%; unemployed: 25% and traditional caste based work: 2%.	17 Brick Kilns in the Village. NTPC's plant in Jajru	Same as in 1970-1980	Wheat main *Rabi* crop. Main *Kharif* crop; *Jowar* (for fodder) and Paddy. Some vegetables

Village Analysists: Suresh Gautam, Kamal, Nand Kishore Sharma, Shamevir, Puran Singh, Dhirendra, Shivchandi, Charanjit Lal, Ashok Gautam.

Facilitator: Sudipta Roy.

Table 6.11

Historical Transect by Men's Group in Hawelliwalle Muhalla

Decade	*Livelihood*	*Industry*	*Farming System*	*Cropping Pattern*
1940-1950	98% in agriculture and rest in caste-based occupation or in the Army	None	Irrigation by *Rehant*; organic manure; ploughing with bullocks; harvesting with sickle; own seeds, rains for water	*Jowar*, Pulses Gram, Sugarcane, Wheat (less), *Bajra*, barley
1950-1960	95% in agriculture and rest in caste-based occupation or Army	Escort and Bata	Same as in 1940-1950	Same as in 1940-1950
1960-1970	90% in agriculture; 20 % in milk vending; 3% in military service; 1% in industry and rest in caste-based occupation. 2% unemployed. Teaching 1%	Gadore Company	Tubewell and canal irrigation; country seeds; tractor for ploughing; organic manure	Same as in 1950-1960, but paddy introduced on commercial basis
1970-1980	Agriculture: 80%; industry: 2%; labourers: 6%; government service: 2%; milk selling 30%; unemployed 5%; traditional caste-based occupation: 3%		Tubewell and canal irrigation; HYV wheat seeds; tractor for ploughing and harvesting; chemical fertilisers, pesticides, pesticides	Main *Rabi* Crop: Wheat. Main *Kharif* Crop: *Bajra*. Gram stopped

contd...

contd...

Decade	*Livelihood*	*Industry*	*Farming System*	*Cropping Pattern*
1980-1990	Agriculture: 70%; industry: 6%; govt. service: 3%; milk: 70%; unemployed: 10%; labourer ^%; business: 1% and milk: 35%	Pyala's LPG Bottling Plant	Same as in 1970-1980	Same as in 1970-1980, but mustard declined and cotton stopped.
1990-1999	Agriculture: 60%; milk: 95%; govt. service: 2%; labourer: 10%; unemployed: 16% and traditional caste based work: 2%. Industry 40%.	17 Brick Kilns in the Village. NTPC's plant in Jajru	Same as in 1970-1980	Wheat main *Rabi* crop. Main *Kharif* crop *Jowar* (for fodder) and Paddy. Some vegetables

Village Analysists: Harchandi, Mohan Singh, Balbir Singh, Ram Swaroop Singh, Rishal Singh, Nathu Ram, Dharamveer, Sant Singh.

Facilitator: Sudipta Roy.

Let us look at the food security question from a class perspective. On the significance of agriculture, large, medium and small farmers (constituting 15 per cent of the population) are categorical about storing their produce for household consumption and then selling the remaining surplus to the government's procurement agency or in the *Mandi* (Market). The first harvest during the first week of April, which yield the best quality grains are stored for household consumption by the households, which cultivate them. And even the portion of this first class crop, which is sold, is also purchased by net buyers of food for domestic consumption. Only second class wheat is sold to the government. Food grown is deemed as the basis of life. The farmers accord a high priority to food security. Those who sell wheat covers only 15 per cent of the villagers.

The remaining 85 per cent have a different story to tell.

Landless people constitute 10 per cent of the village population, who work as agricultural labourers and they are not fully employed all through the year. Generally they are out of employment for half the year. Hence accessing food during the period they remain unemployed or in partial employment is always a difficult achievement.

The case of the marginal farmers, who constitute the remaining 75 per cent of the village population, stands on a different footing. Of the marginal farmers, those who own less than one acre of land, suffer from food insecurity. Because for a family of 6-8 people, food grown on less than 1 acre of land, which according to the farmers' reckoning yields about 14 quintals of foodgrains is insufficient to feed the family for a full year. If total food output on 1 acre of land is 14 quintals, it means that net food availability with the family is even less (after factoring in the cost of production and saving of seed for the next season). Thus, ensuring food availability for the whole family throughout the year, in household of marginal farmers, is impossible.

On the balance, therefore, 15 per cent of the villagers in Sagarpur have assured food to eat throughout the year from their own farms. Almost 10 per cent of the villagers who are landless, depending wholly on daily wages, suffer hunger for large parts of the year. The marginal farmers with 1-1.5 acres of land, who constitute 75 per cent of the village population, do not have enough food from their own land. They have to access food from the open market, out of income earned from off-farm livelihoods like selling milk and from income earned from employment in the nearby industrial complex of Ballabgarh and in Faridabad.

If we bring in the nutrition element into the picture, things worsen. Reference is invited to last column of Table 6.12. The crops grown in the village have dwindled down from *jowar*, gram, *bajra*, barley and sugarcane, to wheat and a small crop of paddy. *Jowar* is currently cultivated only for fodder. The current scenario shows that the variety and palate in the food of the villagers have declined. Hence, even when 10 per cent of the villagers of Sagarpur are able to produce enough food to feed the household throughout the year, it does not imply that the food they eat has the required nutritional value.

Table 6.12

Historical Transect of Farming System and Crops (Male Group, Saini Muhalla) Uncha Gaon

Decade	*Occupation*	*Cropping Pattern*
1940	100% agriculture	Wheat, *jowar*, *bajra*, barley, gram, maize, Moat, Henna
1950	95% in agriculture. Rest in industry, government and labourers	Ditto
1960	95% in agriculture, 2% labourers, 3% service and 50% milk.	Same as in 1950s but pulses reduced
1970	90% agriculture 55 % milk, rest as in 1960	Vegetables started to be grown on a commercial basis
1980	Same as 1970 except 60% in milk	Onion added to the list of items grown on a commercial basis
1990	80% agriculture, 60% milk, 5% private service, 7% petty trade/ business, 3% labourer and 2% in government	Wheat, *jowar*. mustard, cauliflower, potatoes, cabbage, brinjals, chilli, gourds of all variety

Facilitator: Sudipta Ray.

Village Analysts: Villagers of Uncha Gaon.

Hunger in a Vegetable Growing Village: Village Uncha Gaon

Uncha Gaon is a peri-urban village in Faridabad District of Haryana. Like Sagarpur, it is not only located in the heartland of Green Revolution, in Haryana, but also in one of the most industrialised districts of the country and very near to the industrial township of Ballabgarh, with a big market for agricultural produce.

From the seasonality analysis as at Table 6.13, it seems that throughout the year the villagers had something or other to harvest, gather or collect, something to sow, something to transplant and something to sell. These activities absorb considerable portion of the energy and resources, including time, at the disposal of the farmers and their households all through the year.

The villagers perceive certain changes (as reflected in Table 6.12) in cropping pattern, agricultural practices and yield and crop quality, which have a bearing on the state of hunger in the village. Let us take 1940s as the point of departure when a large number of crops were cultivated, which were a mixture of coarse grains (barley and *bajra*) and cereals (wheat, *jowar* and maize). All that the farmers cultivated were for household consumption in the village. Farming was both subsistence and sustenance activity. The variety of crops grown allowed the farmers to diffuse risks. The poly-culture also ensured that consumption basket of the households contained fibre, fat, vitamins and protein. In the 1950s, the position remained largely the same.

In the 1960s, winds of change began to sweep Uncha Gaon. Pulses were reduced. By the time Uncha Gaon reached the 1970s, vegetable was introduced as a commercial crop. In the next decade, as HYV seeds gained ground, wheat became the main *rabi* crop and *bajra* held on as the main *kharif* crop. Cultivation of gram stopped. In the 1980s, mustard and onion took roots as a cash crop in the hope of high returns.

All through the 1990s and currently the farmers in Uncha Gaon are left with wheat and *jowar* as principal (non-commercial), *rabi* and *kharif* crops respectively, with a sprinkling of *bajra*. Food crops are grown in 50 per cent of the gross cropped area of the village. Wheat is now grown both for household consumption as also for sale in the market. Cash crops are grown on the other 50 per cent of arable land, which are mainly vegetables and grown, in the main, for sale. Amongst the vegetables that now grow during *rabi*, potato is by far the most important and is grown on 50 per cent of the land which is earmarked for cash crops, or 25 per cent of the total arable land of Uncha Gaon. The variety and diversity, therefore, of crops grown are markedly low when one compares the variety and diversity of crops obtaining in the 1940s and 1950s. To that extent, the capacity of the farmers to diffuse risk was pruned.

As we move from the 1940 into the last decade of the last century, it signals a reduction in palate and nutritional value of the food consumed in farm households of Uncha Gaon. Additionally, whereas in the 1950s and 1960s much of the agricultural operations were for ensuring self-sufficiency in food, currently the emphasis is on generating income for self-sufficiency in income. There is a movement from growing crops for meeting the food requirements of households and of the community, to growing crops for consumption by outsiders.

From the Seasonal Analysis of agricultural activities by Men's Group in Saini Muhalla, reproduced in Table 6.13, the state of hunger in the village is clear. *Sawan*, *Bhado* and *Kuar* (mid-July to mid-October) are the three hunger months for the people at large. The letter 'H' denotes the hunger months. During these three months, the typical diet of a farm household consists of *chapattis* and pickle or chilli chutney, twice a day. The diet is about the same in *Baisakh* (mid-April to mid-May), with addition of vegetables from their own fields, generally brinjals and onions. Though people generally do not face starvation, there is hunger and the variety and palate of the meals are very limited. The nutritional component of food intake is suspect. During the remaining eight months people are less in distress and the consumption basket is a little more varied. It includes cereals, some fibre, protein and occasional dash of dairy products. Apparently, people do not face acute hunger for eight months in a year but they face food insecurity. Their consumption basket indicate that they eat three meals a day but the quantity and quality of food consumed leave much to be desired.

Because farmers of Uncha Gaon have migrated from agriculture for sustenance and subsistence (in their broadest connotations) and from food self-sufficiency to income self-sufficiency, hunger stalks the villagers whenever income dips. Column 3, of Table 6.13, indicate that in all those months where the villagers have something to sell, they eat well. In the three months of *Sawan*, *Bhado* and *Kuar* (mid-June to mid-October) the farmers generally have nothing significant to sell, and hence are cash-strapped. They, therefore, hack back consumption. This is also the period, the villagers explained, when diseases are usually at their full fury: Malaria, diarrhqea and dengue, apart from the chronic ones in the form of *najla*, headache, gastritis and white discharge amongst women. The villagers are, therefore, forced to spend sizeable portions of their income on treatment during these months, making further inroads into their resource base and forcing them in turn to cut their consumption basket even more. The intensity of hunger for Uncha Gaon is, thus, a function of cash sales and incidence of diseases. Uncha Gaon's people suffer from hunger in some form, for at least four months, because the farmers have migrated from endowment-based entitlement to food in favour of exchange-based entitlement.

Table 6.13

Seasonality Analysis of Agricultural Activities and Food Consumption (Men's Group Saini Muhalla)

Months	*Food Consumption*	*Agricultural Activities*
Baisakh (mid-April to mid-May)	*Chapattis* with pickle or chilli chutney. Vegetables from their own fields.	Harvesting of wheat and selling the produce. Brinjal, melon and onion sold. Sow seeds for lady's finger, bottle gourd, *torai*, chilli, pumpkin, cucumber, bitter gourd. Income is 50%.
Jeth (mid-May to mid-June)	*Chapattis* with pickle or chilli chutney. Occasionally vegetables, fruits, *dalia*, *lassi* or milk and tea. 3 meals plus an evening meal of tea/ milk.	Irrigation and weeding in the fields. Collection of fodder, like cutting grass and harvesting *jowar*. Sowing of *jowar* and maize seeds. Selling cucumber, *kakri* and melon.
Asarh (mid-June to mid-July)	Same as *Jeth*	Irrigating fields. Cutting Fodder. Selling vegetables sown in *Baisakh*. Income 25%. Sowing *bajra*.
Sawan H (mid-July to mid-August)	2 meals of *chapattis*, pickle or chilli chutney. Some Vegetable	Seedling of cauliflower and brinjal raised. Cutting some *jowar* for fodder.
Bhado H (mid-August to mid-Sept.)	Same as *Sawan*	Cutting *jowar*. Sowing radish, carrot, spinach cabbage seeds. Transplanting cauliflower brinjal seedlings.
Kuar H (mid-Sept. to mid-October)	Same as *Bhado*	Irrigating and weeding fields. Cutting some *jowar.*
Katak (mid-October to mid-Nov.)	*chapattis* with pickle or chilli chutney. Occasionally vegetables, fruits, milk tea. 3 meals plus an evening meal of tea or milk.	Harvesting *jowar* and *bajra*. Selling spinach, cauliflower, fenugreek, coriander, brinjal, radish. Income is upto 20%.
Aghan (mid-Nov. to mid-Dec.)	Same as *Kartick*	Sowing wheat seeds. Selling spinach cauliflower, fenugreek, coriander, brinjal, radish, cabbage. Income upto 40%.
Poos (mid-Dec. to mid-January)	*bajra chapattis* with *sarson da saag*, pickle or chilli chutney. Occasionally vegetables. 3 meals plus an evening meal of tea or milk.	Irrigating land. Selling spinach cauliflower, fenugreek, coriander, brinjal, radish, cabbage. Income upto 45%.
Magh (mid-Jan. to mid-February)	Same as *Poos*	Selling spinach cauliflower, fenugreek, coriander, brinjal, radish, cabbage. Income upto 40%. Irrigating fields. Sowing cucumber and melon seeds.
Fagun (mid-Feb. to mid-March)	Same as *Magh*	Selling cauliflower, potato, brinjal, fenugreek, spinach, carrot, radish. Income is 45%. Irrigating and weeding fields.
Chaitra (mid-March to mid-April)	Same as *Magh.*	Fenugreek, spinach, coriander, carrot and *sarson da saag* sold. Income is 35%. Irrigate fields.

Note: H indicates hunger periods.

Village Analysts: Balbir, Bansi, Harish, Omprakash, Bhagawat, Krisen, Mahesh, Babloo.

Facilitator: Sudipta Ray.

The success of the community to avoid hunger revolves around producing vegetables, with which they acquire exchange entitlement to food. With high levels of unemployment, people of Uncha Gaon have little hope of securing exchange entitlement to food through selling their labour and earned wages. The gender disparity within the households, leading to utilisation of household income for indulging in alcoholism, make serious inroads into the ability of the households to access food. Then finally, the fear of hunger that stalks the people of Uncha Gaon due to anticipated acquisition of their agricultural land by the state is oppressing.

Hunger in Contemporary Orissa

Hunger in a Cyclone Devastated District: Netakundi

Though hunger and food insecurity are major problems for vast tracts of the country but for rural Orissa it has always been a key fixture that has kept the state perpetually in the news. Netakundi was devastated by the super-cyclone that hit Orissa in October 1999. The devastation caused by the super cyclone, '*a priori*' must have taken a toll of the very fragile food security that people of Netakundi had lived with for years. An attempt was made to assess the state of hunger in the village as it was before the super cyclone and as it stands after the super cyclone. The state of hunger for men and women were separately examined in Netakundi. The Food Calendars prepared by men's group and women's group are presented in Tables 6.14 and 6.15.

The Food Calendars for men shows the proverbial inter-month variations in food consumed by people throughout the year. The food basket shown in men's Food Calendar comprises rice, potherb (*sag*) and vegetables. This was the case for both before the super cyclone and remains the same after the super cyclone as well. Rice constitutes the bulk of the diet for the villagers. Rice consumption reaches its peak in *Kartick* (mid-October to mid-November) and continues at that level till *Magh* (mid-January to mid-February). It starts falling in *Falgun* (mid-February to mid-March) though it still remains at a high level and then continues to decline till *Sraban* (mid-July to mid-August). The hunger period starts in *Jestha* (mid-May to mid-June), but the really difficult months are *Sraban, Bhadra* and *Aswin* (mid-July to mid-October). The levels of consumption of *sag* and vegetables also show serious gyrations on a month to month basis. While consumption of *sag* and vegetables are high from *Margsira* (mid-November to mid-December), it dips in summer months of *Baisakh* (mid-April to mid-May) and then picks up with the onset of monsoons in *Asarh* (mid-June to mid-July). The other items of consumption such as fruits, fish and potatoes are at best marginal and occasional.

Table 6.14

Food Calendar by Men's Group of the Village, Netakundi

Months		*Rice*	*Pulse*	*Sag*	*Vegetables*	*Fish*	*Fruits*	*Coconut*	*Potato*
Baisakh	B	•••••5	•1	••2	•1	••2	•1	•1	••2
	A	••2	0	•••3	-	-	0	0	•1
Jestha	B	••••4	0	••2	0	0	•1	•1	••2
	A	••2	0	•••3	••2	0	0	0	•1
Asarh	B	•••3	0	•••••5	•••3	•1	0	•1	•1
	A	•1	0	••••4	•1	•1	0	0	•1
Shraban	B	••2	0	•••••5	•••3	0	0	•1	•1
	A	•1	0	•••••5	•••3	0	0	0	•1
Bhadra	B	•1	0	•••••5	•••3	0	0	•1	•1
	A	0	0	0	•1	0	0	0	0
Aswin	B	•1	0	••2	•1	0	•1	•1	•1
	A	0	0	0	0	0	0	0	0
Kartik	B	•••••10 •••••	0	•1	•1	0	•1	•1	•1
	A	•1	0	0	0	0	0	••••4	0
Margsira	B	••••• •••••10	0	•••3	•1	•1	0	•1	0
	A	•••3	0	0	0	0	0	0	0
Pauso	B	••••• •••••10	0	•••3	•••3	0	0	•1	0
	A	•••3	0	••2	0	0	0	0	0
Magh	B	••••• •••••10	0	••••4	•••3	•1	0	•1	••2
	A	••2	0	•••••5	•••3	0	0	0	0
Falgun	B	••••• •••8	•1	••••4	•••3	•1	0	•1	•••3
	A	••2	0	•••••5	••••4	0	0	0	••2
Chaitra	B	••••• ••7	•1	••••4	••2	•1	0	•1	•••3
	A	••2	0	•••••5	•••••5	0	0	0	••2

Note: The dots represent the number of stones used by the villagers to indicate the levels of their consumption. The Fixed Scoring Method was used.

Facilitator: Meera Jayaswal.

Village Analysts: Men of Netakundi.

Table 6.15

Seasonal Food Calendar of Women in the Village, Netakundi

Months		*Rice*	*Sag*	*Vegetable*	*Potato*	*Fruit*
Baisakh	B	•••3	•1	•••3	••2	•1
	A	••2	•1	••2	•1	0
Jestha	B	•••3	•1	••2	•1	•1
	A	•1 ••	•1	•1	•1	0
Asarh	B	•••3	•••••5	•••3	•1	0
	A	•1	•••••5	••2	•1	0
Shraban	B	••2	•••••5	•••3	•1	0
	A	•1	•••3	••2	•1	0
Bhadra	B	•1	••••4	•••3	•1	0
	A	0	0	••2	0	0
Aswin	B	•1	0	•••3	•1	0
	A	0	0	••2	0	0
Kartik	B	•••••10 •••••	0	•••3	•1	0
	A	•1	0	0	0	0
Margsira	B	•••••10 •••••	•••••5	•••3	•1	0
	A	•••••10 •••••	•••3	0	•1	0
Pauso	B	•••••10 •••••	•••••5	•••3	•••3	0
	A	•••••5	••••4	0	•1	0
Magh	B	•••••10 •••••	•••••5	•••3	•••3	0
	A	••••4	••••4	•1	•1	0
Falgun	B	•••••10 •••••	••2	•••3	•••3	0
	A	•••3	•1	•1	•1	0
Chaitra	B	••••4	•••••5	•••3	•••3	0
	A	••2	•••3	•1	•1	0

Note: The dots represent the number of stones used by the villagers to indicate the levels of their consumption. The Fixed Scoring Method was used.

Facilitator: Meera Jayaswal.

Village Analysts: Women of Netakundi.

The pattern of consumption remains the same after the cyclone also. But the levels of each element in the food basket has gone down after the super-cyclone, *vis-à-vis* their levels prior to October 1999. A striking feature of the food basket for Netakundi is that rice consumption increases when the price of rice fall and the systemic availability of rice increases. But the case of *sag* and vegetable was different. People consumes *sag* and vegetables which they grow and what they grow in their kitchen gardens and whatever they gather and collect from common property resources. Thus, consumption of *sag* and vegetables increases significantly during rainy seasons, when these *sag* and vegetables sprout in abundance.

The consumption pattern for women is similar to the consumption pattern of men. The difference is that the absolute quantity of food women consume is less than what men consume. In fact, the quality of food generally consumed by women is poorer, for women have no pulses in their food basket. Fish is generally reserved for men's diet. Coconut is either consumed by men only or is used in cooking as an ingredient of Oriya Cuisine.

For both men and women, the nutritional quality of food is always poor, and after October 1999, it is even poorer. There is a preponderance of starch and little of protein and fibre in the villagers' diet, except what they get from eating *sag* and vegetables, in small quantities.

The two Food Calendars when interviewed with the villagers of Netakundi, gave the following trends:

- The level of food consumed generally leaves the villagers of Netakundi hungry for long periods. And the situation continues to be so today.
- As for the quantity of food consumed by the villagers except for the four months following harvest from *Kartick* (mid-October to mid-November) they suffer hunger of different degrees all through the year, reaching its nadir in the summer and monsoon months.
- Due to the super cyclone, the quantity of food consumed has been reduced drastically even from the earlier low level.
- Rice is the staple food for the people. Rice consumption is sufficient from *Kartick* (mid-October to mid-November) to *Chaitra* (mid-March to mid-April) but from *Baisakha* (mid-April to mid-May) consumption of rice fall very significantly.
- After the super cyclone, the villagers of Netakundi consumed rice in extremely small quantities till *Margsira*. Only after paddy was harvested in the *Kharif* of 2000, that the quantity of rice consumed was sufficient in the villagers' perception.
- Women have fewer food items in their food basket than men do.

Hunger in Dinasingh, Patna

An exercise similar to what was done in Netakundi was carried out in village Dinasingh, Patna. Food items were listed in a focus group discussion with men's and women's groups and then they were requested to score the amount they consume in terms of their sufficiency and/or insufficiency. The range of score was 1-10, and was expressed by placing stones from 1-10 stones. The names of the food consumed along with scoring is presented in the Tables 6.16 and Table 6.17.

The general picture of food consumption by men in Dinasingh Patna looks familiar. Like in many other villages in the state, the food basket consists of rice, vegetables and *sag* in varying quantities throughout the year, with rice being the staple. There is a sprinkling of potato and coconut, fish, milk and banana in certain months and an occasional mango in small quantity during the summer months. The quantities of food in the food basket changes during the year. During the months of *Margasira, Pousa, Magh* and *Falgun* (mid-November to mid-March), the level of food consumed is at the highest. The decline starts with *Chaitra* (mid-March to mid-April) and then get trapped in a low level equilibrium throughout the summer and early monsoon months of *Baisakh, Jeth,* and *Asarh* (mid-April to mid-June). The quantity of food fall further during the three months of *Sravan, Bhadra, Aswin* and *Kartick* (mid-July to mid-November) to the lowest level. That is, the villagers in Dinasingh, Patna suffer seven months of considerable hunger, from *Baisakh* to *Kartick* (mid-April to mid-November) of which the last four months are severe. Indeed even the additional employment generated during the cultivation season never comes to the rescue of the villagers. The villagers of Dinasingh, Patna explained that the cultivation and harvesting seasons for the marginal farmers and share-croppers were particularly stressful as they have to garner all their resources to carry out the agricultural operations. For the daily wage earners, the picture is not much different because they get employment for short periods (all concentrated when the rains comes) for ploughing, puddling, repairing the paddy fields and carrying seedlings from the adjoining nurseries to the paddy fields. Similarly, they are employed during harvesting, threshing and winnowing. And much of these employment opportunities are in lieu of work elsewhere. The position worsened even further once the super cyclone hit, because wages are now being paid as, not cash or goods, but as labour-in-exchange. Therefore, wages earned no longer add to the household income, which could be used for increased economic access to food. Hunger in the post super cyclone scenario has been further exacerbated as the levels of food consumption have declined in absolute terms from the pre-super cyclone levels. A look at Column 3 of Table 6.16 will reveal the story.

The general picture of food consumption depicted by women's group in Dinasingh, Patna also looks familiar. Like men, the food basket is heaviest in *Margasira* (mid-November to mid-December) and *Pauso* (mid-December to mid-January), and starts declining in *Magh* (mid-January to mid-February) itself but remains at a tolerable level. The slide continues till *Baisakh* (mid-April to mid-May) and *Jestha* (mid-May to mid-June) when it starts rising and then fall till Margsira (mid-November to mid-December). The basket of consumption for women is pretty much like the basket of food for men. Like men the women also suffer long periods of hunger and periods of severe hunger in the summer and monsoon months when the energy requirement is highest.

Table 6.16

Seasonal Food Calendar of Men's Group in the Village, Dinasingh, Patna

Months		*Rice*	*Pulse*	*Potato*	*Veg-etable*	*Papaya*	*Aru (root veg)*	*Milk*	*Sag*	*Coco-nut*
Baisakh	B	••••4	••2	••••4	••2	••2	•1	••2	0	0
	A	•••3	0	••2	•1	0	0	0	0	0
Jestha	B	••••4	••2	•••3	•••3	0	••2	•••3	0	•1
	A	•••3	0	•1	•1	0	0	0	•1	0
Asarh	B	••••4	••2	•1	••••4	0	••2	0	••••4	•1
	A	•••3	0	•1	••2	0	0	0	•1	0
Shraban	B	•1	••2	•1	•••3	0	••2	0	••2	•1
	A	•••3	0	•1	••2	0	0	0	•1	0
Bhadra	B	•1	••2	•1	••2	0	••2	0	0	•1
	A	0	0	•1	0	0	0	0	0	0
Aswin	B	•1	••2	•1	•1	0	••2	0	0	•1
	A	0	0	0	0	0	0	0	0	0
Kartik	B	•1	••2	•1	•1	0	••2	0	•1	
	A	0	0	0	0	0	0	0	0	0
Margsira	B	••••• ••••••10	••2	••2	•••3	••2	•1	0	•1	0
	A	••2	0	0	0	0	0	0	0	0
Pauso	B	••••••10 •••••	••2	•1	•••3	•1	•1	0	•1	0
	A	••2	0	0	•1	0	0	0	0	0
Magh	B	••••8 ••••	••2	•••3	••2	0	•1	0	•1	01
	A	••2	0	•1	•1	0	0	0	•1	0
Falgun	B	••••8 ••••	••2	•••3	•1	0	0	0	0	0
	A	••2	0	••2	•1	0	0	0	0	0
Chaitra	B	••••4	••2	••••4	•1	0	0	0	0	0
	A	•••3	0	••2	•1	0	0	0	•1	0

Village Analysts: Abhinayu Singh, Tajeshwar Singh, Sudhir Singh.
Facilitator: Meera Jayaswal.
Interpreter: Jyotirmay Das.
Date: 26.7.2000.

In terms of the relative quantity of food consumed by men and women, it is not possible to establish through the Food Calendars any differentiation or discrimination, but while interviewing the Food Calendars, it did emerge that women, as an age old tradition, eat after men their meals. The general perception is that women eat less than men. How much of this is coloured, at least in part, by social conditioning of the women and how much of this perception is based on conscious observation of the quality and quantity of food consumed by women *vis-à-vis* men, is hard to decipher. But it certainly is the case that the decline food consumption sets in earlier in the year for women than in case of men and the diet of women is less varied and less nutritious than men's diet. To that extent women suffer more from hunger than men do.

From the discussion above and Tables 6.16 and 6.17, the following general trends are discernible:

- Both men and women suffer moderate to severe hunger for almost eight months in a year. In general, the diets of both men and women in Dinasingh, Patna are without variety and palate.
- The levels of absolute amounts of food consumed by both men and the women have been adversely affected by the super cyclone. The amount of food intake got reduced and so has the variety after the super cyclone.
- Women, in villagers' perception, generally consume lesser amounts of food as compared to the men. And women conformed to the stereotype that women eat last.
- The hunger months for the women are greater than those of the men.
- Rice, pulses and potherb (*sag*) are the most commonly consumed food (in that order of magnitude) in Dinasingh, Patna. Vegetable and animal protein are rarely part of the villagers' diet.
- After the super-cyclone, men stopped consuming pulses which prior to the cyclone was a regular item in men's diet. Women's food basket never contained pulses, (both before or after the super cyclone) during *Shraban, Bhadra, Aswin* and *Kartick* (mid-July to mid-October) because they lack sufficient income in the household to buy pulses for the women. That is, the diet consumed by the women is less varied and less nutritious than the diet consumed by men.

Table 6.17

Seasonal Food Calendar of Women's Group in the Village, Dinasingh, Patna

Months		*Rice*	*Pulse*	*Veg-etables*	*Sag*	*Potato*	*Fish*	*Coconut*	*Banana*	*Milk*
Baisakh	B	••••6 ••	••2	•1	•1	••2	0	0	•••3	••2
	A	••••4	0	0	0	0	0	0	0 *1	•1
Jestha	B	••••6 •••	••2	•••3	•1	•••3	0	0	••2	•1
	A	•••3	0	••2	0	0	•1	0	0 *1	0
Asarh	B	•••3	••2	••••4	••2	0	0	•1	•1	0
	A	••1	•1	•••3	•1	0	0	0 *1	0	0
Shraban	B	•••3	0	••2	••2	0	•••3	•1	•1	•1
	A	••2	0	••••4	0	0	0	0	0	0
Bhadra	B	••2	0	••2	••2	0	•••3	•1	•1	0
	A	•1	0	0	0	0	0	0	0	0
Aswin	B	••2	0	••2	••2	0	•••3	•1	••2	0
	A	0	0	0	0	0	0	0	0	0
Kartik	B	•1	0	•1	••2	0	0	•1	•••••5	0
	A	•1	0	0	0	0	0	0	0	0
Margsira	B	•••••7 ••	•1	•••3	••2	0	•1	•1	••••4	•1
	A	•••3	0	0	•1	0	•1	0	0	0
Pauso	B	•••••8 •••	••2	•••3	••2	0	0	0	•••3	•1
	A	••2	0	0	•1	0	•1	0	0	0
Magh	B	•••••6 •	••2	••4 ••	••2	0	0	0	•••••5	•1
	A	•••3	•1	0	•1	0	••2	0	0	0
Falgun	B	•••••5	••2	••2	••2	0	0	0	••••4	0
	A	•••3	•1	•1	•1	0	0	0	0	0
Chaitra	B	••••4	••2	••2	••2	0	0	0	••••4	0
	A	••2	•1	•1	•1	0	0	0	0	0

Note: The * in column 10 indicates, consumption of mangoes from commons.
Village Analysts: Hemlata Singh, Sangita Singh, Brijbala Singh.
Facilitator: Meera Jayaswal.
Date: 26.7.2000.

Conclusions

Having described briefly the food security situation in different districts and states, it is now possible to compare them. Let us begin by identifying the similarities.

First, is the persistence of long hunger periods depicted by all the communities through the Food Calendars. Despite all the talk of our national food security, pockets of hunger in large numbers remain a sad reality. This lends credence to the fact that despite enough food being produced nationally (in the aggregate sense), there being enough (in fact far in excess of warranted level) buffer stocks held in godowns of the government (read STC), a policy of making available food to vulnerable sections of society, through the PDS and a plethora of government programmes, aimed at eliminating hunger, hunger at the community level persists.

Hunger is not uniform throughout the year. On certain months it is severest, whereas in others it is not so and in some there is none of it. Hunger has to be viewed from a temporal dimension. Straightforward statements that 360 million people are hungry and the balance over 540 million are not, conceal a large part of the harrowing picture. Thus, data such as the one dished out by the National Family Health Survey, 1998-99 that 95 per cent of Indians get two square meals a day is not a true and fair account of the state of "India's Hunger".

Second, though the intensity and duration of the hunger periods may be different in different states, even in the best scenario people go hungry for at least three months in a year and in those months when people need the highest energy intake. Therefore, despite there being no systemic shortage of food available from the primary food system, and a burgeoning buffer stock with the government, hunger is a common feature. In one state, it has been there since 1993 through 1995 till 1998.

Third, even if the food intake in the non-hungry months, as it were, is enough in quantitative terms, the quality of food and the consequent nutritional element are areas of major concern. Dominance of starch in the diet of the villagers remains unaffected in all these years. This may be a cultural phenomenon. This is similar to what Beck (1994) observed in respect of some other villages studied by him around the same time, through the questionnaire method. He noted that during the discussion with the villagers there is a common agreement that it is only rice, the staple grain that would make the stomach happy. "The stomach won't understand unless it gets rice", as one villager puts it, to him. Beck even notes that when sufficient quantity of rice was not available, many poor villagers with whom he interacted would take the water left over from boiling rice (usually fed to livestock in richer households) which would fill the stomach. Be that as it may, the absence of other elements like protein, fibre etc., implies that people may not be starving in the non-hungry months, but their nutritional intake is seriously jeopardised by poor nutritional quality of their diet.

Fourth, in the hunger situation in different villages in all the states, for the poor households the major source of protein nutrition remains the food collected from the CPRs, particularly water bodies and forests and micro-environments. More particularly, the relative dependence on food from the secondary food system, particularly for protein has increased in good measure in some cases. However, it is not possible to identify whether the absolute amounts of protein intake from this source have actually increased or decreased over a period of time.

Fifth, the consumption of food is the lowest during the summer months and rainy season as also in the post harvest season, from *Baisakh* to *Kartick* (mid-April to November). Consumption of food is, therefore, the least during the period when the poor have to work the hardest. During *Asarh, Sravan* and *Bhadra* (mid-June to mid-September) the villagers work in agricultural operations, while during *Aswin, Kartick* and *Poush* (mid-September to mid-December) when they work in harvesting operations as also gleaning from the paddy fields. The former period is also the period when the workload of the women increases on account of collecting fuel, making dung "cakes" and then storing them for future use. Poorest households meet their fuel needs for cooking by collecting fuel from the CPRs (collection of fuel is considered a traditional and unspoken right) which is mainly in the form of fallen leaves, animal dung, notably cow/bullock dung and dry branches. Crop residues and other forms of fuel are also gathered from homesteads, paddy fields, paths, area around ponds or wherever. Gathering of fuel is the exclusive responsibility of women and girl children. But, collection of animal dung or other forms of fuel during monsoon or rainy season, is not possible (as leaves do not fall during the rainy season) and cattle, goats/sheep are kept in the animal-sheds and stall fed. This is done to protect both these animals from rain and prevent them from trampling and grazing the standing crops. Poor households, therefore, store "cow/bullock dung cakes" made by the women out of dung gathered in the dry season. This increases the workload of the women.

Sixth, in at least one case, the hunger period is increasing. The 1993 Food Calendar for Krishna Rakshit Chak, had depicted two hunger periods (from *Chaitra* to *Jyestha* was the first hunger period and *Aswin* to *Kartick* was the second hunger period) with some respite in between. From the 1995 and 1998 Food Calendars it is apparent that Krishna Rakshit Chak suffers one long hunger period from *Chaitra* to *Kartick* (both months inclusive), spanning almost eight months and increasing in intensity during the latter part of the hunger period, *viz.*, from *Bhadra* to *Kartick*. The longer hunger period in 1998

Food Calendar, however, seems to be a little less painful *vis-à-vis* the long hunger period depicted by the 1995 Food Calendar, because of the availability of fishes, snails etc., (which were virtually missing in 1995) from Rajbandh, by accident and unlikely to be sustainable.

Finally, wherever CPRs exist, its role in helping food security is critical. The consumption of food from the secondary food system increases during the months when the consumption of other food, particularly rice, is to be curtailed. Thus, food from the secondary food system substitutes food from the primary food system, particularly potatoes and rice, when these become too expensive for the poor villagers to afford. It also means that villagers in different villages are saved from greater hunger during the summer months by food from the secondary food system, though they go still hungry.

The Policy Recommendations

The reality is much more complex than commonly believed. Indeed the concept of hunger itself is complex. We have found that different people are affected differently; different kinds of people are affected differently and most importantly men and women are affected differently. Of the six conditions necessary for eliminating hunger we have only fully met the condition of food availability (at the aggregate level only) and partially the condition of providing physical access to food for only some people through the PDS. All the other conditions that must be satisfied for elimination of hunger stand violated.

A programme to conquer hunger must, therefore, be comprehensive and include, in the long run, along with more food production:

- Measures to promote and sustain sustainable agriculture, with emphasis on organic farming, poly-culture and low external input for higher output as opposed to higher production. The distinction between higher output and higher productivity is of fundamental importance.
- Measures for enhancement of general economic growth and diversification of production, expansion of employment and decent rewards for work, all of which will increase economic access of people to food. The strict implementation of laws relating to minimum wages and pulling the government out of domains where it has no comparative or competitive advantage, will be particularly important measures.
- Enhancement of medical and health care, which will increase, *inter alia*, physical access to family planning facilities, because accessing such facilities will help restrict the size of families. A general improvement in the status of health reduces the risk of infant and child mortality rates that go a long way to boost the psychological strength of people to take the "risk" of opting for smaller families, reducing the strain of large families on food available in the household.

- Arrangements of special access to food for marginalised people, including deprived mothers, aged, disabled and small children, in the nature of a functioning and well targeted PDS, with preponderance of food-for-work programme to build infrastructure, operated by the *Gram Panchayats* (village level elected bodies). This will increase economic and physical access to food for those who are otherwise unable to do so or are seriously handicapped to do so.
- Spread of basic education and literacy, both of which will increase physical and economic access to food, by not only increasing the capability of the people but also encouraging them to use birth control measures.
- Reduction in gender based inequalities, which will help women access food within the households and improve intra-familial distribution of food.

To misquote Sen, "these different requirements call for an adequately broad policy alive of the diversity of causal antecedents that lie behind the many sided reality of hunger in contemporary India". Because, the reality itself has to be changed and it has to be done by the state. There is no other agency, which can do so. For the state to galvanise its resources and reach, it needs a comprehensive strategy. It needs to put in place an appropriate explicit food policy in the medium to longer run, which the country of nearly 360 million hungry people sadly lacks. The former will form the basis for the latter (almost as a counterpart of the Agricultural Policy). And in the immediate run, in the stress areas like Kalahandi, Bolangir and Koraput there is an urgent need of, what Jean Dreze (2001) calls "social security arrangements of a permanent nature. The country's massive foodgrain stock presents a unique opportunity to put such arrangements in place".

With the coming into force of the WTO Agreements, hunger and food security of India are no longer affected by only national forces. They are deeply influenced by international forces. The dismantling of the quantitative restrictions, imposition of bound rates of tariff for agricultural and dairy products, full implementation of the Agreement on Trade Related Intellectual Property Rights (TRIPS) and the Agreement on Agriculture, amongst others, will shape in a fundamental way how our hunger and food security pictures will look like in the years ahead. Experts like Verghese Kurien (2000) and M.S. Swaminathan (2000) believe tough times are ahead.

References

Beck, Tony (1994). *The Experience of Poverty.* London: Intermediate Technology Press.

Chambers, Robert (1992). *Micro-environment Unobserved,* Gatekeeper Series. London: Institute for Environment and Development.

Dreze, Jean (2001). "No More Lifelines, Political Economy of Hunger in Orissa", *Times of India*, 17th September, p.10.

Ghaia, Raghav and Kulkarni, Vani S.: "Look at the Pyramids Base", *Indian Express*, New Delhi, 5 January.

Hindustan Times (2008). "Food For Thought", *Hindustan Times* Editorial, 3 January, New Delhi Edition.

Hunger Project (2001). *Women in Panchayati Raj: Change Agents for a New Future for India.* New York: The Hunger Project.

Kurien, Verghese (2000). "Farmers Might Have to Sell Their Milch Cows", *Outlook*, February, p.26.

Menon, Meena (1999). *The Unseen Workers, On the Trail of the Girl Child.* Writings by Fellows of the National Foundation for India. Bangalore: Books for Change.

Mukherjee, Amitava (1994). *Participatory Rural Appraisal and Rural Planning.* Chapter 2. New Delhi: Vikas Publishing Co.

———. (1994a). *Structural Adjustment and Food Security.* Aldershot, Hong Kong etc.: Avebury.

———. (2001). *Perspectives of the Silent Majority: Air Pollution, Crop Yield and Food Security,* SOAS Studies in Development Geography, School of Oriental and African Studies, University of London. London and Aldershot, Burlington USA, Singapore Sydney: Ashgate.

———. (2002). *Hunger, Theory, Perspectives and Reality: An Analysis through Participatory Methods,* Kings College, University of London, London and Aldershot, Burlington USA, Singapore, Sydney: Ashgate.

Mukherjee, Neela (2002). *Participatory Learning and Action with 100 Field Methods.* New Delhi: Concept Publishing Co.

NCAER (1999). *India Human Development Report.* New Delhi: Oxford University Press.

Scrimshaw, Nevin (1998). "The Lasting Damage of Early Malnutrition", *World Food Program*, May 31.

Sen, Amartya (1985). *Commodities and Capabilities.* North Holland, Amsterdam.

———. (1986). *Poverty and famines: An Essay in Entitlement and Deprivation.* Oxford: The Clarendon Press.

———. (1998). *Hunger in the Contemporary World,* STICERD. London: London School of Economics.

Sharma, Davinder (2001). "Paradox of Plenty", *Times of India,* 11th September, p.8.

Swaminathan, M. S. (2000). "Import of Food, or of Unemployment", *Outlook*, February.

Working Group on Children Under Six: "Strategies for Children under Six", *Economic and Political Weekly,* 29 December.

7

Participatory Poverty Assessment

Knowing is not enough: we must apply.
Willing is not enough: we must do.

—Johann Wolfgang von Goethe

Introduction

Gopalpur village, in Jamaldah *Gram Panchayat*, Block Mekliganj, District Cooch Behar, is a fairly large village, with about 118 households. The village is organised around localities called *baris*. There are at least 14 *baris* in Gopalpur, *Khariza* 188.

The population of Gopalpur is a mixture of Muslims, Rishis, Raj Bangshis and Hindus (many of them are refugees from erstwhile East Pakistan). Each of these communities is organised into *baris*. Hence, there is a Muslim *bari*, a Raj Bangshi *bari*, Rishi *bari* etc. Participatory sessions for the current PPA were held in Khenir *bari*. The general state of housing, as it appears on approaching the village, gives a picture of relative prosperity. Though most of the houses are *kucha* houses and some are brick walled houses with tinned roofs, they are well maintained.

The village has straight roads, some of which are *kucha* and some are metalled roads. The metalled roads are all constructed under the PMGSY. For instance, the road connecting Jamaldah Hat and Kesar Hat, passing through Gopalpur is a metalled road.

The village has 2 ponds, 27 tube wells and 25 wells (*kuwa*). It has a Palli Mangal Sangha and a Kishore Sangha (Youth Club). There are two temples in the village: a Shiv Mandir and a Devi Mandir. There is a Health Sub-centre at a distance of 2 kms from the village. An ICDS Centre, the Nodal Centre for District Literacy Committee and a primary school are all functioning in Gopalpur. The village also boasts of a few shops, selling grocery and provisions to the villagers. (Attention is invited to Chart No. 1 which shows the map of the village, where these institutions are all marked.) The village, from first inspection, clearly appeared to be primarily an agricultural village.

Trends

The current status of Gopalpur village has evolved over a long period of time. There are some original settlers in the village but there are many others who have been settled there from outside the village. The different trends, that visited the village over the last 15 years or so, have been captured in Table 7.7.

Wages: Wages are an important element of the village economy which affects almost everyone in Gopalpur. Daily wages have risen from Rs. 5–6 per day and a meal or 1 kg of rice, in 1990, to Rs. 25–62 per day now, the higher wages being paid to the men. Given that the price of a kg of rice was about Rs. 3–4 per kg, daily wages in 1990 hovered around Rs. 8–10 per day. In 15 years time, daily wages have risen by almost 300 per cent. The rise in daily wages has been impressive and the increase has been both in nominal and real terms. However, between all these years, the wages have been consistently below the prescribed minimum wages for the state and discriminatory against women and continues to be so despite progressive governance.

Prices: Prices have also risen over these years, the prices being represented by price of lentil and rice (*daal-bhaat*). The price of rice rose by almost 100 per cent between 1990 and 1995 (from Rs. 3–4 per kg to Rs. 6 per kg), but between 1995 and 2000 the price level increased by about 70–100 per cent and it stabilised thereafter. On probing, it appeared that the price of rice rose according as the price of rice in the ration shops was jacked up in the public distribution system. It seems the initial jerk imparted to the price-level, in the 1990s, followed the cut back on subsidies consequent upon implementation of the structural adjustment programme in 1991. When the increase in prices is compared with the increase in wages, it seems the price-effect was smaller than the income effect. Consequently *prima facie* it seems the well-being of households, at least of those who depend upon daily wage earnings, has improved over these years, though the well-being is pegged at a relatively low level and has been eroded by increases in population and contraction of employment opportunities as we will discuss later.

Availability of food: While discussing well-being and prices, the issue of food emerged as a major factor, since food occupied a central place in the lives of people in Gopalpur, abundantly exemplified by the fact that even the movement of prices is indicated by movement in price of rice. The question of availability of food, over the years was, therefore, analysed by the villagers. During the late 80s and early 90s, the number of people in each household being relatively low, even with low wages most households had managed a reasonable access to food. However, after 10 years, the number of people to be fed in each household has increased without a commensurate rise in employment opportunities and hence household incomes. During the current phase, the situation has worsened as population increase is unabated whereas employment opportunities, has shrunk. As a result, availability of food per capita has declined. Food poverty in Gopalpur has set in gradually over the years and is a relatively recent phenomenon. To cope with the decline in employment opportunities *vis-a-vis* the number of people available for employment, migration out of the village has become common coping strategy. Some young men migrate on a cyclical basis whereas others seek employment in Jamaldah and Mekliganj. How many young men are emigrants at any point in time could not be ascertained but all young men are potential emigrants.

Quality of food: Row 14 of Table 7.7 also provides important data on the food front. During the late 1980s, rice gruel (*daan bhat*) and roti into were the staple diets of the villagers. By mid 1995, the diet underwent a significant change, with rice, *roti* and broken–rice gruel (*khudi-chaal*), becoming the basic diet. By 2000, only rice remained the basic food and currently, though rice continues to be the main item in their diet, the variety in their diet has decreased. The reasons for this are not far to seek. For one, the cropping pattern changed, with millets no longer cultivated. For the other, with falling economic access to food, represented by lack of employment opportunities, villagers in Gopalpur settled for fairly stale and "undiversified", as it were, food basket. In food security terms, the people were food insecure as the nutritive value of their food were suspect, even if the quantity value is assumed to be of acceptable level, *viz.*, 510 grams per capita per day.

Asset Base: Over the years, the asset bases of households have also varied and this is understandable given that wages and the number of people have changed significantly. During the late 1980s, most people had thatched houses. In the early 1990s, villagers started replacing their thatched roofs with tiles. Of late, the number of houses has increased but most houses have thatched roofs and bamboo walls. Tinned roofs or tiled roofs are for houses belonging to the *Dhoni Shreni* and *Madhyam Shreni* (rich and middle classes) that constitute about 12 per cent of the villagers. However, the quality of houses for the poorer sections of the village, namely, the *Nishwa Shreni* and *Gorib Khet Mazor*, has improved due to assistance received under Indira Awas Yojna. Generally, the asset holdings of the different households have not changed much quantitatively, though significant qualitative changes have been affected.

Vulnerability: Gopalpur has been vulnerable to shocks to some extent. During the 1980s and the early 1990s, cyclonic weather and excessive rainfall alternated with droughts, causing damage to crops (up to 30 per cent), cattle and property in Gopalpur. The situation continued till the mid-1990s. Over the last 10 years, the situation has changed. Rainfall received by Gopalpur has generally declined. Drought and hailstorm are the current natural calamities that visit the village of late and the net crops loss is still upto 30 per cent. Thus, the quantum of crop lost due to natural calamities has not changed much over the years but the nature of the calamity has changed from cyclonic weather and floods as it were to, droughts and hailstorm. Unfortunately there is no insurance available against these calamities to villagers of Gopalpur, which is why they are keen on irrigation as a development intervention to which we shall revert later.

Migration: It was mentioned briefly earlier, that migration has been adopted as a coping mechanism by the villagers, especially the youth, against growing unemployment. It seems in the late 80s and early 90s, most people who sought work did so in Gopalpur itself and generally got employment in the village, mostly in agricultural operation. Row 7 of Table 7.7 indicates that the tendency to migrate emerged in the late 1990s, as existing agricultural operations were unable to absorb the labour force (as historically agriculture was plagued by disguised unemployment) in the village, migration started. The tendency to migrate is very significant now and is on the rise. The current urge to seek job outside is both for earning better livelihood and to seek the things that people in the cities have access to. This has implication for both the income and health status of Gopalpur.

Access to Health: In the 1980s and even the early 1990s, the facility for immunisation was available at Jamaldah and Mekliganj but not many people from Gopalpur accessed these facilities. There being no medical facility in the village, only the rich or those who could afford to pay for treatment and medical care, secured health services. In or around the year 2000, a Health Centre was established in the village. However, many of the villagers still do not access the health care services provided, for several reasons. The availability of medical staff was during hours, which do not suit the villagers always. Secondly, there is lack of interest in accessing the health facility due to an overall lack of awareness and the fact that for several tests and medicines they have to pay which at times are beyond their capability. Moreover, the villagers have in any case to travel to either Jamaldah or Mekliganj to purchase the medicines and obtain laboratory services.

Social Problems: There are not many social problems that Gopalpur faces. The problem of dowry and the social standing of the poor are two most important issues mentioned by the villagers. Dowry as a social custom existed in Gopalpur for ages, as is the case elsewhere in the country. And the problem afflicts all sections of the community irrespective of social class or religious affiliation. But still even as late as in the 80s, though dowry was prevalent it was manageable. Over the years, especially over the last 10 years or\so, the problem has increased rapidly and is rising over time. The villagers think that exposure of the young men to the amenities in the cities and towns, made possible by migration for work, has raised in them the urge to acquire them without having the means to do so. They look upon marriage as an opportunity which helps them to satisfy some of their urges for the luxuries of a city life. Currently, a single marriage costs at least Rs. 50,000, a princely sum for the poor people of Gopalpur. Dowry in that sense also partakes the nature of an economic problem which erodes the asset base of poor households and increases indebtedness, which in turn cuts into consumption level of the poor people, low it already is.

Over the same period of time, the poorer people have lost social standing. There was respect for the poor in the 80s. That is, people were not despised on account of poverty but that has changed during the last one decade or so. Poor people are looked down upon. Flaunting richness is considered a virtue while poverty is looked down upon as a curse.

The two phenomena of increasing demands for dowry and sizing up the poor, are symptomatic of a society moving towards market economy and a social system where "money" is the critical variable. The change in mindset is significant. The villagers perceive this as being the flip side of migration and a decline in societal values where human beings are considered as rich or poor rather than as neighbours and fellow villagers.

Connectivity: The villagers feel that connectivity of the village, ushered in by better roads, has something to do with changing mindset. The metalled road that one now finds in Gopalpur came about only in the late 90s. Earlier the road was a fair–weather *kucha* road. The metalled (pitched) road has facilitated communication of Gopalpur with Jamaldah, Mekliganj and Cooch Behar and has enabled girls to go to school and *haat-bazar* in Jamaldah on bicycle. The road connectivity and "Government development Programmes such as IAY houses" have also led to improved sanitary conditions in the village. Thus, while there were very few, if any toilets in the village in 1995, several of these got constructed with the IAY houses in 2000 (or there about) and few more households, on their own, have constructed toilets. On the downside, the metalled road has also caused the advent of middlemen in the village and lured the villagers, especially the young men (and women), towards life styles and aspirations, more appropriate for peri-urban and urban environments, which in turn has exacerbated the social problems discussed above.

Poverty Grouping

Class Classification: The households in Gopalpur are fairly heterogeneous. These generally fall into two large groups: *Gorib* and *Khet Mazoor* and *Nishwa Shreni*, comprising 56.25 per cent (in the terminology of villagers, 9 Anna out of 16 Annas) and 31 per cent (approximately) of the households respectively. There are *Dhoni Shreni* and *Madhyam Shreni* households also but they comprise about 6.25 per cent each (1 Anna each). Considered on a hierarchical basis there is the *Dhoni Shreni* (1 Anna or 6.25 per cent), *Madhyam Shreni* (1 Anna or 6.25 per cent), *Gorib* and *Khet Mazoor* (9 Annas or 56.25 per cent) and *Nishwa Shreni* (5 Annas or 31 per cent). The majority of the households are thus poor or very poor.

Asset Base: The asset base of the different classes of households is different, as would be expected. All the above categories of households are marked by significant differences in their landholdings, the single most important productive asset-base in a rural economy. The villagers did not categorise their households on the basis of income, though by implication, those who have a higher asset base are probably with higher income levels as well.

The *Dhoni Shreni* households have bamboo and tin walls and tin roofs for their houses;[1] have furniture (such as chairs, tables, cots, racks or what villagers call *alna* and almirah); possess up to 15 *bigha* of land to cultivate paddy, jute, potatoes, tobacco (in that order of importance) and maintain a flock of buffaloes, cows, goats and poultry birds.

The *Madhyam Shreni* households have houses of inferior quality with bamboo walls and tin roofs. They too possess a minimum of furniture (like cots, *chowki,* and some households even have chairs), have control on an average over about 5-7 *bighas* of cultivable land with cropping pattern similar to that of the *Dhoni Shreni*. They also maintain cows, goats, ducks and hens, but fewer in numbers.

The *Gorib* and *Khet Mazoor* households live in houses with bamboo walls and thatched roofs. In the four cases, from amongst the *Gorib* and *Khet Mazoor* households, which have received assistance under IAY, the houses have tin roof. They too have cows, goats, ducks and hens, but have no other asset except a few cooking utensils. These households typically hold 1½ to 3 *bigha* of land, for cultivating paddy, for much of which they borrow capital from the village money lender (*Mahajan*) both in cash and in kind, primarily seeds and fertilisers.

The *Nishwa Gorib* households live in an assortment of houses, some made of jute reeds and thatched roofs, others are mere sheds made from any freely available materials such as plastic sheets, palm leaves, thatch etc. The landholding of these *Nishwa Gorib* households measure up to 1½ *bighas* (in several cases due to land reforms) and some have no cultivable land at all. Their "other" assets comprise cooking utensils, some ducks, and hens and a few pigs.

The general picture of asset holdings of households in Gopalpur is typical of a poor village. About 85 per cent of the households (*Gorib* and *Khet Mazoor* and *Nishwa Shreni*) are asset poor and suffer from poverty born out of assetlessness. As stated earlier, thanks to land reforms, many of them have some land due to *Pattas* for land given by the government, providing them with income, food and above all social standing. On the balance, only about 13 per cent of the households in Gopalpur are not asset poor.

The capability status of Gopalpur looks similar to the asset base of the households. Children from *Dhoni Shreni* and *Madhyam Shreni* households,

1. The PPA team visited two such households where tea was served.

have all access to schools and all children from *Dhoni Shreni* households are literate. However, the *Gorib* and *Khet Mazoor* households are keen to send their children to school but all of them cannot do so due to lack of money, implying poverty. Though school is free, there are incidental expenses which parents of these children are not always able to spare. In case of the *Nishwa Shreni*, they do not think of sending their children to school. The reasons for the two poorer segments are different. *Gorib* and *Khet Mazoor* cannot afford the "ancillary cost" (*Anusangik Kroroch* as the villagers put it) of education and hence keep their wards from attending school. Children from *Nishwa Shreni* households, however, do not send their children to school both because of their attitudes and their poverty. For one, they "deploy" their children to help them in their work (and earn a little income), help their parents in household chores, look after their siblings and take care of their pigs, ducks and hens, a situation similar to many other parts of the country. For the other, many of the parents from these households still do not see the utility of an education system, which does not prepare them for employment. Thus, they perceive teaching their children their traditional skills stand them a better chance to survive than educating them which does not prepare them for anything (*Ei kool oi kool, du kooli jabe*).

In case of both *Gorib* and *Din Mazoor* households and *Nishwa* households, an additional factor that militates against sending their children to school is a lack of awareness, which with income poverty form a strong constellation of forces to keep the poor and the poorest in the village in "capability poverty".

Clearly, there is a class difference in capability of the households in Gopalpur. Children from about 85 per cent of the households have no education or little education; children from the 13 per cent or so of households, belonging to richer classes of people (*Dhoni* and *Madhyam Shreni*) get access to education which is primarily designed to serve the poor. Girl children from the richer classes go to school even in Jamaldah.[2] Thus, a majority of the children in Gopalpur are capability poor, and in almost all cases their parents are also "capability poor".

There is an inter-generational question here which warrants a few comments. The capability poverty of the last generation has succeeded in ensuring that their children get trapped into capability poverty in the present generation. Given the asset base, income levels and attitudes of the villagers in Gopalpur, it seems very likely that a majority of the next generation parents (the present children) will also be in capability poverty, leading to their children being capability poor and the cycle going on repeating itself, unless something dramatic happens in the foreseeable future.

---

2. In itself it is very heartening that girls education in high school would lead to gender empowerment.

Resources/Capital Base

Natural Resources/Capital: Like many other villages in Cooch Behar, Gopalpur also has a wealth of natural resources. The village has ponds, areca nut orchards, and jackfruit orchards, betel vine, betelnut trees, a plethora of fruit trees from banana to mangoes, coconut and jackfruits. The village has a sizeable number of timber trees especially *sheesum* and *gambhar* and robust bamboo bushes (*Baans Jhaard*). However, except for the ponds situated in the northwest corner of the village, much of the natural resources are held as private property. There are no significant common property resources or forests etc. As a result, access to natural resources is differentiated on the basis of ownership. The *Gorib* and *Khet Mazoor* and *Nishwa Shreni* households have no access to much of the natural resources except their small parcel of agricultural land and homestead land and whatever grows on them. For Table 7.2, row 1 is revealing. It seemed that trees (both timber and fruit bearing) that stand on public lands as "road-margin" are few and far between while demands on them are very large. Since the village is divided into *Baris*, access to natural resources on public land is also confined, in the main, to whatever lies at or near the respective *Baris* and the connecting roads.

Physical Capital: The physical capital of the village comprises the ICDS centre, the roads network, the Health Sub-Centre, the wells, temples, tube wells, the Nodal Centre for the District Literacy Committee and the school buildings. It is important to recognise that the physical capitals are all in good shape. The *Gorib* and *Khet Mazoor* and *Nishwa Shreni* households find the ICDS centre as the most accessible physical capital for their purposes.

Social Capital: The social capital of the village is fairly strong. There exists considerable bonding and goodwill amongst the inhabitants of Gopalpur. The temple, the Palli Mangal, Kishore Sargha (The Youth Club) and Samabay Krishi Unnayan Samittee (Agricultural Co-operative) have contributed much in this regard. Unfortunately, as elsewhere in the country, the Agricultural co-operative has run into problems of poor governance and leakages. Equally unfortunate is the fact that the women's SHG formed under the DWCRA programme is also wound up.

Human Capital: The human capital base of the village is large but poor. As we discussed earlier, the *Gorib* and *Khet Mazoor* and *Nishwa Shreni* households are uneducated and most of their children cannot and/or do not attend school. And 75 per cent of the adults in these households are also illiterate. Hence, generally in 85 per cent of the households, the human capital base is poor. Amongst the villagers, the relatively better human capital, consisting of the more enterprising and industrious young men, migrate to "other" places for employment. Of the human capital available from the remaining 15 per cent (*Dhoni Shreni* and *Madhyam Shreni*) of the population, most of them lack any technical expertise, though they are educated.

Financial Capital: Poor human capital base also gets reflected in the poor financial capital base of Gopalpur. Barring income from agricultural operation and daily wage earnings and plying of "Vans" by some, the villagers have no source to build their financial capital. Consequently, the *Dhoni Shreni* households with food and cash crops to sell have a fairly sound financial base but for the others, it is almost at zero savings level. The absence of any bank or co-operative credit institutions have not helped matters either. Indeed the *Gorib* and *Khet Mazoor* households face considerable erosion of potential financial capital or fail to build financial capital, as they are forced and borrow from the *Mahajan* to cultivate their small landholdings, as discussed earlier.

In sum then, Gopalpur is well endowed with natural resources capital and has a reserve of social capital, though access to natural capital is skewed in favour of the *Dhoni Shreni* and *Madhyam Shreni* households. The human capital and financial capital bases for the village are poor. The need to borrow money from the village moneylenders for the *Gorib* and *Khet Mazoor* households (comprising over 56 per cent of the households) for agricultural operation eats into their financial capital as well.

Livelihoods

Livelihoods: Gopalpur is a typical West Bengal village, connected to nearest *Panchayat* and Block headquarters by a metalled road. It is also connected to Jamaldah *Haat* and Kesar *Haat* to its South and North respectively. The livelihood pattern in Gopalpur is also typical of a village in rural Bengal.

Agriculture is the principal source of livelihood. Almost all the households of *Dhoni* and *Madhyam Shreni* have agricultural operations as their source of food and work throughout the year. For the *Gorib* and *Khet Mazoor* households, agriculture provides employment and food for five months or so in a year, given their small landholdings. These households depend on wage employment in Gopalpur or in Jamaldah and Mekliganj during the remaining seven months. The *Nishwa Shreni* households, by definition, has to fall back up on their labour, almost always as daily wage labourers for their livelihood. During cultivation and harvesting reasons, they luckily get employment in the village. During the lean season they travel to other villages, or the block headquarters in search of work. On an average, they find work for 15 days a month during the lean season at wage rates ranging between Rs. 30–35 per day.

Some households from the *Gorib* and *Khet Mazoor* households also ply "Vans" (essentially cycle carts) to ferry goods and human beings. Some of these vans are used to carry goods to the *Haats* in Kerhar *Haat* and market in Jamaldah for the relatively large agriculturists and to fetch goods for petty traders, petty trade occupying a small place in the livelihood scenario of Gopalpur.

Agriculture provides most of the employment for the *Dhoni* and *Madhyam Shreni* households, because, one, the use of HYV seed and fertilisers and two, diversified agriculture with paddy, tobacco, jute and potatoes, grown in the same chain of cultivation. Thus, the *Dhoni* and *Madhyam Shreni* households take full advantage of the diversified agriculture in Gopalpur. Paddy is used principally for consumption and only the surplus is sold. Tobacco and potatoes are generally for cash income. Fruit trees, betel nut trees, betel leaves (*paan*) and coconut trees abound but these are not cultivated as livelihoods. They provide supplementary food and add palate as well as variety to the diet of the villagers.

The surplus in paddy has come about ever since mid-1990s, after HYV seeds, and NPK fertiliser use were accepted by the farmers. The economics of paddy cultivation and just cultivation is given in Tables—GP-1 and GP-2.

The issue of improvements in agriculture has important bearing on the well-being of the people of Gopalpur, which will be discussed later.

Table GP-1

Economics of Paddy Cultivation in Gopalpur

Expenditure in Cultivating Paddy on one Bigha of Land (Average)		*Recovery from Paddy Grown on one Bigha of Land (Average)*	
Items	*Cost (in Rs.)*	*Items*	*Price Received (in Rs.)*
Seed	25	Seed retained	25
Labour	750*	Grains	1800**
Fertilisers and Pesticides	150	Hay	200***
Hiring of Bullocks and Plough	200		
Total	1125	Total	2025

Note: * For all operations from ploghing till harvesting

** Assuming 10 maunds of output

*** Assuming 600 bundles ("Aanti") are produced

Table GP-2

Returns from Tobacco Cultivation in Gopalpur

Kind of Tobacco	*Sale Price per Maund (in Rs.)*
Good Tobacco-L2	800-900
Chaloo Girian	400
Standard Girian	600

Problems

With a low capital base, poor human capital and high dependency upon agriculture, mostly rainfed, for livelihoods, as expected, Gopalpur has significant problems. Reference is invited to Table 7.3 prepared by the men. The Male Group listed 10 major problems confronting them. These problems can be classified into three broad heads: economic problems, social problems and problems of social development.

Problems at serial number 1 to 3 of Table 7.3 are economic problems. Problems at serial numbers 4 to 6 and 9 and 10 of the Table relate to social development or delivery of basic services. Problems of serial numbers 7 and 8 are social problems.

Of the economic problems, lack of capital is ranked as the most important, in line with the status of financial capital base of Gopalpur discussed in Section 4 above. Interestingly the nature of the problem as articulated by the villagers is the absence of Swa Nirbhar Dal (Self Help Group), implying that they could neither inculcate the habit of savings nor of using credit fruitfully to increase their income and well-being. Additionally, the villagers could not derive the benefits of their entailments under the Government of India's poverty alleviation programmes like the SGSY where SHGs have a very important role. And the fundamental reason for this failure to sustain their SHG has been lack of training and the capability to take forward and run SHGs.

Since agriculture is the main stay of livelihoods in Gopalpur, lack of irrigation facility is high on the prioritised list of problems for men in Gopalpur. Improved agricultural practices have brought a certain level of prosperity to the village, but being principally rainfed agriculture, the farmers do not reap the full benefits unless the rain-gods are merciful. The farmers are unable to deal with uneven distribution of rainfall in years with good monsoon, and deficit in availability of water when the rain-gods fail. In consequence the full benefits of "new-technology" in agriculture have not accrued to the farmers. The farmers feel, (since ground water availability is not yet a problem) that boring deep tube wells could well meet the irrigation needs of Gopalpur and allow the farmers to reap the full advantages of using HYV seeds and fertilisers (in the main NPK).

Lack of capital and rain fed agriculture naturally leads to lack of employment opportunities. Because the economy of Gopalpur is not diversified, employment opportunities dry up once agricultural operations are over in two installments: cultivation and harvesting, including minor post-harvesting operations like winnowing, threshing, parboiling and dehusking. There being no traditional occupation and no cottage/village industry in the village, the solution suggested lies in introducing small scale industry and improved agricultural practices but for both of these to be sustained there is the need to build capacity of the villagers on various aspects of starting and managing tiny sector units and on practising improved agriculture, which in turn means revamping the extension services, both in quantitative and qualitative terms. The near extinction of extension services in the village has been a serious bottleneck in achieving higher agricultural productivity.

The community perceives that the social sector problems, pertaining to lack of schools, hospitals (health centres), electricity and proper housing, (in that order of priority), are all symptomatic of gross under-spending in infrastructure development by the state. Lack of doctors, beds and medicines; absence of connection to individual households from electric poles and absence of a high school in the vicinity of Gopalpur (the nearest is in Jamaldah) can be circumvented by a well planned investment programme.

The social evils of early pregnancy (consequent upon child marriage) and dowry system, are natural concomitant of an underdeveloped social structure, illiteracy and poor economic status. The villagers did suggest social action (read communal action) and legal measures to tackle the menace of dowry and early marriage, which are important in themselves but for the legal measures to succeed there is need to increase awareness, spread literacy and empower the community economically.

The notable feature of the solutions suggested by the villagers in Gopalpur, and especially, "who" should be responsible for introducing those solutions, is that the government, *panchayats*, (at *zilla*, block and village levels), non-government organisations and the Legislatures, have been squarely relied upon. Self-help, community action and social action are conspicuous by their absence. Dependency syndrome seems deeply entrenched in the psyche of the people. 50 years or so of "subsidy raj" has created an impression in the public mind that the solution for all problems rests with the state rather than the individual initiative and community mobilisation, as was the case for centuries. There is need to attract serious attention of the powers that be to this problem.

Seasonality Problem: These problems in Table 7.3 do not all affect the inhabitants of Gopalpur uniformly throughout the year. These problems have a differentiated impact in terms of time: in some months these problems are severe while in others they may be only at the margin. The seasonality analysis in Table 7.8 gives a quick view of the seasonality situation. Five months–*Asarh, Shravan, Aghrayan, Poush* and *Falgun* are good months. These months provide employment and food grown in the village. The crises months are *Baisakh, Jyasthya, Bhadra, Aswin* and *Kartik,* when there is no work in the village and crops are still not available to mitigate their suffering. And of these months the even worse months are *Bhadra* and *Aswin*.

These months become even worse because during *Baisakh* and *Jyasthya* as also *Bhadra, Aswin* and *Kartik* a variety of diseases visit Gopalpur: fever, asthma and diarrhoea. There being poor medical care in the village, diseases take a heavy toll of the earnings/savings or dis-savings of the poor villagers.

Institutional Analysis

These are several institutions in Gopalpur, but the villagers consider seven of those as significant. In Table 7.4 the villagers have analysed the status of these institutions and suggested some corrective measures.

The ICDS Centre, the Sakirta Siksha Samittee and the primary schools, are passing through a difficult phase. They lack the basic facilities, like rooms, proper medicines in the Health Sub-Centre and drinking water in the schools. In fact, the Sakirta Siksha Samittee is closed.

The *Gram Panchayat* and the *Panchayat Samittee* exist, but these institutions lack transparency and hence credibility. There is no way how the *Gram Panchayat* even communicates with the villagers the contents of their village development plan. The identification of beneficiaries is questioned, a familiar refrain throughout the state.

The bank credit through the Gramin Bank, Jamaldah Branch has reached at best 20 per cent of the households. And being defaulters in repayment of credit extended to them, many of the households are unable to reap any further benefit from credit facilities available from the formed sector. The villagers assert that the defaulters are unable to repay, presumably because they cannot generate enough income. This could be partly explained by the fact that the villagers are "capability poor", as is apparent from Table 7.3. This already difficult situation is made worse by the collapse of the institution of extension services.

The task of rebuilding the institutions, even the basic ones, in Gopalpur is critical in any poverty alleviation strategy. And the communal perception is that the task of building or rebuilding these institutions lie in the domain of the states responsibilities

Government Poverty Alleviation Programmes

The villagers in Gopalpur see the hand of the state in a large number of development schemes, as described in Table 7.5. There are 10 schemes mentioned in the Table and the villagers have benefited from these schemes. Nevertheless the schemes are either poor in quantitative or qualitative terms. For example, the houses under Indira Awas Yojna are under-financed (including cuts the potential beneficiaries, have to part with). The pond and well constructed under SGSY are wrongly "targeted": they benefit the *Madhyabitto* households. The road constructed under SGRY is a fair-weather road—it is a *kucha* road.

When the villagers talked of the qualitative problems of development schemes the point to the ICDS Centre, the Primary Health Centre and Shishu Siksha Kendra: the food distributed at the ICDS Centre is inadequate and improper; the Health Centre has no medicine and lacks health workers; the Shishu Siksha Kendra need more workers. Krishi Pension and Old Age Pension apart from reaching just one person each are not released every month and amount of pension is just Rs. 75 per month. The request is to increase these pensions to over Rs. 100 per month!

These development schemes implemented in Gopalpur leave, much to be desired. Poor targeting, poor delivery and poor quality, all visit the government poverty alleviation programme. Consequently, the impact of these programmes up on the well-being of Gopalpur is nothing to write house about. It is not surprising that Gopalpur is still besit with the problems discussed in Table 7.3 and the section above.

Problems of Women

Women's problems were different from men's problems in several ways. In Table 7.6 the problems outlined by women's group have been shown.

Women in Gopalpur are more concerned about their non-economic problems than the economic issues. Privacy, unity amongst women, and putting an end to the indignity perpetrated by the dowry system are their primary concerns. Provision for income generating activity is last in their priority.

Given the problems faced by women, the status of their empowerment was probed. In Chart 2, the empowerment circle created by the women of Gopalpur is presented. The women identified six elements which make up for women's empowerment: economic independence, control over resources, society in the village, knowledge and literacy, decision making ability and having information. In all these counts, the women placed their personal status between 0 to less than 50 and in two cases (literacy and knowledge, and decision making ability), their personal status were between 0 to 25, on a scale of 0 to 100. Women of Gopalpur seemed disempowered. Economic dependence, lack of reproductive rights, illiteracy, social discrimination reflected in "poor village *samaj*", and lack of decision making authority, speak volumes about measure necessary to tackle women's problems.

The question of decision-making (or lack of it) within the households was probed further. The decision matrix prepared by a mixed group of men and women, at Table 7.9, make interesting reading. On all major issues, decision in the households are made by men. Control over income, sale of produce expenditure, saving (keeping money) and size of the family are areas where decisions are made by men. Women have no role. Women decide on child immunisation and visits to fairs and festivals. Women in Gopalpur, conditioned by social construction, saw nothing unusual about this decision-making arrangement. In what environment was this exercise being carried out and how much of the same emanated from entrenched belief, could not be ascertained, despite the fact that the women were vocal. Given the fact that women lack economic independence and had low literacy levels and lacked information, Table 7.9 seems to be a reasonable representation of reality.

Women's health did not figure in the test of problems in Table GP—1 or in Chart 2, where solutions to their problems were enunciated. With Table 7.8, showing seasonality of diseases, women's group was requested to discuss which of the diseases mentioned in Table 7.8 affected them most. The women's group indicated that apart from the diseases outlined in Table 7.8 women have special problems. A health diagram as at Chart 3 was prepared by the women to indicate the diseases that they suffer. Chest pain, severe headache and gynecological diseases were the most common diseases. Complications following childbirth were fairly common but remedies were rare. The women in Gopalpur believed that their chest pain and severe headaches were due to the hard labour that they had to put in throughout the year. The diagnosis of the women is based on their own perception or what the 'traditional healers" tell them. There was never any attempt to diagnose the problems in any health care outfit—a phenomenon that reflects on the status of women in Gopalpur.

Women's Empowerment

That the women are pretty much moulded in their traditional roles is also evidenced by the decision matrix as at Table 7.9. By all accounts, major decisions affecting the households, such as agricultural operations, accessing health services, marrying children, purchasing household assets, family planning and expending household income are in the exclusive domain of men. Only on issues relating to household chores do women have a decisive role. To that extent there is considerable scope for interventions in empowering women.

That women are disempowered and that they suffer from severe dependency syndrome, was also reflected in the section on problem analysis above. If the problems confronting women, including domestic violence and dowry, are read with the decision-matrix, it seems that government efforts at empowering women have not yielded the desired results.

Inferences

The picture from the participatory sessions in Ratherhat paints a complex picture of poverty in the village.

Trends: Several trends are clearly discernible.

(i) The livelihood pattern in Ratherhat is dominated by agriculture, with migration and some daily wage earnings being the other two major sources of livelihoods. Selling of products from CPRs and duckery/poultry is supplementary source of livelihood.

(ii) The technology and mode of production in the lead sector, namely, agriculture, has not changed much. Use of High Yielding Variety Seeds, Fertilisers (NPK) and application of irrigation have caught on but there is room for considerable improvement.

(iii) Wages have over the years increased fairly rapidly, especially over the 80s. But the continuous rise in the price level has made the increase in real wages much more modest. There is discrimination in wages paid to women *vis-à-vis* men for the same amount of work. Wages are well below the legal minimum wages.

(iv) The general well-being of the people have changed as the income effect of a rising trend in wages outstripped the price effect significantly.

(v) The state of household assets has not changed much.

(vi) Communication with the outside world, and road connection have improved over the years but these are far from being satisfactory.

Nature of Poverty: The nature of poverty is multi-dimensional in Ratherhat. It has the following features:

(i) There is class structure amongst the households. There are four classes, *Shochaal Paribar*, *Krishak*, *Prantik Krishak* and *Din Mazoor,* with the latter two comprising 93 per cent of the households. However, poverty afflicts different classes of people differently.

(ii) There is no income poverty amongst the *Krishak*, *Prantik Krishak* and *Din Mazoor* households in Ratherhat, but the *Prantik* and *Din Mazoor* households face problem of income poverty acutely, which they seek to mitigate through migration. That implies that over 93 per cent of the villagers in Ratherhat suffer from income poverty.

(iii) There is no poverty on account of "assetlessness" especially amongst the *Shochaal Paribar* and *Krishak* households. Thanks to land reforms in the state.

(iv) However, the *Prantik Krishak* and *Din Mazoor* households suffer from some amount of poverty on account of assetlessness, which means 93 per cent of the village suffer some form of poverty due to assetlessness.

(v) Poverty on account of material deprivation affects the *Prantik Krishak* and *Din Mazoor* households.

(vi) There is food poverty amongst the vast majority of the households especially those belonging to *Prantik* and *Din Mazoor* households.

(vii) There is capability poverty especially amongst the women. The status of health and education leaves much to be desired.

(viii) Women in Ratherhat have special needs especially of income and access to health. Women in Ratherhat clearly demonstrate that they are disempowered and are subject to male domination manifested by domestic violence and rising dowry

Livelihoods: The livelihood pattern has not changed much over the years, as mentioned earlier. Agriculture remains the principal source of livelihoods for most of the villagers of Ratherhat. The mode of production in agriculture has remained almost unchanged over the last two decades but agriculture is diversified and there is some off-farm supplementary income from sale of ducks, poultry and vegetables. Daily wage earning and migration, are the other sources of livelihood. Problems relating to raising the current levels of income and tackling unemployment levels confront both men and women.

Capital Base: Ratherhat has all kinds of capital in some form or other: physical capital, natural capital, human capital, financial capital and social capital. Except for natural capital, none of the other capital holdings of the community is of high quality.

Well-being: The well-being of the people in the village is mired by lack of improved agriculture, lack of employment opportunities, poor capital base and disempowered women. The gradual reduction in the number of people living in poverty in Ratherhat has come about, because of improvements in agriculture, a few government programmes and the initiative of the people.

Government Programmes: The people of the village are not aware of major poverty alleviation programmes except the Indira Awas Yojana and Prime Minister's Gram Sadak Yojana and social security schemes. They are not aware of even the SGSY, the major poverty reduction programme of the government. However, government programmes, whatever their scale and quality of implementation, have contributed to the improvement in the sense of well-being of the people, such as land reforms, Indira Awas Yojana and construction of the *kuccha* road between the village and main road to Monaguri. The flow diagram at Figure 7.1 depicts the situation.

Policy Recommendations

The policy recommendations from the inferences and the recital can be classified under three headings: implementation of policies and programmes, amendment of policies and programme design and three, suggesting new policies.

Implementation of Policies and Programmes

Clearly there are gaps in implementation of policies and programmes. The following could be the possible steps:

- There is a need to raise awareness about the government programmes and establish a "connect" between the people and the line departments concerned. Awareness will, hopefully, lead to demand for these programmes and their utilisation.
- The role of NGOs in this regard may be explored especially in mobilisation of communities for formations of SHGs so that benefits from government

programmes (like SGSY) can reach the poor. Provision must be made to build capacities of the people to change their mindsets from one of looking at the government as the saviour to self help and community action.

- The plan expenditure may have to be reviewed so that investments required to build infrastructure or provide supplementary infrastructure (like building irrigation facilities and *pucca* road to the *Haat*) are made available.
- All allocation of resources for primary health care and elementary education should be reviewed. Allocation for these sectors could follow internationally recommended norm of allocating 20 per cent of budget for social sectors.
- The need to introduce improved farming technology, better seeds and use of soil nutrients could not have been over emphasised by the villagers.
- Several institutions have to be built. The extension services in agriculture and allied activities need to be revived or restored.

Amendment of Policies and Programme Design

Many of the programmes and policies are well designed but their manner of implementation may warrant improvement. It may be worth recording the following comments in this regard:

- In several government programmes, like the SGSY, there should be cent per cent reservation for women. This is likely to succeed following the experiences from large development organisations in India and neighbouring countries
- The various pension schemes run by the government need reworking. The quantum of the pensions as also the number of poor people covered by them have to be revamped.
- Politicisation of development schemes has to be stopped. While there is great merit in *Panchayat* elections being fought along party lines, distribution of benefits under anti-poverty programmes should not be coloured by party affiliations. Poor are poor whatever be their party affiliation.

Suggesting Policies

There is need to look at the policies of the government afresh. The following are a few suggestions:

- Whatever prosperity that the people in Ratherhat has seen has been due basically to three anti-poverty programmes, namely, land reforms; housing under IAY, and road. Reference is invited to Figure 7.1. Thus, even when liberalisation and privatisation are buzz words, there is a need for the state to continue to perform its basic functions for ensuring that the rights of its citizens are not violated. In so far as the poor are concerned the market cannot substitute the state.

- There is a need to usher in the "Green Revolution", for Ratherhat to gain fully from new technology.
- There is a need to build the capacity and provide technical support to the villagers in Ratherhat for developing their capacity to generate off-farm employment (such as poultry and pisciculture) which some of the households are resorting to on a small scale and help them develop into a class of modern artisans using traditional knowledge. The access to market that the villagers have to Moinaguri and Dhupguri should be put to full use.
- There is a need to diversify the rural economies, using local know how and local resources, in which the roles of TVEs/SMEs could be vital, given that Ratherhat is near the district headquarters of Jalpaiguri District. These will provide employment to both youth and women.
- There could be partnerships developed between the community based organisations to be developed, the private sector and the public sector, including the banks, to diversify the rural economy of Ratherhat.
- Actively promote the participation of NGOs and CBOs in development activities in Ratherhat, especially where they have comparative advantages.

Table 7.1

Social Groups in Village Gopalpur, Cooch Behar

Social Group	*Dhoni Shreni*	*Madhyam Shreni*	*Gorib and Khet Mazoor*	*Nishwa Shreni*
1. HH in Anna = 0-16 (0% to 100%)	1	1	9	5
2. Type of Dwellings	Bamboo and tin wall and tin roof.	Tin roof and bamboo wall.	Straw roof, bamboo wall, tin roof in Indira Awas.	Straw, roof, any how a shed is there.
3. Household Possessions	Chair, table, cot, *palang*, *alna*, almirah.	Cot, *chowki*, a few have chair.	Nothing other than cooking utensils.	Nothing other than cooking utensils.
4. Livestock	Cow, buffalo, goat, duck, hen.	Cow, goat, duck, hen.	Cow, goat, duck, hen.	Duck, hen, pig.
5. Landholding	Up to 15 *bighas* paddy, jute, potatoes, tobacco are cultivated.	Up to 7 *bighas* paddy, jute, potatoes, tobacco are cultivated.	Up to 3 *bighas* potatoes are cultivated by borrowing money from *Mahajan*.	Many have 1½ *bigha* land, few don't have land.
6. School	All children go to school, no one is illiterate.	All children go to school.	Despite aspiration, children cannot go to school due to lack of money.	Children do not go to school.
7. Health	All children are immunised against polio.	All children are immunised against polio.	All children are immunised against polio. Toilets have been constructed by Indira Awas Yojna.	All children are immunised against polio. Toilets have been constructed by Indira Awas Yojna.
8. Livelihood	Earning from cultivation, specially from tobacco and potato.	Earning from cultivation, specially from tobacco and potato.	Daily wage labour and cultivation.	Daily wage labourer.
9. Social Capital	Samabay Krishi Unnayan Samittee. There is no controversy in the *samittee*.	Samabay Krishi Unnayan Samittee. There is no controversy in the *samittee*.	SHG was formed by DWCRA but it is not functional.	SHG was formed by DWCRA but it is not functional.

Table 7.2

Resources in Village Gopalpur, Cooch Behar

	Dhoni Shreni	*Madhyam Shreni*	*Gorib and Khet Mazoor*	*Nishwa*
1. Natural Resources	Pond, small pond, land, areca nut orchard, coconut orchard, jackfruit orchard and betel vine.	1-2 small pond agricultural land, pond.	*Bastu bhita*	Landless, many don't have even *Bastu bhita*.
2. Physical Resources	School, well machine, pump set, motorcycle, cycle, TV and other household materials.	School, well machine, pump set, motorcycle, cycle, TV and other household materials.	School, ICDS.	School, ICDS.
3. Human Resources	Education (technical education is not there).	Education (technical education is not there).	Due to lack of awareness, there is no education	Due to lack of awareness, there is no education
4. Social Resources	Temple—all go there.	Temple—all go there.	Temple—all go there.	Temple—all go there.
5. Economic Resources	Earn from paddy, tobacco and betel vine. Cultivate potato by borrowing money from *Mahajan*.	Earn from cultivation. In addition, they are involved in tobacco and rice making business.	Work as wage labourer during cultivation. In lean season work as domestic labourer.	Work as wage labourer during cultivation. In lean season work as domestic labourer.

Table 7.3

Problems in the Village and Suggested Solutions, Village Gopalpur, Cooch Behar

Problems		*Description*	*How the Problem will be Reduced*	*Who Will Do and How Will be Done*
1. Lack of Irrigation Facility	3	Irrigation is dependention on rain. The rainwater is not absolved.	Deep boring tubewell to be installed.	*Panchayat*, Block and *Zila Parishad.*
2. Lack of Work throughout the Year	3	The cultivation and yield is not stable. There is no work other than agricultural works.	• Small-scale industry should be organised. • Introduction of modern agro-technology in cultivation	Voluntary organisation and *Panchayat*.
3. Lack of Money and Capital	1	Due to absence of Swa Nirbhan Dal.	Various types of work should be undertaken after training.	Non-government organisation and government.
4. Lack of Hospital		Lack of doctors, beds and medicines.	Health centre should be equipped with infrastructure.	Government.
5. No High School		Children have to go to other places for study. Girls cannot go for higher studies.	High school should be managed.	Government.
6. Problem of Electricity		The electric posts are installed but connection has not been given.	-	-
7. Problem of early Mother-hood (pregnancy)		The girls are married at an early age after suitable grooms are identified. They deliver child within 1 to 1½ years of marriage.	In order to check early motherhood, a committee should be formed in villages and the responsibility should be entrusted to the committee.	-
8. Dowry System		Now-a-days the girls are married after mortgaging land and utensils.	It should be prohibited by making law.	-
9. Lack of Training		There is no training centre in the village.	The training should be organised at the government and non-government level	NGO and *Zila Parishad.*
10. Problem of House		Indira Awas supports but all are not receiving.	All should be supported by Indira Awas.	

Table 7.4

Institutions in Village Gopalpur, Cooch Behar

Institutions	*Problem*	*Solution*
1. ICDS	• There is no ICDS worker. • The food distributed is not adequate and the quality is also not proper. • It has no room. • Many children do not go to ICDS. • The teaching is not proper.	• ICDS work should be appointed. • The amount of food to be increased. • The teaching of children should be managed. The villages should be provided the facility of ICDS.
2. Sakirta Siksha Samittee	It is closed. Adults do not want to go there.	
3. Primary School (I) Harnath Primary School. (II) Magora Burman Netaji Prathamik Vidyalaya.	The teaching is up to class IV. There is paucity of drinking water.	High school should be constructed.
4. VEC	-	-
5. Gramin Bank. (Jamaldah Branch)	• Only 100 HH out of 500 HH have received loan. • People cannot repay loan. • The manager visits only their HH for payment of loan.	The government should support.
6. Health Sub-Centre	Gives only white and yellow medicine e.g. Paracetamol and Depandal. Hence, the villagers go to private doctor by paying rupees 40.	The government can solve the problem.
7. *Gram Panchayat* and *Panchayat Samittee*	The village developmental plans are discussed in *Gram Samsad*. These are not known by the village.	Proper beneficiaries should be identified and supported by the government.

Table 7.5

Schemes Implemented in Village Gopalpur, Cooch Behar

Schemes	*For whom implemented*	*How it could be improved*	*Any new schemes*
1. Indira Awas	Proper persons have been supported.	There are many problems.	The amount of support to be increased.
2. Pond (SGRY)	For *Madhya bitto*	It should been constructed after consulting all villagers.	
3. Road Construction (SGRY)	For all villagers.	The road should be pitched.	
4. ICDS (SGRY)	For the poor.	The food distributed are not adequate.	
5. House			
6. Primary Health Centre	For the villagers.	There is no medicine, the worker is not available, does not reside in the village.	
7. Shishu Siksha Kendra	For boys and girls.	More workers are needed for proper service delivery.	
8. Well Construction	For the villagers (*Madhya bitto*)	If the wells are constructed near the agricultural land, irrigation can be done.	
9. Krishi Pension (one person)	Proper persons have been supported.	More persons should be supported. If pension is released monthly, it would be better.	If the amount is increased to Rs. 500.
10. Old Age Person (One person)	Proper persons have been supported.	More persons should be supported. If pension is released monthly, it would be better.	If it is increased more than 100 rupees, it will be better.

Village Participants: Women = 4, Men = 9.

Table 7.6

Problems (Women's Group)

Sl. No.	*Problems*	*Rank*	*Remarks*
1	Lack of toilet facilities.	1	Loss of vegetative cover has exacerbated the problem.
2	Lack of village and cottage industry.	6	Women have no work other than in agricultural season.
3	Absence of women's organisation.	2	Discrimination amongst women.
4	Illiteracy amongst women.	4	-
5	Problems of dowry.	3	It is on the rise amongst all groups.
6	Discrimination against girl children in some households.	5	-

Date: 17/05/2004.
Facilitator: Amitava Mukherjee
Number of Village Participants: Male: 2. Female: 14.

Table 7.7

History of Village Gopalpur, Cooch Behar

	1990	*1995*	*2000*	*2004*
1. Wage Rate	Rs. 5-6 meals and 1 kg rice	Rs. 7-8	Rs. 15-20.	Rs. 25-30
2. Rate of Rice per kg	Rs. 3-4 Rs. 16.	Rs. 6 -	Rs. 10-12 -	Rs. 10.00 Rs. 30.00
3. Amount of Meals	As the number of persons was less, the meals could be afforded in lower wage.	As the number of persons was less, the meals could be afforded in lower wage.	Population increased but work not increased.	Population increased but the work decreased.
4. Household Possessions	The straw dwelling was very small. A few persons had land.	A few had houses made of *khapra* (earthen tiles) roof.	The number of houses increased.	The number of houses increased.
5. Natural Calamities	Crops were damaged due to heavy rain, scanty and untimely rain.	Crops were damaged due to heavy rain, scanty and untimely rain.	Due to scanty rain, there was severe drought. Hail storm was also there.	Due to scanty rain, there was severe drought. Hail storm was also there.

contd. ...

...*contd.* ...

	1990	*1995*	*2000*	*2004*
6. Treatment	Medical facility was not in the village. Those who had money, used to go to another place for treatment.	Medical facility was not in the village. Those who had money, used to go to another place for treatment.	Health sub-centre was constructed in the village.	Health sub-centre was constructed in the village. Many people do not come to the centre.
7. Migration	Did not migrate because agricultural work was available.	Did not migrate because agricultural work was available.	The desire for migration initiated in order to get employment.	The desire to migrate is increasing.
8. Dowry System	Dowry was existent but not pervasive.	Increasing.	Increasing.	Increasing.
9. Respect for the Poor	Was more	Decreasing.	Decreasing.	Decreasing.
10. Agricultural Charge	Ordinarily paddy (*kolam*) and jute (*suti*) was cultivated.	High yielding cultivation started.	High yielding cultivation started.	Various types of paddy are cultivated.
11. Loan	The loan received was not more than Rs. 2000 for goat rearing or their works. The *Awastha Panna* were getting more.	The loan received was not more than Rs. 2000 for goat rearing or their works. The *Awastha Panna* were getting more.	Could not repay loan.	Who have repaid the loan are received under SGSY Scheme.
12. Social Net Capital	The road was *kuccha*.	The road was *kuccha*.	The road has been pitched.	The girls are going to school and bazaar by bicycle.
13. Toilet	No	No.	Under IAY can toilets have been constructed	A few more are being constructed.
14. Livelihood Problem	There was severe problem.	There was several problems but people consume rice, *roti* and *khudi* rice.	Consumed rice.	The food problem had reduced.

Village Participants: Male = 9.

Table 7.8

Seasonality of Poverty in Village Gopalpur, Cooch Behar

	Baisakh	*Jaisthya*	*Asardh*	*Srabon*	*Bhadro*	*Aswin*	*Kartik*	*Aghrayan*	*Poush*	*Magh*	*Falgun*	*Chaitra*
Good months								Paddy cultivation *Pat* cultivation.			Cultivation of potato	
Pat cultivation.												
Crises months (*Abhaber* months)	There is no work in the village											
Acute scarcity					There is no work.							
More Expenditure								Purchasing winter garments.				
Income								Daily wage labour is available.				
Health problem	Diarrhoea, *Amasa*, fever.				Fever and diarrhoea affect children more.							
Festival							Durga puja, Kali puja			Anukul Jhakun	Baroni puja	Dol purnima.

Table 7.9

Decision Matrix: Men and Women

Major Decisions of Households	*Decisions Taken by Men (M)*	*Decisions Taken by Women (M)*	*Decisions Taken Jointly*	*Who has Major Role (M vs. W)*
What clothes to wear—(Expenditure).	✓	✓		✓ M
The quality of food to eat.	✓	✓	✓	✓ M
Repair of houses and rarely buying and construction of house.	✓			✓M
Education of children.			✓	✓ M
Child immunisation.	✓	✓		✓W
Practice of "Family Operation".	✓			✓ M
Voting in elections.	✓	✓		✓ M
Sale of household produce.	✓			✓ M
Festival and visit to 'fairs'.			✓	✓ W
Keeping money.	✓			✓ M
Children's marriage.	✓		✓	✓ W M

Chart 1

Chart 2

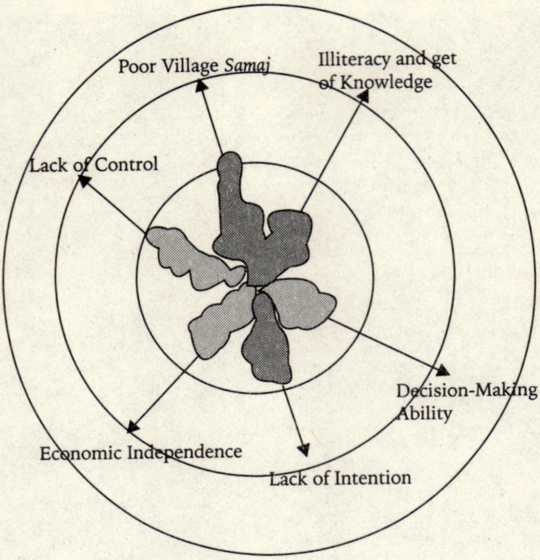
Poor Village *Samaj*
Illiteracy and get of Knowledge
Lack of Control
Decision-Making Ability
Economic Independence
Lack of Intention

Chart 3

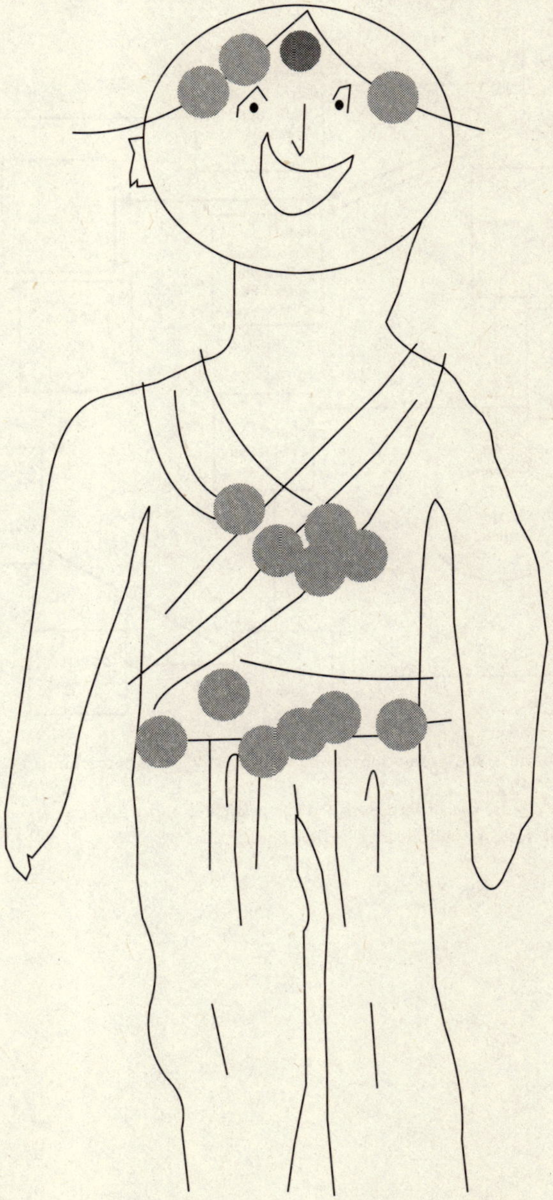

Figure 7.1

Flow Diagram of Development Process in Ratherhat

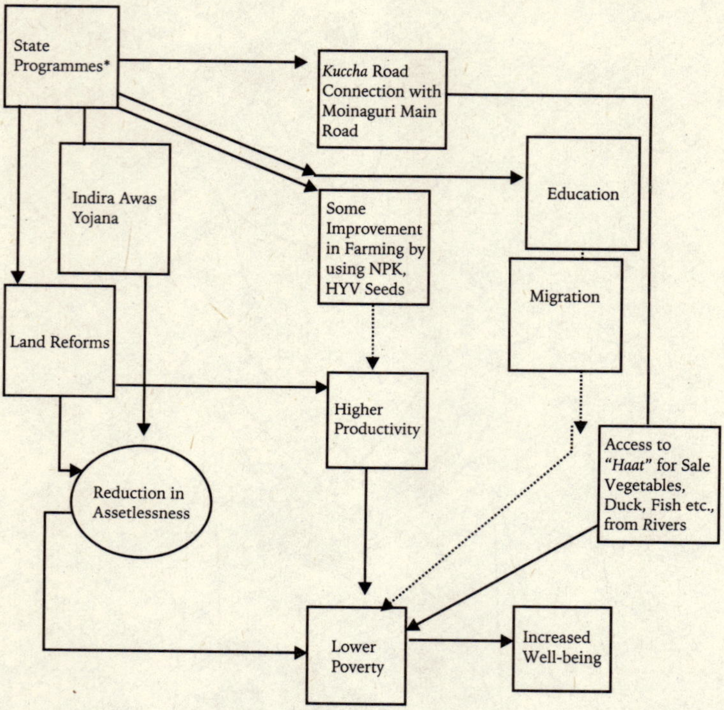

Note: *Land reform; some promotion of the use of HYV seeds, etc.; housing under IAY and road connectivity.

** HYV seeds, use of fertilisers (NPK), pesticides and irrigation.

Weak force is indicated by broken line ....

Figure 7.2

Flow Diagram for Gopalpur

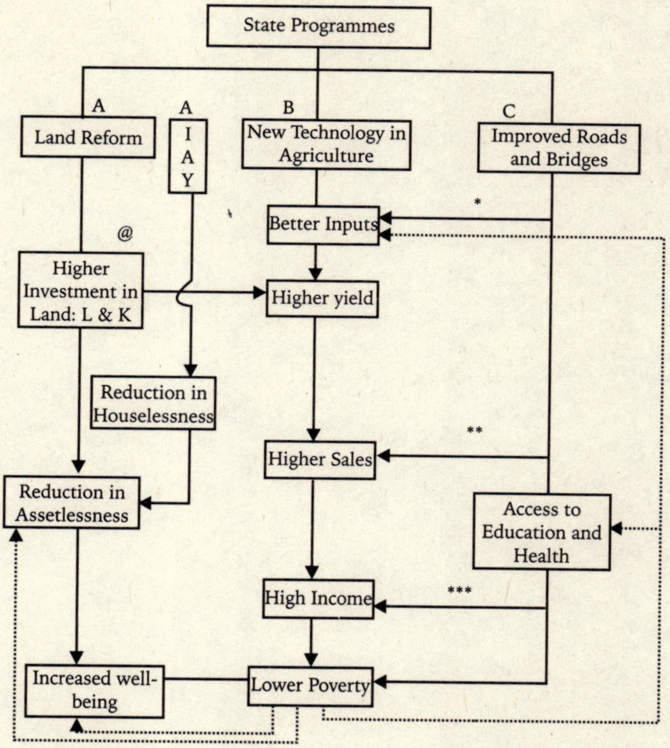

Punch Lines

- Ö State works!
- Ö Long-term meaures yield sustainable results
- Ö The cost of diesel works as an involunatary rationing of water use.

*		Ease in bringing and information from Baneswar and Block
**		Ease in Marketing Surplus Produce
***		For source.
A,B,C	=	Long-term measures.
@	=	Large landlords do not cultivate well because they have hired labour.

8

Global Concerns

Loss in Biodiversity and its Impact on Agriculture Assessed Through Participatory Methods

Deal with things in their state of not-yet-being,
Put them in order before they have got into confusion,
For the 'Tree Big as Man's Embrace' began as a tiny sprout,
The tower nine storeys high began with a heap of earth.

—*Lao Zi in Dao De Jing*

Introduction

Agriculture supports a huge number of people round the globe. However, the kinds of agriculture that support people vary from region to region. Fundamentally there are three systems of agriculture that support people worldwide. In the industrialised countries of the OECD and eastern Europe, some 1.2 billion people are supported by agriculture relying heavily on external inputs, or what has been called high external input agriculture (HEIA). In these regions, agriculture is highly productive, but also too often degrades and damages natural resources.

In the countries of the Third World, some 2.3-2.6 billion people are supported by agricultural systems characterised by modern technologies brought by the Green Revolution, characterised by high-yielding cereal varieties which, when cultivated with modern fertilisers and pesticides, transformed many agricultural systems, or what has been called Green Revolution agriculture. These systems have good soils and reliable water, and are close to roads, markets and input supplies. Plains of Punjab, Haryana and western Uttar Pradesh are representative of such agriculture. The area of these lands is some 215 million ha, and they currently produce 60 per cent of the grain in Third World countries.

Once we net out these types of agriculture, some 1.9-2.2 billion people are left out largely untouched by modern technology. Much of these people tend to be in the poorer countries which has no—or little if at all—capacity to buy external inputs for agriculture such as fertilisers, pesticides and insecticides, from the outside world. The agricultural systems in these areas are complex and diverse, and are in the humid and semi-humid lowlands, the hills and mountains, and the drylands afflicted perpetually by the vagaries of nature, more particularly uncertainty of rainfall. Rajasthan, Madhya Pradesh and parts of Uttar Pradesh in India are typical examples of such agriculture. They are remote from services and roads, and they commonly produce one-fifth to one-tenth as much food per hectare as farms in the industrialised and Green Revolution lands.

First Stage Loss in Biodiversity: The Record of Modernised Agriculture

The impact of modern agriculture has been astounding with about half of the rice, wheat and maize areas in the Third World countries planted by modern varieties. This has resulted in fertiliser and pesticide consumption growing rapidly. Nitrogen consumption, for example, increased from 2 to 75 million tonnes between 1950 and 1997, and pesticide consumption in many individual countries has increased by 10-30 per cent during the 1980s alone. Farmers have intensified their use of external resources and expanded into previously uncultivated lands. As a result, food production per capita has, since the mid-1960s, risen by 7 per cent for the world as a whole, with greatest increases, according to a FAO estimate, in Asia, where per capita food production has grown by about 40 per cent.

Between 70-90 per cent of the recent increases in production have been due to increased yields rather than greater area under agriculture (World Bank, 1993). This has been described by Donald Plunkett (1993), scientific adviser to the CGIAR, as "the greatest agricultural transformation in the history of humankind, and most of it has taken place during our lifetime. The change was brought about by the rise of science-based agriculture which permitted higher and more stable food production, ensuring food stability and security for a constantly growing world population" (As quoted in Elwell, 2007).

However, agricultural modernisation has transformed many rural communities, both in the developing and industrialised countries, which is seen by large sections of the population as being injurious to general welfare and well-being. The process has had many impacts, through events which include the loss of jobs, the further economic disadvantaging of women where they do not have access to the use and benefits of the new technology, the increasing specialisation of livelihoods, the expanding gap between the rich and the poor, and the co-option of village institutions by the state.

A second major problem of modernised agriculture is that benefits flowing from it have been poorly distributed. Many people have missed out and hunger still persists in many parts of the world. The situation is best typified by India, which produces nearly 206 million tonnes of food and has in store something of the order of 32 million tonnes of food in government godowns rotting, yet hundreds of millions of people suffer from hunger in some degree or the other, and millions face the prospect of starvation in large parts of the country.

In Africa food production per capita fell by 20 per cent between 1964-1992. According to estimates by the international agencies like FAO, WHO and the Hunger Project around 1 billion people in the world have food consumption that is energy deficient for work. Of these, an estimated 480 million live in households "too poor to obtain the energy required for healthy growth of children and minimal activity of adults" (Hunger Project, 1991).

The final problem with modern agriculture is where production has been improved through modern technologies, often there have been concomitant adverse impacts on environment and biodiversity, which include, but are not restricted to:

- Contamination of water by pesticides, insecticides, nitrates, soil and livestock wastes, causing harm to wildlife, disruption of ecosystems and the consequent damage to biodiversity.
- Contamination of water by pesticides, insecticides, nitrates, soil and livestock wastes leading to deterioration in the quality of drinking water and harming human health.
- Contamination of foods and fodder by residues of insecticides, pesticides, nitrates and antibiotics endangering food safety.
- Damage to farm and natural resources by insecticides, pesticides, etc., causing harm to farm workers in particular and the public in general, disruption of ecosystems and harm to wildlife, causing loss to biodiversity.
- Contamination of the atmosphere by ammonia, nitrous oxide, methane and the products of burning, which play a role in ozone depletion, global warming and atmospheric pollution.
- Overuse of natural resources, causing depletion of groundwater, and loss of wild foods and habitats (and of their capacity to discharge their sink function, causing water logging and increased salinity) resulting in damage to biodiversity.
- The tendency in agriculture to standardise and specialise by focusing on modern varieties, causing the displacement of traditional varieties and breeds leading to loss in biodiversity.

The last effect warrants a few comments. The introduction of modern varieties and breeds has almost always displaced traditional varieties and breeds. During the twentieth century, some 75 per cent of the genetic diversity of agricultural crops has been lost. Only about 150 plant species are now cultivated, of which just 3 supply almost 60 per cent of calories derived from plants downwards in many countries. In India, where once more than 30,000 rice varieties were grown, now just 10 cover 75 per cent of the whole area under rice. Fowler and Mooney (1990) carried out a comprehensive study on biodiversity in the USA during the last century. For 65 types of vegetable, they record a consistent loss of between 80-100 per cent of the varieties of each during the last century. Of the 8207 varieties listed for these vegetables in 1903, only 607 are now held by the National Seed Storage Laboratory.

Most modern scientists have seen mixture as a problem to be overcome. Rockefeller sponsored a team of experts to assess wheat cultivation as a precursor to establishing the national wheat-breeding programme in Mexico in the 1940s. The low yielding traditional fields were condemned by the team after their first visit. They maintained that because "most fields were a mix of many different types, tall and short, bearded and beardless, early ripening and late ripening, fields usually ripened so unevenly that it was impossible to harvest them at one time without losing too much over-ripe grain or including too much under-ripe grain in the harvests" (Stakman *et al.*, 1967). These mixtures of traditional varieties may have lower yield. But yield is not the only yardstick with which to judge a farming or agricultural system. Mixtures of different types of crops not only insures the farmers from pest, insect and disease attack but also provide higher output since output from mixtures of different crops are higher than the output of a single crop, though yield from a single crop in a mixed cropping agriculture may be lower than the yield from a single or two crop agriculture. The variable to look at for judging agriculture is not yield *per se*, but the output. The team failed to make this vital distinction between output and yield and hence see the benefits of growing a mixture of traditional varieties of crop instead of just one or two crops. Modern wheat varieties introduced in Mexico in the 1940s and 1950s were soon susceptible to new races of rust, and were quickly overcome.

Similar experience during rice modernisation in Asia, considerably buttress the findings in Mexico. For example, in Central Luzon, in the Philippines, 25 varieties of traditional rice were grown in the mid-1960s. By 1980, the total number of rice varieties cultivated had fallen only to 19, of which only just 2 were traditional varieties (Cordova, Gascon and Yambao, 1981), and now an estimated 95 per cent of the rice cultivation plants modern varieties. In the early part of the 20th century, USA had a mixture of wheat and oats, oats and barley, sorghum and alfalfa, maize and soybean (Bussell, 1937; Bailey, 1994). Farmers in the US today grow all these as mainly mono-crop farming. The incentive structures provided by cheap and available inputs have encouraged farmers to specialise abandoning their time tested mixed cropping patterns. Indeed in some countries, farmers have even been forbidden by law from growing traditional varieties and reportedly traditional crops were either burned or destroyed (Soetrisna, 1982).

These are significant losses of genetic diversity and with such loss, humankind could have lost future opportunities as well. Crops or livestock that are locally adapted are at times critical in dealing with the challenges posed by pests, insects or diseases. During the 1970s, the Grassy-Stunt Virus devastated rice from India to Indonesia and it took scientists almost four years to find a solution to the problem in terms of a disease resistant rice, and screen over 17,000 cultivated and wild rice samples before a disease resistance was found. One population of the wild species, *Oreyza Nivara*, growing near Gonda in Uttar Pradesh, was found to have a single gene for resistance to Grassy-Stunt Virus Stain 1. Today, resistant rice hybrids containing the wild Indian gene are grown across some 110,000 square km of Asian rice fields (FAO, 1993). Genetic erosion, the reduction of diversity within a species, is a global threat to agriculture.

Table 8.1 gives a summary of the loss of diversity seen in different parts of the world.

Despite these problems, many scientists and policy makers still argue vigorously that modern agriculture, characterised by externally developed packages of technologies that rely on externally produced inputs, is the best, and probably the only road to agricultural development. Table 8.2 contains a sample of the types of perspectives brought by leading experts and institutions to debates on the future of agricultural development that support modernist, high-external input themes. These perspectives point out that the route to agricultural production is through modern agricultural practices involving deployment of high external inputs. Some experts, such as the Nobel Laureate, Norman Borlaug himself, have gone so far as to suggest that all alternatives to modern agriculture have to be put down and even suggesting that the claims made on behalf of alternative or sustainable agriculture are suspect.

The reason why this is so is perhaps because there is a comparison between traditional agriculture and HEIA on the basis of yield. The protagonists of Green Revolution and industrial agriculture (which we are calling modern agriculture) to establish that productivity in the paradigm of modern agriculture is higher than in traditional agriculture. Without going into the myriad of data on the subject, it is important to recognise, first, that the dominant productivity calculus of the modern agriculture paradigm is not cognisant of the environmental costs and benefits of the different agricultural practices, and the full economic costs and benefits that go with different agricultural systems. Second, the dominant productivity paradigm only measures partial outputs, which have a commercial value for dominant interests and financial incomes derived from partial outputs. Third, the productivity paradigm does not fully reflect the additional financial costs when agricultural practices shift from low internal input (LEISA) to high external input agriculture (HEISA).

The dominant productivity paradigm has the modern plant breeding concepts like HYV at its heart, which reduces farming systems to individual crops and parts of crops, and then compares the productivity of crops. Table 8.3 below helps illustrate the point.

Table 8.1

Decline in Diversity of Crops and Livestock in a Selection of Locations

India	Once more than 30,000 rice varieties grown; now expected that just 10 rice varieties will soon cover 75 per cent of rice area.
The Philippines	Before the modernisation of early 1970s, 3500 varieties of rice existed; now only 3-5 are grown in irrigated areas.
Europe	Half of all the breeds of domestic animals (horses, cattle, sheep, goats, pigs and poultry) have become extinct since the beginning of the 20th century; a third of the remaining 770 breeds are in danger of disappearing by 2010.
France	71 per cent of apple production from one variety, Golden Delicious; 30 per cent of bread wheat from 2 varieties and 70 per cent from 10 varieties; in the SE, the Provincial diet contained 250 plant species at the beginning of 20th century; now it comprises only 30-60.
Greece	95 per cent of local wheat varieties lost since 1920s.
The Netherlands	A single potato variety covers 80 per cent of potato land;
	90 per cent of wheat planted to 3 varieties;
	75 per cent of barley planted to 1 variety.
UK	68 per cent of early potatoes planted to 3 varieties;
	4 wheat varieties account for 71 per cent of wheat area.
USA	Since 1900:
	6121 apple varieties lost (85 per cent)
	2354 pear varieties lost (88 per cent)
	546 garden pea varieties lost (95 per cent)
	516 cabbage varieties lost (95 per cent)
	394 field maize varieties lost (91 per cent)
	383 pea varieties lost (94 per cent)
	329 tomato varieties lost (81 per cent)
	295 sweet corn varieties lost (96 per cent)
	Now:
	71 per cent maize area planted to 6 varieties
	96 per cent pea area planted to 2 varieties
	65 per cent rice area planted to 4 varieties
	76 per cent snap bean area planted to 3 varieties

Source: Pretty, 1995.

Table 8.2

Modernist Perspectives on Future Strategies for Agricultural Development

Technical Assistance Committee of the CGIAR (1988):

Indigenous farm populations have learned to manage their systems quite efficiently, making it difficult to increase their production without resort to external inputs.

FAO (1991):

It seems likely that much of the growth in agricultural production will take place through increased use of external inputs.

Norman Borlaug, the Nobel Laureate (1992):

Some agricultural professionals contend that small-scale subsistence producers can be lifted out of poverty without the use of purchased inputs, such as modern crop varieties, fertiliser and agricultural chemicals. They recommend, instead, the adoption of so-called 'sustainable' technologies that do not require fertilisers and improved varieties. The advent of cheap and plentiful fertilisers has been one of the great agricultural breakthroughs of humankind. The adoption of science—based agricultural technologies is crucial to slowing—and even reversing—Africa's environmental meltdown.

Norman Borlaug, the Nobel Laureate (1992):

Development specialists must stop 'romanticising' the virtues of traditional agriculture in the Third World. Moreover, leaders in developing countries must not be duped into believing that future food requirements can be met through continuing reliance on the new complicated and sophisticated `low-input, low-output' technologies that are impractical for the farmers to adopt.

International Fertiliser Development Center (1992):

Higher yields per hectare produced by fertilisers will be the most persuasive argument to coax developing country farmers to abandon their environmentally destructive farming practices.

The World Bank (1993):

Experience such as obtained with the Green Revolution in parts of Asia has shown that broad-based agricultural growth, involving small and medium sized farms and driven by productivity-enhancing technological change, offers the only way to create productive employment and alleviate poverty on the scale required.

FAO (1993a):

When managed well, external inputs can lead to greater yields and improved nutrient content. This reduces the pressure to convert land to agriculture and improves food security. Few developing countries can therefore, afford to forgo the benefits of external inputs. Used incorrectly, however, they can result in environmental pollution, threats to human and animal health, greater volatility in production levels, and reduced production and incomes.

Source: Pretty, 1995.

If we look at Table 8.3, it is apparent that for a fair account, the real scientific comparisons should be between the two farming systems, FS1 and FS2, with the full range of inputs and outputs included. This is often not done because FS2 is given by the immunity from ecological evaluations. Thus, only PC1 is compared with PC2 and the conclusion is arrived at that FS2 has higher productivity and hence better than PC1 under FS1. The comparison should be between FS1 and FS2 as a whole. It will then be apparent that while PC2 > PC1, FS1 > FS2. And when FS1 is taken as the dominant paradigm, it is sustainable *vis-à-vis* the inherent unsustainability of any system which is highly dependent upon external inputs.

When FS1 is compared to FS2, only then is crop components of one system measured with crop component of another system. Since modern agriculture increases the output of a single component of a farm, irrespective of what happens to other components of the output and increasing external inputs, it has to inherent bias of making the new agricultural system as generating higher yield, when actually that is not the case at the systems level. In contrast, traditional farming system, based on mixed and rotational cropping system of producing cereals, pulses, oilseeds with diverse varieties of each crop as against uniform monocultures of the modern agriculture system. No realistic assessment are made of the yield of the diverse crop outputs in the mixed and rotational systems. Usually the yield of a single crop like wheat, rice or maize of the traditional system is compared with yields of these crops of new varieties. The comparisons are not flawless and hence the results certainly needs midway corrections.

Table 8.3

Comparison of Traditional and Modern Agriculture

Traditional Farming System (FS1)	Modern Farming System (FS2)
Mixed Farming System	Green Revolution Mono culture
Diverse crops of cereals, pulses, millets, nuts, oilseed etc.	Cereals crops of wheat or rice
Reduced to	Reduced to
Part of Crop: PC1 (GRAIN)	Parts of Crop: PC2 (GRAIN)

Source: Shiva, 1995.

The fact that the distinction between total output and total yield is important is best substantiated by the analysis of Fransica Bray which is depicted as Figures 8.1 and 8.2.

Assuming for the purpose of argument, though not accepting, that yields from all crops are included in a comparison of the two systems and it is found that total yield from modern agriculture of new varieties is higher than the total yields from all crops in the traditional system of agriculture, even then the comparison cannot give a true and fair account of yield. The reasons are not far to seek. It is difficult for example, to convert a measure of wheat, because in human diet and in the ecosystem they have different contributions to make. The protein value of pulses and the calorific value of cereals are both essential for nutrition security but in different ways, and one cannot replace the other. Similarly the nitrogen fixing capacity of pulses is an invisible ecological contribution to the yield of associated cereals. The complex and diverse cropping systems which are based on indigenous varieties are, therefore, not easily comparable to the simplified monocultures of modern agriculture propagated under the currently dominant paradigm. Any comparison of the two systems must involve entire systems of the two paradigms and cannot be restricted to a comparison of a fragment of the farming system, *viz.*, yield of a crop or two crops.

What has Happened in India: Voices of the Farmers[1]

The Case of Chandpur

The kinds and number of crops grown in Chandpur have changed over time. While in the 40s, the principal crops were barley, *bare, sawa,* sugarcane and vegetables, during the 50s wheat, paddy, peas, Bengal gram, maize and red gram, began to be cultivated, and cultivation of barley and sugarcane was discontinued. That is, there was a diversification in production, between the 1940s and the 1950s. From the 1960s, this diversification lost its sway and the number of crops being cultivated got reduced to Paddy and wheat besides vegetables. The trend continues till today, through the 1970s and 1980s. The cropping pattern has, therefore, seen substantial changes over the years but has stabilised during the 1990s. The transect at Table 8.4 is revealing.

Interestingly, while the cropping pattern was changing, the yield was also changing. The yield increased quite dramatically during the 1960s and then again fell during the 1970s, and continued at that level throughout the 1980s and 1990s. In 1988 there was a sharp drop in yield both for paddy and for wheat. Though the yields in the 1988 were higher than those obtaining in the 1950s, it is a cause for concern, unless one is prepared to treat it as an aberration.

Why have the changes taken place?

We are reviewing a period in our economic history which saw rapid changes in every direction. Changes were many and some with quite far reaching consequences, such as mechanisation of agriculture and the introduction of "new technology", to which we made a brief reference above. A tentative answer to the questions relating to changes in cropping pattern and yield in Chandpur is best provided by timeline drawn by the senior citizens of Naipurwa Hamlet of Chandpur village which bears repetition here as Table 8.5.

1. (Mukherjee, 2001)

Table 8.4

Historical Transect of Main Crops and their Yield in Naipurwa Hamlet, Chandpur Village

By Men's Group

Decade	*Principal Crops*	*Yield (Quintal/acre)*
1940s	Barley, *bare,*	04
	Sawa,	0.5
	Sugarcane,	
	Vegetables	
1950s	Wheat,	3.5-4
	Paddy,	3.5-4
	Peas,	2.4-2.5
	Bengal Gram,	2.4-2.5
	Red Gram,	3.5-4
	Maize	2.4-2.5
	Barley discontinued	
1960s	Wheat,	16-18
	Paddy	16-18
	Vegetables	
1970s	Wheat,	10
	Paddy	10-12
	Vegetables	
1980s	Wheat,	10
	Paddy	10-12
	Vegetables	
1990s	Wheat,	10
	Paddy	10-12
	Vegetables	
1998	Wheat,	10
	Paddy	08
	Vegetables	

Village Analysts: Mohan Patel, Rajendra Prasad, Dhanilal, Shyamdayal Patel.

Facilitator: Ms. Meera Jayaswal.

In the 1960s, new variety of seeds came, improved variety of wheat was introduced, lift irrigation through pumpsets and electrification of the pumpsets commenced. There was a sharp rise in productivity in wheat and paddy as we saw in Table 8.4 earlier. This sharp rise in productivity in wheat and paddy during the 1960s, was clearly due to the introduction of new varieties of seeds as also the introduction of pumpsets for irrigation. This also marked a significant change in the mindset of the people depending on the sky for succour. Thus, not only did they resort to improved variety of wheat and paddy seeds, as opposed to traditional varieties of seeds, but also shifted their dependence from "Rain gods" to their own ingenuity of making water available through pump irrigation. The use of chemical fertilisers also started. However, after the initial spurt in yield due to "new technology", in the 1960s, the yield fell as the chemical composition of the soil changed, no further improved varieties of seed were introduced and the extension work could not keep pace with changing times. The initial spurt during the 1960s in much higher yields was lost during the 1970s and in the subsequent decades. The use of HYV seeds, chemical fertilisers and pesticides etc., has adverse consequence which, has been noticed in several parts of the country.

Table 8.5

Time Line: Historical Events as Recalled by the Senior Men of Naipurwa Hamlet of Chandpur Village

Decade	*Year*	*Events*
1940s	1942	Food in River Baruna; bridge washed away
	1947	India wins Independence
	1947	Single Stage coach started from Vitari to Morai
1950s	1950-51	Locust attack
	1959-60	Transportation by truck started.
	1959-60	Birdi making unit started
	1959-60	Reinforced Concrete Construction (RCC) of houses started
1960s	1962	New varieties of seeds introduced
	1964	New wheat variety (RR21) started
	1969	Electric supply started. 2-3 pumpsets introduced.
1970s	1972-73	Tractor introduced
	1975	Four new pumpsets introduced
	1975	Sardar Ballab Bhai Cross Road (Chaumahani) constructed
	1976	Torrential rain leading to damage of crops (in November-December) which lasted for 7 days
1980s	1981(?)	Rudrax Garland Making Unit started
1990s	1990	School constructed

Village Analysts: Mohan Patel, Rajendra Prasad Singh, Dhanilal, Shamdayal Patel.
Facilitator: Ms. Meera Jayaswal.
Date: 11.11.98.

It is to be noted that the variety in principal crops in Chandpur has come down to three or so, because of major shifts in yields in other crops. Green peas, for instance, used to be grown earlier with traditional variety of seeds but with the introduction of improved variety of seeds, the productivity fell so dramatically that the villagers abandoned the crop altogether. The production of *jowar* has stopped because it has been replaced by a cash crop, namely, cauliflower. *Jowar* gets ready for harvest in October-November, if it is sown in August, whereas cauliflower seedlings have to be planted in September-October. Since income from growing cauliflower is much higher than what *jowar* could provide, villagers have opted for the former. Cultivation of lentil (*arhar*) has been almost abandoned since last 10-12 years because of its high vulnerability to pest attack and also because the same land on which *arhar* used to be cultivated competed with wheat as a crop. Given that people have incentive for growing wheat from the government's support price and procurement price, which was not available for growing *arhar*, it got pushed out.

The Case in Tikri

The kinds and number of crops grown in Tikri have changed over time just as in Chandpur. It is important to put in perspective the general socio-economic and political changes that have been faced by the villagers in Tikri, to better appreciate the changes in cropping pattern and agricultural practices. The historical transect by the villagers of Mahato Basti which is reproduced as Table 8.6, gives a graphic account of these changes.

In the 60 years covered by the historical transects in Tables 8.6 and 8.7, Tikri has seen major changes generally and in the agricultural sector in particular. Because agriculture became HEIA, yield, income and cost of cultivation became the dominant determinants in deciding what crops would be chosen for cultivation; not taste, not cultural acceptability, not nutritional value, not staying power, not even tradition. There are five phases in the cropping pattern:

(a) Through most of the 1940s and 1950s a wide range of crops were grown: *bajra*, barley, some paddy, some wheat, grams, chillies, peas and the like. There was an unfailing sign of poly-culture and crop diversity.

(b) In the 1960s, the "new-technology" in agriculture had its influence on Tikri and cultivation of wheat and paddy was increased, and other crops slipped down the ladder of importance. Vegetable cultivation was carried out for sale in the adjoining towns and not for consumption at the household level.

(c) Then came the 1970s, when again a wide variety of crops (barley, chilli, pigeon peas, grams, pea, *bajra* and sunui) came to be cultivated. Wheat was cultivated but on a limited scale. Again productivity remained at about the same level as was the case in 1960s.

(d) By the time we came to the 1980s, intensive cultivation of wheat had begun and cultivation of barley, chilli, peas and grams fell considerably. This had the villagers explained, was because the use of fertilisers, rendered the soil unsuitable for cultivating these crops. The non-existence of improved variety of seeds in some of crops, such as barley, led to a reduction in farming them. And then the predatory attacks by the *Nilgais* made life for those farmers who cultivated these crops somewhat more difficult.

(e) In the 1990s, wheat became the dominant crop and those vegetables which had higher commercial value, such as cauliflowers, potatoes, onion, and *ninwa* (a kind of ridge gourd) came to be included in the cropping pattern, to the exclusion of others. *Jowar* was still cultivated, but for fodder.

Table 8.6

Time Line: Historical Events as Recalled by Men of Mahato Basti of Tikri Village

Period	*Events*	*Cropping Pattern*	*Agricultural Practices*	*Yield Per Bigha*
1940s	Flood in the village	*Bajra*, barley, paddy (in limited quantity), wheat (in limited quantity), gram, peas & chilli (as specialisation).	Ploughing by ox. Irrigation by moat. Organic manure in use. Traditional seeds used.	Yield 4-5 *maunds* per *Bigha*
1950s	Middle School started	Same as in 1940s	Aluminum sulphate introduced. Tubewell installed for irrigation.	Yield 8-10 *maund* per *Bigha*
1960s	Brick Houses constructed	Increased wheat and paddy. Cultivation of vegetables like potatoes started	Irrigation by Pumpsets. Fertilisers, new-Hybrid seeds and Pesticides introduced. Tractors came.	Same as in 1950s
1970s	Irrigation canal constructed. Washed away by floods.	*Moong*, barley, peas, grams, chillies, pigeon peas, *bajra* and *sunui* dominated cultivation. Wheat as second fiddle.	Same as in the 1960s.	Same as in 1960s
1980s	Outbreak of measles. Increase in fertiliser use. Famine in 1986-1987. Bank opened	Intensive wheat cultivation overtakes all other crops. Cultivation of *moong*, barley, gram, peas and chilli reduced.	Same as in the 1970s.	Yield 10-15 *maunds* per *Bigha*
1990s	1995: Vaccination on mass scale. Girl's School started. 1997: Metalled Roads laid. 1998: Hails before Diwali	Wheat, peas, potatoes, paddy, *ninua* (snake gourd), cauliflower, tomatoes etc. *Jowar* cultivated as fodder.	Same as in the 1980s. Weedicides introduced in the farming of wheat.	12-14 *maund* for wheat. 10-12 *maunds* for paddy

***Note:* that these are the major constraints indicated by the farmers. There are other constraints which they narrated during the analysis and prioritisation of agricultural constraints.

Village Analysts: Pratap Narain, Hiralal, Radheysham, Ramesh Kumar Patel, Bahadur Patel, Munnalal, Ashok, Krishan.

Facilitator: Sudipta Roy.

Dates: 2.11.98 and 8.11.98.

Table 8.7

Historical Transect of Main Crops and their Yield (Maunds/Acre) in Tikri Village

Main Crops	*1940s*	*1950s*	*1960s*	*1970s*	*1980s*	*1990s*
Monsoon (*Kharif*) Crops						
Paddy	10	10	20	40	45	50
Maize	30	40	40	50	50	40
Pearl Millet (*bajra*)	10	10	20	25	20	15
Red Gram (*arhar*)	12	12	12	6	3	1
Green Gram (*moong*)	5	5	10	--	--	--
Urad	5	5	10	--	--	--
Kodo	5	5	10	--	--	--
Utalia	5	5	--	--	--	--
Winter Crops (*Rabi*)						
Wheat	10	10	20	45	45	50
Barley	10	10	5	--	--	--
Bengal Gram	10	10	5	--	--	--
Bare	10	10	5	--	--	--
Peas	10	10	5	2	--	--
Alsi	2	2	2	--	--	--
Mustard	3	3	3	2	1	0.50

Village Analysts: Pannalal, Kanhaiyalal, Laxman Mourya, Musseram and Chhatanki.
Facilitator: Meera Jayaswal.
Date: 6.11.99.

Clearly there has been changes both in terms of diversity and yield. The number of *Rabi* (winter) crops got reduced to two in the 1990s, from seven in the 1940s, 1950s and 1960s. It came down initially to three in the 1970s and then from the 80s it got to two. Similarly, in case of *Kharif* crops, from a basket of eight crops grown in 1940s, by the time Tikri reached the 70s, the basket had only four crops, a pattern that continues till today. Similarly with vegetables, only potatoes are grown as the main vegetable. Reduction in crop diversity means that distribution of risk has also shrunk and the vulnerability of the farmers to natural or man made calamity has increased. It has led to the abandonment of several time tested practices known to the community such as crop rotation which is possible when a large number of and different kinds of crops are grown, for restoration of soil vitality and reduce the risk of failure (See Murakami, 1991; Wijewardene and Waidyantha, 1994).

Prior to the 1960s, (pre-new-technology or "Green Revolution" days), the villagers explained, they practised crop rotation, field rotation, mixed cropping, rotational grazing and applied green manure to ensure better yield from farming. Field rotation and rotational grazing were complementary activities: fields were left fallow deliberately for restoring nutritional strength of the soil and allowing animals to graze on fallow fields, a process which also naturally manured the fields from animal droppings. Depending on the nature of the crops, farmers cultivated crops in a series sequence to ensure that subsequent crop replenished nutrients used by the earlier one. And in some cases, crops were cultivated concurrently in the same field for reasons similar to crop rotation. For instance, mustard and wheat were farmed concurrently. Grass was grown in the arable areas, to be ploughed back into the same fields to manure them. After the 1960s (post-new-technology or "Green Revolution" days), these systems lost out to the use of chemical fertilisers, improved variety of seeds etc.

The Case of Khadaoli

Changes are agriculture in Kadhaoli has to be viewed in the larger context of other changes that were taking place in Kadhaoli over the years. The historical transect by men's group in Aat Bisa puts all the changes in Kadhaoli in total perspective. Reference is invited to Tables 8.8 and 8.9.

Let us take 1950s as the point of departure. In 1950s, a large number of crops were cultivated, though the villagers did not specify on what percentage of arable land each crop was grown. The crops were a mixture of staple, coarse cereals, lentils, pulses and condiments and sugarcane (for jaggery). The main crops were coarse grains (barley and *bajra*) and grams. Most of the crops grown were for consumption in the households in the village. By growing this diverse mosaic of crops, the farmers not only diffused their risk of failure, on account of pests, insects, drought, flood, disease or whatever, but also ensured that their households consumed a basket of food which contained fibre, nutrition and protein: carbohydrates, cereals and pulses.

In the 1960s, winds of change had begun to hit Kadhaoli. Some of the crops started being looked at with less of interest. Wheat, horse bean and sesamum got pushed out a bit. By the time Kadhaoli reached 1970s, wheat was back with a vengeance, paddy was introduced, but several of the other crops fell by the way side. As of now (1990s) farmers in Kadhaoli are left with wheat, a dash of mustard, and some vegetables like cauliflower and radish, as principal *Rabi* crops. During *Kharif* paddy constitutes the main crop, with bits of *bajra, moong, arhar, dhencha* and sesamum. *Jowar* is grown for fodder.

Uncha Gaon and Agricultural Practices that have taken Place

The group of men who met us in Unchagaon told us an interesting story. We first prodded them to recall the significant events of their lives over the last 50 years or so. The group responded remarkably well and told us that in the 1940s the wells were *kuccha* (unbricked), India won Independence and Punjabi Refugees from Pakistan were allotted land in Faridabad for resettlement and rehabilitation. In the 1950s, they recalled, the *kuccha* wells were all brick laid as the government gave incentives for doing so and Bata Shoe factory came to be established. In the 1960s, tractor and electricity were first used in cultivation, and fertilisers were used too. It was not until the 70s that the

HYV seeds came to Uncha Gaon. They then went about drawing the historical transect at Tables 8.10 and 8.11.

Table 8.8

Historical Transect by Men's Group in Aat Bisa, Khadhaoli

Decade	*Occupational Structure*	*Industrial Establishment*	*Farming System*	*Cropping Pattern*
1940	99% in agriculture and rest in traditional caste related occupation	Nil	Irrigation with bullock and *rehant*; manure; ploughing with bullocks; rainfed; traditional harvesting; seeds from own field.	Barley and gram as main crops. *Jowar, bajra, moong, arhar*, sugarcane, pulses, *chora*, mustard; sesamum, horse bean.
1950	98.5% in agriculture and others as in the 1940s	Escort and Bata	Same as in 1940s.	Barley and gram main crops. *Jowar, bajra, moong, arhar,* sugarcane, pulses, *chora*, mustard; sesamum, horse bean.
1960	98% in agriculture and others in private service/ non-agricultural labour		Manure and traditional seeds continue. Electrification leads to use of tubewells for irrigation. Tractors used for ploughing and harvesting.	Barley and gram as main crops but area under wheat fell. *Jowar, bajra, moong, arhar,* sugarcane, pulses, *chora* and mustard. Area under sesamum and horse bean reduced.
1970	90% in agriculture; 40% in milk business; 7% works as labourers; 1% in government service; 2% in private service		Fertiliser; hybrid seeds; electricity use for tubewells to irrigate. Tractors used for ploughing and harvesting. Insecticides and pesticides formed part of inputs.	Wheat cultivation increased. Gram discontinued. Paddy and *jowar* introduced.
1980	85% in agriculture; 50% in milk business; 8% labourers; job in private sector 3%; government service 2%; and 2% in Gulf and other business.	Kelly's Pharmaceutical Company	Fertilisers; hybrid seeds; electricity use for tubewells to irrigate. Tractor used for ploughing and harvesting	The cropping pattern of 1970s continued but mustard cultivation reduced.
1990	Agriculture 75%; Gulf 2%; Government service 2%; private service 4%; business 2%, labourer 15%; in milk business 60%.	Brick kilns, plastic & rubber factories. iron melting	Fertilisers; hybrid seeds; electricity for tubewells. Tractors for ploughing and harvesting. Insecticides and pesticides used	Wheat is main *Rabi* crop. Main *Kharif* Crops: Paddy, *jowar* (for fodder). Vegetable cultivation as commercial crops on land near canal.

Facilitator: Sudipta Ray.

Village Analysts: Haji Karim Khan, Karim, Hamid, Jakir, Fajruddin, Rashi, Tyab Husain, Rati Khan, Yakub.

Table 8.9

Changes in Agricultural Output by Men's Group, Aat Bisa, Khadaoli

Decade	*Yield Wheat*	*Size of Wheat Grains*	*Taste of Wheat*	*Colour of Wheat*
1940	4 quintal per acre	Fat and long	Nutritious and tasty (Sweet)	Golden yellow
1950	Same as in 1940s	Fat and long	Same as in 1940s	Same as in 1950s
1960	7-8 quintal per acre	Fat and long	Same as in 1950s	Same as in 1960s
1970	16 quintal per acre	Relatively smaller	Less tasty and make not good *chapattis*	Reddish yellow
1980	Same as in 1970s	Relatively smaller	Same as in 1970s	Reddish yellow
1990	13-15 quintal per acre	Relatively smaller	Same as in 1980s	Reddish yellow

Analysts: Karim Khan, Karim, Hamid, Jakir, Rashi, Tyab Husain, Rati Khan, Yakub.
Facilitator: Sudipta Ray.

Villagers perceived distinct changes in cropping pattern, agricultural practices and yield and crop quality. Let us take the decade of the 40s as the point of departure and Tables 8.10 and 8.11 as reference data. Refer to first column of Table 8.10 and last of Table 8.11. In that decade, a large number of crops were cultivated, though it is difficult to reconstruct the exact percentage of arable land on which each crop was grown. The crops were a mixture of staples, coarse cereals and pulses and henna for use as cosmetic, usually worn as intricate designs on palms/hands and feet during weddings. The main crops were coarse grains (barley and *bajra*) and cereals (wheat, *jowar* and maize). All the crops grown were for household consumption in the village. Farming was both subsistence and sustenance activity. The variety of crops grown gave the farmers not only the opportunity to diffuse their risks of failure but also ensured that consumption basket of the households had a combination of food which contained fibre, nutrition and protein.

In the 1950s, the position remained largely the same.

In the 1960s, winds of change began to sweep Uncha Gaon. Pulses were reduced. By the time Uncha Gaon reached 1970s, vegetable was introduced as a commercial crop and it is important to recognise this fact. In the next decade, as HYV seeds take ground, wheat remains the only main *Rabi* crop and *bajra* hold on as the main *kharif* crop. Cultivation of gram stops. In the 1980s, mustard and onion take roots as a cash crop in the hope of a high return.

Table 8.10

Historical Transect of Farming System and Crops (Male Group, Saini Muhalla) Uncha Gaon

Decade	*Occupation*	*Cropping Pattern*	*Farming System*	*Constraints*
1940	100% Agriculture	Wheat, *jowar, bajra,* barley, gram, maize, moat, henna	Irrigation by *rehant* and rains. Organic manure. Seeds from previous year's harvest. Ploughing with bullock. Cart for transporting produce	None
1950	95% in agriculture. Rest in industry, government and labourers	Ditto	Ditto	None
1960	95% in agriculture, 2% labourers, 3% service and 50% milk.	Same as in 1950s but pulses reduced	Late 60s HYV seeds introduced. Tractor for ploughing. Electric pump for irrigating.	Increase in *nagfal* (weed)
1970	90% agriculture 55% milk, rest as in 1960	Vegetables started to be grown on a commercial basis	Hybrid seeds in full force. Pesticides. Tractor for ploughing. Electric pump for irrigation. Fertilisers are in thing.	*Jai* and *mundi* appear in wheat field. *Kanduwa* in wheat fields.
1980	Same as 1970 except 60% in milk	Onion added to the list of items grown on a commercial basis	Ditto	Termites emerge. *Nilgais* start grazing.
1990	80% agriculture, 60% milk, 5% private service, 7% petty trade/business, 3% labourer and 2% in government	Wheat, *jowar.* mustard, cauliflower, potatoes, cabbage, brinjals, chilli, gourds of all variety	Ditto	Termites increase. *Nilgais* continue grazing. Weeds: *Doob* grass, *motha, zinzri, makra, Sati,* congress grass. Green *tidda* in *lobia* and cauliflower. Increase in caterpillar. Water Table has gone below 85 feet. *Moriya* in chillies.

Facilitator: Sudipta Ray.

Table 8.11

Historical Transect of Changes in Farm Produce (Male Group)
Saini Muhalla, Uncha Gaon

Decade	*Yield of Wheat*	*Size of Wheat Grains*	*Colour of Wheat Grains*	*Industrial Growth*
1940	3-4 quintals/ acre	Long and fat	Golden	Nil
1950	3-4 quintals/ acre	Ditto	Ditto	Bata and Escorts
1960	16 quintals/acre	Relatively small and thin	Orangeish red	Steel factory
1970	16 quintals/acre	Ditto	Yellow	Ajit Rubber and Thermocol factories
1980	13 quintals. Yield started falling in late 80s	From late 80s less grain per year of corn and small in size	From the late 80s, creamish	Khanna Thermocol Factory
1990	Wheat yield 13 quintals/acre. Yield of lady's finger, cucumber, small melon and onion falling since last 4-5 years.	Small in size and less grain	Creamish. Height of standing wheat crop has declined. Wheat corn size has fallen by 1%.	

Note: The villagers also indicated that bottle gourd no longer tastes as good as it used to be. Cauliflower since last 10-12 years develop black stains, which when washed turns creamish, spoiling the white colour of cauliflower, considered a mark of its good quality.

Facilitator: Sudipta Ray.

As of now (1990s) farmers in Uncha Gaon are left with wheat and *jowar* as principal *Rabi* and *Kharif* non-commercial crops respectively, with a sprinkling of *bajra*. Food crops are grown in 50 per cent of the gross cropped area of the village. Wheat is grown for household consumption as also for sale in the market.

Cash crops are grown on the other 50 per cent of arable land, which are mainly vegetables and grown, in the main, for sale. Amongst the vegetables now grown, in *Rabi*, potato is by far the most important and is grown on 50 per cent of the land which is earmarked for cash crops, or 25 per cent of the total arable land of Uncha Gaon. The variety and diversity, therefore, of crops grown are markedly reduced. To that extent, the capacity of the farmers to diffuse risk is pruned.

As we move from the 1940 into the last decade of this century, Tables 8.10 and 8.11 brings us near the truth that the mosaic of crops grown in Uncha Gaon is also becoming boring. The present day crops are basically three: vegetables, wheat and *jowar* (as fodder). This reduction in diversity of crops signals a movement away from polyculture towards standard monoculture. There is a movement from growing crops for meeting the food requirements of households and of the community, to growing crops for consumption of outsiders, who can buy in the market and for money. Thus, in a sense and certainly partially, production in Uncha Gaon has shifted from catering to the needs of the "have-nots" of the village to the needs of the "haves" outside the village, by exhausting the natural resources meant to serve the essential needs of the "have-nots". This has serious inter-generational questions and somebody needs to address them. Recall that the villagers have mentioned the falling of the water table to below 85 feet which makes irrigation difficult. This may be interpreted to mean that water resources are being used up beyond sustainable (read replenishable limits), to cater to the needs of "haves" outside the village at the expense of conserving resources for future generations.

The philosophy of the Green Revolution thus clearly gives the impression that diversity militates against productivity. Thus, the imperatives of uniformity and monocultures emerge. This has resulted in the situation where modern plant improvement has been based on destruction of the biodiversity, which it uses as raw material. Forestry development projects for long introduced monocultures of industrial species, like eucalyptus which pushes into extinction the diversity of local species which meets local needs. Agricultural modernisation schemes introduce new and uniform crops into farmer's fields and destroy the diversity of local varieties. Similarly modernisation of animal husbandry destroys diverse breeds and introduces factory farming. This strategy of basing productivity increases on the destruction of diversity, is dangerous and unnecessary. Because monocultures are ecologically and social unstable because they destroy both nature's economy and people's economy (Shiva, 1991).

But Why is Diversity Necessary?

Given that farmers are at the riskiest end of the farming system and given that farmers operate under stochastic conditions, farmers are disinclined to standardise their practices and maintain a diversity of crops grown, develop a variety of strategies and by so doing spread the risks associated with agriculture. A good mixture of crops varieties clearly provide farmers with a range of outputs, and represents a logical approach to coping with variable environments particularly the vagaries of nature. "Mixed crops can also be less variable in time and space, and combined yields are often greater, particularly if differences in root and shoot geometry allow the crops to use light, nutrients and water more efficiently" (Pretty, 1995; Vandermeer, 1989; Francis, 1986). Inter-cropping very often reduces weed problems, and hence lower labour requirements; can lead to increased returns to labour; and reduce the risks associated with soil erosion and run-off by the greater ground cover given by the mixture of crops and vegetation.

All these explains why the Indonesian farmers in rainfed conditions plant a greater mix of crop combinations during the more risky seasons (Castillo, 1992). For instance in the dry season, the Indonesian farmers plant 42 combinations of crop; in the uncertain middle season, they plant 25 crop varieties and in the rainy season, they plant just 7. John Vandermeer the author of a recent comprehensive review of inter-cropping, has put it: "In personal conversation with [farmers] in southern Mexico, Costa Rica and Nicaragua, I have frequently been told that two crops make a good combination because one is taller than the other and 'fits in' to the spaces where the other does not, or that the root systems go to different depths and thus use nutrients from different parts of the soil. Such popular knowledge is common."

The picture is similar in case of farmers operating the non-irrigated rice systems in Cambodia, Indonesia, Laos, Madagascar, Myanmar, Nepal, the Philippines and Thailand. Farmers in these systems have been found to manage their highly diverse conditions with different land-use strategies (Fujisaka, 1990; 1991) and adopt different combinations of rice varieties and management practices. In as much as, for example, farmers distinguished 20 different types of soil upland Laos, with each growing up to four varieties of rice. It has also been found that as high as 29 varieties of rice are grown in the two regions of Luang Prabang and Oudomasay. And farmers continuously change the mixtures of crop according to demands of the circumstances and are continually experimenting with new varieties or readopting old or existing ones. For example, in Bukidnon, in the Philippines, farmers were found to be currently cultivating 18 varieties of rice and had dropped six rice varieties in recent years. Nearer home, in Mayanmar, 52 different varieties of rice are grown in the rainfed uplands and lowlands, and in deepwater conditions. Reference is invited to Table 8.12. Farmers in these areas do not seek to maximisation of yield, and they do not have any particular preference for any variety. They seek variety of crops to get different tastes, colours, pest resistance, growth pattern, duration, flood and drought tolerance, milling recovery and market price qualities.

The Value of Wild Diversity

Wild resources are often called wastes or wastelands, and are seen as symptom of backwardness and underdevelopment. During the agricultural revolution of the 17th to 19th centuries in Britain, many officials described the common property resources as the "trifling fruits of overstocked and ill-kept lands" (Humphries, 1990). To large landowners, commons "burdened a village with beggarly cottages and idle people. They were better enclosed for agriculture" (Thirsk, 1985). In India, common resources are still called wastelands by some and their destruction rampant, without any policy or thinking on the issue (Jodha, 2000).

Table 8.12

Numbers of Rice Varieties and their Qualities Encountered in Three Non-irrigated Rice Regions of Myanmar

Region	*Number of Varieties*	*Qualities of Rice Varieties*
Rainfed uplands	18	115 to 180 day duration, red and white, glutinous and sticky, long and short awned and awnless, drought tolerant and intolerant, 100-150 cm in height for eating or for rice wine grain size
Deepwater rice	18	length of time in stomach, yields from 1.0 to 2.0 t/ha, elongation from water expansion when cooked, eating quality
Rainfed low-lands	16	yellow and white, resistance to stem border, yield from 1.5 to 1.8 t/ha, 125-200 day duration, flood or drought tolerant, glutinous or not yellow, white or black, length of time in stomach, fertiliser responsiveness, distinctive aroma, expansion when cooked, yields from 1.2 to 6.2 t/ha

It is well recognised that many communities, such as the Kung San in Botswana or Indian groups in the Amazon, depend on wild resources for their complete livelihoods. In India in the semi-arid and arid parts of the country, people derive as much as 35 per cent of their income from common property resources (Jodha, 1986; Mukherjee, 2001a). What is less widely recognised is that farming households also rely heavily on wild resources (Table 8.13). If wild habitats are lost, these resources will no longer be available to rural households. And those who will suffer most are the poorest, who most often rely on wild resources as key sources of food, fuel, medicines and fodder. Many agricultural institutions were indicating during the 1980s that agricultural area would have to expand substantially if growing world populations would be fed (Technical Assistance Committee, 1988). More recently, these calls have been toned down, as it is being increasingly recognised that expansion on this scale will incur significant costs to rural households and national economies alike in terms of loss of biodiversity.

This explains why it has been found that farmers, given the choice, instead of replacing local varieties entirely with a single modern variety, prefer to add a modern variety to their existing mix of options. In Indonesia, for instance, local variety called *Rajolele* was found that compared well with IR64, a modern variety from International Rice Research Institute (Soetomo, 1992). IR64 yields better but, because it needs more water, weeding and fertiliser, it gives lower returns to farmers. *Rajolele* is also favoured for its distinctive taste and fragrance, as well as being fairly resistant to brown plant hopper, rats and birds, unlike IR64. Farmers can also produce it locally in community seed banks, which are growing in popularity in Indonesia, despite them being contrary to existing government policy that holds that germplasm should be managed only in official gene banks.

Table 8.13

Use of Wild Plants for Food and Medicine by Farming Communities

Brazil	Kernels of *babbasu* palm provide 25 per cent of household income for 300,000 families in Maranhao State.
China, West Sichuan	1320 tonnes of wild pepper production; 2000 tonne fungi collected and sold; 500 tonne ferns collected and sold.
Ghana	16-20 per cent of food supply from wild animals and plants.
India, West Bengal	155 of wild plants collected for food, fodder, medicine and fuel.
Kenya, Bungoma	100 species of wild plants collected; 47 per cent of households collected plants from the wild and 49 per cent maintained wild species within their farms to domesticate certain species.
Kenya, Machakos	120 medicinal plants used, plus many wild foods.
Nigeria, near Oban, National Park	150 species of wild food plants.
South Africa, Natal/KwaZulu	400 indigenous medicinal plants are sold in the area.
Sub-Saharan, Africa	60 wild grass species in desert, savanna and swamp lands utilised as food.
Swaziland	200 species collected for food.
Thailand, NE	50 per cent of all foods consumed are wild foods from paddy fields, including fish, snakes, insects, mushrooms, fruit and vegetables.
South West of USA	375 plant species used by native Indians.
Zaire	20 tonnes Chanterelle mushrooms collected and consumed by people of Upper Shaba.
Zimbabwe	20 wild vegetables, 42 wild fruits, 29 insects, 4 edible grasses and one wild finger millet; tree fruits in dry season provide 25 per cent of poor people's diet.

Source: Amitava Mukherjee (2001).

When farmers are given the choice about new technology, they also prefer to absorb the new technology into their existing systems. This is quite different to the way that agricultural modernisation has worked so far, with farmers having to adopt the whole package or nothing at all. Recent participatory research with women farmers in Andhra Pradesh conducted by ICRISAT scientists has shown how important is the principle of supporting local biodiversity. Women experimented with new varieties of pigeon pea that were resistant to the pod borer, *Helicoverpa armigera*, which can devastate whole crops in bad years (Pimbert, 1991). Although some varieties were rejected because of bitter taste, interest was generated by the resistance to pod borer. Women farmers, though said they would not replace their traditional varieties, but incorporate the new varieties of pigeon pea into their current mix of land races. The new technology, in this case, has been adapted to suit local farming and livelihood conditions.

Finally, the stagnating capacity in modern systems of agriculture has led to diversity-based agriculture. Modern systems of agriculture will continue to be immensely important for many farmers and economies, but the potential for significant further improvements in cereal yields and their sustainability through high external input has become doubtful. All countries and areas where modern systems of agriculture has had a significant impact, including areas in India, have seen average annual growth rates in the agricultural sector fall during the 1980s, and the 1990s, compared with the post-revolution period of 1965-1980 (World Bank, 1994). A growing body of evidence has come to light that high cereal yields in the high-external input agriculture areas cannot be sustained. Concurrently, monocropped modern cereals appear to be unable to maintain their initial yield levels, whether fertilised or not. The reasons for this decline or stagnation of outputs have not been as yet decisively determined. Pests, plant diseases, chemical toxicity, changing soil carbon-nitrogen ratios and chemical deficiencies could be possible explanations but the issues are far from settled. There is a virtual unanimity however that a result of this changed micro-environment for cereal production has been the need for increased input requirements for sustaining current yields, with declining profitability of monoculture systems. Kenmore (1991) wrote early in the beginning of the last decade: "the degradation of the paddy environment, whether by micro-nutrient depletion, atmospheric population, pest pressure or accumulative toxic change in soil chemistry, is greater than the capacity for genetic improvements in yield potential that breeders can select." (As quoted in Mulleriyawa, 2008.)

The quest, therefore, has started at finding ways and means of having high yields on a sustainable basis and through a sustainable means of agricultural production. Sustainable agriculture requires sun, water, nitrogen, minerals, weed and pest control, energy, seed, management decisions and information, animals, cropping system, varieties of plants, labour and capital. Their internal and external sources and processes are shown in Table 8.14.

When these components come together, farming becomes integrated, with resources used more efficiently and effectively. Sustainable agriculture, therefore, strives for the integrated use of a wide range of pest, nutrient, soil and water management technologies. These are integrated at farm level to give a strategy specific to the biophysical and socioeconomic conditions of individual farms. Sustainable agriculture aims for an increased diversity of enterprises within farms, combined with increased linkages and flows between them. By-products or wastes from one component or enterprise become inputs to another. As natural processes increasingly substitute for external inputs, so the impact on the environment is reduced.

Table 8.14

Internal and External Resources for Agro-Ecosystems

	Internal resources and processes	*External resources and processes*
Sun	Main source of energy	Supplemented by fossil fuels
Water	Mainly rain and small irrigation schemes	Large dams, centralised distribution and deep wells
Nitrogen	Fixed from the air and recycled in soil organic matter.	Primarily from inorganic fertiliser
Minerals	Released from soil reserves and recycled	Mined, processed and imported
Weed and pest control	Biological, cultural, mechanical and locally available chemicals	With pesticides and herbicides
Energy	Some generated and collected on farm Some produced on farm	Dependence on fossil fuel
Seed	By farmer and community gathered locally and regularly	All purchased
Management decisions and information	Integrated on farm	Some provided by input suppliers, researchers, extensionists, assumed to be similar across farms
Animals	Rotations and diversity	Production at separate locations
Cropping system varieties of plants	Thrive with lower fertility and moisture	Monocropping Need high input levels to thrive
Labour	Labour requirement greater—work done by family living on farm and hired labour	Labour requirement lower—most work done by hired labour and mechanical replacement of manual labour
Capital	Initial source is family and community; any accumulation invested locally	Initial source is external indebtedness or equity; any accumulation leaves community

Source: Adapted from Rodale, 1990.

The Second Stage Loss of Biodiversity: The Genetic Engineering Paradigm

The Green Revolution Modern Agriculture Paradigm had, thus, narrowed down the basis of biodiversity by spreading monocultures of rice, wheat and maize. However, the Green Revolution has focused on a staple food and their yields. But it still could not feed the earth's population and even today an estimated eight billion people go to bed hungry everyday. There is an urgent need to get food to these people. Even the World Food Summit held in November 1996 very seriously debated the issue. Search for alternatives have been on for a long time, and it has now been suggested that geometrically modified food or genetic engineering has the *armoire*.

The genetic engineering revolution will undo the narrow gains of the Green Revolution both by neglecting the diversity of staples and at once not addressing the issue of yields. The table below shows that the element of yield increases in food crops do not even exist in the list of traits being introduced in genetically modified or transgenic crops accounted for by herbicide resistance which implies increased use of herbicide, not increased production of food. As it has been noted by an industry briefing paper: "The herbicide tolerant gene has no effect on yield *per se*" (James, 1997).

Table 8.15

Global Area of Transgenic Crop in 1996 and 1997 (By Trait)

	1996			*1997*			*1996-97*		
Crops	*Ha*	*Acres*	*%*	*Ha*	*Acres*	*%*	*Ha*	*Acres*	*%*
Herbicide resistance	0.6	1.6	23	6.9	17.0	5.4	6.2	15.4	10.7
Insect resistance	1.1	2.6	37	4.0	9.9	31	2.9	7.3	3.8
Insect resistance & Herbicide resistance	-	-	-	<0.1	0.1	<0.1	<0.1	0.1	-
Quality Traits	<0.1	<0.1	<0.1	<0.1	<0.1	<0.1	<0.1	<0.1	<2.0
TOTAL	2.8	7.0	100	12.8	31.5	100	9.9	24.5	4.5

Source: James, 1997.

There are four ways in which genetic engineering destroys biodiversity in agriculture:

- Genetic engineering is pushing out crop diversity and narrowing the genetic base of agriculture to a few crops.
- Genetic engineering is accelerating the expansion of monocultures in these crops.
- Genetic engineering is breeding to the destruction of on-farm biodiversity through use of broad spectrum herbicides like Round-up associated with Round-up Ready Resistant Crops.

- Genetic engineering is threatening the survival of species especially through the ecological import of Bt. crops (Shiva, 1998).

The global trend of the growth of genetically engineered crops is as follows:

Soybean	40%	Cotton	11%
Corn	25%	Conola	10%
Tobacco	13%	Tomato	1%
		Potato	1%

A report on a recent study by RAFI stated that of "some 3,20,000 vascular plant varieties, about 3000 species (both wild and domesticated) are regularly exploited as food while the total number of plant species cultivated and collected by human beings exceeds 7000. A study by Christine and Robert Prescolt-Allen used per capita food supply data from 146 countries and found that 103 species contribute 90 per cent of the world's plant food supply. However, thousands of species contribute to the food supply of the other 10 per cent which have considerable importance from a nutritional viewpoint and for poor people.

As against this, the trends of genetically engineered crops indicate a clear narrowing of the genetic basis of our food supply. The currently commercialised staple food crops are only two. In place of hundreds of legumes and beans eaten around the world, there is only soybean. In place of diverse varieties of millets, wheat and rice there is only corn. In place of diversity of oil seeds there is only canola. Furthermore, genetic engineering is also pushing the expansion of non-food crops like tobacco and cotton, leading to larger areas going out of food production and hence aggravating food insecurity.

The trends in cultivated of transgenic crops show that genetic engineering is displacing the diverse food crops that people of diverse cultures have used in their diets. By focusing on non-food commercial crops like tobacco and cotton and on crops like soybean which have not been the staples of most cultures outside East Asia. Since food security has cultural dimensions, soybean will not provide food security for *dal* eating Indians and corn will not provide security in the sorghum belt of Africa. Similarly, transgenic tobacco, cotton and tomato are not food staples.

The fact that genetically engineered based cropping systems are based on expanding monocultures of the same variety evolved for single function response, is lent considerable credence by the fact that in 1996 only two varieties of Bt.cotton was planted in 1.9 million hectares and the same Round-up Ready Soybean was planted in 1.3 million hectares. It is anticipated that as the biotechnology industry globalises, these monoculture tendencies will increase, thus further reducing agricultural biodiversity and creating ecological vulnerability.

This can be best illustrated by examining some real life cases. Take the case of Round-up Ready Soybean. Monsanto has this to say:

> Many of you heard of Monsanto's Round-up and it is very effective at killing weeds—so collective, in fact, that Round-up would control soyabeans as well as weeds if it should come in contact with both.
>
> At least, that was the case until Monsanto developed Round-up Ready Soybean. Round-up Ready Soyabeans expenses a novel protein which allows them to thrive, even when sprayed with enough Round-up to control competing weeds (ASSINSEL, 1997).

Broad spectrum herbicides (like Round-up) are directly aimed at destruction of biodiversity. The total destruction of biodiversity is however, promoted as ecologically friendly by the protagonists of genetic engineering. The danger of expanding Round-up Ready crops in the biodiversity rich agro-systems of the third world will be even more dangerous. The direct destruction of biodiversity will in fact lead to more rapid soil and water erosion since without, what is called "cover crops"; there will be no protection against the tropical sun and rain. Round-up ready crops will lead to increased use of round-up and hence destruction of both cultivated and wild biodiversity.

In Indian agriculture, as we briefly mentioned earlier, women can use up to 150 different species of plants (which are called weeds) as medicine, food and fodder. In West Bengal, as many as 124 weed species collected from rice fields have economic importance to local farmers. In Tanzania in a village over 80 per cent of vegetables are derived from uncultivated plants (Rissler and Mellon, 1996). It is feared that broad spectrum herbicides, like Round-up for example, destroys the economies of the farmers and local population, especially women. What is a weed to the protagonists of genetic engineering is a mediaeval plant or food for the rural households. Crops like Round-up Ready crops will, thus, destroy biodiversity rich areas and with it, the sustainable economy of the poor (Shiva, 1995).

How herbicide resistant crops destroy biodiversity, increase soil erosion and increase herbicide use in the last analysis is depicted in Figure 8.2, which is self-explanatory.

The reality at the ground level has been tested even in degraded ecosystem. Three plots of land, each measuring 10×10 metres were selected in different areas. The three plots were different in different respects. The first plot was on a farm level which had not be cultivated in the season. The second plot was a plot by the wayside and in a rural side. The third plot was a roadside plot in an urban area, near Dilshad Garden, New Delhi.

At first a survey was done on the three plots of land to catalogue all the plants, weeds, herbs, grasses and crops that grew on the plots separately. These results were as under in Tables 8.16, 8.17 and 8.18.

The Round-up was applied to all the three plots. The results were dramatic. All the plants in each of the three plots were destroyed. Extrapolated to the fields and farms of the developing countries, the introduction of genetically engineered crops becomes a major source of biodiversity destruction.

Table 8.16

Plot Number 1, Farmland in Panchgaon

Sl. No.	*Plant*	*No.*	*Properties*
1	*Partheneum*	24	Weed
2	*Sharpunkha*	13	Used for treating liver disorders
3	*Bhuiamla*	60	Treatment of jaundice and liver disorders
4	*Purnarawa*	44	Treatment of urinary tract infections, blood pressure and inflammation.
5	*Sadahari*	18	Treatment of cuts, burns and dysentery
6	*Aak*	5	Innumerable uses including appetiser and treatment of piles
7	*Sarkanda*	6	Root is used as medicine and plant is used for making *modas* (sitting stool).
8	*Cokharu* (patented)	15	Diuretic and anti-inflammatory drug.
9	*Apamarg*	21	Used for treatment of children's diseases and spleen and liver disorders
10	Various grasses		Good source of nutritious fodder

Source: Shiva, 1998.

Genetic engineering has its own vulnerability as well. For instance engineering a toxin into a plant variety can have its own hazards as well. Plants engineered to genetic their own pesticides can harm organisms other than their intended targets and no one knows for sure how and when. "Soil inhabiting organisms that degrade the organic matter containing the insecticidal toxins produced by the soil bacterium. Basically *thuringienses* can be harmed by the toxin. Then herbicide resistant crops like Round-up Ready cotton can create the risk of super weeds. By transferring herbicide resistance to weeds, in one case, it was found that a notorious Australian weed, rue grass has developed tolerance to the herbicide Round-up, thus rendering genetic engineering of herbicide resistant crops a useless strategy" (Shiva, 1998).

It is these and such other related concerns which provided the impetus for the Bio-Safety Protocol under the Convention on Biological Diversity 1992 (following the Earth Summit in Rio-de Janerio) which includes three dimensions:

- Ecological impact of GMOs on biodiversity and the environment.
- The socio-economic impact of genetic engineering on third world producers.
- The health impact of genetically engineered foods for public health.

Table 8.17

Plot Number 2, Farmland by the Roadside in Panchgaon

Sl. No.	*Plant*	*No.*	*Properties*
1	*Partheneum*	35	Weed
2	*Sharpunkha*	6	Used for treating liver disorders
3	*Ban Tulsi*	20	Treatment of cough and cold
4	*Purnarawa*	22	Treatment of urinary tract infections, blood pressure and inflammation.
5	*Chakramard*	5	Treatment of gastro-intestinal and liver disorders
6	*Aak*	6	Innumerable uses including appetiser and treatment of piles
7	*Apamarg*	100	Used for treating *Shwet* and *Rakt* diseases and spleen and liver disorders
8	Various grasses		Good source of nutritious fodder
9	Wild berries		Source of food for a variety of birds
10	*Arhar*		Highly priced lentil which when grows in the wild is a very good source of nutrition

Source: Shiva, 1998.

Third Stage of Biodiversity Loss

The final stage of biodiversity loss emerges from the international institutional arrangements worked out by the governments in terms of the World Trade Organization and the agreements entered under its auspices. In particular the Agreement on Agriculture (AOA) and Agreement on Trade Related Intellectual Property Rights (TRIPS). Indeed genetic engineering cannot be commercialised without patents on seeds and plants. Patents prevent farmers from exercising their age old freedoms of saving and exchanging seeds. It is true that biotechnology industry often argues that farmers are free to use their own seeds, but it is as much true that industrialisation of agriculture has also created systems to prevent farmers from using farmers varieties.

Briefly stated the TRIPS enjoins upon the Member States that they provide protection for intellectual property rights of various forms through protection of trade marks, copy rights, industrial designs, geographical indications and patents. The provision relating to patents is the most controversial of these provisions and they affect the whole question of biodiversity. Article 27 of

TRIPS Agreement enjoins that Member State shall ensure by law that patents are available in principle for any invention whether they concern products or processes in all fields of technology. For patents to be available, the invention must be new, involve an inventive step and be capable of industrial application. The Agreement under reference further defines in footnote 5 thereto that: "For the purposes of this Article" (meaning article 27) the term 'inventive step' and 'capable of industrial application' may be deemed by a Member to be synonymous with the term 'non-obvious' and 'useful' respectively.

Table 8.18

Plot Number 3, Farmland by the Roadside in Delhi.

Sl. No.	*Plant*	*No.*	*Properties*
1	*Partheneum*	50	Weed
2	*Sadahari*	35	Used for treating cuts, burns and dysentery
3	*Gokru* (patented)	11	Diuretic and anti-inflammatory
4	Castor (patented)	3	Laxative
5	*Apamarg*	15	Used for treating *Shwet* and *Rakt* diseases and spleen and liver disorders
6	*Aak*	4	Innumerable uses including appetiser and treatment of piles
7	*Bathua*		Food and a good source of iron.
8	*Kaner*	8	Has a number of medicinal properties
9	Wild berries		Source of food for variety of birds.
10	*Ban Tulsi*	5	Treatment of cough and cold.
11	*Dudhi* (patented)	12	Treatment of diarrhea and dysentery
12	*Ashwagandha* (patented)	4	Rejuvenator

Source: Shiva, 1998.

The requirement of patentability is subject to two kinds of exceptions. Firstly, some inventions to be excluded from patentability on the grounds of protection of public order or morality, human, animal or plant life or the environment.

Secondly, under Article 27(3) of the TRIPS Agreement "Members may exclude from patentability:

(a) diagnostic, therapeutic and surgical methods for the treatment of humans or animals;

(b) plants and animals other than micro-organisms and essentially biological processes for the production of plants or animals other than non-biological and micro-biological processes. However, countries shall provide for the protection of plant varieties either by patents or be effective *sui generis* system or by any combination thereof"(MVIRDC, 2000).

There are two phrases which are key for biodiversity. One, the phrase that 'inventive step' and 'capable of industrial application' may be deemed by a Member to be synonymous with the term 'non-obvious' and 'useful' respectively and that micro-organisms and micro-biological processes will not be excluded from patentability. The term 'inventive step' meaning something 'non-obvious' in effect means that hidden properties of nature, which are discovered (as opposed to invention) will also be patentable. Thus, over 40 patents mainly for *neem* pesticides are being held by American and European laboratories in respect of *neem*; patents have been granted for anti-viral property of a pharmaceutical composition made from *amla*; a compound called Piperine found in black pepper has been patented for nutritional use; two American scientists were given patents for healing properties of Turmeric (which was fortunately challenged by Government of India); a protein isolated from bitter gourd (*karela*) plant by scientists for treating tumours and HIV infection; an anti viral agent found in pomegranate (*anar*) has been patented in the US and so on. Even a strain of *Basmati* rice was patented in the US under the name of Texmati. The Agreement by providing for products or processes patents have enjoined upon the Member States to nullify the exclusions built into national patent laws for protection of public and national interest. For example, in India the patent laws did not allow for product patents but to make the law WTO compatible, the products in food, medicines, drugs and chemical products have to be made patentable.

The TRIPS Agreement is an agreement born out of the needs of the Transnational Corporations, conceived by the Intellectual Property Committee (IPC) with a coalition of 13 major US Corporations and have been imposed by them by manipulating the governments of the North. James Enyat of Monsanto commenting on the IPEC's contribution to the framing of the TRIPS Agreement remarked which bears repetition here:

> Besides selling our concepts at home we went to Geneva where we presented (our) document to the staff of the GATT Secretariat. We also took the opportunity to present it to the Geneva based representatives of a large number of countries. What I have described to you is absolutely unprecedented GATT. Industry has identified a major problem in international trade. It crafted a solution, reduced it to concrete proposal and sold it to our own and other governments. Industries and traders of the world commerce have played simultaneously the role of patients, the diagnosticians and the prescribing physicians" (GATT Secretariat, 1994).

The TRIPS agreement is the embodiment of the values and interests of Northern Corporations and imposed on diverse societies and cultures of the world, through their unsuspecting negotiators.

The shift from common to private rights is inimical to biodiversity. The preamble to the TRIPS Agreement reads that intellectual property rights are recognised as private rights, which excludes all kinds of knowledge, ideas and innovations that continually take place in the "intellectual commons" in villages among farmers, in forests among tribal people and even in academic and research institutions. TRIPS Agreement therefore, has the ingredients to privatise the intellectual commons and de-intellectualise civil society, so that in effect the mind becomes a corporate monopoly, and all monopolies by nature of things. The TRIPS Agreement recognise intellectual property rights only when knowledge and innovations generate profits, not otherwise, not when they meet social needs. Thus only profits and capital accumulation are recognised as viable end-use of creativity, under the control of corporations. Social creativity and social good in terms of diversity is therefore at a serious discount. As a natural concomitant it enforces rights of the corporations to monopolise all production and distribution at the cost of all citizens and small producers. Thus, diversity created through innovations of women peasants and tribal people in farming, in agricultural production and perpetuating life forms for domestic, local and public use will receive a serious setback.

Worse still seeds will be patentable and the rights of the farmers to use seeds as they like will be extinguished. Farming decisions, which need to be taken at the farm level, will be taken at the international level; not on the basis of farmers' livelihood interest but in the interest of MNCs' business needs.

Policy Implication

There are several policy implications that flow from the above. We will briefly mention just a few.

Given that we are living in an age of extraordinary changes, there is an urgent need to assess the ecological costs of globalising agriculture using a biodiversity based productivity framework to reflect the health of nature's economy and people's economy. Such a framework has to have the following elements:

Provide documentation of the biodiversity status of a farm including crop, tree and arrival—biodiversity.

Indicate the contribution of biodiversity to provisioning of internal inputs and to the building and maintenance of nature's economy through the conservation of soil, water and biodiversity.

Indicate the contribution of biodiversity to self-provisioning of food needs by the agricultural families and communities and to the building and maintenance of people's economy.

Reflect the market economy of the farm in terms of incomes from sale of agricultural produce, and of additional costs for purchase of external inputs and food items, where benefits from biodiversity are foregone.

The biodiversity based productivity framework has to be kept simple so as to allow participatory evaluation by farmers on the basis of needs of the land and needs of the farming communities and to allow for comparisons across diverse ecosystem and farming systems. It has to be flexible to be adaptable to meet the needs of the complex socio-economic context of farming.

There has to be a conscious effort to preserve traditional agriculture and make a clear break from intensive agriculture. Austria has begun doing so in the face of several diseases like the Mad Cow disease and the Foot and Mouth disease, that have afflicted Northern Agriculture.

The WTO Agreements have to be re-negotiated to serve the interest of the farmers and maintaining biodiversity. In particular, TRIPS Agreement should be amended to disallow patenting of any life form, whatever it may be for the simple reason that life forms are inventions. They are at best discoveries. The time now is opportune.

Figure 8.1

Polyculture (16th Century S.E. China)

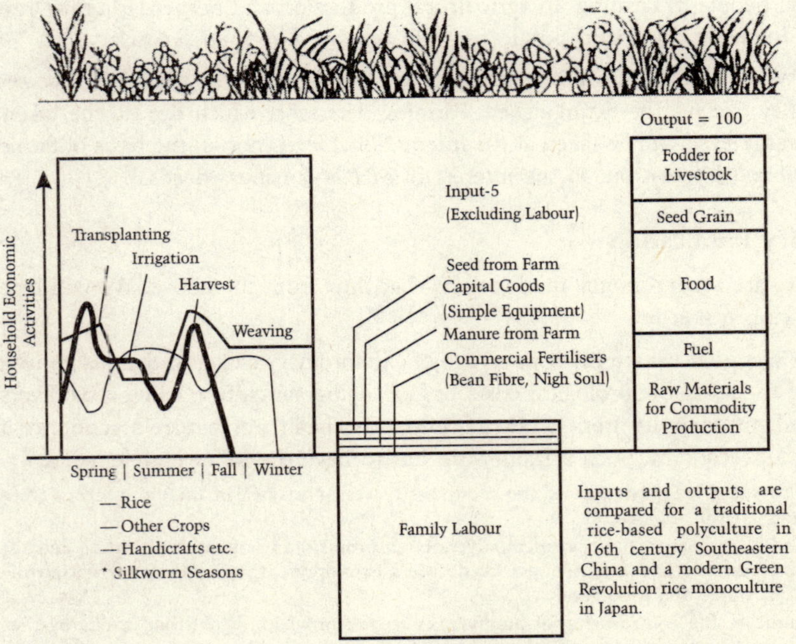

Source: Bray, Francesca (1994). "Agriculture for Developing Nations", *Scientific American*, July pp. 33-35.

Figure 8.2

Green Revolution, High-Tech Rice Manoculture (Contemporary Japan)

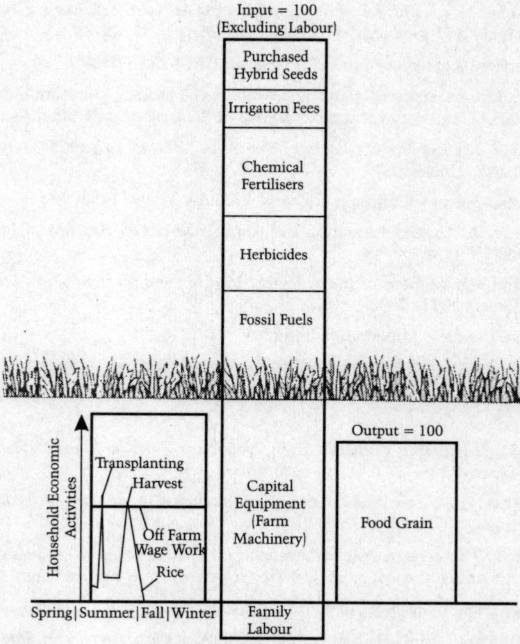

Note: The height of the labelled bars reflects the relative amount of that input or output. The curves at the bottom left of each diagram indicate how the people of the farm household apportion their productive time. In the polyculture the women do little work in the fields but are heavily involved in handicrafts such as silk production. In the monoculture economy, women do more of the field work because many of the men have off-site jobs.

Source: Bray, Francesca (1994). "Agriculture for Developing Nations", *Scientific American*, July pp. 33-35.

References

ASSINSEL (International Association of Plant Breeders) (1997). *Feeding the 8 Billion and Preserving the Planet* (Chemin du Reposoir 7, 1260, Nyon, Switzerland).

Bailey, C. H. (1994). "The composition and quality of wheat grown in mixtures with oats", in Argon 6: 204-210.

Busell, F. P. (1937). "Oats and barley on New-York farms", *Cornell Extension Bulletin* 376.

Bray, Francesca (1994). "Agriculture for Developing Nations" *Scientific American*: 33-35, July.

Castillo, G.T. (1992). "Sustainable agriculture in concept and in deed", ODI Agricultural Administration (R&E) *Network Paper* 36: 1-32. London: Overseas Development Institute.

Cordova, V.; Herdt, R. W., Gascon, F. B. and Yambao, L. (1981): "Changes in rice production technology and their impact on rice farm earnings on Central Luzon, Philippines 1966-1979", Department of Agricultural Economics Paper, International Rice Research Institute, Los Banos, Philippines.

Elwell, H.A. (2007). "The effects of high-input, green revolution group production in Limbabire's smallholder sector", November 4. *http:/africanagriculture.blogspot.com/2007/effects-of/-high-input-green-resolution.html. accesed* on 16.03.09.

Food and Agricultural Organisation of the UN (1993). State of Food and Agriculture (Rome: FAO).

Fowler, C. and Mooney, Pat (1990). *The Threatened Gene: Food, Policies and the Loss of Genetic Diversity.* Cambridge: The Lutterworth Press.

Fransis, C. A. (1986). *Multiple Cropping Systems.* London: John Wiley and Sons.

Fujisaka, S. (1990). "Rainfed lowland rice: building research on farmer practice and technical knowledge", *Agriculture, Ecosystem and Environment* 33: 57-74.

Fujisaka, S. (1991). "A Diagnostic study of shifting cultivation in northern Laos: targeting research to improve sustainability and productivity", *Agroforestry Systems* 13: 20-23.

GATT Secretariat (1994). Final Agreement of GATT. Geneva: GATT Secretariat.

Humphries, J. (1990). "Enclosures, common rights and women: the proletarianisation of families in the late eighteenth and early nineteenth centuries", *Journal of Economic History* 50: 17-42.

Hunger Project (1991). The Hunger Project Update: The Alan Shawan Feinstein World Hunger Project (Rhode Island: Brown University).

James, Clive (1997). "Global Status of Transgenic Crops", ASSAA Briefs, 1997: 14.

Jodha, N. S. (1986). "Common Property Resources and Rural Poor in Dry Regions of India", *Economic and Political weekly* 21(27): 1986.

———. (2000) Wasteland Management in India: Myths, Motives and Mechanisms", *Economic and Political Weekly* 35(6), February 5-11, 2000.

MVIRDC (2000). WTO in The New Millennium (Mumbai: MVIRDC)

Mukherjee, Amitava (2001). *Air Pollution, Crop Yield and Livelihood.* Aldershot, Hong Kong, Sydney etc: Ashgate.

Mukherjee, Amitava (2001a). *Hunger: Theory, Perspectives and Reality.* Aldershot, Hong Kong, Sydney etc: Ashgate. Chapter-8.

Mulleriyawa, Ranjit (2008). "Increasing Domestic Food Production", in *The Island Online, http://www.island.ltc/2008/09/22/Features 7.html*

Murakami, Shimpei (1991). *Lessons from Nature: A Guide to Ecological Agriculture in the Topics.* Manickganj. Bangladesh: Proshika.

Pimpert, M. (1991). Designing Integrated Pest Management for sustainable and Productive Future, London. International Institute for Environment and Development, Gate Keeper Series No. 29.

Pretty, Jules (1995). *Regenerating Agriculture.* London: Earthscan.

Rissler, Jane and Mellon, Margaret (1996). *The Ecology Risks of Engineered Crops.* Cambridge, Mass: The MIT Press.

Rodale, R. (1990). "Sustainability: An opportunity for leadership", in Clive A. Edwards *et al.* (eds.), *Sustainable Agricultural Systems.* Ankeny: Soil and Water Conversation Society.

Shiva, Vandana (1991). *Violence of the Green Revolution.* London: Zed Books.

———. (1995). *Biodiversity Based Productivity: A Framework for An Alternative Economic Assessment for Sustainable Agriculture.* New Delhi: Research Foundation for Science, Technology and Ecology.

———. (1998). *Betting on biodiversity: Why Genetic Engineering will not Feed the Hungry.* New Delhi: Research Foundation for Science, Technology and Ecology.

Soestrisna, L. (1982). "Further agricultural intensification in Indonesia: who gains and who loses?", paper for Working Group Meeting on Agricultural Intensification in Indonesia, Puncak, June, 1982.

Soetomo, D. (1992). "Growing Community seed banks in Indonesia" in Cooper, D; Velle, R. and Hobbelink, H. (eds.): *Growing Diversity: Genetic Resources and Local Food Security.* London: Intermediate Technology Press.

Stakman, E. C. *et al.* (1967). *Campaign Against Hunger.* Cambridge, Mass.: Belknap Press.

Technical Assistance Committee of the CGIAR (1988). "Sustainable Agricultural Production: Implications for International Agricultural Research". Rome: Technical Assistance Committee Secretariat.

Thirsk, J. (1985). "Agricultural innovations and their diffusion" in Thirsk, J. (ed.): The Agrarian History of England and Wales, Vol. V. Cambridge: Cambridge University Press.

Vandermeer, J. (1989). *The Ecology of Inter-cropping.* Cambridge: Cambridge University Press.

Wijewardene, R. and Waidyantha (1994). *Systems Techniques and Tools for Small Farmers in Humid Topics.* Colombo: Department of Agriculture, Government of Sri Lanka.

World Bank (1993). Agricultural Sector Review. Washington D.C.: The World Bank, Agricultural and Natural Resources Department)

World Bank (1994). Agricultural Factor Review. Washington D.C.: The World Bank.

9

Livelihoods, Eco-Tourism and Conflict in Sharing Natural Resources

The Case of Keoladeo Ghana National Park: An Analysis from the Stakeholders' Perspectives

Strength does not come from physical capacity.
It comes from an indomitable will.

—*Mahatma Gandhi*

Introduction

Keoladeo National Park or KNP (also called Keoladeo Bird Sanctuary), Bharatpur, India is a world heritage site under the World Heritage Convention, since 1985. Situated in the western state of Rajasthan with an area of just 29 sq. km, KNP has several species of birds and, also attracts hundreds of species of them from all over India and, the world. Many of the migratory birds come for nesting and breeding and many use it as their winter home. KNP is also rich in micro-flora and micro-fauna, macro-invertebrates, amphibions, reptiles and mammals, some threatened with extinction. Chauhan and Gopal, 2001 and Singh, 1999 have extensively documented the names of the species of birds and animals in KNP. It naturally attracts tourists from across the country and the world that have interest in birds, animals and nature.

The Keoladeo National Park

The Location

KNP is situated on the Bharatpur Jaipur Highway and is elongated in shape, stretching from north to south. The main gate of the park is on the northern front of KNP from which a straight metalled road runs for about three and a half kms, right upto the centre of the park where a temple of Keoladeo (Shiva) is situated, after whom the park is named. There are several brick laid trails and mud tracks inside the park on which tourists and visitors walk around or cycle. At about the mid-point on the road from the main gate to the Keoladeo Temple, there was a barrier. Vehicular traffic was allowed upto this barrier.

To the left of the road, as one enters the park from the main gate, near the barrier, there are two lodges, one run by India Tourism Development Corporation and the other by the Forest Department, Government of Rajasthan.

The office of the park director is also located adjoining the Forest Lodge. A map of the KNP indicating these features is at Figure 9.1. KNP has an area of 29 sq. km, comprising of wetlands and dry uplands. Originally the area of the wetland was 8.5 to 11 sq. km, which varies from year to year. The average rainfall received by the Park is 662 mm over a period of 60 days usually from mid June. There is a dam called Ajan Bundh lying to the west of KNP (outside its boundary) from which a canal called Ghana Canal, runs into the Park, till the Keoladeo Temple. There is a second canal from the Ajan Bundh which skirts the southeastern portion of KNP. In the vicinity of the Keoladeo Temple, is the third canal, called Jatoli Canal that carries water from the Ghana Canal to the eastern and northern wetlands of the KNP. Water from the Jatoli Canal runs through the eastern boundary of KNP and flows into the adjoining villages, like Jatoli, Barso and Ghasaula, through sluice gates. These canals form the lifeline for KNP for they not only bring water to the wetlands in the park but also along with the water, bring aquatic life from the Ajan Bundh and beyond which are critical in sustaining birds and other life forms in KNP.

To protect the Park from predation, both by human beings and animals, a boundary wall was constructed around the Park, with several inhabited villages situated just outside the boundary wall such as Mallah, Ramnagar, Aghapur, Barpura, Darpoura, Babnera, Ghausaula, Barso and Jatoli. There were differences of view on the origin of the boundary wall. While Park Authorities maintained that the wall was constructed to keep human beings and milch animals at bay, the villagers argued that they wanted the wall for their protection from wild animals inhabiting the KNP. Unlike many national parks in India and elsewhere there was no buffer zone between the KNP and the villages. The absence of a buffer zone meant that the communities and the KNP interfaced directly on an ongoing basis, everyday. This was an issue of importance for the villagers and the park.

Classes of Tourists and Visitors

Being en route to the golden triangle of Delhi, Agra and Jaipur, KNP attracted hordes of casual tourists as well. Tourists came to KNP throughout the year especially during October to February, when migratory birds came to the Park from different parts of the world, for nesting, breeding and making it their winter home. The classes of tourists who came to KNP are identified by Svalastog (1994) as under:

- The wilderness tourists, who want to be close to nature and to learn more about the self, and who want unspoilt areas, clean water, good hunting ground, fishing waters and an intact flora and fauna. They make great demands on natural resources.
- The anti-tourists, who want to be part of the normal activities of the community being visited, adopting local standards in food, water etc.

- The emigrant tourists, who want to get away from their home.
- The sightseeing tourists, who "pick places" which means they have a subject of conversation, photography etc., for later use in a social context at home.
- The knowledge seekers or the connoisseur tourists, who want to learn more about a place and experience its environment, culture etc.
- The sun and snow worshippers, are tourists who seek plenty of sun and a good climate, and consider the host environment and community rather uninteresting.
- The activity tourists, who visit the place for physical exercise and do not necessarily damage resources.
- The utility tourists who want leisure to pick berries, fish, gather flora etc.

KNP also received visitors who came for prestige or what has been called 'ego-enhancement' (Dann, 1977).

There was also clear evidence that KNP was also being used as a product for tourism, much in the same sense as the term has been defined by Voase (1995). The Royal Train Ride that took tourists (mostly foreigners and non-resident Indians) around the historical places in Rajasthan and Agra, made a halt at Bharatpur Station to allow all the passengers a chance to visit KNP for one hour or so. These passengers usually arrived at the barrier (see Figure 9.1) inside the park on a bus and then went inside the restricted area of the park during the evening on the cycle-rickshaws licensed to ferry such passengers.

Why This Study?

Tourists who came to KNP naturally brought to the park, their lifestyles as reflected in their modes of travel, food and food containers, cameras, photograph accessories, clothes and even entertainment material. The advent of these materials inside the Park have had their impact on the biodiversity of KNP with nearly 400 species of birds, many species of animals and 379 species of flowering plants (including 96 species of wetland flowering plants). There have been efforts on the part of the Park authorities (the Forest Development) to manage the flow of tourists through eco-tourism. The attempt all along has been to ensure that tourism was encouraged (it was a source of revenue to the government) while the adverse impact of tourism is eliminated or kept within tolerable limits.

The establishment of the KNP also meant that the environments—economic, social, natural and psychological—around the Park have also been altered. Such alterations have often generated conflicts with local communities, which have a bearing on eco-tourism and on the Park itself. The World Conference on Sustainable Tourism 1995 at Lanzarote, as a thematic successor to the

Rio Conference, generated "The Charter for Sustainable Tourism" and "The Sustainable Tourism Plan of Action". The Sustainable Tourism Plan of Action laid down at Lanzarote Conference, set out 18 principles for how tourism should be managed so that it can be included in the global strategy for sustainable development. An important mandate of the conference was that the interests of local communities should be given utmost importance (Sustainable Tourism, World Conference, 1995). Agenda 21 for the Tourism Industry explicitly maintained that cooperation with the local communities, amongst others, has to be enlisted and environmentally dangerous substances were to be replaced. (Aronsson, 2000). In keeping, as it were, with the spirit of the above documents, attempts have also been made to resolve conflicts with local communities living around, and having interest in, KNP (WWF-I, 1996) in the past.

This study is an attempt to examine:

- How eco-tourism was managed in KNP, from the perspective of different stakeholders?
- How the concepts of sustainable tourism were being operationalised?
- How the conflicts arising of such parks were being resolved?
- And to what extent problems identified earlier have been resolved?

The study was attempted through participatory methods.[1]

The Stakeholders

The stakeholders in KNP are:

(i) The Forest Department, Government of Rajasthan.
(ii) The staff of KNP Park Authorities.
(iii) People who depend on the KNP for their livelihoods: hoteliers, cycle-rickshaw pullers, *tongawallas* (horse carriage owners), guides, vendors, temple priests and villagers in villages surrounding the park.
(iv) The tourists and the avid bird watchers.
(v) Conservationists.
(vi) Donors and others interested in preservation of birds, wild life and indeed the ecosystem itself.

The perspectives of the different stakeholders were probed as under:

(i) The director and deputy director of the park through semi-structured interview.
(ii) The cycle-rickshaw pullers-cum-guides through conversation and biodiversity mapping.
(iii) Conservationists through semi-structured interview.
(iv) Tourists through direct observation between 1/1/2002 and 2/1/2002.

1. As per the Director of the Park and the Assistant Director in a conversation in KNP on 2 January 2002.

(v) Villagers (of adjoining village) through pine line, livelihood analysis, anecdotal evidence.

(vi) Review of secondary literature.

The discussion in the subsequent paragraphs has been developed on the basis of the foregoing participatory methods carried out in separate sessions on 1st and 2nd January 2002 at Bharatpur. But the discussion has not followed the chronology in which the participatory sessions were carried out.

The Origin of the Park and its Problems

The origin of KNP has been beautifully projected by the villagers of village Mallah that borders KNP (see Table 9.1) through a Time Line. The Time Line is at Table 9.1. From the Time Line it seems that the Rulers of Bharatpur State created a *bundh* (a dam) called Ajan Bundh at the confluence of two rivers, Gambhir and Ban Ganga, some 400 years ago or so, primarily as a flood control measure. This *bundh* inundated a natural depression, which lies to the west of the present KNP. The inundation of the natural depression resulted in production of aquatic vegetation, which in turn attracted large number of migratory birds, both from India and abroad. A reserve for birds started to form, which over the centuries evolved into what came to be recognised as a Duck Shooting Reserve in the beginning of the last century. The Duck Shooting Reserve was inaugurated by the then Viceroy of India in 1902.

Table 9.1

Time Line of Ghana Keoladeo National Park

18th Century	Ajan Bundh created at the confluence of Gambhir and Ban Ganga Rivers. The consequent inundation resulted in production of aquatic vegetation. This attracted a large number of migratory birds.
1902	Duckshoot Reserve inaugurated by the *Laat Sahab* (Viceroy) of India.
1938	Lord Linlithgo shot 4273 birds.
1954	Salim Ali started working.
1956	Notified as Bird Sanctuary. Started attracting lot of attention from outside.
1962	Last shooting of Birds.
1972	Creation of prohibited area. Shooting banned.
1979	Cycle-rickshaws were introduced for visiting the park.
1980	More rickshaws came. (*) Training of cycle-rickshaw pullers started.
1981	Ramsar site (*)
1982	Declared a National Park. Banned grazing and grass cutting.
1985	Trained cycle-rickshaw pullers and *tongawallas* introduced. World Heritage site. (*)
1986	Grass permits were introduced.
1999	Supreme Court of India ordered stoppage of grass permit.
2000	Rainfall deficient. Seven Saras Cranes died of eating wheat from fields in neighbouring villages.
2001	Canteens inside the Park near the Keoladeo Temple closed. Decline in arrival of birds and tourists.

Note: * One of the villagers was a guide working in KNP who provided these details.

A noted ornithologist Dr. Salim Ali began working in the Park in 1956. KNP was notified as a bird sanctuary in 1956, shooting was banned in 1972, declared a Ramsar site in 1981, and made a national park in 1982 and a world heritage site in 1985. These incidents, according to the villagers, created problems of two kinds. One, they attracted a huge number of tourists and a large number of outsiders who poured alien material into the area. We will call this the "Problems of Visitors/Tourists". Two, the upgradation of the Duck Shooting Reserve to a National Park and World Heritage Site etc., seriously endangered the livelihood of the villagers living in villages in the periphery of KNP. We will call this the "Problems of Livelihood".

Nature has created a third problem. A biodiversity map produced by one set of stakeholders, *viz.*, rickshaw pullers, at Figure 9.1 indicates that parts of the KNP which were earlier wetlands and marshes have since dried up for want of adequate rainfall for the last two years. Because the wetlands are not flooded and the water discharged for the Ajan Bundh was not enough to make good water shortage due to deficient rainfall, wetlands were disappearing and the existence of the KNP was under threat. The arrival of migratory birds had substantially reduced in 2001 as against 2000. The reason, the cycle-rickshaw pullers opined, was that the vegetation and aquatic life in KNP was not enough to support the winged migrants. Thus, shortage of water was a major problem. We will call this the "Problem for the KNP". The rickshaw pullers also felt that a subsidiary factor that contributed to shrinking of the wetlands has been want of imagination on the part of authorities to clean up the impoundments of weeds, deadwood etc.

Problems of Visitors/Tourists

Environmental and Attitudinal Problems

Let us deal with "Problem of Tourists" first caused by the influx of tourists and outsiders in the Park. The tourists who came into the KNP brought with them materials and food, which did not synchronise with the KNP, its environment and biodiversity. One, the steady rise in use of plastic bags as "carry bags", has resulted in the tourists bringing into KNP food, drinks and other materials in plastic bags, which were left behind in the KNP, as litter, either in the litter bins or elsewhere. Though the movement of traffic, men and materials inside the KNP were strictly restricted to the mud trails, brick paths and the only one metalled road, nevertheless the plastic bags left behind by the tourists and other visitors, were carried to all corners of the KNP by wind and monkeys. Second, the pockets wrappers, cups, and glasses, made of non-biodegradable matter, were also left behind as litter which was also strewn all over the KNP. Third, the noise pollution that large number of tourists and human visitors brought into the park in the form of transistors, cassette players and feed for the birds and animals. The noise pollution so created

Figure 9.1

KNP: Bio-Diversity Map

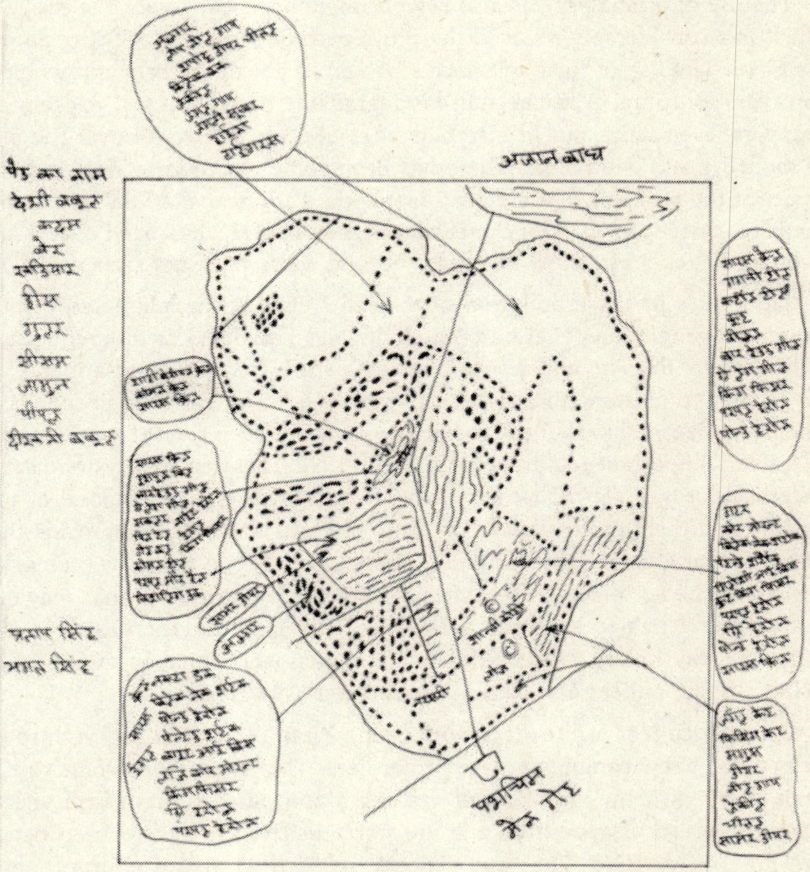

disturbed the birds and animals as also the unique sounds of the forest. The feed brought in by the visitors often caused injuries to the birds, animals and insects. Finally, the attitude and behaviour of the "outsiders" were not conducive to the peaceful life of the Park. While the KNP was a nesting and breeding place for the birds, which required quiet and tranquility, the visitors treated the place more for fun and frolic than as a bird sanctuary.

The Official Responses

The official responses have been varied and some very innovative. The Park authorities banned the use of vehicle beyond the "barrier" near the Forest Lodge and Forest Headquarter of the Park. This took care of vehicular pollution that afflicted the park. However, to facilitate the movement of tourists and visitors, cycle-rickshaws that were introduced as cheap mode of transportation, within KNP, helped reduce the hardship of tourists/visitors.

The use of plastic bag has also been banned in the Park since the early 90s, which has considerably reduced the prevalence of plastic bags flying all over the place. The use of food and drinks packed in plastic packets and wrappers however, continue. And the non-biodegradable cups, glasses, packets and wrappers, even when put in litterbins after use, are strewn all over the place by monkeys and wind alike. There has been some response to deal with this aspect of the problem. The cafeteria inside the Park near the Keoladeo Temple has been closed down. The canteen near the "barrier" has been downscaled to only sell tea and coffee. Measures beyond these have not been taken.

The issues of noise pollution have been sought to be addressed through awareness generation. There are handbills and hoardings at different places, which exhort tourists and visitors not to disturb the birds and animals and not to play transistors and cassette players inside the Park. In an innovative scheme, cycle-rickshaw pullers and *tongawallas* have been trained as guides who play a very important role in protecting the KNP. These trained cycle-rickshaw pullers and *tongawallas* advise the tourists/outside visitors on disposal of solid waste, guide them professionally on birds and bird watching and provide them with tips that enhance their interest. These trained cycle-rickshaw pullers and *tongawallas* are so sensitive to environmental needs of the KNP that they even pick plastic litters to keep the park clean. The fact that the future of KNP is inextricably linked to their livelihood acts as additional incentive to the cycle-rickshaw pullers and *tongawallas* to keep KNP clean.

On "attitudes" of tourists/outsiders that require a lot of midway corrections, a few comments are in order here. The visitors who come to KNP often come with the approach of visiting a zoo. Such tourists and visitors naturally return disappointed and are not sensitive enough to keep decibel level low inside KNP. The "zoo-visitors' mentality" also prompts them to feed animals, a common sight in most Indian zoos. Some visitors also come expecting KNP to be a picnic spot and tend to use the park as a venue for an excursion. Food, music and fun and frolic, as we mentioned earlier, are parts of such excursions. These excursions, therefore, bring their own set of problems to KNP. And then there are school children that are brought during the Diwali and Christmas holidays. School children and their accompanying adults are not always conversant with requirements of keeping KNP free from plastic and other non-biodegradable matter, noisy conversation, teasing and feeding of birds and animals.

Though there has been limited effort at dealing with the problems of "attitudes and behaviour", the decisive interventions are under implementation. Dr. Salim Ali Interpretation Centre as also the programme being implemented by the World Wide Fund for Nature-India, and funded by D. Swarovski Company, Austria, would disseminate effective environmental information and run awareness programme, establish infrastructure for environmental information and awareness programme, build capacity of the KNP management to run environmental information programme. Once the Interpretation Centre becomes operational and its outreach programme is implemented in full, some of the problems associated with inappropriate "attitudes and behaviour" of tourists and visitors could be circumvented.

The Second Problem: The Livelihood Problems

With the development of KNP and its migration from a Duckshoot Reserve to a Bird Sanctuary to National Park and then on to Heritage Site, tourists and visitors, from across the globe were attracted to the Park. While these developments caused cheers for the Forest Department, Government of Rajasthan, for the villagers who resided along the periphery of KNP, the developments caused major disruptions in their livelihood. The evolution of the KNP, therefore, necessitated changes in livelihoods and exacerbation of problems of people, living along the periphery of KNP. This is best shown by the Historical Transect at Table 9.2 prepared by the villagers of Mallah, a village adjoining the park (see Figure 9.1).

Four Remarkable Features

There were four remarkable features. The KNP gained in status and importance, which attracted several policy measures. Apart from upgrading the park from a reserve to sanctuary to a national park and having it declared as a world heritage site, several other steps were taken. 50 years ago, when KNP was a Duckshoot reserve the villagers had free access to the park and usually used it for grazing cattle, accessing fodder and some wild fruits. The villagers of Mallah being vegetarians did not hunt birds, animals and fish.

In 1956, when the Reserve was upgraded to a sanctuary, *status quo* was maintained because, people residing in or around a sanctuary, except those which were prohibited. Grazing, cutting of grass, accessing wild fruits etc., were not prohibited activities.

In 1982, the sanctuary was upgraded to a national park. This is where the first problem started. As soon as KNP was declared a national park, grazing of animals, accessing fodder etc., were banned. This was likely to adversely affect the villagers of Mallah and such other villages along the KNP boundary. There were protests and agitation by the villagers. In order to mitigate the suffering of the villagers, it was agreed by the government that cost of fodder will be reimbursed to the villagers and employment opportunities created by the KNP will provide employment to some of the villagers. The transition of the sanctuary to a national park was completed without further events.

Subsequently, according to the villagers of Mallah the promise of employment was not honoured and the reimbursement of cost of fodder was discontinued.

Table 9.2

Historical Transect of Village Mallah, Bharatpur

No. of Birds	*Condition of Ghana*	*Relationship of the Villagers with Ghana*	*Livelihood of Villagers*	*Changes in Livelihood Pattern*	*Remarks*
********** ********** **********	50 Years ago: Duck reserve of Maharaja of Bharatpur. No bird shooting except for Maharaja's guests.	Grazing area, source of fodder and food.	Village Mallah was a small village.	25 per cent agriculture and 75 per cent milk vending.	Villagers had large herds of milch animals from which they sold milk at 0 marginal cost.
********** ********** **********	Ghana National Park 1982. Boundary wall started several years back, completed. Shooting banned.	Grazing, cutting grass etc. stopped. Park Authorities started paying for cost of fodder to villagers and promised employment in KNP for villagers.	Village Mallah a big village. Stall feeding animals started. People also started taking up employment in neighbouring industry.	15 per cent agriculture, 10 per cent industry and 75 per cent milk vending.	Villagers who had large herds of milch animals from which they sold milk started reducing the number of animals they kept.
*********** **********	KNP around 1985 declared World Heritage Site. Growth in the number of animals.	Permit to cut grass during summer started. Promise of employment broken. Cost of fodder stopped earlier.	Mallah—an expanded village now. Stall feeding of animals continued. People also started taking up agriculture as a major source of livelihood. Grazing still banned.	25 per cent agriculture, 10 per cent industry and 65 per cent milk vending.	Livelihood from sale of milk substantially reduced. More reliance on agriculture, especially *Rabi* (summer) crops.

contd...

...contd...

*********** **********	KNP around 1988	Illegal grazing, illegal grass cutting and "informal" tax payment started.	Villagers in a quandary.	35 per cent agriculture, 60 per cent milk and 10 per cent industry.	More or less as in 1985.
*********** *****	KNP in 2002 in crisis of water.	Illegal grazing, illegal grass cutting and "informal" tax payment. Attack by animals on the crops of villagers. Competition for water.	Mallah Village a big village of 500 households.	25 per cent on sale of milk and 75 per cent on agriculture.	Livelihood primarily dependent on agriculture in *Rabi*. Milch animals reduced dramatically. Employment in industry stopped as major industries closed down.

Village Analysts: Tulsi Ram Pandit, Vijan Pahelwan, Udai Singh Thakur, Nitra Pal Pahlwan, Bhim Singh (*Sarpanch*), Ratan Singh *Rickshaw-walla* and others.

Facilitator: Amitava Mukherjee. Date: 2/01/2002.

The Beginning of the Second Problem

This started the second problem and the major problem. The villagers faced with the prospect of losing the principal source of fodder and grazing rights, started to change their livelihood pattern. In 1982, they depended roughly 75 per cent on sale of milk (from their herd of milch animals), 15 per cent on agriculture and 10 per cent on employment in the industrial and service sector for their livelihood. Over the years, the proportion of dependence on milch animals and employment in the industrial and service sectors for livelihood have declined sharply. In 2002, people depended primarily on agriculture for their livelihood or what the villagers said their dependence on agriculture and milch animals for their livelihood was now in the proportion of 75 per cent and 25 per cent respectively. These changes have been induced by two factors. Dependence on milch animals for livelihood has been reduced as fodder as grazing area has shrunk. Dependence on industrial employment for livelihood has vanished because several industries such as Dalmia Dairy, SIMCO, GWD Lock Factory and China Cigarettes have been shut down. In effect, the villagers in around KNP have turned into settled agriculturist from pastoralists. And the change was almost irreversible.

Thus, currently villagers maintained only as many milch animals as they were able to stall-feed and have migrated to agriculture (during *rabi*, that is, summer cultivation) in a big way, depending primarily on irrigation. They have not migrated to *kharif* (or monsoon) cultivation, because the villagers perceived that the monsoon rains were insufficient to support paddy, the principal *kharif* crop, in their kind of soil. Since agriculture is dependent on irrigation, there was fight for water. The fight for water was with KNP because the source of water both for KNP and the villagers was the good old Ajan Bundh. In years when rainfall was normal or above normal, the wetlands of KNP got inundated in the natural course of things and the problem of water got sorted out automatically.

The Genesis of the Tripartite Dispute

However, when Bharatpur received less than normal rainfall, such as in 1999 and 2000, KNP needed water from Ajan Bundh for inundating the marshes and wetlands. In such years tripartite disputes arose. The first dispute was raised by villagers inhabiting villages like Mallah lying on the western boundary of KNP. They protested and prevented water being released to KNP, because that would mean that water for *Rabi* cultivation from Ajan Bundh would not come (or would not come in desired quantity) to their villages. This would have meant loss of livelihoods. The second dispute was raised by the Park authorities of KNP, who wanted water to be released to KNP from Ajan Bundh or else the wetlands could not be flooded. This would have resulted in a loss of habitation for birds, loss of food for the birds and animals and shortage of water for the animals and birds to drink. The third dispute was raised by villagers inhabiting villages like Jatoli and Ghasaula lying to the east of KNP. They also wanted water to be released to KNP and then allowed to run out of the Park through the sluice gates located on the eastern boundary of KNP, because they would get none of the water from the Ajan Bundh unless the same passes through KNP. Consequently livelihoods in these villages depended upon both the release of water from Ajan Bundh to KNP and the opening up of sluice gates of the Park to let water flow out of wetlands.

Availability of water and its distribution between KNP, villages on the west of KNP and the villages on the east of KNP held the key to the survival of the park and the livelihoods of all the villagers residing along the Park boundary. Amongst all of them, the need for distribution of water partook the nature of a fight between survival of human beings and survival of birds and animals.

The Third Problem

This brings us to the third problem. The upgradation of KNP to a national park and the ban on hunting and shooting, have seen a steady rise in the number of mammals particularly the herbivores, the blue bell (called *nilgai*), chital and wild boar. The rise in the number of herbivores, blue bull and wild boar had ushered in the third problem for the villagers. Though there was a boundary wall around the KNP to prevent grazing and other forms of trespassing, there are breeches in the wall. Blue bulls, sambars and wild boar from KNP jump over the boundary walls and pass through the breaches to invade and graze standing crops of the villagers. Since the villagers of Mallah are vegetarians and since the animals were protected animals under the Wild Life Protection Act, these animals cannot be killed. The loss in crops and damage to croplands put severe strain on the villagers. And interestingly enough, the animals and human beings competed for the crops more when there was greater scarcity of food, *viz.*, in the years when rainfall was deficient. Shortage of rains meant lower availability of food for the wild animals and they in consequence scouted around for food outside the KNP. Unfortunately these were also the years when due to deficient rain water, the productivity of crops were lower. Thus, the villagers complained, the attack on their crops were the severest when they needed their crops most.

The villagers argued that the absence of the buffer zone for the KNP was a major source of problem. They perceived that the presence of a buffer zone would have prevented animals from KNP grazing and trampling their crops less. This would have resulted in reducing the adverse impact of the KNP on their current livelihood, thrust upon them by the Park itself.

Ratio Decidendi of Problems

From the villagers' perspective the establishment of KNP, therefore, have had threefold effect on them. One, they have been forced to abandon their traditional livelihood, that of selling milk, by stoppage of grazing and accessing fodder. Two, they were deprived of the use of water from Ajan Bundh when they needed it most. Three, they were deprived of their produce due to the predatory activities of the blue bulls, wild boars and other animals from KNP.

Closed Access and Increased Vulnerability

Finally, the villagers perceived that the closed access regime has actually rendered the KNP more vulnerable to destruction. Their reasoning is given in Figure 9.2. The villagers argued that closure of the park to grazing automatically reduced the availability of feed for the birds, through lesser nutrient replenishment and proliferation of insects and the consequent reduction of the number of birds which have visited KNP over the years, particularly in 2000 and 2001. At the same time, non-grazing was instrumental in increasing the quantum of weeds and grass beyond the warranted level, which in its turn increased the vulnerability of the park to fire hazards. While the former had caused a decline in the number of birds visiting Ghana of late, the latter may obliterate the flora, fauna, mammals, reptiles and other animals in the Park in not too distant future. The future of the Park lies in allowing grazing so that surplus vegetation may be removed in a natural process.

Figure 9.2

The Cause and Effect Relationship of Closed Access Regime in KNP

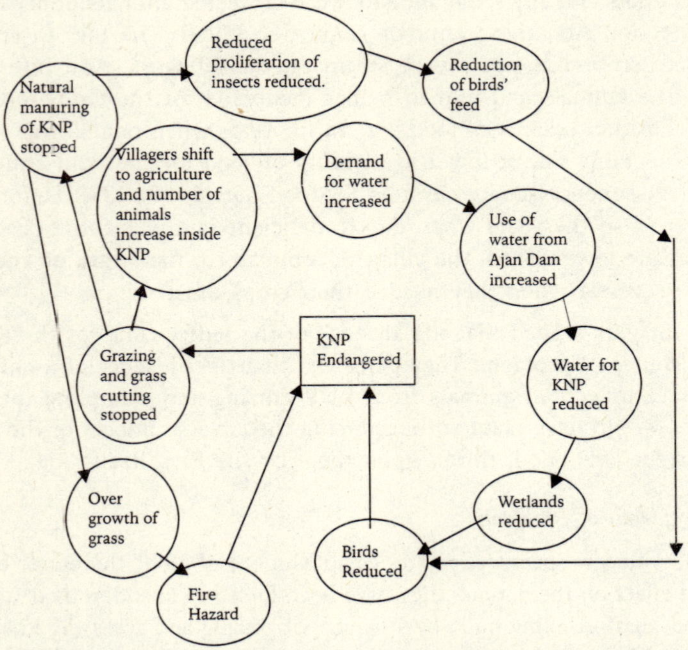

Village Analysts: Tulsi Ram Pandit, Vijan Pahelwan, Udai Singh Thakur, Nitra Pal Pahlwan, Bhim Singh (*Sarpanch*), Ratan Singh *Rickshaw-walla* and others.

Facilitator: Amitava Mukherjee.

Date: 2/01/2002

The villagers' perception about the problems non-grazing causes has substantial backing of the scientific community. "The available studies of wetland suggest that the interactions with the surrounding terrestrial vegetation as well as herbivores play significant roles in the structure and functioning of wetland systems" (see Patten *et al.*, 1989). Buffaloes would have also played an important role in checking the formation of marl crusts which interferes with the growth of aquatic plants, sprouting and seed germination, sediments aeration and microbial activity. Several bird species feed upon the rhizomes, tubers and benthic animals, and, therefore are directly affected" (Gopal, 1989). And the solution suggested by the villagers was indeed a solution that was suggested earlier by the Bombay Natural History Society in 1990.

The Responses to Tackle Communities' Problem of Livelihood

There have been responses to all these problems both from the side of the Park authorities and the villagers. It would be worthwhile spending some time on the issues.

The Problem of Fodder

To tackle the problem of fodder, villagers maintained that they per force illegally graze their milch animals in KNP (to the extent possibly because they have to pay an informal tax to the Forest Guards in KNP) and illegally cut grasses (again by paying informal taxes). While during the regime of limited access, villagers were allowed to cut grass during summer months only, a period in the year when the Park was least populated, now under the closed access regime, villagers cut grass whenever they can. (We saw villages cutting grass even in January, a peak season in the park for migratory birds.)

To tackle the problems of water for the Park and the villagers, the villagers have come to an agreement with the Park authorities (through the Village Water Users Committee) that water beyond 7 feet in Ajan Bundh may be released into the Park through the Ghana Canal. Once the water table in the Ajan Bundh fell to 7 feet, such water as there may still be in the Bundh was left to be used by the villagers for cultivation. As a consequence KNP received about 180 million cubic feet of water as against its requirement of 500 million cubic feet of water in 2001. The Park, therefore, received far too little water. As a consequence, there are large patches which were wetlands earlier have dried up. Reference is invited to the biodiversity map prepared by the cycle-rickshaw pullers and guides (Figure 9.1). Such dry patches were visible even to visitors. One noted visitor remarked: "Beyond the barrier, the scene was desolate. The marsh was all dry. There not even a small pool of water in evidence for upto 3 kms. Areas that used to be overflowing with water were empty" (Dang, 2001-02). And the wetlands have also been subjected to terrestrialisation such that in 1998 a "total intake of only 12 million^3 water from Ajan Bundh (against an estimated requirement of 15 million^3) could fill the depressions near the Park's entrance" (Chauhan and Gopal, 2001).

The Park authorities have also attempted to flood the wetlands of KNP during the drought affected years of 2000 and 2001, by drawing ground water. It was thought that this would enable the authorities to provide more water to villagers lying to the west of Ajan Bundh and through the sluice gates, to the villagers lying to the east of KNP. However, the impact of such discharge of ground water had limited efficacy because such water did not bring with it aquatic lives that came into the park from the Ajan *Bundh* and the flooding the impounments inside KNP was insufficient to allow the sluice gates to be opened.

On the last problem of crops being grazed and damaged by the animals from the KNP, there has as yet been no response from any quarter.

Table 9.3

Problems Faced by Cycle-Rickshaw Pullers

Sl. No.	*Problems Identified in WWF-1996*	*Problems Currently Faced*	*Remarks*
1	Seasonality of work	Seasonality of employment.	The peak season was from November to January.
2	General decline in the number of birds	General decline in the number of birds, which was particularly severe in 2000 and 2001.	Some of them believed that the war in Afghanistan will reduce the arrival of migratory birds next year.
3	Some tourists are generous and others are miserly.	Some tourists are good pay masters (some even gift away their binoculars to them) and others are miserly.	Rana Singh was one cycle-rickshaw puller who during a long conversation with us showed us the binocular he had received as a gift.
4	Competition* from cycles (50), *tongas* or horse carraiges (20), electra vans (25) and boats (60).	Competition from private cycle-rickshaws, boats and cycle.	Private cycle-rickshaws are allowed during christmas holidays.
5	Authorised guides	Authorised guides who crowd the booking counter at the main gate.	
6	Connivance between guides and personnel at the counter		
7	(Mal) treatment meted out by the Park staff in terms of free rides to the city		
8	Increased prices for entry tickets		
9		Absence of a good map of the Park at the main gate.	
10			
11		Absence of rickshaw shed.	

Note: * Figures in the parenthesis indicate through free scores the intensity of competition in ordinal terms.

Problems of a Significant Stakeholder

There are several significant players, as was apparent from the discussion above. The first was the cycle-rickshaw pullers. These operators play a vital role in eco-tourism. But they have problems confronting them, which have persisted over time. Table 9.3 gives the problems faced by them over the years.

The cycle-rickshaw pullers played a significant role in KNP. Apart from providing clean transportation, they played crucial roles in creating a proper environment in the Park by educating and informing the visitors and tourists, creating awareness about the need to keep the park free of wastes (especially non-bio-degradable wastes) and often cleaning the park of filth. They had problems but some of them were being looked after by the State.

Conclusions

The foregoing discussion leads us to the following conclusions.

Problems on the Upswing

Firstly, KNP and the communities living around the Park both had problems galore. Unfortunate as it was, both KNP and the communities got no benefit from each other. An adversarial relationship was writ large all over. And one of the reasons has been that not much has been done to tackle the problems over time. The problems faced by the Park were clearly identified by Gopal (1989) and the problems faced by the communities were comprehensively documented in WWF-India, 1996. Efforts have been made to deal with problems facing the Park. These problems nevertheless persisted and have indeed now increased. The tonics and elixirs to sort out the maladies have not worked. Table 9.4 illustrates the situation.

Table 9.4

Comparative Table of Problems Faced by the Community and KNP

Sl. No.	*Problems found by Gopal (1989)**	*Problems found in WWF-India, 1996*	*Current problems*	*Remarks*
		Problems Faced by the KNP		
1	Erratic rainfall and consequent water shortage		Erratic rainfall and consequent water shortage**	
2	Eutrophication from fertilisers and toxic effects of pesticides		Birds dying of eating pesticide laced grains outside the park**	
3	Insufficient tree cover for roosting and brooding		Insufficient tree cover for roosting and brooding@	

contd...

...contd...

Sl. No.	*Problems found by Gopal (1989)**	*Problems found in WWF-India, 1996*	*Current problems*	*Remarks*
4	Growth of weeds		Growth of weeds like water hyacinth**	Heaps of water hyacinth manually being removed and dried can be seen.
5	Unwanted vegetation which used to be consumed by milch animals	Unwanted vegetation (mainly *Paspalum distichum*) which used to be consumed by milch animals	Unwanted vegetation which used to be consumed by milch animals	
5	Management of surrounding forest area	Destruction of trees like kadam	Management of forest area**@	
6	Keeping humans and milch animals out of the Park		Keeping humans and milch animals out of the Park@	
7			Problems of grazing round the year (by paying informal tax) which caused disturbance to birds, damaging eggs, damaging aquatic vegetation during peak season and stirring up mud.**@	
8	Fire Hazard		Fire Hazard**.	
9			Pollution from plastic bags and other non-bio-degradable substance**@.	
10			Multiplication of visitors with attitudes not conducive to KNP's environment**@.	
11		Release of unproductive and disabled cows into the park by the villagers	Release of diseased and disabled cows into the park from the adjoining village	
12			Sharing of development cess collected with entry tickets etc., not yet worked out@.	

contd...

...contd...

Sl. No.	*Problems found by Gopal (1989)**	*Problems found in WWF-India, 1996*	*Current problems*	*Remarks*
		Problems Faced by the Communities Living Around the Park		
13			Problems of collecting fodder and fuel from the park**.	
14		Problems of wild animals attacking crops	Problems of animals of KNP attacking crops**	
15			Problems of paying informal taxes to forest guards**.	
16		Problems of sharing water from Ajan Bundh between the communities and park	Problems of sharing water from Ajan Bundh between the communities and park**	
17			Fall in the number of birds**.	
18			The development fees collected, which should be used for the community's benefit (at least partly), diverted to other uses**.	
19		Entry to temple for villagers should be legalised.		
20		Water logging due to obstruction of natural drainage by the Boundary Wall		
21		Unemployment	Unemployment	Currently because of closure of factories around Bharatpur

Note: * The Paper does not speak about the problems of the communities as the paper focussed on the problems of (mis) management of the Park only.

** Perceived by the villagers, cycle-rickshaw pullers, and guides, as elicited in participatory sessions.

@ Perceived by the Park authorities, as elicited through semi structured interviews in participatory sessions.

Whereas as of late there were 19 problems faced by the Park and the communities, there were six such problems identified by WWF-1996. Gopal (1989) had identified seven problems for the KNP. While numbers *per se* do not mean much, but the disturbing fact is that the same problems persists and have been exacerbated, as perceived by the communities.

Water is the Critical Variable

Secondly, water is vital for the survival of the Park. The water that inundates KNP through the Ghana Canal emanating from the Ajan Bundh holds the lifeline for the birds, animals, insects, flora and fauna of KNP. Ground water can help the life in KNP only to limited extent. The same Ajan Bundh also holds the lifeline for the communities around KNP and the communities on the one hand and KNP on the other, are competing for water that Ajan Bundh holds. One gets a measure of how problems have transformed by nature over the years when one ponders over the fact that Ajan Bundh which was started as a flood control instrument, is today struggling to survive because of want of water.

Customary Right: Right to Graze Cattle

Thirdly, because the KNP has denied access to the villagers to graze their cattle in the Park and to collect fodder (grass etc.) from KNP, the villagers have shifted their livelihood pattern in a major way. They have dramatically reduced their dependence on rearing milch animals for sale of milk to make a living, to settled agriculture during the winter and *rabi* (summer) cultivation seasons, which were mostly irrigated agriculture. The major crops grown were wheat and mustard and some grams. Water for such irrigation only came from the Ajan Bundh. This had the serious implication in that the villagers, living in the periphery of the Park, now depended on the same source of water, *viz.*, the Ajan Bundh upon which the existence of KNP critically hinges. In effect, the water that Ajan Bundh provided was the source of life for both the villagers living in villages outside KNP and for the birds, animals, insects, flora and fauna and the entire vegetation of KNP. Additionally, while closing the Park to grazing and access to human beings for other purposes, was intended to protect the Park, it had the effect of endangering the Park. Because the move forced the villagers to migrate to a livelihood (irrigated agriculture) which depended heavily on the basic resource that sustained the Park, *viz.*, water. It had the effect of creating conflicting claims on water from the source that fed the KNP.

Deprivation and Entitlement

Fourthly, there is sense of deprivation that the villagers feel. The feeling of deprivation is because KNP has denied access to the villagers to graze their cattle in the Park and to collect fodder (grass etc.), which was a classic case of a secondary conflict arising out of what could be called "scarcity of means" (Mulder, 1980). The fact that the villagers had both customary and legal rights to graze their cattle in and to collect fodder (grass etc.) from KNP is undeniable. When such rights were taken away and the relationship between the livelihood system of the villages and the Park was severed or at least permanently altered, when National Park was established, not much effort was made to minimise the adverse consequences on the villagers. The compensation for fodder was stopped and promise of providing employment to some of the youth was never fulfilled. Indeed setting up of the KNP appeared like a classic case of taking the villagers, mostly illiterate, for a ride by the government by making incorrect promises and raising unachievable expectations. Public memory is not short when it comes to events that puncture their livelihoods!

The situation has been further exacerbated by the fact that the government had furthered reneged on promises made even in the late 90s. The government (following the WWF, 1996 study) started collecting development funds from different classes and kinds of visitors. Table 9.5 provides a break-up of the different charges levied by the Forest Department for using the facilities of KNP.

Table 9.5

Schedule of Rates Charged by KNP (In Indian Rupees)

Sl. No.	*Category of Visitors*	*Fees*	*Development Fund*	*Total*
1	Indian visitor	5	20	25
2	Foreign visitor			
3	Student	1	4	5
4	Bus	25	75	100
5	Gypsy, jeep, car, etc.	12	38	50
6	Motor cycle	03	07	10
7	Boating charges per head	5	20	25
8	Small boat	15	60	75
9	Big boat	30	120	150
10	Electra van per head	5	15	20
11	Photography 8 mm video	50	150	200
12	Video by Indian professional photographers	1000	2000	3000
13	Movie/Video for film production	5000	15000	20,000
14	Video by foreign professional photographers	2000	3000	5000

A look at the levy structure showed that the major component of the levies was the development fund. The development fund, which was to be used in Eco-tourism (defined elsewhere in this paper), was never used for the purpose. The entire exaction goes into the state coffers. Since funds created by the state by pooling amounts deposited in the from different sources was highly "fungible", it was difficult to locate where all the money collected as development fees went. The communities around the park perceive that the development fees collected by the Park authorities should have been spent on their development, but that has not happened. The communities, therefore, feel deprived once again.

Summary of Villagers' Perception

In sum the villagers' perception of the role of KNP in their lives looked like the following:

- Their customary right to graze animals in the park has been violated.
- Their customary right to collect fuel wood, fruits and food from the park has also been violated.
- They have been forced to abandon their pastoralist way of life to that of settled agriculturists.
- Their principal source of livelihood now, agriculture, was threatened by appropriation of water for the birds and animals in the park, reducing the issue to a fight between survival of human beings versus survival of birds and animals.
- Animals from the KNP damaged their crops and agricultural land.
- The government has not honoured the promises of employment and compensation for taking away their right to graze milch animals.
- Money collected for their development was being diverted to other uses, not known to them.

Relationship between the Park and the Communities

Fifthly, because of the foregoing, the relationship between the villages and the KNP is one of confrontation and conflict. The villagers perceive that they derive no benefit from KNP whatsoever. Indeed the overwhelming perception is that KNP is the principal source of their major problems. And the villagers can only be hapless spectators, given that such animals like the blue bulls etc., are protected animals which cannot be attacked by the villagers, which they might otherwise have done. As one villager remarked: "*Aare, ya to dana do, ya chara do, ya pani do.*" (Either give us food, or give us fodder or give us water.)

Clearly all the stakeholders have not been involved in the formation and management of the KNP. This was apparent from the problem analysis of different stakeholders. The perspectives of the state government in the forest department, of the environmentalists (read ornithologist) and to a lesser extent of the tourists were dominant influences in the formation and management of KNP. In one sense, it was a top-down approach adopted for ensuring a good future for KNP. Probably this was a pivotal factor that ensured that the problems of the park in establishing a working relationship with the surrounding communities, was exacerbated over the years. There was a lesson to be learnt.

Ingenuity in Tackling the Problems Created by the Tourists

Seventhly, while the powers that be did not demonstrate much ingenuity in tackling the problems of the livelihood of those living in the periphery of the KNP, showed considerable foresight in dealing with the menace of the tourists. They had in their management of KNP showed elements of eco-tourism when it was still not the flavour of the time, as it were. Hark these points:

(i) To reduce pollution, vehicular traffic has been banned inside the park except upto a certain point. Second, the introduction of cycle-rickshaws and bicycles and even *tongas* (horse drawn carriages) as principal means of transportation within the Park, all of which were available on hire in abundance, ensured that pollution inside the park is kept under check.

(ii) Educating the cycle-rickshaw pullers and the *tongawallas* on the environmental needs of KNP and the art of bird watching (including names of birds), helped in good measure in building public awareness on how to deal with KNP generally and the birds and animals particularly.

(iii) Indeed, these cycle-rickshaw pullers and the *tongawallas* are put through a three months course after which they have to pass an oral exam and only then are they licensed to act as guides and ply cycle-rickshaws and *tongas*. There is a refresher course held to up date these cycle-rickshaw pullers and the *tongawallas* so that they serve the tourists and visitors (especially the discerning/interested ones) better. This has ensured, additionally, a means of sustainable livelihoods for these cycle-rickshaw pullers and the *tongawallas* and guides.

(iv) The use of plastic bags has been banned which had the effect of restricting the preponderance of non-biodegradable material reaching in the heart of KNP. In fact, use of plastic bags within the perimeter of KNP is an offence.

(v) The closing down of the cafeteria in the vicinity of the Keoladeo Temple had the benefit of bringing down in substantial measure input into the Park's environment with plastic cups, plates, spoons, food packets and other of the non-biodegradable material and thus reduce agents known for polluting the Park.

Partnership with the Private Sector

Finally, the partnership between the private sector multinational company M/s

Swarovski & Co. of Austria, the World Wide Fund for Nature-India and the Government of Rajasthan for developing Dr. Salim Ali Interpretation Center and Programme, is excellent in conception. It will, when implemented fully, go a long way to develop awareness and the right attitudes amongst the tourists and visitors, to preserve and protect KNP, unique as it may in many ways. For a government, which had a record of adopting a top-down approach in the establishment and management of KNP, the wide ranging consultation with the community (WWF, 1996) that preceded the decision to set up the Interpretation Centre was indeed remarkable. The chances that the centre will achieve sustainability is much higher that what it would have been had the top-down approach been adopted.

Policy Implications

There are several policy implications that emerge from the study. These policy implications should be taken as suggestive.

Management of Emotional Relationship

Firstly, in all acts of the state, there should be more effort at managing the emotional content of the process. In case of KNP, where the livelihood as also the rights of the villagers were being jeopardised (for a worthy cause) yet not much attention was paid to manage the emotional upheaval of the communities affected. In consequence, there is a permanent adversarial relationship that evolved between the KNP and the communities who ring the Park. It needs to be understood clearly that those who manage the Park (and its establishment) are temporarily associated with KNP, whereas the relationship between the Park and the community living around (and previously dependent on) the Park is permanent and carry on for generations. There is even now the need to manage the emotional relationship between KNP and the people most affected by it. Hark these words: "*Ladhai hogee, aur ham mauke par ladhenge*" (There will be a fight and we will fight at the right moment). And "*Garib ke bad dua bahut jor lagtee hai.*" (The curse of a poor person hurts very badly). Managing the emotional relationship is critical in building the psychological capital of the villagers in adjoining villages for the ultimate benefit of KNP. As is well known now, sustainable livelihood requires five kinds of capital: physical, financial, natural, psychological and social capital. Similarly for the KNP to survive and prosper, the existence of all these capital are indispensable.

State as the Facilitator

Secondly, following from the foregoing, the role of the state must change from that of a controller and giver to that of a facilitator. Because the state in now projected as the controller, it had two damaging psychological effect. One, for every problem of the community *vis-à-vis* KNP, the communities look up to the state as the saviour and as they got disappointed, their antagonism to the park was exacerbated. Secondly, the state having taken upon itself the responsibility of controlling the park, its inefficiencies have also injected into the management of the park. The sooner the state gets rid of its role as the controller, the better it is for KNP. The state, in its new incarnation in KNP, should be promoting, encouraging, guiding and making possible the wide scale participation of the communities living around the KNP in developing and applying more productive and sustainable forms of protecting the Park and their own livelihood. The participation in the special context of KNP must be interactive participation.

Revamping the Resources of Ajan Bundh

Thirdly, there is a need to revamp the sources that feed into the Ajan Bundh. Given that the vagaries of nature affect Bharatpur, unless the feeders of the Ajan Bundh are activated, it is impossible to save KNP and the communities from further injury. The Ajan Bundh is the last dam downstream of Banganga and Gambhir Rivers. Dams on the upper reaches of the rivers at Jamuar Ramgarh and Pachna Dam at Karoli have reduced the inflow into Ajan Bundh. Indeed because of dams upstream Banganga has totally dried up. One suggestion that came from the cycle-rickshaw pullers was that the Chambal River should be linked to Ajan Bundh to make it alive again.

Management of the Demand for Water

Fourthly, for the villagers to prosecute their irrigated agriculture without prejudice to the interest of KNP, they have to be weaned away from using the waters of Ajan Bundh. There are two alternatives. The first alternative was from the demand side, to adopt a two pronged approach on the water issue: one, make suitable arrangements be made for sharing water from the Ajan Bundh and two, hold and conserve as much of surface water as much as possible. Given that the area received on an average 662 mm of rains over a 60 day period, it is possible to harvest surface water successfully. Effectiveness of surface water harvesting, through watershed management practices has been demonstrated in the neighbouring district of Alwar by the pioneering work of Tarun Bharat Sangh and its Director, Sri Rajender Singh who won the Ramon Magsasay Award in 2001 (*Down to Earth*, 2001). Wherever possible, lift irrigation (not an easy option) should supplement the use of surface water for agriculture.

It needs to be underscored that the current system of having a Village Water Users Committee to decide on sharing of the Ajan Bundh water was termed as ineffective by both the parties. From the perspective of the communities, the committee usually met in one of the villages only once in a year, in or around the middle of October (*Kuar* in local language). This single meeting did not take care and failed to address all their problems. From the perspective of the Park authorities, the meeting of the Village Water Users Committee was of little consequence, because the Park had to take decisions about sharing and releasing of water around June–July, at the start of the monsoon season, while the committee met in October. The Park authorities confirmed that the Village Water Users Committee was almost defunct. Thus, an alternative system of resource and water sharing was imperative. To do so the role of the Village Water Users Committee has to be redefined from merely rubber stamping a *fait accompli* to planning for water use, planning for forest protection,[2] implementation of the plans jointly with the government (Park authorities), awareness generation and dispute settlement forum. There should be a study on the inter-relationship between water in the impoundments in the park and the ground water table in the adjoining villages. Intuitively, it seemed there was a positive co-relationship between ground water level in the villagers and the water in the impoundments in the Park.[3] Once this was established, it would be easier for the Village Water Users Committee to take a more sympathetic view of water for KNP.

Management of Water Supply

The second alternative was that from the supply side: methods for augmenting more water for Ajan Bundh was necessary. The cycle-rickshaw pullers and the communities indicated that the death knell for Ajan Bundh was sounded by the setting up of the Pachna Dam upstream on river Gambhir in Sawai Madhopur and Jamwa Ramgarh Dam near Jaipur on Ram Ganga, which had reduced the flow of the rivers very substantially. And indeed, one of the rivers has since become dry. According to the communities perspective, there was an urgent need of connecting river Chambal with Ajan Bundh.

Promoting "Alternative" Livelihoods

Fifthly, "alternative" off-farm livelihoods have to be explored and opened up. As Claridge and O'Callaghan (1997) noted "frequently it will be necessary to assist communities to develop alternative livelihood sources to compensate for restrictions that need to be placed on utilisation of former sources in order to protect important biodiversity values". It was seen that when employment in the industrial sector and service sector dried up in Bharatpur, the people increased their dependence upon agriculture. That is, there is a need to diversify the rural economy of Bharatpur, so that alternative livelihoods are created outside the government. This has been tried and tested several times elsewhere (Ayres *et al.*, 1997) such as in the Amazonian Flooded Forests.

2. Dr. Brij Gopal, professor, Jawaharlal Nehru University, New Delhi pointed this out to me, during a personal conversation with Dr. Amitava Mukherjee.
3. The experience of Joint Forest Management, of which the Forest departments were integral parts, in different parts of the country have enough lessons to offer.

Just as the partnership between the private sector multinational company M/s Swarovski & Co. of Austria, the World Wide Fund for Nature-India and the Government of Rajasthan is working towards developing the Dr. Salim Ali Interpretation Center and Programme, there is need to involve the corporate world and the NGOs as well. The corporate sector should be encouraged to generate green industry to diversify the local economy and ease the pressure on the park and the Ajan Bundh water. As Claridge and O'Callaghan (1997) noted "Livelihood projects provide an opportunity to involve the business sector in the wetland management process. Project personnel can build on this connection not only to increase the level of involvement in community development but also make the business community more aware of wetland conservation issues". NGOs like Partners-in-Change, New Delhi who are in the business of developing good corporate citizenship would be willing to act as a bridge between the Park authorities, the communities and the corporate sector. Additionally NGOs, like Development Alternatives, New Delhi, could play an effective role in building capacities of the communities to enable them to take up alternative livelihoods and provide ideas on appropriate technology and marketing.

Sixthly, there is an urgent need to put an end to the informal taxes that the communities pay for grazing the animals and cutting grass from KNP. Because not only are the communities losing out, even the environment of KNP and the birds are being hurt because by paying the informal taxes, the villagers are grazing their cattle and cutting grass throughout the year, including during the peak season when such activities should be closed. There has to be serious attempts at finding out a way to make sure that while the communities get a chance to graze their animals and access fodder while not disturbing the environment of the Park. The sooner KNP goes on to regulated access from the closed access regime, better it so for the KNP and the communities who live in the periphery of the Park. The happenings in the KNP is yet another instance of failure of the government to implement its own orders, despite there being human resources, the technical competence and awareness to do so.

Sharing the Development Fund

Finally, if the powers that be are serious about eco-tourism then it is important that policy shifts be made, so that local communities are benefited from the KNP. The noted taxonomist Sir Ghillean Prance remarked "*We need to promote tourism without the destruction of the natural habitat. And Eco-tourism can be one of the ways for this. In this, tourists visit the natural areas at a premium cost and the benefit goes to local population*" (Rahid, 2002) (Emphasis added). While steps have been taken to ensure that tourists bear a premium cost, the benefit to local population is yet to be seen. There is need to take action on this front.

This is particularly so when large resources were being raised as development fund from every man, woman, vehicle, camera and video and what you have. The issue when raised with the park authorities, evinced a positive reply but it was as yet fluid. "The issue of how to appropriate the development fund collected from the visitors and tourists as also their vehicles and equipment, was being sorted out."

References

Aronsson, Lars (2000). *The Development of Sustainable Tourism*. London and New York: Continuum.

Ayres, Jose Marcio *et al.* (1997). "Mamiruaua: The Conservation of Amazonian Flooded Forests", in Claridge, Gordon and O'Callaghan, Bernard (eds.): *Community Involvement in Wetland Management: Lessons from the Field*, Incorporating the Proceedings of Workshop 3:Wetlands, Local People and Development, of the International Conference on Wetlands and Development held in Kuala Lumpur, Malaysia, 9-13 October 1995. Kuala Lumpur: Wetland International.

Centre for Science and Environment (2002). "How Rainwater Harvesting Created a River, Arvari: a Video", *Down to Earth*, January, 15th, inside back cover, New Delhi.

Chauhan, Malavika and Brij Gopal (2001). "Biodiversity and Management of Keoladeo National Park (India)- A Wetland of International Importance", in Gopal, B. Junk, J. A. and Davis, J. A.: *Biodiversity in Wetlands: assessment, function and conservation*. Leiden, The Netherlands: Backhuys Publishers.

Dang, Rajiv. "Wildways (2001-02). A Date with Pelicans", *Holiday Travel India*, December/January: 32-36.

Dann, G.M.S (1977). "Anomie, ego-enhancement and tourism", *Annals of Tourism Research* 4(4): 184-194.

Deputy Chief Wildlife Warden and Director, KNP. Keoladeo National Park, Bharatpur, A Park that Inspires Migrants the World Over (Bharatpur: Gang Printers) undated.

Gopal, B. (1989). "Wetland (Mis)Management by Keeping People Out: Two Examples from India" in Marchand, M. and Jdo De Haes, H.A. (eds.). *The People's Role in Wetland Management* Lieden: Centre for Environmental Studies.

Malhi, C.S. (2001). "Unearthed", *Down to Earth*, December 15.

Mulder, M. (1980). "Conflicthantering, theorie en praktijk in organisaties", Stenfert Kroese B.V., Leiden, The Netherlands as quoted in de Soet, M.C. and de Wit, A.B.: " Overview Paper: Conflict in Handling Wetland management" in Marchand, M. and Jdo De Haes, H.A. (eds.): loc. cit.

Oakley, P. (1987). *People's Participation in Conservation: A Review*, SADCC (Geneva: International Labour Organisation).

Palten, D.T. and J.C. Stormberg (1989). "Instream flow requirements for riparian vegetation" in Baumli, G.R. (1989) (ed.). Legal, Institutional, Financial and Environmental Aspects of Water Issues. New-York, American Society for Civil Engineers.

Rashid, Toufiq (2002). "India has much to tell the world about conservation, says British Scientist", *Express Newsline*, New Delhi, 12th January, p.3.

Singh, Rajpal (1999). *Keoladeo National Park Bharatpur*. Jaipur: Piyush International.

Sustainable Tourism, World Conference (1995). *Charter for Sustainable Development*. Lazarote, Canary Islands, Spain Sustainable Tourism, World Conference April.

Svalastog, S. (1994). *Lokalisering av reiseliv: Om resursonalyser; den romlige fordelning og lokal innpassing*.2. itgave/2. oolag. Skriftserien. No. 92, Hogskolen i Llehammer as quoted in Aronsson, Lars: *The Development of Sustainable Tourism*. London and New York: Continuum.

Voase, Richard (1995). *Tourism: the Human Perspective*. London: Hodder & Stoughton.

World Wide Fund for Nature(WWF-India) (1996). *Participatory Management Planning for Keoladeo National Park*. New Delhi: World Wide Fund for Nature.

World Wide Fund for Nature-India (2002). *Dr. Salim Ali Interpretation Centre and Program, Keoladeo National Park, Bharatpur, An Overview*, mimeograph. Bharatpur: Forest Department, Govt. of Rajasthan.

Part III

Policy Analysis

10

Voices of the Poor for Review of Poverty Reduction Strategy Paper for Armenia

The ultimate measure of a man is not where he stands in moments of comfort and conveniences, but where he stands at times of challenge and controversy
—Dr. Martin Luther King

Introduction

The PRSP for Armenia was adopted in 2003. The preparation of the PRSP was made participatory as enjoined by the World Bank. However, as the concept of "participation" was relatively new in Armenia, the process was huge and participation of every description was included. From April to November 2002, two agencies selected by the Government of Armenia to organise public participation, organised "(i) public discussions with representations from civil society, deputies of the national assembly, local government and the press; (ii) seminars in all regions of the country with the participation of civil society, the private sector, central, regional and local governments; (iii) preparation, publication and dissemination of information and analytical material for the public, including through the internet;[1] (iv) TV and radio programmes; (v) articles in the provincial and national press; (vi) public opinion surveys; and public awareness campaigns in communities, various representative groups of the population, educational institutions etc."[2] According to the PRSP, an "Internet site including information on the participatory process has been set up and is regularly updated."[3]

The Governmental bodies through their representatives on the PRSP Steering Committee and Working Group and participation of Deputies in Seminar, topic discussion and round tables; regions through discussions and round tables; local self-governments through feedback on the draft PRSP and participation in a three day workshop on the issues of Local Self Government; NGOs, scholarly and educational structures, mass media, private sector and trade unions; international agencies through joint comments on TOR/Draft PRSP seminars and technical support; and the diaspora through participation of organisations representing them in joint discussions on the PRSP, all participated in the writing of the PRSP under reference. "More than

1. See *www.gov.am/en/gov/iprsp, www.undp.am/pubs/pover/index.htm*
2. PRSP Armenia, 2003 page 17.
3. Ibid.

100 written recommendations were received. These were mainly incorporated in the draft PRSP. More than 1800 people participated in events organised within the framework of the participatory process. Overall, about 700 recommendations were recorded based on questionnaires completed at the end of discussions."[4]

Some Problems with Participation in the Preparation of the PRSP

From the discussions with Government functionaries, donors, civil society actors and international agencies the following features emerged:

(i) It was widely believed that the participatory process followed in the preparation of the PRSP was extensive. Several stakeholders participated.

(ii) Since the concept of participation was new to Armenia and to many development actors in the country, quality and the process of the participatory exercises were not as good as was desired.

(iii) There was, however, some disappointment that in the processes the direct consultation of with the key stakeholders (namely the poor) on a significant scale did not take place.

(iv) All the outcomes of the participatory process(es) were not incorporated into the final PRSP document. According to some key civil society actors, this had resulted in cynicism amongst the people about the PRSP.

(v) There was a general feeling amongst NGOs and development actors that there will be lack of motivation on the part of the people to engage in the PRSP review process. However, it was felt across the board that direct consultation with the people, as inputs to reviewing the PRSP and seeking feedback from the people on a draft revised PRSP, would be important.

(vi) The Government of Armenia was keen on the participation of people in the revision of the PRSP but it did not wish to "radically" disturb the exiting institutional arrangements for revision of the PRSP.

While civil society actors felt that lack of political will to incorporate the outcomes of the participatory process(es) was mainly responsible for the disappointments with participation in the preparation of the PRSP, Experts who Drafted the PRSP felt that views from the participatory process(es) could not be better incorporated because "thousands of pages" of material presented to them could not be put to best use within the available resources (including time) because of the sheer volume. They thought the "Voices of the Poor" would be very important in drafting the PRSP and would also be keen to have feedback from the people once the PRSP is drafted.

4. Ibid.

Revision of PRSP

There were two tracks of the PRSP revision process. One, based on the monitoring of the PRSP implementation so far and other inputs, the Expert Group were to draft the revised PRSP document in a manner it deemed fit. Two, there was a participatory track, in which views and opinions of the people (especially the poor people) in revising the PRSP were be elicited through a participatory process and the outcome of the process (called for brevity, "Voices of the Poor") were to be taken cognisance of in revising the PRSP. The second exercise and its outcome relate to people's direct participation. The present volume is that "Voices of the Poor."

The Framework

In order to facilitate the process of people's participation ("Voices of the Poor") in the revision of the PRSP, a framework was devised which is presented in summary format in Annexure A-10.1. In preparing the framework for the principal concern of the Government of Armenia (that the institutional arrangements are not required to be radically changed), the concerns of the civil society (that PRSP should be cognisant of the outcomes of the participatory processes) and the concern of the Expert Group (that they may be presented with outcomes of the participatory process in useable form) were all taken into account.

To complete the process it was estimated that 3 months time would be necessary. The process actually started in August 2006, and the "Voices of the Poor" was finally available by the beginning of November 2006.

Methodology and Methods

The methodology for eliciting views of the people was anchored on what has come to be known as the Participatory Action and Learning.[5] The basic tenets of the methodology are that people "know their condition best", can provide the data based on their knowledge, they can analyse their situation, they can identify their problems, they can find solutions to their problemmes and they can monitor and evaluate policies, strategies, plans and program designed for them. The outsiders act as facilitators and help them to make informed choices.

A fairly wide range of methods was used. These included:

- Mapping and modelling
- Transects

5. The earlier incarnation of this methodology was encapsulated in what was called Participatory Rural Appraisal (PRA). There were diverse versions of PRA.

- Seasonality analysis
- Time lines
- Historical transects
- Mobility mapping
- Scoring, ranking and matrix analysis
- Venn diagramming for institutional analysis
- Relational matrices
- Causality analysis
- Empowerment diagramming
- Semi-structured interviews
- Participatory SWOL Analysis
- Participatory force field analysis.

These methods are inherently flexible, both in theory and practice and improvisation is very strongly encouraged, as every human formation is unique. The facilitators, therefore, improvised these methods depending on local conditions.

The Process Followed

The Process as a Whole

The PRSP revision process was under way when work began on attempting to incorporate the "Voices of the Poor" directly into the PRSP revision process. As stated there were two tracks in revising the PRSP: one an Expert Group drafting the revised PRSP and a participatory process where, the public directly provided their inputs into the revision process under reference. There existed an institutional arrangement for revising the PRSP and for making it "participatory". The methodology adopted for this exercise did not require radical changes in the existing institutional arrangements for revising the PRSP but make small adjustments to achieve the objective of inputting "Voices of the Poor" in the revision of the PRSP.

The process involved the following elements:

(a) Reviewing the process of preparing the PRSP of Armenia and the various poverty reduction programme of the Government of Armenia.

(b) Ascertaining the views of the different stakeholders on the feasibility and utility of bringing the voices of the poor into the PRSP revision process.

(c) Devising a framework for eliciting the views of the people on the different dimensions of the PRSP, using participatory methods.

(d) Developing, to the extent possible, the capacity of the key government functionaries and selected agencies on the technology of eliciting the views of the people and reflecting them in the PRSP process, as indicated above.

(e) Carrying out participatory sessions in various locations.

(f) Preparing write ups on the participatory sessions.

(g) Sharing and disseminating the outcomes of the participatory exercises.

(h) Providing to the Expert Group, drafting the revised PRSP, a consolidated view of the people for incorporation in the revised PRSP.

The participatory process was carried out under the auspices of the PRSP Secretariat and supported by the UN System. The steps involved the following:

(a) A Special Group of animators was recruited under the auspices of the PRSP Secretariat (funded by UNDP). They were trained (for 10 days approximately) in the use of participatory methods.

(b) These animators carried out participatory sessions, using the methods outlined in 10 (c) above, or some combination thereof, on the PRSP in about 10 per cent of the villages in each region (subject to a minimum of two in each region), chosen randomly. [See section 5 below on the method for selection of the villages and communities]. The groups of people in each village/locality in towns who participated included the marginalised people/excluded people of the village/community. Where necessary, separate participatory sessions were conducted with the marginalised groups.

(c) In each town, the participatory sessions were conducted in different locations, selected through purposive sampling so that all localities/groups of people are represented in the participatory exercises, using the methods outlined in above, or some combination thereof.

(d) The reports on the outcomes of the participatory sessions in the villages and towns were prepared at the community level and shared at the community levels.

(e) The report on the outcomes of the participatory sessions in the villages (and towns) was consolidated in Yerevan with technical support from UN System. First, the issues as emerging from each village were collated in Tables, such as in Table 10.1 on issues relating to poverty. Then the common issues and exceptional issues were collated region-wise as Regional Tables. From these Regional Tables, the national issues were collated, as in Box 10.1 and 10.2 for poverty. [For brevity other tables relating to other sectors, like education, health, agriculture etc., have not been included in this publication]. A similar process was followed for finding solutions to the issues raised. Finally, these issues and solutions have been packaged in policy formats.

(f) Finally, the reports were then condensed in a publishable form for the Expert Group as "Voices of the Poor" being micro-level perspective possibly as a supplement to the macro perspective presented as Chapter 2 of the PRSP. As far as possible, the language used by the people has been retained, noting that there has been loss of local flavour due to translation from Armenian to English.

Based on the "*Voices of the Poor*", it was expected the experts revising the PRSP might wish to revise the PRSP Goals and Main Policy Directions.

A graphical presentation of the process is at Annexure A-10.1.

A Sample of Process Followed in One Community

There is no one-way of conducting participatory sessions. Indeed the technology of participation as also the philosophy of participation, enjoins that facilitators should avoid blueprint and improvise, innovate and improve all the time. Thus, the processes for the participatory sessions followed by different facilitators in the 11 regions were very different. Described below is a summary of steps followed in one village, to give an indication of the nature and character of the process.

- The name of the village is Teghut in Tavush Marz.
- The date when the participatory session was conducted is September 29, 2006.
- The methods used were the ones mentioned earlier.
- A village meeting was held in the middle of the village.
- Requested the villagers to choose a place for discussion.
- People were very active.
- Visited the Town Hall at 10.30 am and met the staff.
- Started Session in the school building at 11.00 am.
- Described the programme and answered villagers' question as a start up activity.
- Divided the people into two focus groups with men and women equally represented.
- Used previously prepared formats.
- Did not express our opinions.
- Took down dialectical expressions.
- Used historical transects, social map, problem matrix etc.
- And people chose the methods.
- Distributed evaluation sheets on the PLA and animators.
- Finished at 19.00 hours.
- Thanked for the discussion and said "we hope for positive social change."

Selection of the Communities

Armenia has a total of eleven regions and the urban agglomeration of Yerevan. All the regions and the urban agglomeration of Yerevan were chosen for conducting participatory sessions. It was originally envisaged that 10 per cent of villages from each region would be selected at random from each region and 10 per cent of the communities would be chosen at random from Yerevan. However, since the regions varied in size, in terms of the number of villages, it was decided that participatory session would be held in 10 per cent of the villages in each region subject to a minimum of four or even five communities per region. Based on the above, the villages and communities mentioned in Annexure A-10.2 were chosen for participatory sessions and participatory sessions were conducted.

Participatory sessions were also held in Yerevan but not as exhaustively as one would have ideally wished to.

Results of Participatory Sessions with the Communities: The Many Faces of Poverty

How People Define Poverty?

It is almost a truism that there are many faces of poverty and poverty has been defined in as many ways as there are experts in the field. The concepts of poverty such as income poverty, capability poverty, human poverty, poverty of "unfreedom" (from hunger, fear and want) and poverty born out of powerlessness, voicelessness and vulnerability from the tyranny of nature and man, are too well-known to be paraded here. The concepts of poverty that people in Armenia have demonstrated include the above concepts as also those that portray that there are localised forms of poverty. They have also spoken of the existence of such forms of poverty in different locations. These together make what we call the State of Poverty in Armenia to which we may presently turn.

The State of Poverty

The fifth column of Table 10.1 makes an interesting reading. In at least 21 of the villages and communities studied, people experienced a rise in poverty and in another four of the villages and communities, the state of well-being has remained unchanged. In three villages and communities studied, people perceive that poverty has actually decreased. That is, in at least 31.3 per cent (approximately) of the villages and communities, across the country, the state of deterioration of poverty has gone unabated over the years; and in at least 37.2 per cent of the villages and communities, the state of poverty has either deteriorated or remained as they were before.

Against this backdrop, it seems that a high rate of economic growth experienced by Armenia (of around 12 per annum for the past few years) has not translated itself into reduction in poverty uniformly across the country. The structure of growth as also the redistributive policies may need to be examined *de novo*. The views expressed by the people are different from what has been the recent position of the World Bank.[6]

Box 10.1

People's Criteria for Defining Poverty: Non-traditional Ones

Voice and Power Deficit

i. Powerlessness against the tyranny of nature: hailstorm;
ii. Being ethnic minority (Ezide);
iii. No voice: voicelessness in political process;
iv. Powerlessness/ voicelessness;
v. Yezidi (minority), sense of insecurity born out of government apathy;
vi. Violation of human rights;
vii. Proximity to border with Azerbaijan: vulnerability;
viii. Work without rest;

Gender and Relative Income Deficit

ix. Women headed households without paid employment;
x. Food poverty;
xi. A situation where the cost price of agricultural production is more than the sale price of the produce;
xii. The ratio of monthly incomes to indispensable cost per household is less than 1;
xiii. Imbalance between income and expenditure;
xiv. Not having anyone from their relatives helping from Russia;
xv. Lack of entitlements to pensions and welfare;

Social Obligation Deficit

xvi. "Inability to attend funeral or a wedding";
xvii. Inability to pay taxes;
xviii. Inability to pay public utility bills;

Capability Deficit

xix. Lack of intellectual and material capacities;
xx. Inability to sustain a student;

Privacy and Hygiene Deficit

xxi. "In the 21st century we still have no baths, there is not even a single public bath in the village. If that does not make us poor, what does?"
xxii. Not washed for weeks.

Criteria for Definition of Poverty

The fourth column of Table 10.1 also makes as interesting a reading as the fifth one. People have a very complex and comprehensive set of criteria to locate poverty. The depth of perception and width of tacit knowledge that people have in judging poverty are demonstrated by the wide range of criteria identified by them. Some of these are well known but some are rarely heard.

6. World Bank (2006). *Armenia, The Caucasian Tiger*. Washington D.C.: The World Bank. 23 June.

Hark these criteria outlined in Boxes 10.1 and 10.2. In Box 10.1, what we call for want of better expression, "non-traditional criteria", are catalogued and in Box 10.2 the "traditional criteria" are set out.

Let us look at the Boxes under reference.

Box 10.2

People's Criteria for Defining Poverty: Traditional Ones

Technology Deficit

i. No means to cultivate land;
ii. Lack of opportunity to cultivate land and engage in animal husbandry;
iii. Inability to cultivate land, keeping land fallow;
iv. Inefficient farming methods;
v. Low farming incomes;
vi. Low income caused by poor and inefficient cultivation of land;

Asset Deficit

vii. Landlessness;
viii. Lack of houses (living in shelters);
ix. Not owning vehicle, not owning cattle;
x. Distress sale of land plots and property;
xi. Bad housing;

Income Deficit

xii. Depressing living conditions;
xiii. Joblessness, not having at least one working member in the family; low income and have poorly paid jobs; not having a monthly income above 50,000 AMD;
xiv. Inability to provide for their basic needs and unemployment;
xv. Mounting debts; "Here, if you do not owe money to anyone, you are not alive";
xvi. Alcoholism;
xvii. Lack of assistance from outside the household.

Table 10.1

People's Concept of Poverty in Armenia

S.No.	*Village*	*Region*	*Criteria for definition of poverty*	*Has poverty increased or decreased*
1	Ohanavan	Aragatsotn	Powerlessness against the tyranny of nature: hailstorm.	The village is not poor but refugee-families and fallen freedom fighters are vulnerable.
2	Gyalto	Aragatsotn	Being ethnic minority (Ezide). No voice: voicelessness in political process.	
3	Zovassar	Aragatsotn	None	Not indicated

contd...

...contd...

S.No.	Village	Region	Criteria for definition of poverty	Has poverty increased or decreased
4	Nor Amanos	Aragatzotn	None mentioned. "20 families are in dire straits since they do not have anyone from their relatives helping from Russia".	Not indicated but majority members are so poor that they can not afford paying the land tax.
5	Derek	Aragatzotn	Yezidi (minority)	Not mentioned. There is no out-migration now.
6	Nerqin Sasnashen Community	Aratagzotn	Sense of insecurity born out of government apathy,	Not indicated
7	Tzaxkashen	Aragatzotn	Not indicated	Not indicated
8	Verin Artashat	Ararat	Women headed households without paid employment.	There is no one in extreme poverty.
9	Nor Kyurin	Ararat	Unemployment, low income caused by poor and inefficient cultivation of land, bad housing.	The number of extremely poor families has sharply grown.
10	Mragagav	Ararat	Low farming incomes	No indication but 10 per cent of the population are poor.
11	Urtsadorz	RA Ararat	Not mentioned	Not mentioned
12	Yeghegnavan	Ararat	People who use cultivate land badly, keep land fallow and have poorly paid jobs.	Not indicated
13	Paruyr	RA Ararat	Unemployment, depressing living conditions and inefficient farming methods.	Not indicated
14	Yeghenoot	Armavir	Lack of opportunity to cultivate land and engage in animal husbandry and landlessness.	Number of poor people have grown.
15	Doghs	Armavir	Joblessness, low income, sale of land plots and property.	Poverty is high and the number of vulnerable families and unemployed have risen.
16	Koghbavan	Armavir	Alcoholism	There is only one family in the village which is extremely poor.

contd...

...contd...

S.No.	*Village*	*Region*	*Criteria for definition of poverty*	*Has poverty increased or decreased*
17	Nalbandyan	Armavir	Lack of property, lack of houses (living in shelters), lack of assistance from outside the household,	No indication. 86 families are on welface and 580 are pensioners (out of 1760). 80 families are extremely poor.
18	Baghramyan	Armavir	Not having at least one working member in the family.	Poverty is decreasing compared to 1991-1997.
19	Metzamor	Armavir	Not indicated	Not indicated
20	Akhpradzor	Gegharkunik	"In the 21st century we still have no baths, there is not even a single public bath in the village. If that does not make us poor, what does?" Lack of income and no paid jobs.	Poverty has increased.
21	Geghamasar Community	Gegharkunik	Inability to provide for their basic needs and unemployment.	Poverty has increased. The "farmer is poor when the actual cost of production is higher than the market price and the difference increases by the year".
22	Ttujur	Gegharkunik	Mounting debts, inalbility to derfay cost of their minimal needs, unemployment, "getting by whatever we have in that month".	There is more poverty now than before.
23	Hayravank	Gegharkunik	"Inability to attend funeral or a wedding". Inability to defray the costs of meeting basic minimal needs (is the best indicator of poverty), joblessness, decline in cash incomes. In the past they "spent more because and wore clothes that remained (read lasted) since the Soviet times but now those, too, are gone".	There is more poverty in the community than ever before.

contd...

...contd...

S.No.	*Village*	*Region*	*Criteria for definition of poverty*	*Has poverty increased or decreased*
24	Gegharkunik	Gegharkunik	Inability to defray the costs of meeting basic minimal needs (is the best indicator of poverty),	There is more poverty in the community than before.
25	Astghadzor	Gegharkunik	Inability to defray the costs of meeting basic minimal needs (is the best indicator of poverty), joblessness and food poverty. But "Friends, speaking frankly none of us go hungry".	There is more poverty in the community than before.
26	Mets	Gegharkunik	Failure to bear expenses for their own minimal requirements and a situation where the cost price of agricultural production is more than the sale price of the produce.	Poverty has increased in the community.
27	Tsovagyugh	Geharkunik	Lack of land, lack of job, falling income	90% of the community are jobless and things have not changed.
28	Bozhakan	RA Kotayk	Ratio of family income and necessary expenditure.	In 1988, more than 50% of the community could be considered poor. Now the percentage is 80%.
29	Zovuni	Kotayk	The ratio of monthly incomes to indispensable cost per household.	Compared to 1990s, socio economic condition of village has not improved. If in 1988 only 5% of the population could be considered as poor, today that number has gone up to 20%. Number of unemployed has increased.
30	Gehhashen	Kotayk	The ratio of monthly incomes to indispensable cost per household and unemployment.	From 1990s, some improvement of socio-economic character have been recorded. But if in

contd...

...contd...

S.No.	*Village*	*Region*	*Criteria for definition of poverty*	*Has poverty increased or decreased*
				1988 only 7% of the population could be considered as poor, today that number has gone up to 50%.
31	Charentsavan	RA Kotayk	Not indicated.	Poverty has decreased, "more or less".
32	Arzni	RA Kotayk	Not indicated.	Poverty has situation has not improved.
33	Fatan	RA Kotayk	Ratio of monthly family income to needed expenditure.	Poverty has situation has not changed positively. 57% are poor.
34	Arjut	RA Lory	Not indicated.	Not indicated. Many village youth abandoned the village and left the burden of rural troubles on the shoulders of elderly parents. "They come, bury their parents and leave".
35	Berdshen	Lori	Not indicated	Incomes of the community declines day after day and they sell their livestock just ot put bread on the table.
36	Mgchart	Lori	Imbalance between income and expenditure.	Overall economic situation has a tendency to deteriorated. Per capital income has been decreasing every year compared to expenses.
37	Noramut	Lori	Not indicated	Not indicated
38	Fioletovo	Lori	Not indicated	Poverty has not changed much but has a tendency to become worse due to out migration of young poeple to Russia.

contd...

...contd...

S.No.	*Village*	*Region*	*Criteria for definition of poverty*	*Has poverty increased or decreased*
39	Khnokoyan	Lori	Not indicated. Not indicated.	Not indicated but 80% of the village are poor.
40	Noramut	Lori	Not indicated.	Deteriorating. "Sunny, you can see you're your eyes that the village is dying and all of us together with it". "Only those who leave the village will be saved".
41	Lorut	Lori	Inability to cultivate land, not owning vehicle, not owning cattle. Those owning satellite dishes are considered to be better off.	Living standard is low but none in extreme poverty
42	Armanis district	Lory	Not indicated.	No indication if population is increasing or decreasing. But 70% of the population of the district is poor.
43	Khoznavar	Syunik	No employed member, lack of arable land, lack of cattle and menas to pay for seed and fuel.	Not indicated. 16 families receive welfare benefits
44	Toruniq	Syunik	Lack of property, land or cattle, non recipient of state benefits, inability to pay taxes, unemployed people with children.	90% of the village are poor.
45	Barcraven	Syunik	Lack of work, sources of income, productive land, animals, entitlements to pensions and welfare and no means to cultivate land.	There are 3 families (out of 36) who are poor as per their criteria. No indication.
46	Cghuk	Syunik	Owning land but inability to cultivate the same, lack of cattle and faming equipment	Five families (out of 136) are poor. No indication.

contd...

...contd...

S.No.	*Village*	*Region*	*Criteria for definition of poverty*	*Has poverty increased or decreased*
47	Lernadzore	Syunik	Not mentioned	Not Mentioned
48	Meghri	Syunik	Not indicated	Not indicated
49	Newvadi (Nrnadzor)	Syunik	Lack of minimum income, a job, a cow, a land (sic), a decent house, money to buy bread, intellectual and non-receipt of welfare benefits.	Not indicated
50	Srashen	Syunik	Not indicated	Not indicated
51	Tavshut	RA Shirak	Not indicated	Not indicated
52	Akhurik	Shirak	Not indicated	Not indicated
53	Hogmik	Shirak	Lock of cattle and land. "If a villager has no flour and has to pay money for it. He is poor, isn't he...?"	50% of the population is poor.
54	Sarakap	Shirak	Lack of land (newly formed families that at the time of privatization were not separate households) or inability to cultivate it.	About 50% of the people are poor.
55	Sarpat	Shirak	Lack of means of subsistence,	The economic situation is very bad and does not change. The tendency is to become worse due to out-migration of younger population to Russia.
56	Teghut	Tavush	Severe disproportion between incomes and expenditure, lack of land resources, lack of land resources, unemployment and low salaries,	Not indicated.
57	Berd	Tavush	Inadequate quantity and condition of jobs, landlessness and proximity to border with Azerbaijan and indebtedness. "Here, if you do not owe money to anyone, you are not alive."	Increased

contd...

...contd...

S.No.	Village	Region	Criteria for definition of poverty	Has poverty increased or decreased
58	Azatamoot	RA Tavush	No indication.	55% of the residents are poor but no indication on increase or decline in poverty.
59	Berdavan	Tavush	Lack of jobs, insufficient land resources, lack of agricultural machiney, dilapidated and devastated housing conditions, long-term indebtedness.	Community is extremely poor. The situation has not changed.
60	Chinari	Tavush	Not indicated but only those who had relatives and friends abroad are better off.	No improvements in living standards over the last several years.
61	Khashtarak	Tavush	Powerlessness/ voicelessness, lack of job, lack of land and irrigation,	Not indicated
62	Zaritap	Vayots	Lack of employment, lack of land, lack of housing, lack of livestock, or some additional income.	Not indicated but out-migration has ceased over the last two years. There are 150 poor families (out of 505 households) and 50 families receive social aid.
63	Rind	Vayots Dzor	Lack of house and land, inability to renovate house for the last 15 years, lack of monthly income of atleast 10-15000 AMD, receives no wages or pensions, inability to pay public utility bills, unable to buy bread and cannot sustain a student.	20-30 families are poor and a "worsening tendency can be traced for living conditions".
64	Hermon	Vayots Dzor	Not indicated	Not indicated
65	Artavan	Vayots Dzor	Owning less than 3 heads of cattle, lack of job and land, lack of working hands in the family	10 families (out of 135) are poor

contd...

...contd...

S.No.	*Village*	*Region*	*Criteria for definition of poverty*	*Has poverty increased or decreased*
66	Vernashen	Vayots Dzor	Lack place of residence, financial in income, employment, social allowance, adequate living conditions, remain hungry, not washed for weeks, work without rest and have a monthly income below 50,000 AMD.	50% of the village population is poor and the number of needy people is increasing.
67	Davitashen community	Yerevan	Unemployment, low wages, violation of human rights, imbalance between income and expenditure	Not indicated

Even under the traditional criteria for defining poverty as given in Box 10.2, people think beyond asset deficit (assetlessness) and income deficit (income poverty) to define and determine poverty. People talk about technology deficit as being a criterion to judge a community as poor (such as inefficient farming methods and old farm machinery and equipment). Though the link between technology, productivity and income is seen in the agriculture, people were inclined to name technology deficits as criteria for recognising poverty. Significantly, belonging to a minority community or group is considered as a criterion for poverty, which by implication means that either for historical factors or because of the current socio-politico-economic situation, the minorities face deprivation of some form. This may or may not be a huge problem for the present but it needs to be tackled. Good democracy is always cognisant of the needs of the minorities because democracy is the rule of the majority with the acquiescence of the minorities.

In the non-traditional criteria (see Box 10.2), people outlined five sets of criteria: voice and power deficits, gender and relative income deficits, social obligation deficit, capability and privacy hygiene deficits. Powerlessness against tyranny of man and nature, powerlessness and voicelessness in the political process, violation of rights, inability to meet social and legal obligations, lack of privacy and personal hygiene are among the prominent criteria identified by the people. While doing so, the people were not oblivious of the fact that capability poverty is also an important element in the poverty scenario. It is worth mentioning that a vast majority of respondents put high importance on the establishment or reopening of the "cultural clubs" as key centre of communities' cultural and social life. In fine then people were concerned with income and non-income poverty in equal measure. In consequence, the common people do provide glimpses of many faces of poverty and do remind that poverty reduction strategies need also to be multi-dimensional.

Interim Policy Implications

These criteria, therefore, have important implications for strategies and policies for the Government of Armenia. Poverty reduction strategies have to address a wide range of issues, if poverty is to be tackled substantially if not wholly, and "well-being" of the people increased significantly. While rapid economic growth does provide one way of reducing poverty, it is not the only way to do so. Poverty reduction strategies could, at first glance, include, but not be restricted to, measures for:

(i) increasing the income levels of the people—to remove income poverty, poverty born out of social deficit—through such measures as provision of micro-credit and launching of wage-employment programmes;

(ii) increasing the asset base of people—to remove poverty due to assetlessness—micro-credit and launching of self employment programmes;

(iii) increasing the "voice" of the people in the political (and development) processes—to remove poverty due to voicelessness—through a process of decentralisation of development administration, planning and project implementation to the lower level on the basis of the principle of subsidiarity;

(iv) empowering the people—to eliminate poverty due to powerlessness and violation of rights—may be through organising the poor, promoting community based organisation and encouraging the voluntary sector to flourish. This would entail a paradigm shift, a movement away from welfarist approach inherent in some socialist societies. It needs to be underscored that rights are violated, not necessarily by the State, but by a range of actors and circumstances;

(v) increasing the capability of the people through improved education, healthcare and personal hygiene; and

(vi) increasing incomes relative to expenditure to eliminate relative income deficit, primarily through reduction of input prices through a benevolent regulatory mechanism, social risk management (to minimise loss) through provision of micro-insurance and elimination of exploitative intermediation by better marketing of goods and services produced by the people and providing minimum support price.

Specific policies and strategies will be dealt with in the last section.

The criteria set out by the people and the knowledge they shared during the participatory sessions also indicate that the causes of poverty are as varied as the faces of poverty that the people have outlined. A reading of the output from the participatory sessions in the villages/communities indicates that poverty in different regions of Armenia has been caused by:

(i) processes—e.g., degradation of land, environmental degradation, loss in soil fertility, decline in quality of seeds;

(ii) policies—e.g., poor targeting for providing social welfare benefits, unregulated prices of inputs etc.,

(iii) institutions—e.g., recalcitrant government officials, lack of support institutions to provide technical advice and technical knowledge to farmers, to eliminate exploitative intermediation and market agricultural products and provide social risk management cover.

Thus if the voices of the people are heard there is a need to propel the boat of poverty alleviation with oars of remodeled institutions, new policies and "reversed processes" to eliminate poverty of different hues. Care has to be taken not to lose sight of poverty caused by powerlessness, voicelessness, vulnerability, violations of rights and privacy and hygiene deficits.

It needs to be underscored that the criteria for defining poverty that people have articulated also brings forth in bold relief the inherent goodness of the people and their urge to have a freer and fuller life. For example, people are concerned about their income (or low income), but only in relation to their expenditure to meet their basic needs—food, fuel, shelter and clothing. People are concerned that those who are unable to meet their legal and social obligations are poor, because they are unable to discharge their responsibilities as good members of society and responsible citizens, which in turn leads to an erosion of social capital. People know that they do not live by bread alone: they need dignity, privacy and capability. They perceive, and rightly so, that they deserve their right to be respected and their entitlement not denied. These issues need to be dealt with in any poverty reduction strategy.

Poverty: Regional Dimensions

The regional dimensions of poverty are noticeable in the Armenian context. It is debatable whether these differences are strong except perhaps in the domain of livelihoods, primarily agriculture. The following observations are in order.

"Unemployment" as a criterion has been used in all regions in some form or the other: Aragatston, Ararat, Armavir, Gegharkunik, Kotayk, Synik, Shirak, Tavush, Vayots Dorz and Yerevan. This is symptomatic of the fact that the economy of Armenia is not diversified, especially after independence when many factories have been closed, which is reflected in the fact that people in many villages have urged that the factories be re-opened and that people are migrating to Russia and to a moderate extent to Yerevan in search of livelihood and to better their prospects. For example, villagers in Meghri, has urged for re-opening of the wine factory and indicated that their well-being improved because of the resumption of operation of the Agarak Copper-Molybdenum Combine (the gold mine) a few months back in 2006. Again in Noramut Village, Lori Marz, villagers were keen that processing factories (read agro-processing) are opened to provide jobs and help farmers add value to their produce.

Not surprisingly, "landlessness" as an indicator of poverty has been voiced in all parts of the country: from regions like Lory, Shirak and Tavush in the north to Synik and Vayots Dorz in the south, to Armavir and Gegharkunik in the vicinity of Yerevan. People were quite categorical that ownership of land alone does not necessarily lead to poverty alleviation. Owning land but inability to cultivate land, or use of inefficient methods of cultivation have also been identified in several regions as indicators of poverty. This is especially true of Ararat, Armavir, Lori, Synik and Shirak. While these issues will be dealt with in the section on agriculture, suffice is to underscore here that people did flag the point of dated technology and absence of technical advice (also called agricultural extension), being major determinants of poverty.

The issue of "rights" has been raised from different perspectives. In some cases, the rights relate to minority rights, like those of minorities like Yezdis in Aragatsotn (it is surprising that no one raised the issue of Kurds also a minority in Armenia and in the same Region) and in other cases, relates to violation of human rights (as in case of Yerevan). In case of Khashtarak, Tavush Marz, political right as it relates to the possibility of raising their voices in a free and fair democratic election, was mentioned. This is significant. In case of a village in Vayots Dorz, the right to privacy and what Johan Galtung had once said "right to excretion" were mentioned up front. There are other rights, like right to food, to education and to information, being not exercised, which have been mentioned, but people presented them from the "deprivation perspective" rather than a violation of rights perspective.

In the context of income poverty, the communities considered both absolute levels of income and relative levels of income as indicators of poverty. In two communities, people held that incomes below a certain level would indicate poverty. For example, people thought that income levels at less than 10000 to 15000 Drams per month in case of village Rind and 50,000 Drams per month in case of village Vernashen in Vayot Dorz Marz would indicate poverty. But in several places, income poverty was relative. For instance in some communities in Tavush Marz, severe disproportion between incomes and expenditure was an indicator of poverty or in case of certain communities in Kotayk Marz, ratio of monthly income to indispensable expenditure was an indicator of poverty. Communities in Geharkunik Marz introduced the concept of a farmer's cost of production being higher than the market price as an indicator of poverty, thereby injecting the element of non-viability of agricultural operations as a sign that the people (read the farmers) are poor. Non-viability of agriculture impinges upon a major portion of the livelihood sector.

It needs to be indicated that the criteria for identifying poverty (or poor for that matter) used by the people have been a mixture of both income poverty, capability or non-income poverty in some combination, except in case of Argatsotn and Yerevan where minority issues and violation of rights were raised. Indeed, in case of Vayots Dorz, the communities indicated at least 20 criteria to identify poverty. By conservative interpretation, therefore, it seems that the poor suffer from multiple poverty and, in turn it may, therefore, be necessary to have policies with multiple strategies to tackle poverty in Armenia. People have also recommended certain measures to improve their lot, to which we shall revert later, and they too are aimed at reducing different aspects of poverty.

Having discussed the state of poverty, it may be useful to see at some of the key sectors: education, health and social security and agriculture.

Education Sector in Armenia

Participatory assessment of education-related issues was undertaken in 11 regions of Armenia. People, both women and men, and more importantly teachers and students, freely expressed their views and opinions based on their daily experience and local knowledge. The villagers from different *Marzes* of Armenia and communities in Yerevan listed 14 key issues in education sector (see Box below) and also suggested changes in education-related programmes and strengthening of the education system.

Schools are operating almost everywhere and only in rare cases do children have to go to a neighbouring village to take lessons as in village Gyalto, in Aragatsotn *Marz* children need to go to a support school in the neighbouring village of Pirmalak. School is an institution, which receives a lot of public attention, because, *inter alia,* education is a high priority for the people in Armenia. In only one case, in Gegharqunik Marz, did the community maintain that education was not a priority. Generally, there are no families whose children do not attend school due to social issues. The schools give textbooks with a discount to a number of children from vulnerable families. However, some children cannot afford to go to school due to their families' poverty. The principal issues raised by the people are in Box 10.3 below.

The Issues in the Education Sector

(i) **Insufficient or poor condition of building and infrastructure in schools:** Building and infrastructure across the regions stand in need of renovation. In some cases, the condition of school buildings is deplorable while in one case the school is being held in temporary structures. Leaking roofs, cracked window glass and single frame windows are not uncommon. Insufficient number of classrooms has also been spoken of. This has resulted in holding of what people call, in several cases, "combined classes", where students of different classes study in one classroom. In one case in Shiraz *Marz* all the nine students of the school study in the same classroom. Some communities want a modern school building with proper fixtures and equipment.

Box 10.3

Issues for the Education Sector raised by the People

(i) Insufficient or poor condition of building and infrastructure in schools
(ii) Poor physical environment of schools
(iii) Lack of or poor personal hygiene and absence of water and toilets
(iv) Teachers and their capability
(v) Old or inadequate furniture, equipments and inventory
(vi) Inadequate library
(vii) Ill-equipped or absence of laboratory and computers and computer-rooms
(viii) Ill-equipped, or absence of gymnasium and extra curricular activity
(ix) State of Kindergarten
(x) Poverty as a hindrance to education
(xi) Health of students
(xii) Neglect of schools by social institutions and Parent's Council
(xiii) Adverse impact of "Recent Education Policies" of the Government of RA
(xiv) Others: attitudes, budgets.

Box 10.4

Partnership in Nutritional Programme in Village Hogmik

It is already six years that KARITAS has been carrying out a food programme directed towards the pupils of elementary classes: the organisation distributes vegetable oil, lentil and flour. On their part, community members donated a baking oven, gas-stove and utensils to the school. Besides, community members provide the school with requisite food—potato, and other vegetables.

Within infrastructure, heating is a major problem. Various forms of heating are used from heating with liquid fuel to fuelwood. When heated with kerosene stoves, classes are filled with smoke causing considerable discomfort to students. In some cases chimneys create problems. In some cases stoves are old and hazardous. Poor heating is generally the case, often leading to diseases. "In winter the classroom temperature is below 0 (degrees). But they do not allow to make the classes shorter" said one villager. A teacher even argued that cold has led to decrease in fertility of the girl children later in their lives.

Many schools did not have provision of drinking water. In some cases there is no drinking water supply in the school at all while in others the source for accessing drinking water is far away from the school.

Box 10.5

Good Practices to Augment Resources

Owing to the industrious and persistent efforts of the present school management they have been able to win projects and draw the attention of benefactors.

At present, "Save the Children Fund" is implementing a sewerage repair project in the school while USAID is supporting light repair works in the school building and its heating system.

Benefactors Karo and Aida Mirikyans have funded renovation of the second floor of the school. After renovation, the teachers' room, the headmaster's office, the IT laboratory and grades 5-9 have moved here.

(ii) **Poor physical environment of schools:** Environment of the school is an area that bothers people considerably. Construction activities in the villages are a spontaneous enterprise and are not always done in accordance with the village plan. In some villages, presently the construction works undertaken in the school area, as well as the nearby shops, seriously interfere with the teaching process. In one case, the households of the village dump their garbage by the school fence. Sewers too contaminate the school territory. There are cattle sheds constructed next to a school in a village; and manure is piled up in and around the place.

(iii) **Lack of, or poor, personal hygiene and absence of water and toilets:** The issue of personal hygiene came in for comments at many places. There are no toilets and no running water in several schools. In some other cases, where toilets exist, they are not useable in the absence of running water supply. Pupils and teachers often use Open Pit Toilets. There are schools, which have neither separate toilet for the girl children or for children with disabilities.

(iv) **Teachers and their capability:** Schools are generally well staffed and teachers are perceived as being well educated and well trained. There are both men and women teachers. Students respect teachers and their positive attitude is appreciated. Technical teachers are in short supply especially in specialised subjects such as Physics, Chemistry, Geography, History, Armenian, English and Russian. In some cases, however, teachers are seen as lacking proper training in the art of teaching and do not know the modern pedagogy.

Box 10.6

On Capability of Teachers

"They avoid the army by hanging out here for four years and then they leave. They can't even tell the difference between wheat and barley." ....Villagers in Akhpradzor, Gegharqunik *Marz.*

In most cases, teachers are from the local area but there are communities where teachers are not community residents and commute from nearby places or even walk. In these places, teaching becomes problematic during the winter season when public transport gets dislocated due to snow.

Private tuition has been mentioned as an area of concern. Though in many schools, private tuition is not encouraged, in some cases, students have resorted to private tuition. Members of some communities want this to be discouraged because they maintain that private tutoring has a negative impact on the quality of education in the schools generally, as teachers are not interested in ensuring good standards of teaching at school.

(v) **Old or inadequate furniture, equipments and inventory and didactic materials:** It is a fact that schools generally have furniture and equipment. What people perceive is that in some cases they are not adequate to meet the needs of the school and in most cases these are worn out and need replacement. In some cases, additional furniture are necessary. Similarly inventory and stocks and didactic materials are also in most schools old and need urgent replacement. In several places, supplies have not been received since 1970. Equipments and inventory as also didactic materials are considered inadequate in several cases. Given the importance of inventory and stocks and didactic materials, and given the state of resources made available to the school management, existing inventory of a school has been occasionally repaired by the efforts of teachers and villagers.

(vi) **Inadequate library:** The communities consider libraries as important. Many schools have libraries. Some libraries are rich. But there are several schools with a limited number of books inherited from the old Soviet times. In some cases, the school library does not meet the new requirements of foreign literature and training materials on information technology. There is shortage of fiction and does not meet the standard for literature set for school programmes. There are schools as well, which do not have a library at all. Stacking school libraries is an important need for the schools.

(vii) **Ill-equipped or absence of laboratory and computer rooms:** Many schools have laboratories. And there are schools, which have no science laboratory especially for physics and chemistry, which prevents them from properly teaching these subjects. Teaching of biology is also hampered by lack of laboratory. People complained in many places that though there is a laboratory in the school, laboratory equipments are in short supply and in some cases, they are old or even missing.

Computer rooms were also in for discussion. Some schools have computer classroom with computers and some even had Internet connection. Others did not have either computer rooms or computers. Some of the schools have their computer classroom (with even upto six computers). The School Reforms Programme has provided computers to Schools. Computers were also brought in 2006 through World Bank's co-financing, credit programme. Having an information technology teacher was a problem for many schools.

(viii) **Ill-equipped or absence of gymnasium and extra curricular activity:** People in most of the villages and *marzes* were keen to see that the school going children have a disciplined body and that they get opportunities to develop their talents outside the class. While some schools also do not have any gymnasium at all, in many schools there are gymnasiums but these lack equipment or the equipment is old. Some schools lack playing fields, while others have no recreation room.

(ix) **State of kindergarten:** Except in one village, kindergartens are highly valued by the people. There is a mixed picture that one gathers about the state of kindergartens. There are kindergartens, which are well run and in good buildings and people in these communities are happy with the kindergarten's work. Such kindergartens are accessible to everybody in terms of fees and location.

But there are cases where kindergartens have fallen in bad times and in other cases they are conducted in old buildings. In one case the roof of the kindergarten building is flat and has become obsolete. Rainwater penetrates into the building and damages the entire building, furniture and other inventory. And there are some villages, which have no kindergarten or where the kindergarten has been closed and needs re-opening. Complaints about lack of linen, toys and stationery were also heard. The kindergartens are financed through the local self-government budget but in many cases they are also funded by international NGOs like World Vision and other charitable Trusts. Recently, in Meghri, Ararat *Marz*, a contract was signed with the Australian owner of the gold mine, to sponsor the kindergarten (covering the cost of food and salaries).

(x) **Poverty as a hindrance to education:** Poverty is a major stumbling block for children's education in several communities. In some villages, due to socio-economic hardships that the population has to cope with, students are not sent to school. In all *Marzes*, while most of the children have their textbooks, the teachers mentioned that the parents in some communities are so poor that they can hardly afford buying the textbooks. Lack of money to buy clothes, as well as children's involvement in cattle farming and household chores (due to parent's poverty) prevent children from going to school.

Teachers have also indicated that in several communities, few school graduates and talented children continue their education in institutions of higher learning because it is in a faraway village and because of families' "grave socio-economic condition". There are even cases where due to poverty, parents cannot bear full costs of kindergarten operation (approximately AMD

4-5 thousand per child). One woman from Village in Nor Kyurin, Ararat *Marz* explained that her two daughters do not attend school because of health problems, and she has no means of seeking medical assistance. She is a single mother.

(xi) **Health issues of students:** It is in winter and fall months that the number of cases of pneumonia and flu grows because of bad heating. One of the teachers said angrily that many girls develop sterility because they sit on cold desks in the school. A system of immunisation is also needed.

(xii) **Neglect of schools by social institutions and parent's council:** Though schools were highly sought after by the people, social institutions did not pay much attention to the schools. Even the Parents' Councils set up to act as bridges between the schools and the respective communities are in most cases inactive. In some cases they are active and where they are so, they make valuable contributions.

(xiii) **Adverse impact of "Recent Education Policies" of the government of RA:** In case there are small groups (small number of students) in the class, the classes are combined in one. For example the 2nd and 3rd and/or 4th grade classes will have class in one room and within the 45 minute (official class time). This means that teachers have to complete explaining the topic for each class as well as accomplish asking and giving assignments, within one "class time" otherwise devoted to a separate class. Thus, if two classes are combined, it would imply that a teacher devotes 22.5 minutes per class instead of 45 minutes to a given class. The teachers complained that this seriously impaired teaching. Secondly, from 2006 the school education became 12 years instead of 11. It also meant that while earlier a child's age of entry to a school was 7 years, it now became 5-6 years. There, the key complaints by the people and teachers about this change were that young children need special equipment and/or teaching materials, methodology, toys, etc. But none of these was provided to schools. Thus, the teachers explained that schools were not prepared properly for this reform.

In one village, the teachers are also concerned about the Education Ministry's decision to convert their school into an eight-grade school and set a base high school in one of the nearby communities to serve several villages. They are afraid that such a decision will foster emigration.

Policies regarding schools for children with disabilities leave much to be desired. It was indicated that generally there are no schools for children with disabilities. For example, in one case in Gegharqunik Marz, virtually all of the school-age children in the community attend the school, with the exception of nine children that are mentally retarded or have physical disabilities. Only one of them attends school and the others do not do so. Owing to financial problems and lack of desire on the part of the parents of such children, the other eight cannot attend special educational institutions.

(xiv) **Others:** Budget insufficiency is a major problem for the school management in some cases. Local self-governments have little leeway to fund either capital or recurring expenditure in schools that operate within their jurisdiction.

People's Solutions

Having discussed the issues in the education sector, people provided their solutions to tackle the problems. The solutions have not been presented here in the same sequence in which the problems have been enumerated for the reason that the solutions are interrelated and the same solution or more than one solution, applies to a particular issue highlighted by the people. A summary of the solutions presented is in Box 10.7.

A brief discussion of the solutions is presented below.

Box 10.7

People's Solution in the Education Sector

(i) Provide transportation
(ii) Medical attention in schools
(iii) Nutritional programme
(iv) Institutional reforms
(v) Curriculum development and capacity building of teachers
(vi) Reopen or establish kindergartens
(vii) Building school infrastructure, equipment and hygiene and sanitation
(viii) Affirmative action for vulnerable groups
(ix) Raising resources from non-conventional sources
(x) Policy changes
(xi) Rights of the students be recognised

Provide Transportation

In winter where a school is not properly heated or teachers cannot come, school transportation should be provided so that students can go to a nearby school. Even though this seems like a seasonal measure, it has to be institutionalised. For example, the children of a village go to Dzorashen owing to the benefactor A. Aghababyan who has provided a jeep to take them to school and back.

Repair of community streets is very important as in bad weather (meaning winter) it is almost impossible to get to the schools. Only providing transportation without a minimum of roads will not carry the communities very far. The complementarity of the two is well realised by the people.

Provide Medical Attention in Schools

Health issues are important for the community. All, promotive, preventive and curative health care for students and teachers were considered essential for improvements in school education. Medical examination of the schoolchildren and specialist visits more frequently were strongly recommended. Along with students, teachers should also be provided with free medical examination and treatment. Teachers should additionally benefit from reduced fees for utility services.

One model for providing medical care to students and teachers in schools is the "Open Door Days" model. "Open Door Days" held once or twice a year when the doctors from a nearby hospital visit the school and examine the students. In addition, once a month the nurse conducts a sanitation day. This should be extended to all Schools. An example of "Open Door Days" is in village Tavshut, Shirak Marz. Another model is that provided by the School in Noramut village, Lori, where a nurse, carries out the mandatory vaccinations of school children, together with the nurse of the medical post.

Start Nutritional Programme

Nutritional programmes should be started in the schools as both an enabling step and as a health measure. Nutritional programmes would not only improve school attendance of children from relatively poor families (by increasing the real income of the respective parents) but improve the health status of children in general, enabling them to study better, specially in harsh weather conditions where nutritional requirements of the body are not easily met. There are several models available in Armenia, which can be adopted or upscaled.

Box 10.8

On Good Practices in School Nutritional Programme

In Hogmik Village, Shirak Marz, for six years CARITAS has been carrying out a food programme directed towards the pupils of elementary classes. The organisation distributes vegetable oil, lentil and flour. On their part, community members donated a baking oven, gas-stove and utensils to the school. Besides, community members provide the school with requisite food—potato, and other vegetables.

One kindergarten, in Noramut Village, Lori Region, has two groups with 35 children in each. Children are fed three times a day. Save the Children Funds programme supports the food provision. 2000 Drams are collected from each child for food and the village administration transfers 50 Drams per day for each child.

The UN Food Program has been supplying food for elementary school students for 3 years in Village Arjut. Jointly, the school and the parents renovated one classroom, which is used as a dining room. CARITAS provided the dining room with tables and chairs. The parents support the project either by money or with food.

Institutional Reforms

It is important to revitalise the Parents' Council. The Parents' Council acts as a bridge between the community and the schools. A revitalised Parents'

Council can act as a watchdog against violation of students' rights and arbitrary behaviour of teachers and eschew corporal punishment meted out to students. Above all, an active Parents' Council would help the school management to raise resources including community contribution to help repair buildings etc., run nutritional programmes and enlist the support of social institutions for the schools.

Curriculum Development and Capacity Building of Teachers

Needs for additional teacher of Armenian and Russian languages and in technical subjects such as Geography, History, Physics, Chemistry, Biology and Information Technology should be met. The Education Department of the *Marzes* should be mandated to help schools, when school management approaches them for assistance. An example is the case of the school in Hogmik, Shirak Marz, which was assured that a specialist will be sent, by the Education Department, Gyumri and the assurance was carried out.

Box 10.9

Good Practices in Institutional Reforms

The Parents' Council is registered as an NGO, "Tavshut School Parents' Council." The governing body is a ten-member board. Acting as a legal entity, the parents' council has been repeatedly helping the school. Recently they were awarded a project and repaired the gym and purchases sports equipment.

Parents' committee, the Office of the Village Head, the Church and philanthropists could join hands to help schools.

Appointment of Physical Education teacher and as well as teachers in Arts and Craft are important. The potential impact of these teachers, according to the people, on the students is that they would not only enhance the overall development and personality of the children but also inculcate in them healthy habits.

Local language should be used as a medium of instruction. Use of local language would improve the learning process and elicit more interest from parents and the community in school's activities. It is also in this context that appointments of language teachers mentioned above assumes greater importance.

Box 10.10

Learning in Your Own Tongue

In the school at Fioletov, Lori Region, the language of education is Russian. In Village Gjalto, Aragatsotn Marz, the school offers instruction in the Ezide language. In the school in village Arzni, Kotayk Marz, the Assyrian students have the opportunity to study in their native language, though the school is Russian.

Introduction of English language in the school curriculum found much favour. The villagers attach great importance to the learning of English, as they believe it gives greater possibilities for professional growth than from learning other foreign languages.

The pedagogy of teaching should be modernised. Many of the teachers have positive attitudes and have earned the respect of the students. But they have not been able to keep up with modern methods of imparting education. Training of teachers has, therefore, been emphasised which will positively impact on the quality of education.

According to some participants, it is necessary to raise the teachers' salaries and their responsibility for work and measures must be taken to enhance the role of teachers in the society, both of which will improve the quality of teaching in schools. One reason why raising salary commends itself is that a higher salary would reduce the need of the teachers to undertake private tuition, to which we shall revert again later.

The school curriculum needs to be upgraded along with upgrading the skills of the teachers and make the schools more relevant to the ground realities. It may be done either by including into the school curriculum subjects for professional application, like viticulture, tractor and car-driving classes or vocational schools be started for building capacity of young men and women in these and such other areas, such that they become more employable. It is believed that these measures would help in reducing the problem of unemployment.

Promote Kindergartens

Kindergartens are highly prized by the communities. They have a strong gender dimension. People recommended reopening kindergartens where they are closed; renovating buildings where they stand in need of repair and equipping them with toys and other materials necessary for children's initial initiation into the schooling system. Promoting kindergartens was also recommended as a measure to help reduce the loads of teachers in secondary schools.

Building School Infrastructure, Equipment and Hygiene and Sanitation

There is a need to make investments in building and renovating the infrastructure of the schools. The Governments both of RA and local levels should provide inventory, furniture, physical plant especially heating facilities, Gymnasium and recreation centre. Acquisition of didactic materials, computers, equipment and other materials needed for practical training and laboratory classes must be made a priority for the government. It seems there is under-investment in these areas of the education sector.

Box 10.11

Save the Children and USAID

At present, "Save the Children Fund" is implementing a sewerage repair project in one of the school in Lorut Village in Lori Marz. While USAID is supporting light repair works in the school building and its heating system.

Take Affirmative Action for Vulnerable Groups

Poverty being a serious issue and being an impediment to educating children from disadvantaged families, the communities had various suggestions to make in this regard. Summaries of these are:

- To provide the vulnerable children with books and stationery free of charge in addition to financial aid.
- Provide preferential treatment to applicants from high-mountainous villages in admissions to schools of education in Yerevan.
- Children from socially disadvantaged families should be allowed to attend school exempted from paying the required fees/fees for textbooks etc.
- Children from minorities like Assyrians have serious problems with enrolment in universities. As children from a minority group they have no privileges, while competing with Armenians is hard. This must be addressed by making special reservations for minorities in institutions of higher learning.
- Legitimate exemption from classes for both pupils belonging to disadvantaged families and teachers during the harvesting period allowing children to participate in income generation activities.

Raise Resources from Non-Conventional Sources

Communities when they catalogued the foregoing list of "things to do", for the government, were aware that to implement the suggestions, there will be need for additional resources. While the government has the responsibility to implement the recommendations in the education sector, people thought that alternative means of financing should be devised and there are enough examples of such alternative sources of funding in Armenia. A sample of good practices is in Box 10.12.

Box 10.12

Innovative ways of Raising Resources

In village Lorut, Lori Marz, owing to the industrious and persistent efforts of the school management they have been able to win projects and draw the attention of benefactors. In the same village, benefactors Karo and Aida Mirikyans have funded renovation of the second floor of the school building. In village Khnkoyan also in Lori Region, in 2006 the Social Investment Fund is planning to build the roof of the school, as the flat roofs of the previous period are not well suited for Armenia and especially the climatic conditions of Lori. The same school in Khnkoyan had a problem with textbooks but the headmaster has managed to bring them from School #2 of Spitak using his personal ties. Every year free-of-charge textbooks are being provided to 7 orphan children (1 with a single parent and 6 with no parent at all). Syunik Marz.

Policy Issue

On educational reforms and related issues, the teachers were more vocal than the communities because they understood the technicalities, based on their professional experience, better than the communities in general. The following suggestions emerged:

- To declare invalid the decree of the ministry of education on class mergers, even if the enrolment in classes is too small.
- Competent authorities, including the *Marz* Governor's office, RA Ministry of Education, RA Government, RA President, should be responsive to the needs of the schools.
- The education reform mentioned earlier is problematic in that its implementation is not supported either financially or technically. Hence, they should be implemented only after necessary groundwork is done in terms of proving technology and resources for aids and materials to the schools in question.
- The government should organise inspections in the classrooms thus contributing to increased sense of responsibility on the part of both the teachers and the pupils. This is considered important by the communities to respect the rights of the children and ensure quality in education.
- The students should not be asked to contribute to the everyday needs of the school.
- Pupils have to take private classes both in the village and in the town to be admitted to institutions of higher education. This must be discontinued and teachers made to improve their performance in the schools. This regulatory step should essentially be accompanied by the incentive of a higher salary as people have recommended earlier.

The local people consider per capita financing of the village school wrong. Financing of school should be based on the resources required to run the school in an efficient manner.

Respect Rights of the Students

The students made the following recommendations:

- students' rights should be respected,
- teachers should not beat students,
- students' opinions should be respected,
- students' knowledge should be assessed impartially,
- students should take part in laying down the school rules,
- students should have a say in selecting their class supervisor, and
- some activities should be organised for leisure time.

In conclusion, it seems that the areas of concern voiced by the people demonstrate that people want their children to have a disciplined mind and a disciplined body. These concerns reflect that because people generally are satisfied with the education imparted to their children in terms of quantity and attitude and the behaviour of the teachers, the focus of improvement in the education sector should be on software part of the sector as well. The impact of advancements in information technology is much sought after by the communities. Thus, the emphasis of strategies to improve education should be on the quality of schools, their technology, didactic material, plant and machinery and, the most important, the teachers. It may not be out of place to mention here that the communities exhibited their awareness of the need to find innovative ways of finding some of which have been suggested above.

Health Issues as Indicated by the Voices of the Poor from Armenia

Participatory assessment of health-related issues and services was undertaken in 11 regions of Armenia. Village-wise issues were elicited first; then region-wise issues were distilled and finally national health related issues were identified.

The villagers from 60 study villages of Armenia (across 11 regions) listed nine key issues in health (see Box 10.13) and also suggested changes in health-related interventions and strengthening of health-related infrastructure and services. In terms of common issues, which were voiced to be crucial, the villagers flagged the first six issues in most regions covered by this study.

Box 10.13

Key Issues in Health from the Voices of the Poor in Armenia

(i) Limited availability of local health services and medication
(ii) Infrastructural constraints in local health post and maintenance
(iii) Constraints to approaching health care outside village
(iv) Difficult transportation and no ambulance allotted
(v) Lack of financial capacity to access health care
(vi) Problems in emergency health services
(vii) Lack of local village pharmacy store
(viii) Lack of provision of anti-snake venom
(ix) Polluted water, climate and morbidity

Key Health Problems

Selected local dimensions of the key issues indicated by the people are described below:

(i) **Limited Availability of Local Health Services and Medication:** Local health services are limited to child vaccination, counseling and first aid, check up and registration of pregnancy and timely injections. Medication for primary health care is insufficient. There is a lack of medical equipment. Medicaments (sic) are too expensive. In a few study villages, the health post is almost always closed. Even if it is open, the required medication is not to be found. For other study villages there is no primary health post functioning and the residents need to travel long distances for health care. The local nurse performs only the mandatory vaccination of children, provides consultation and first aid, the latter being generally free of charge in the village.

(ii) **Infrastructural Constraints in Local Health Post and Maintenance:** In some villages, the primary health post is located in a small shabby room with no running water, sewage, toilet, telephone, basic furniture or equipment. Due to lack of funds, for years, many villages have experienced such deprived semi-dilapidated ambulatory. This is also the reason for the decline of health care quality and affordability. There exists first aid post in many villages for vaccination programme, which has no running water, sanitary arrangements, essential equipments, no refrigerator for keeping vaccines; and the first aid items available are not adequate in quantity. The lack of refrigeration accounts for failures to organise several important vaccinations in good time. In many villages, the first aid post cannot pay for its electricity bills and often power gets disrupted. Some have full time/part time nurse who is over-loaded and rarely a visiting dentist. In absence of heating in winter the health post is forced to remain closed and the nurse attends patients at her own home.

Box 10.14

First Aid Box gets Updated with Improved Infrastructure, Village Hogmik, Shirak Marz

Until last year, the village's first-aid post had been located in a 32 years old wagon. Last year the NOVA organisation renovated two rooms in the village administrative building, and since then the first aid-post has been removed to these rooms. The aid-post has water supply and working sanitary arrangements. The NOVA also donated some inventory and medical equipments. The only worker of the aid-post is the nurse who is paid 12,000 drams monthly. Participants were content with medical services provided by the nurse. According to them, one can go to her house for an urgent help even at night.

(iii) **Constraints to Approaching Health Care Outside Village:** With difficulty the villagers go to health care institutions in the provincial centre. In serious cases people have difficulty going to hospitals at a distance for which they need money for travel or need to pay for fuel charge for getting ambulance service. Though in many hospitals treatment is provided free of charge the attitude of health staff is not always pro-client and in some cases some payments are also required to be made to get health services.

(iv) **Difficult Transportation and No Ambulance Allotted:** This is a serious problem not only in terms of financial costs, but also in terms of bad roads and lack of transportation. There are no ambulances allotted to many villages and patients tend to use any available vehicle by paying for it. Residents are often asked to pay money by hospitals in order to supply fuel for ambulance service.

Box 10.15

No Health Care comes Free of Charge Shirak Marz—Village Hogmik

"There is nothing free of charge nowadays." One of the participants told us: "When my daughter-in-law was about to deliver, I approached the doctor and told that the only money I have is 10000 drams. He replied that 10000 drams is a very small amount to be divided among 6 people: So, give me at least 20000 drams. Take into account that I had already paid 2000 drams to the pediatrician and 1000 drams additionally for seeing the child. If there is a need for doctor, they have him/her visited from the Health Centre by a phone call. Sometimes they have to pay for the visits. There is a private dentist in the nearby village of Goghovit, whom the population of Hoghmik mainly goes to see in time of need.

As for the availability of medicine, people can get it from the first-aid post, which, on the whole, has medicine in necessary quantities. Regarding the medicine prescribed by doctors, people get it from the pharmacies in Amasia or Gyumri. The village authorities assist the first-aid post by paying the latter's electricity bills."

Box 10.16

Services Rated as Good by Local Users Shirak Marz—Village Tavshut

Open door days are held often when the doctors from Ashotsk hospital visit. A radio telephone was given to the ambulatory by the hospital, and this year, a cell phone, for uninterrupted communication between the community and the hospital. Ashotsk hospital also provides the ambulance service. The ambulance reaches the village in 10-15 minutes. The residents do not pay for the ambulance. The residents are satisfied with health care. Vaccination is done on time; there are monthly vaccination days. Medication is distributed by the ambulance free of charge; sometimes medication is not sufficient. When visiting the ambulatory for special health care, the patients are always treated well. For treatment, the patients go to Ashotsk hospital. Hospital treatment here is free of charge. The hospital also provides the patient with food and medication.

(v) **Lack of Financial Capacity to Access Health Care:** According to the participants, medical aid presently is more costly than in the 1980s. Medicines are expensive and approaching hospitals are also costly due to high transportation cost and health costs. It is wise to avoid illness and avoid going to hospitals to the extent possible.

(vi) **Problems in Emergency Health Services:** As there is no proper telephone communication, the villagers themselves handle emergency cases by taking the patients to different health outfits generally at a good distance from their villages. It is not possible to provide childbirth assistance locally. Roads are closed in winter months and there have been cases where women gave birth at home. Ensuring telephone communications, transport and resolving the issue of the ambulance are urgent problems for the community.

(vii) **Lack of Local Village Pharmacy Store:** Many villages do not have a drugstore or people who would sell medicines as intermediaries. The problem is due to the small size of the population residing in a village, a drug store may not be viable.

Box 10.17

Doctors with Good Attitude and Ready Service Ararat Marz, Village Urtsadzor

In the community members' words the doctor and nurses can be easily reached and use their best efforts to help the patients. They perform vaccinations, give checkups to outpatient visitors and patients with chronic diseases and render first aid service. All these services are low cost or free and for this reason affordable to the community. The village has a dentist and dental technician who work in a private clinic. The village does not have a pharmacy. People have to travel to Vedi in order to buy necessary drugs. Vedi is a destination for birth deliveries too. The villagers say that if the newly born is a girl, they spend AMD 20,000. If it is a boy, they spend AMD 25,000.

Box 10.18

Trying to Escape Medical Services by not Falling Sick
Gegharqunik Marz, Village Mets Masrik

Health care to community members is provided by medical institutions of Vardenis, Martuni and Yerevan. However, they mention that they try not to fall sick "as far as possible as it's a crime to go to hospital". The main reason for escaping medical services is the fact that these services are inaccessible because of being rather expensive while to get qualified medical aid they are constrained to go to hospital in Yerevan as far as the hospitals of their region are lack of not only qualified specialists but also kind attitude. They report that the hospital in Vardenis hasn't completed either its staff or equipment within recent fifteen years. "Medical operations are made using forty-year tools, what should we do there?"

People were complaining of first aid services as well. They report that it has been fifteen years that any ambulance car has visited the village. One of the villagers told that currently the first aid station in Vardenis has got only one Mercedes, which doesn't reach their village because it's impossible for this car to overcome the road to Mets Masrik. So if they call for first aid service, and if somebody answers the phone, they will say indeed "We cannot register the call". In response to the question what they do in these cases, they answered: "If there is such a case, we put the patient into a truck basket and take him to hospital".

(vii) **Lack of Provision of Anti-Snake Venom:** Villagers in many villages were worried about abundance of snakes connected with current drought, while there is no antidote vaccine in the first-aid post. Increased number of cases when people are bitten by venomous snakes, tarantulas and scorpions are also cause for concern.

(viii) **Polluted Water, Climate and Morbidity:** A health survey revealed that the most frequent illnesses are cold, flu and pneumonia both among children and adults. The main causes are the severe climate and insufficient heating at the school and in the houses. Decline of the general health status has been noted mainly due to an increase in the number of stomach and intestinal cases caused by water pollution. In recent years there has been an increase in cases of cardio-vascular diseases, cancer, hypertension and cold-related ailing, though there is lack of local health service in these vital aspects.

Box 10.19

Vaccination at Local Health Post is Problematic though getting Ambulance is Easy, Lori Marz—Village Armanis

There is an ambulatory in Armanis located in the school building. The ambulatory has neither water supply, nor sufficient medication needed for primary medical aid.

The ambulatory is staffed with one nurse who, however, is not an Armanis resident. The former nurse was an Armanis resident, but she died last year and due to the lack of the relevant specialist in the district, a nurse was appointed from Stepanavan. The new nurse visits the district once or twice a month referring to the lack of transportation; even vaccination is not done on time. The residents complained about her: "She says, bring the new-born to Stepanavan for vaccination. And if the young parents are unaware of the needed vaccinations and don't inquire, the child remains unvaccinated."

When needed, the residents use the ambulance, which arrives from Stepanavan. According to the residents, they are satisfied with the ambulance service. According to them, only the poor roads slow down the arrival of the ambulance on time and transportation of the patients to Stepanavan. Even in the event of accidents, the residents are reliant on the ambulance, since the ambulatory is almost always closed. In the meantime, neighbours help with bandages, cotton wool, iodine, etc.

Box 10.20

Seasonal Morbidity in Derek and Nerquin, Sashnashen Aragatsoin Marz

Village Derek

According to a seasonal morbidity diagram, the most common illness for the community members is the inflammation of upper respiratory tract, which is very common in winter, beginning of spring and in autumn. One of the main causes is the lack of proper heating. Inadequate quality of drinking water tends to cause gastrointestinal and kidney diseases, which become more acute in spring and autumn. According to the villagers, there is not a single household in the community where at least one member had no gastrointestinal problems. Appendicitis is a common illness.

Village Nerquin Sashnashen

The seasonal morbidity diagram of Nerqin Sasnashen shows that the most common diseases include flu and gastrointestinal conditions. In the former case, epidemic breaks out in winter, spring and fall, when the weather is cold and there is no or little heating (the flu mostly affects children of school age and teachers). "People cough a lot", says Hovik. Gastrointestinal diseases are mostly caused by the quality of water. These diseases also become more common in spring, fall and summer. Due to the poor condition of water sources, manure infiltrates the drinking water system with rain and melted snow.

Village Tsaxkashen

A health survey among the school children revealed that the most frequent illnesses are cold, flu and pneumonia. These are also common among adults. The main causes are the severe climate and insufficient heating at the school and in the houses. One of the teachers, Shushan, informed that most of the students suffer from intestine disorders but the parents tend to disregard that.

Box 10.21

People's Suggestions and Recommendation for the Health Sector

(i) Upgradation of skills in health care services
(ii) Upgradation of facilities at health post
(iii) Overhauling of health care system
(iv) Raising salaries of health staff
(v) Establishing local station for medical aid
(vi) Other health and nutrition measures

People's Suggestions and Recommendations

The villagers across 11 regions suggested several measures towards improvement of the overall situation in health care services. According to many local communities, the health situation is determined by the under-financing of healthcare, by the imperfection of the legislation, regulating health care, by the poor socio-economic condition of people, by corruption, by poor skills of the doctors and public inertia.

The top priorities of the villagers from different regions include the following:

A. **Upgradation of Skills in Health Care Services:** People were concerned with access to health care services as we shall see later but they were as anxious to have quality health care. The health care personnel can upgrade their health care skills and the nurses can be better trained for improved delivery of health services. Just as people asked for capacity building of teachers, they were keen that capacity of medical staff and nurses be built for betterment of the health services.

B. **Upgradation of Facilities at Health Post:** The health posts need total repair; furniture, equipment, and more and different medication are all essential. The health post needs improvement in its sanitary-hygienic conditions, regular water supply, telephone connection, medicines and training opportunities for the health care workers. It has also been suggested that medical institutions should be equipped with modern equipment and first aid station should be provided with technical means and fuel enabling quick transportation of patients to hospital.

C. **Overhauling of Health Care System:** According to the participants, to improve the health care system and its affordability, it is necessary to stipulate appropriate laws for de-politicisation of the sector, to introduce an effective medical insurance system and to initiate the institution of family doctor. In this context, one best practice in health care is that of village Fioletovo in Lori Marz, which has established a Health Protection Project whereby every household pays a certain amount of money on a monthly basis and when the need arises their members are provided with free medication and assistance. What the people were urging in this regard, essentially relates to the domain of either community based health insurance (CBHI) or general insurance.

Some of the local community residents would like to have a specialist doctor, a janitor at the ambulatory, a drugstore and a maternity ward accessible to them in the village. Some local people have suggested that new working places for population should be opened, medical staff should be trained, as well as skilled professionals should be invited.

D. **Raising Salaries of Health Staff:** It is also necessary to raise the doctors' salaries and make free medical service a reality. Low paid staff is less motivated to render intensive service under difficult circumstances.

E. **Establishing Local Station for Medical Aid:** Other improvements proposed: establishing a medical aid station in the village with a doctor on duty on regular basis; opening a pharmacy near the medical aid station or at another densely populated location within the village for buying the necessary medicine; and instituting the practice of free annual check-ups for everybody. The local doctor should be permitted to seal the medical certificates. The health post and hospitals could acquire didactic materials, computers, equipment and other materials needed for practical training and laboratory classes and also switch to gas heating which is much cheaper and efficient.

F. **Other Health and Nutrition Measures:** Some people also suggested to reinstate the practice of providing free baby food; increase up to seven years the age of patients entitled to free outpatients and hospital treatment; include more social groups entitled to free or discounted medicine; and furnish and re-equip the outpatients station. This nutritional aspect has also found resonance in the suggestions for nutritional programme in schools.

To summarise, health care issues have been mapped against each of the 11 study regions in Armenia. Though there are many commonalities amongst the regions in terms of the quality of medical services from hospitals and polyclinics and limitations of services from local health post, some regions, which are located at or near the "centre", have better quality of health services than those located at the periphery and mountainous regions.

The crux of the matter is that incidence of illness and disease are on the rise and health care is fast getting "privatised" across regions of Armenia and poor people are finding it very expensive to tackle health issues and emergency health problems. The profile of health problems in Armenia is also undergoing a change and hospitals and polyclinics need better facilities and experts to attend to the patients. Also see "overhauling the health care system" as suggested above in point (iii) as per people's suggestions and recommendations. The poor people without access to proper health care are also in need of more responsive health care systems. Health issues in each study regions have been described based on participatory assessments as done by local communities. Some best and worst practices have also been highlighted.

Livelihood Issues Impacting on Poverty: Agriculture

The Issues: Agriculture-related Issues—Voices of the Poor

Participatory assessment of agriculture-related issues and services was undertaken in 9 regions of Armenia. The regions covered were: (i) Shirak Marz, (ii) Aragatsoin Marz, (iii) Lori Marz, (iv) Gegharqunik Marz, (v) Ararat Marz, (vi) Tavush Marz, (vii) Syunik Marz, (viii) Armavir Marz, and (ix) Vayots Dzor.

The farmers—both women and men, freely expressed their views and opinions based on their grassroots experience and local knowledge. The villagers from 58 study villages of Armenia (across nine regions) listed 10 key issues in agriculture (see Box 10.22) and also suggested changes in agriculture-related policies and programmes and strengthening of agriculture-related inputs and services. In terms of common issues, which were voiced to be crucial, the farmers flagged the first nine issues in most regions covered in this study.

Box 10.22

Key issues in Agriculture—from the Voices of the Poor

(i) Common occurrence of drought and hailstorm and lack of related services
(ii) Lack of irrigation facilities and network
(iii) Lack of ability to purchase seeds and chemical fertilisers, pesticides, diesel, fuel
(iv) Lack of agricultural machinery
(v) Lack of access to bank credit
(vi) Lack of good roads
(vii) Low selling prices and limited local markets
(viii) Lack of agro-processing facility
(ix) Livestock-related issues and high cost of veterinary medicines
(x) Lack of access to technical information and technology

Selected local dimensions of the key issues are described below.

Common Occurrence of Drought and Hailstorm and Lack of Related Services

Many study regions of Armenia are in the grip of drought and other natural calamities such as hail, whose frequency has increased over the last five years. (Shirak Marz—hail and drought are common occurrences; Aragatsoin Marz and Lori Marz—frequent droughts, frosts and hails especially in the past five years; Gegharqunik Marz—dry weather and frequent droughts; Vayots Dzor—drought conditions.) These natural calamities have taken their toll on yield and productivity in agriculture and have damaged and destroyed crops and made farmers' livelihoods vulnerable. Even livestock-raising as a source of livelihoods has been adversely affected with fodder in short supply and mass slaughter of cattle. The farmers find it difficult to cope with the natural calamities in absence of either an effective government mechanism to tackle drought/hailstorm or insurance to make good the loss to animals, crops and agricultural implements. The farmers, thus, either are not compensated for crop loss or find the compensation from the government as meagre. It appeared from the discussion with the farmers that mechanism to tackle hailstorm was better in the Soviet times as compared to recent periods. In Soviet times hail was tackled quite successfully carried out by cannons that dispersed hail clouds.

Lack of Irrigation Facilities and Network

Lack of irrigation is a major issue in almost all the regions under reference. The land productivity is low due to irrigation problems such as absence of irrigation facility, damaged pumping station and erratic supply of irrigation water. In absence of irrigation, most part of lands is not cultivated, in many villages, being left for haymaking. Some villages have irrigation facilities though local residents complain about high cost of irrigation water and its erratic supply. Cattle breeding are also negatively affected by irrigation problems. Lack of irrigation also makes land cultivation unattractive and unprofitable. In some villages there is no irrigation facility while in other villages such existing facility needs to be renovated and extended. Water consumers are required to pay their water bills irrespective of how and the quality of the service that are provided, whether in timely fashion and in necessary quantities or not.

Lack of Ability to Purchase Seeds and Chemical Fertilisers, Pesticides, Diesel, Fuel

Due to expensive seeds, fuel and agricultural machinery, many villagers find it difficult to cultivate land; and hence use it as pasture. Indeed the high cost of inputs has made agriculture an unviable livelihood option, given the low returns reaped by the farmers from agricultural produce. Discounted fertilisers that are provided by the provincial authorities are not sufficient for returning soil nutrition and the farmers have to buy additional amounts of fertilisers at market prices. Pesticides provided are of poor quality and their use is not effective. The villagers complained that the land fertility was dropping and the state was not taking adequate steps to provide productive land use and crop varieties.

Lack of Agricultural Machinery

There is a gross lack of agricultural machinery in the agricultural sector and wherever equipment is available, they are not functioning. The machinery left from Soviet times is outdated and worn out. Most of the farming is done by traditional means and hand labour is widely used. There is acute shortage of tractors. The farming equipment is obsolete and has been in use for 22 years already, in many villages. In many villages, new equipment is not available even on leasing terms. The old equipment is not leased either as there are no spare parts to repair it. Still, people have to pay property tax for, what they called for want of a better expression, "a piece of scrap that they are not using". In some villages the agricultural machinery is now privatised and the farmers have to lease it from the owners. It is estimated that the cost of harvesting one hectare of arable land, which, when compared to the price of the harvest, renders the farmers' livelihood unprofitable. The farming community also has problem with the availability of qualified operators of agricultural machinery. Hence the importance of reopening secondary technical education institutions is also a related issue that is worth pondering.

Lack of Access to Bank Credit

The farming sector is capital scarce. There is, therefore, an acute problem in accessing credit by farmers. Many farmers are badly in need of long-term loans at low-interest rates for their agricultural operations. The expansion of commercial activities is as well constrained by shortage of financial resources since the available circulating assets are inoperative as a result of huge debts accumulated by villagers in different regions. Aside from a lot of paperwork required and bureaucratic delays, the interest rates are far too high. Loans are provided for a period of one-year at 20 per cent interest rate.

Bank loans are also often denied for lack of a steady income and absence of agro-technical machinery. Banks do not accept land as collateral and require only gold as security for the loans. As collateral the banks do accept livestock, though at a very low estimated cost, which makes the loan amount small.

Micro-credit granting organisations refuse to accept villagers' lands as mortgage, again because of their low yield capacity. Credits can be received only through mortgaging of movable inventory or cattle. Most villagers almost do not make use of such micro-credit services. Banks consider agriculture as a high-risk business.

Many farmers fail to keep up the re-payments of interest and loans, and in consequence lose their property. In several cases, people possessing gold items have already pledged them in security and are unable to repay the loans and are likely to lose them to banks.

Lack of Good Roads

The villagers cannot afford to take their produce to the market due to bad roads. Because of battered roads, merchants frequently refuse visiting many villages with interior location and, if they visit, they tend to buy goods from the farmers at low prices imposing a big burden on the villagers (See Box 10.22).

Low Selling Prices and Limited Local Markets

In comparison to the cost of production, the price of farm produce is very low. Most of the villagers are unable to take their agricultural and animal produce to the market due to high transportation costs. The villagers are discontented about the fact that they are not in a position to reap the price they want (and should get reasonable) on their produce in the market. Whereas dealers who buy agricultural produce in villages pay paltry amounts for the produce they get. As there is no shop in many villages, and the villagers cannot afford to transport their crops/produce to be sold elsewhere, they barter. But again barter is not a profitable proposition: the villagers do not get the actual worth for their crops or dairy products.

The business environment is underdeveloped in many villages, which adds to the woes of the farmers. There are very few small shops in the locality that are stocked primarily with the only essential goods for local residents who for the most part buy on credit. In the available few kiosks in the villages, goods are very expensive and only basic necessity goods are purchased.

Lack of Agro-Processing Facility

At present agro-processing facilities at the local level are rather limited. There are no normal shops available in many villages where agro-processing is supported. Storage of meat is an issue in many villages. As people cannot store meat, they sell or barter it for quite low prices (the traditional problem in economics, of very short run pricing). According to the villagers, it was more profitable to have one cow before than ten cows now. To that extent their conditions have worsened.

Livestock-related Issues and High Cost of Veterinary Medicines

On a limited scale, the veterinary department regulated from the Ministry of Agriculture is an important consultant and service provider. Animal immunisation is timely. Though there is a vet in the village for vaccination, which is carried out periodically free of charge, the medicaments (sic) for livestock are rather expensive and many farmers cannot afford to buy them. The vaccination of cattle and sheep is inexpensive. However, for pigs both vaccination and feed are expensive. The villages have veterinary service though farming and cattle breeding advice is not easily accessible.

Lack of Access to Technical Information and Technology

Some villagers also pointed out that there is lack of information on the quality of medication or pesticide and they buy whatever is available, which is usually not very efficient.

Box 10.23

People's Solution to Agricultural Problems

(i) Protection against natural calamities.
(ii) Regular and adequate water supply for irrigation purposes.
(iii) Procurement of efficient agricultural machinery who important.
(iv) Reasonable prices on fuel, seed and pesticides was important.
(v) Resolution of land problems.
(vi) Provision for agriculture insurance.
(vii) Provision of long-term and low-interest loans and ensuring access to mortgage loans.
(viii) Creation of markets opportunities for selling agricultural produce was important.
(ix) It was important to establish accessible sales points and storing facilities.
(x) To procure pedigree cattle.

People's and Farmers' Suggestions and Recommendations

The villagers of the study villages and regions suggested several measures towards improvement of the overall situation in agriculture and entrepreneurship.

The top priorities of the farmers from different regions included the following:

(i) **Protection against natural calamities:** Natural calamity is a major headache for the farming community. Hail and drought visit them with regularity. According to the farmers, the rehabilitation of the hail-dispelling station is extremely important. It was suggested by some farmer group that farming insurance schemes could be created to extend some protection against hails, which threaten crop almost any year. Such insurance schemes could protect farmers against natural disasters. In essence, people recommended what has come to be called, "social risk management approach" to tackle the problem of co-variant risks of natural calamities.

(ii) **Regular and adequate water supply for irrigation purposes:** It was suggested by most farmers that there was need for irrigation facility and/or its extension and ensuring better supply of irrigation water; there was need to increase irrigation water supply hours and make water fee cheaper. It was suggested that for the irrigation network, water fees could be collected on the basis of consumption and not usage time. There was a request from some farmers that irrigation water fees could be collected after the crop was realised. Many suggested that the irrigation water-usage fees were in need of review as they were too high from farmers' perspectives. It was also suggested that the fees could be calculated on the basis of the service costs as the irrigation water was transported through a gravity-flow system.

There was also a suggestion that creation of separate water users' union in the village so that local communities could organise direct management of irrigation water supply, would be very helpful.

It was also suggested that building an open canal irrigation network was better for transport of irrigation water to the village. As a result, the losses would decrease and the neighbouring communities would have plenty of water to meet their own needs.

Box 10.24

People prefer to receive welfare payments instead of cultivating their own land in the absence of irrigation and low fertility of land.

(iii) **Procurement of efficient agricultural machinery was important.** The villagers expressed their view that farming equipment should be provided at affordable prices. Some villagers also suggested that they were prepared to purchase equipment with credit facilities, if their cost was affordable. Modern equipments (and especially syringes) were needed for efficiently spraying insecticides and pesticides over the grapes and for treating fruit trees.

(iv) **Reasonable prices of fuel, seed and pesticides were important.** There is apparently a clash between private interest (represented by the profit of private dealers in fuel, seeds and pesticides) and social interest (represented by the need to supply farmers with good quality fuel, seeds and pesticides). It was, therefore, suggested that there ought to be state control on the price, quality and distribution of seeds, fertilisers and treatment materials. It was also important to provide credit lines for buying fertilisers and pesticides and to distribute fertilisers on credit as and when necessary.

(v) **Resolution of land problems:** People had considered "landlessness" as an indicator of poverty and it was a serious problem for farmers. Providing access to land is thus, not only an important step for ensuring a viable livelihood for the farmers but also as a means to alleviate poverty. Indeed the two were interlinked. To make available land to farmers, it was suggested that reserve land could be distributed/sold only to the community members and not sold through auctions.

To augment land resources (since technically the supply of land is fixed) people suggested that the government should demine the village land and return it to the community and also provide the village with clearly defined specific programmatic assistance under a "border settlement" clause.

(vi) **Insurance and credit:** With regard to recommendations for credit it was suggested that the government could make provision for agriculture insurance and long-term and low-interest loans and ensuring access to mortgage loans. It was also suggested that a system could be established to ensure that true market value of the property and land placed in collateral against agri-loans are taken cognisance of. This would ensure a fairer quantum of loan from mortgaging assets pledged by the people. Therefore, in this context, expansion of micro-finance institutions and of micro-credit as also appropriate rules to govern them comes to mind immediately.

(vii) **Creation of markets opportunities and price incentives for agricultural produce:** Many of the regions grow good quality fruits. For reasons mentioned earlier and for the fact that the farmers have no means of "value-addition", results in farming getting poor return. Export of fruits was suggested as an option, though people were aware of the competition they would face from farmers of other countries. Creating either state-assisted or partly state-owned processing companies with own transport and up-to-date packaging facilities would help for exporting the fruit to foreign markets.

There could additionally be a state policy for the sale of agricultural products and fixing a minimal threshold price for purchasing agricultural produce by non-farmers and where the market price falls below the threshold price, the state would step in and buy the products,[7] offering real chances for the growers to sell their products on the market etc., at a fair price" [The agricultural goods to be procured by the state can then be used for creation of economic and social overheads under food for work programme, which will have the twin effect of directly attacking poverty while at once creating the much need infrastructure]. Brokering contracts between tinned food processing/packaging factories and villagers and store production regularly could help the farmers as well.

Box 10.25

Exploitative Intermediation

"Imagine they (meaning traders) come to our houses and buy the wheat that we grew, at 80 Drams per kg, while only wheat husks that we buy for pigs cost 100 Drams. Milk is also sold at a low price: 90-100 Drams a litre, to the milk collecting cars of the Ashtarak Kut Company".

(viii) It was important to establish accessible sales points and storing facilities in order to facilitate crop realisation. With government's assistance, farming plants and processing factories could be created for community's use, which will also help to create new jobs. State assistance could be institutionalised for private individuals exporting fruit including waiver/reduction in custom

7. Called "procurement and minimum support price for agricultural produce" in development literature.

duties and taxes, to increase exports instead of putting obstacles in their way. Re-opening/establishing factory for manufacturing capacitors could also be considered.

(viii) **To improve cattle breed:** Bovine wealth was part of the farmers' assets. But the cattle held by the people were not of high breed. It was recommended to build production units and entities, establish collective farming and cattle breeding business, to improve the quality of livestock. Many villagers engaged in livestock were prepared to breed cows in crib-equipped stables for which state assistance is also required.

An important point raised by villagers was the indifference and lack of appropriate education of the members of the Council of Aldermen, which deprived the villages of numerous opportunities to benefit from long-term concessional loans and grants provided by various international and local organisations. Some villagers believed that all their problems were solvable if the state focused on their village and provided low-interest long-term loans. Many were of the opinion that there were several opportunities for business development at the local level, where only limited investment was needed to operate and jobs could be created for more people.

The Social Security Sectors

People's Perception of Social Welfare Programmes in Armenia: The National Picture

Great importance is attached to social services and state allowances. In many villages, people receive social services like: monthly allowances, free of charge health care, first year school-child bonus, "new-baby" bonus. Refugees and families of fallen freedom fighter families get support from the state and office of village head, though people feel they need more. People receive pension in time, barring some exceptions. Pension formalities are easy and quick.

People, from across the *Marzes*, nevertheless had their own story to tell about the welfare programmes and serious suggestions to make for the reforms. Important issues and recommendations to rectify the situation are enumerated below:

(i) **Level of satisfaction is low:** People prefer not to apply for assistance as they feel that if they get adequate crops, they will be fine. In several villages, people are disappointed with social assistance. They do not bother to apply for assistance as the authorities do not respond. There are many families in dire straits and government pays allowances to some of these families but these are not enough. There are some villages where no people receive benefits and no social assistance is provided to needy families in the village despite there being many deserving people. Several villages were discontented with the quality and timeframe of aid received, especially child bonuses which are only paid several months after all the papers are filed.

(ii) **Targeting was indicated as a major issues:** Poor targeting was a common refrain. In some cases villagers said no aid is extended even to the most financially disadvantaged. Some needy families are disqualified for enrolment in welfare programmes under a score-based qualification system. Social workers would rather prefer to make personal decisions on inclusion of fellow citizens in welfare programmes than rely on outdated score-based system which does not reflect the present reality. "Only those who are already well off receive them".

In some villages, the overall distribution of aid is fair but in other cases people said that the principle of fairness is not there. There is a certain lack of transparency as well because people do not know what data is fed into a computerised system. A villager remarked: "....how can the computer know, how many animals a person has, or does he have any animals or not...and who can tell what data was entered onto the computer by the operator......."

Box 10.26

In village Astghadzor, Gegharkunik Marz one villager said "There are people in the village who own several cars and still get allowance".

In some villages, people think that the whole population should get aid as they have no other financial income but they don't.

(iii) **Quantity is not enough:** In some villages a majority of the villagers do not pin hope on pensions, allowances and other compensation provided by the state. The amount of different kinds of pension is insufficient amount or as one set of villagers described, the limited state support (pensions and benefits) "unserious". This was illustrated in one village by the fact that women headed households without employment are considered poor but pensions paid to them fail to eradicate the problem of poverty. Pensions are low even for veterans with 40-50 years seniority. The size of the monthly allowance is too small to take care of even the basic needs of 4-member households. In a few villages, people complained that the number of needy people is high yet they are denied social aid, allegedly because of possessing land or receiving big pensions. Pensions are also few in numbers. In some cases the coverage was deemed inadequate.

Box 10.27

For instance, this year the government allocated mere 1200 kg of seed-stock wheat to the entire village (of 650-655 residents) as a compensation for the drought. Speaking about that fact, the villagers could not resist laughter as the allocated wheat would be sufficient only to sow six hectares of land plots.

—Village Zovasar, Aragatsotn Marz

(iv) **Problems with identification of beneficiaries:** Some villagers think that pensions are calculated "justly" but the amount is small while others think that benefits of pensions not assigned fairly. People generally thought that the methodology for poverty assessment was flawed. As they put it in one place "many people sneak in and take the places of the poor people".

Box 10.28

Whose Reality Counts?

"Four people drive from Kyavar, decide here who is entitled to get aid and then leave. And we do not see them till the next year. It should be the Mayor who should make those lists so that we too know where to go if something goes wrong."

—Villagers of village Geghamasar, Gegharkunik Community

The procedure for compensating damages caused by natural disasters such as hail and frost has revealed that the state insurance mechanism needs re-examination. In one village, the villagers mentioned entry of false and exaggerated data.

(v) **Transparency Issue:** Villagers, in many villages, were not informed about the criteria for receiving social welfare benefits. In other places, people have no information of the social allowances. People do not understand why pensioners whose pensions were increased became ineligible. Some villagers feel that there are no clear and understandable legal provisions concerning their eligibility and ıights. Some people, therefore, went on to complain that the procedure established by the Ministry of Labour and Social Security for distribution of family allowances is full of loopholes.

Box 10.29

Welfare Benefits versus Pensions

People do not understand why pensioners whose pensions were increased became ineligible to receive welfare benefits. "They must be kidding, the increase is only 450 Drams per month (presumably in pensions) , and they take away 4000 to 4500 Drams (presumably in welfare aid) ...Is the Social Ministry not part of the government and works as it pleases.." a villager from Chinari, in Tavush Marz. [Emphasis added]

In some villages people had no idea about the expenses incurred for the use of social services as the village headman deals with these matters. "it is he who submits a list of those who qualify as allowance recipient."

(vi) **Corruption:** As a natural concomitant to lack of information and lack of understanding/information of rules/legal provision governing welfare programmes, people perceive that there is corruption in the system. Villagers of a village in Gegharkunik Marz said upfront "They pocket the four month's allowance money just for putting you on the list of *Paros*.."

In one case (village Teghut, Tavush Marz) the public opinion about officials dealing with social security was: "..they are the wolves with open mouths; they will eat whatever you give them..."

Arbitrariness and discrimination in determining vulnerability status of households were also indicated. Villagers in one village alleged even abuse of family ties by the social workers. "Eligibility did not depend on the actual social condition of a household but rather on how well connected this household was or how it could reciprocate this 'favour'" said a villager in Chinari.

Misuse of pension funds was also mentioned in one village. "They hardly pay us any pension and in addition, they make Post Office employees bring various goods with the pension: coffee, soap, pasta, and sell us at high process...We complained but what's the use...The mayor is well aware and keeps silent..."

(vii) **Institutional aspects:** In some villages, people are unhappy about the social strategy and the policy implemented through regional and local service centres.

Villagers indicated in some villages that the office of social security service is located in another town. People spend resources to go to the office. Nothing is resolved after just a few visits. People in some cases do not even care to apply for this reason and for the fact that even those who file an application for receiving welfare benefits often do not get a response (presumably from the office of the social security service). People left out of the list of beneficiaries get little response from *Marz* and regional officials. People were not familiar with social service office in some villages.

One village complained that the staff of the social service office is undisciplined. In some cases, the villagers believed that the social service office has insufficient technical resources and its property/computers are old. Officers of social service office are believed to lack basic understanding and care when dealing with people, which lead to poor quality of management of the service. Non-governmental organisations and international non-governmental organisations were said to be unhappy with the Ministry of Social Security in one *Marz*.

(viii) **For Yerevan:** Social services are normal. More welfare programmes are offered now than before. The quality of services has improved. However, residents thought that the policy on welfare programme is defective. For example: a resident receiving family benefit is included in the "benefit for work" programme and receives 10,000 Drams from the public work performed. But his right to receive 24,000 Drams of poverty benefit is immediately revoked. There is also corruption. "If you give money you will get special treatment; if you don't give money you won't".

Assessment of families for inclusion in the poverty benefit system is not conducted properly.

Low salaries of employees have adverse impact on the quality of services provided by the social service employees.

What People Say to Set the House in Order?

While people had a fairly clear idea of what needs to be improved in the welfare programmes, they were less forthcoming on what needs to done. For one, they lacked information on the system and the programmes, for the other, they were still engrossed in the concept of an all-pervasive welfare-state. The latter inevitably leading to the widely held view that the state should do everything to set the house in order. Nevertheless the following key suggestions were made which warrant serious consideration:

(i) **Democratise selection of beneficiaries:** Villagers across the *Marzes* wanted some objective criteria for identifying the beneficiaries. For example in one village, people said: "Abolish allowances granted through the *Paros* system and give monthly allowances for minors". In another case, people suggested that welfare benefits be distributed on the basis of number of children in the households. That is, the villagers wanted objective criteria for grant of social welfare benefits. The villagers asked the government to create a Board of Trustees in the community which would decide who would get the welfare benefits and how much. Involving the village head in approving the list of families qualifying for allowances was favoured because he had tacit knowledge of the real socio-economic status of the families in the relative village. Involving the community or the municipality in approving the list of families qualifying for allowances, would improve the transparency of the system.

(ii) **Improve the quantum:** Raise pensions and amounts of allowances. Villagers also thought that it is important for the community to get governmental support to construct houses.

(iii) **Improve the state insurance mechanism:** While people wanted the state welfare system to be improved, they were less sure of what could be done. One suggestion was change staff of the social services entities so that they are more responsive to peoples' needs and at once weed out any vested interest that might have grown.

(iv) **Information is power:** Increasing the awareness amongst the people about the quantity, costs involved, legal provisions, methods of selection of beneficiaries and timeliness of disbursement of welfare allowances was suggested by several communities. A well-informed public is often the first step towards a transparent government and an essential element in weeding out corruption.

Timely distribution of aid and allowances was also very strongly urged.

> **Box 10.30**
>
> *Some Good Practices*
>
> In Mets, Gegharkunik Marz, local government has set benefits of 7000 Drams for new born babies and stationery and dress for all children going to class one from the village budget in one village. Other villages should follow the example.
>
> Community government supports vulnerable families for the education of their children and local municipality members take care of two vagabonds. These practices are worth examining.

(v) **International organisations** like GTZ, World Vision and others should expand their coverage for their social assistance and include as many communities as possible in their list of target communities.

In summary, vulnerable families and refugees have access to various welfare schemes. People were aware and have received pensions, allowances and other compensations provided by the state. While the concept and design of social security measures are appreciated, the major concern of the communities relate to:

i. Inadequacy of the quantum of pensions/allowances and compensations;
ii. Inadequate or improper targeting, which results in needy people getting left out, while non-deserving ones reaping the benefits (in as much as in one village a person owing a car was a beneficiary);
iii. The *Marz* mechanism for collecting and registering information on conditions of the citizens are not always objective;
iv. The big distance between the *Marz* or the regional social security unit and the villages;
v. Artificial improvements in living standard indicators of the village in the database of the corresponding social security agencies;
vi. Arbitrariness and discrimination in determining the vulnerability status of households;
vii. The meagre size and lack of timeliness of payments;
viii. The government apathy towards complaints of citizens; and
ix. Corruption in granting and utilising the welfare amounts.

> **Box 10.31**
>
> ...They're the wolves with open mouths; they will eat whatever you give them...
>
> —A villager of Teghut, Tavush Marz

Summary of Policy Implications

The suggestions emanating from the people range from major macroeconomic policy reform to micro-level interventions benefiting the households. Although it is desirable that all interventions suggested by the people do get reflected in a PRSP document, for brevity they have been clubbed into broad policy recommendation, without compromising the substantive thrust and character of the suggestions made by the people.

Direct Attack on Poverty

(i) ***Tackling income poverty through employment guarantee in the lean season:*** Increasing the income levels of the people—to remove income poverty, poverty born out of social deficit-is high on the agenda of the people. In almost every region, the issue of unemployment and low income as a characteristic and cause of poverty has been identified. Unemployment also affects the young people most and hence has inter-generational implications including, as indicated by the people, the fertility rate.

Increasing employment has to be high on the [policy] agenda of any PRSP for Armenia. Measures at increasing employment must be cognisant of two facts that the most of the people depend on agriculture (including livestock development) for their livelihood and there are seasonal dimensions. On measure used successfully in many developing countries is creation of wage-employment programme during the lean season. In such a programme the government guarantees wage employment to people during the lean season for a fixed period and use the labour so harnessed to build infrastructure and improve service delivery. The "Employment Guarantees Scheme" in the State of Maharashtra, India has been very successful in the past.

(ii) ***Tackling income poverty by creating assets for the poor:*** Increasing the asset base of people—to remove poverty due to assetlessness—is the other aspect of tackling income poverty. This is best done through launching of self-employment programmes. Unlike wage employment, self-employment programmes need not have a seasonal dimension. Under self-employment programme there will be three elements: one, the programme should try to build upon the local knowledge and local technology of the people; two, there will be capacity building of the people in development of products and entrepreneurship, for people who do not have a traditional product or lack the technological capability; and three, most importantly, there will be micro-credit made available to those who either have traditional knowledge or who have received training in development of products and entrepreneurship mentioned earlier. The models for delivery of micro-credit for poverty reduction are several that could be of use to Armenia. Generally, self-employment programmes should be developed as "Off-farm" employment opportunities for those who are landless or as supplementary income generating proposition for those who have unviable land (that is, land which does not yield sufficient income to meet the basic needs of the poor).

Under the self-employment programme, it may be possible for one community or a group of geographically adjacent communities, to specialise in one product, which could be termed as One-Community-One-Product (OCOP). This will help in keeping the cost of external inputs low [increasing the profit margin for the people], maintain the supply chain and keep the quantum of production large enough for ease of marketing. The success achieved by Thailand in creating livelihood opportunities for the rural masses through its "One Thambon One Product" (meaning one village one product) warrants a serious look.

Institutional arrangement for self-employment programmes may take the form of a public sector-community-NGO partnership, where the public sector helps in identifying the technology gaps, provide appropriate technology and capacity building, the NGOs provide micro-credit and the community ensures proper utilisation of resources (including training) and recycling of credit.

Indirect Attack on Poverty

(iii) ***Tackling income poverty by creating a balance between cost of production and realisable price of farm produce:*** In a primarily agricultural economy like Armenia poverty of those dependent on agriculture is a critical area for intervention, for increasing incomes relative to expenditure to eliminate relative income deficit of the farming community. Since issues relating to relative cost of inputs and price of outputs will be the subject to be dealt with under the agriculture sector policies later, suffice it is to state for the present, that a balance between cost of production and realisable price of farm produce will have to be achieved primarily:

a. by reducing input prices through a benevolent regulatory mechanism,

b. by social risk management (to minimise loss especially crop loss),

c. through provision of micro-insurance, and

d. elimination of exploitative intermediation by better marketing of farm goods and providing minimum support price for agricultural produce.

(iv) ***Tackling non-income poverty by eliminating the voicelessness of the poor:*** Increasing the "voice" of the people: in the political (and development) processes—to remove poverty due to "voicelessness"—through a process of decentralisation of development administration, planning and project implementation to the lower levels on the basis of the principle of "subsidiarity". It could be "*Marz* level Planning Based on Community Plans".

There is a burgeoning literature and models on decentralised planning available from the developing world such as in Israel. Indeed there are models already available in Armenia on how community level planning could be carried out both in the NGO sector and in the UN System. The need is to institutionalise the idea of decentralised planning and adopt a system to scale up the Armenian Models of decentralised planning, with or without modification.

Developing a decentralised system of planning can be in stages. Such a system should include, as a first step, building the capacity of relevant functionaries at all levels in the architecture and engineering of decentralised planning. At subsequent steps, elements of "automaticity" in devolution of more finances, greater financial autonomy and powers to plan to *Marzes* and communities, need to be institutionalised. In this regard, models provided by China and Kerala, India would be particularly instructive.

(v) ***Tackling non-income poverty by eliminating powerlessness of the poor:*** Empowering the people—to eliminate poverty due to powerlessness and violation of rights—may be through organising the poor, promoting community based organisations and encouraging the voluntary sector to flourish. This would entail a paradigm shift, a movement away from welfarist approach to an empowerment approach. It needs to be underscored that rights are violated, not necessarily by the state, but by a range of actors and circumstances.

Promoting community-based organisation could be based on the use of social capital available in the country. The Self-Help Group (SHG) concepts available in Armenia as well as the concepts of Self Help Group movement in different parts of the developing world provide important examples of community based organisation. Proactive promotion of community-based organisations (CBOs) could be through creation of an enabling environment, in terms of rules, regulations and laws that make establishment, operation and sustainability of CBOs easier. It ought not to partake the nature of institutions established by the government.

One of the ways to institutionalise the community based organisations like Self Help Groups would be to designate them as programme implementation agencies on behalf of the regional and local self-governments. These Self Help Groups, for instance, could be the conduit for servicing micro-credit referred to above. Self Help Groups could be effective organisations for promotive and preventive health care services like neighbourhood-committees seen to flourish in Israel,[8] to which we shall refer later.

(vi) ***Affirmative action for the minorities:*** While the foregoing measures are likely to help people belonging to the minority communities, in some cases their special circumstances may not allow them to reap the benefits of anti-poverty measures. There may thus, be a need for special programmes for the minorities. These may include but not restricted to, special financial

8. See for an early exposition of this Ram A. Canaan and Joseph Katan (n.d.). "Local Neighborhood Committees in Israel: Potentials for Self-Help Group Activity," *Nonprofit and Voluntary Sector Quarterly* 15(2): 23-46.

aid for children of people belonging to minority communities going to schools and reservation of seats for such children in institutions of higher learning,[9] reservation of jobs in the public sector and the like.[10]

Education Sector

Education is the key sector for development of any developing country, especially for a country like Armenia with high level of literacy. As mentioned earlier, people have enthusiastically come up with a whole range of suggestions for making the education sector better. These suggestions can be broadly combined into four policy options: respecting the rights of the child; improving the quality of teaching by filling critical gaps, capacity building of teachers and curriculum development, affirmative action for vulnerable groups and raising resources through alternative sources. These are briefly discussed below:

(i) ***Respect Rights of the Students:*** In a modern world, rights of children have a special significance and should be given a high priority. The rights specifically relevant in the current context could be incorporated in a Students Charter comprising:

- Right access to school: Provide transportation and school roads as appropriate on a priority basis. Only providing transportation without a minimum of roads and vice versa will not carry the communities very far. The complementarities of the two should be well recognised and realised.
- Right to happy early childhood learning: Kindergartens are highly prized by the communities and have strong gender dimensions. People recommended reopening kindergartens where they are closed; renovating buildings where they stand in need of repair and equipping them with toys and other materials necessary for children's initial initiation into the schooling system. Promoting kindergartens was also recommended as a measure to help reduce the loads of teachers in secondary schools.
- Right to a fear free environment in schools: Ban on corporal punishment commends itself.
- Right to be heard: Putting in place a system where students' opinions, including in laying down the school rules and in selecting their class supervisor, are respected and students' knowledge impartially assessed, would be in keeping with the national ethos of Armenia.
- Right to be taught in their own[11] languages: Use of local language should be used as a medium of instruction. Use of local language would improve the learning process and elicit even more interest from parents and the community in school's activities.

9. This issue will be discussed in the sub-section on education below.
10. The steps taken by the Philippines for the indigenous peoples of that country may be worth an examination.
11. Also referred to a mother-tongue or "father-tongue".

- Right to nutrition and medical attention: Beginning a national nutritional programme as a measure to facilitate attendance because a well designed nutritional programme would not only improve school attendance of children from relatively poor families (by increasing the real income of the respective parents) but improve the health status of children in general, enabling them to study better, specially in harsh weather conditions where nutritional requirements of the body are not easily met. There are several Models available in Armenia, which may be adopted or upscaled.
- Right to full development of their personality: Students need to have a disciplined mind and a disciplined body. Hence, while due emphasis has been placed on academic studies, co-curricular and extra curricular activities need more attention. Some such activities should be organised for leisure time.
- Providing institutional mechanisms to monitor that the rights of the child are not violated: Revitalising the Parents' Council every where will be a very acceptable and effective means towards acting as a watch-dog against violation of students' rights and arbitrary behaviour of teachers. The Parents' Council could act as a bridge between the community and the schools, help the school management to raise resources including community contribution to help repair buildings etc., run nutritional programmes and enlist the support of social institutions for the schools.

(ii) ***Quality of Teaching:*** Filling Critical Gaps, Capacity Building of Teachers and Curriculum Development. Shortages of teachers in certain areas, their capability and modernisation of the curriculum, have been brought out in bold relief.

Needs for additional teachers in Armenian, English and Russian languages and in technical subjects such as Geography, History, Physics, Chemistry, Biology, Information Technology, Physical Education Teacher and Arts and Craft should be met. The impact of these teachers on the quality of education would be very substantial not only to enhance the overall development and personality of the children and inculcate in them healthy habits but also to upgrade the scientific tenor of teaching. In this context, introduction of English language in the school curriculum has found much favour, as it is believed that language competence in English provides greater possibilities for better professional growth.

The pedagogy of teaching should be modernised. Many of the teachers have positive attitudes and have earned the respect of the students but they have not been able to keep up with modern methods of imparting education to school children. Training of teachers has, therefore, been emphasised which will positively impact on the quality of education.

The school curriculum needs to be upgraded along with upgrading the skills of the teachers and make the schools more relevant to the ground realities. It may be done either by including into the school curriculum subjects for professional application, like viticulture, tractor and car-driving classes or vocational schools be started for building capacity of young men in these and such other areas. These measures would help in reducing the problem of unemployment while at the same time making the education system more relevant to present realities of the country.

To take full advantage of improved pedagogy and curriculum development, it is necessary to raise the teachers' salaries as well as their responsibilities including their enhanced role in society, to motivate them, which will ultimately show up in improved quality of teaching in schools. Raising salary particularly commends itself in that a higher salary would reduce the need for the teachers to undertake private tuition, which is detrimental to quality education in school.

In the light of the foregoing, the government may wish to re-examine the current educational reforms underway.

(iii) ***Affirmative Action for Vulnerable Groups:*** Poverty is a serious issue and acts as an impediment to educating children from disadvantaged families. A whole range of steps may be necessary in this regard. A summary of these is:

- Children from socially disadvantaged families should be allowed to attend school exempted from paying the required fees/fees for textbooks etc., and provided with financial aid to meet "other expenses" relating to education.
- Legitimate exemption from classes for both pupils and teachers during the harvesting period to allow children to participate in income generation activities.
- Provide preferential treatment to applicants from high-mountainous villages in admissions to Schools of Education in Yerevan.
- Children from minorities like Assyrians have serious problems with enrolment in the universities. As children from a minority group they have no privileges, while competing with Armenians is hard. This must be addressed by making special reservation for minorities in institutions of higher learning.

There are many examples of such affirmative action in developing countries, which have borne fruits. The treatment of children of indigenous people in New Zealand and India can provide learning in this matter.

(iv) ***Raising Resources from Non-conventional Sources:*** To carry out reforms in the education sector outlined above, there will be need for additional

resources. While the government has the responsibility to implement the recommendations in the education sector, alternative means of financing should be education devised and there are enough examples of such alternative sources of funding in Armenia. A sample of good practices is in Box 10.12 but there are other means of financing that should be explored. There are two programmes that immediately commend themselves.

First, is allowing private sector participation in the education sector, with differentiated fees structure. That is, the private sector may charge higher fees from the parents who are relatively well-off and cross-subsidise the fees charged from parents who are poor or non-rich. Foreign equity participation could also be encouraged in this sector as is being done in several developing countries including in Bangladesh and Indonesia.

Second, a system of child sponsorship should be encouraged where a non-resident Armenian and even others would sponsor one child at home for their education. The amount of sponsorship could vary from US$ 50-100 per annum and the support is for the period till a child reaches 16 years of age. This is what is called a "Child Sponsorship Programme", and is run by many international non-governmental organisations like Oxfam, Foster Parents Plan International, Action Aid UK, Aide et Action,[12] France in different parts of the world including in Bangladesh, Pakistan and China.

These measures would provide the much needed "extra-budgetary" support to make good the "apparent" sub-optimal public-investment in the education sector, especially in building and renovating the infrastructure, inventory, furniture, physical plant especially heating facilities, gymnasium and recreation centre. Acquisition of didactic materials, computers, equipment and other materials much needed for practical training and laboratory classes which must be made a priority for the government, can also be funded through this mechanism, substantially if not wholly.

Health Sector Policies

The picture of health care in the different regions indicates that there are few, if any, communities, which have not been covered by health services. This is quite remarkable given the structural changes that have occurred after the exit of the former Soviet Union. People have, nevertheless, felt that there are areas within the health sector which do not look pretty. They have urged some major changes, which can be encapsulated in the following policy options:

(i) ***Overhauling of Health Care System though Pro-Poor Public Private Partnership (PPPPP), Community Based Health Insurance (CBHI) and Para-medics:*** Looked at from the perspective of the common people, improving

12. Aide et Action, France is especially focused on education sector.

the delivery of health care and making it affordable are the two major dimensions to be cognisant of. Against this backdrop, the following policy options commend themselves:

(a) ***Upgradation of Facilities at Health Posts:*** The health posts need total repair; furniture, equipments and sanitary-hygienic conditions, regular water supply, telephone connection, medicines, specialist doctor, a janitor at the ambulatory, a drugstore and a maternity ward accessible to the people and training for upgrading the technical skills of the healthcare workers all stand in need of essential improvements. The Village Health Posts even need supply of fuel for quick transportation of patients to hospitals who cannot be treated in the Village Health Post. However, given the competing demands on state's resources and quantum of resources required for these measures, it may not be possible for the government to make the required investments to bring about these changes, at least in the short run. However, combining the mandate and reach of the public sector; the entrepreneurial and managerial capability of the private sector and the social capital of the communities, through a pro-poor public-private partnership (PPPPP) could possibly help accomplish these. A PPPPP model has been explored in at least tackling the scourge of HIV/AIDS in Thailand.

Within the PPPPP framework, two supplementary steps are needed:

- Establishment of an affordable medical insurance system such as the community based health insurance (CBHI), which will cut the cost of availing quality health services. There are several success stories in CBHI in different developing countries such as in Senegal and Bangladesh.[13] Indeed, one good practice in Armenia, though in a rudimentary form, is health care provided in village Fioletovo in Lori Marz, through a Health Protection Project where each household in the community pays a certain sum of money every month in a common pool and when the need arises their members are provided with free medication and related assistance.
- Initiation of the institution of family doctor, who would act as a friend, philosopher and guide for the suffering masses and where finding a family doctor is not possible for whatever reason, licensing of Para-medics with an ability to provide first aid and read the symptoms in complicated cases and referring them to referral hospitals would help the poor people. In Thailand for example, people living with HIV/AIDS have been trained to provide psycho-social counselling to "HIV+" people in the use and adherence to anti-retroviral drugs. In the state of West Bengal, India, the services of Self Help Groups have been utilised to identify under-nourished children and connect them with state agencies for supply of supplementary nutrition.

13. See for instance J.P. Juttings (2003). "Do Community Based Health Insurance Schemes Improve People's Access to Health Care?", *World Development* 32(2).

(b) ***Establishing Local Station for Medical Aid:*** Other major improvements proposed are establishing a medical aid station in the village with a doctor on duty on regular basis; opening a pharmacy near the medical aid station or at another densely populated location within the village for buying the necessary medicine. The local doctor should be permitted to seal the medical certificates. The health post and hospitals could acquire didactic materials, computers, equipment and other materials needed for practical training and laboratory classes to help train the "Para-medics" referred to earlier.

(ii) ***Propagating the Ideas of Promotive and Preventive Health:*** Health issues are important for the community. Promotive and preventive health care (apart from curative health facilities) for students and teachers are considered essential for improvements in overall health. Medical examination of the school children and specialist visits more frequently is strongly recommended. Catching them young as it were, to take promotive and preventive health, as serious business would eventually reduce the burden and need of preventive health care, make it lean and more effective.

One model for providing medical care to students and teachers in Schools is the "Open Door Days" model. "Open Door Days" held once or twice a year when the doctors from a nearby hospital visit the school and examine the students. In addition, once a month the nurse conducts a sanitation day. This should be extended to all schools. An example of "Open Door Days" is in Village Tavshut, Shirak Marz. Another model is that in the school in Noramut Village, Lori, a nurse, who carries out the mandatory vaccinations of schoolchildren together with the nurse of the medical post.

(iii) ***Health and Nutrition Measures for Marginalised Groups:*** Marginalised groups need special attention. Since programmes for special groups would essentially be heavily subsidised, these need to be well targeted and tightly administered. Some people have suggested to reinstate the practice of providing free baby food; increasing up to seven years the age of patients entitled to free outpatients and hospital treatment; include more social groups entitled to free or discounted medicine.

Livelihood and Agriculture

The economy of Armenia is largely agricultural and agriculture related like managing livestock. Naturally development and poverty reduction in the country has to pay special attention to this sector. This is particularly so when agriculture has a strong bearing on some of the characteristics of income and non-income poverty like unemployment, inability to cultivate land, imbalance between cost of production and realised price of agricultural production and unemployment. The policy options for this sector, emerging from people's perspective, deserve a serious look. These are within four segments: input supply and regulation; protection against calamities; fair price of outputs and livestock improvement. The following comments are in order here.

(i) ***Resolution of land problems:*** People had considered "landlessness" as an indicator of poverty and it was a serious problem for farmers. Providing access to land is thus, not only an important step for ensuring a viable livelihood for the farmers but also as a means to alleviate poverty. Indeed the two were interlinked. To make available land to farmers, it was suggested that reserve land could be distributed/sold only to the community members and not sold through auctions.

To augment land resources (since technically the supply of land is fixed) as the people suggested that the government should demine the village land and return it to the community and also provide the village with clearly defined specific programmatic assistance under a "border settlement" clause.

(ii) ***Regular and adequate water supply for irrigation purposes:*** Access to land and access to water are fundamental to improving agriculture in Armenia. In fact, in many communities in almost all the Marzes, people believe that if only irrigation can be ensured, it would usher in enough prosperity to tackle most of the problems confronting the communities. While water belongs to the State, the users were primarily individuals who are outside the public sector. A new water policy needs to be devised with the following elements:

- providing irrigation facility and/or its extension and ensuring better supply of irrigation water would be given a priority;
- building an open canal irrigation network was better for transport of irrigation water to the village. As a result, the losses would decrease and the neighbouring communities would have plenty of water to meet their own needs;
- increasing the hours for supply of irrigation water;
- ensuring that water fee would be made cheaper;
- for the irrigation network water fees could be collected on the basis of consumption and not usage time;
- such water fees could be calculated on the basis of the service costs as the irrigation water was transported through a gravity-flow system and could be collected after harvesting of crop was realised; and
- the creation of separate water users' union in the villages so that local communities could organise direct management of irrigation water supply, would be very helpful.

(iii) ***Reasonable prices on fuel, seed and pesticides was important,*** because rising input costs have, at least in part, a major contributory factor making agriculture a non-viable option. The conflict of interest between private interest (profit of private dealers in fuel, seeds, fertilisers and pesticides) raising input prices and social interest (the need to supply farmers with good quality fuel, seeds, fertilisers and pesticides at reasonable prices) can be circumvented by a multi-pronged attack on the problem of rising input costs. First, there ought to be state regulation on the prices, quality and distribution of seeds, fertilisers, insecticides and pesticides, essential for a healthy agricultural economy. Second, facilities to provide credit lines for buying fertilisers and pesticides and to distribute fertilisers on credit as and when necessary, to reduce production cost by keeping the cost of working capital at a reasonable level, should be established. Here the role of micro-finance comes in, in a big way. Third, on long-term loans and ensuring access to mortgage loans, the method of valuation of collateral usually was such that they were "undervalued" and hence the loans the farmers succeeded to secure usually resulted in under-financing of their "tiny enterprises". Hence, a system for valuation of property could be established to ensure that true market value of the property and land placed in collateral against agri-loans are taken cognisance of, to help farmers avail of a fairer quantum of loan from mortgaging assets pledged, is crucial. Therefore, in this context expansion of micro-finance institutions and of micro-credit as also appropriate rules to govern them commend themselves immediately.

While, ensuring availability of fuel, seed and pesticides at reasonable price, farmers also recommended the procurement of efficient and affordable agricultural equipment/machinery was as important, as essential complementary inputs. Modern equipments (and especially syringes) were needed for efficiently spraying insecticides and pesticides over the grapes and for treating fruit trees. Some villagers also suggested that if the state was unable to ensure affordable agricultural equipment/machinery, they were prepared to purchase such equipment/machinery with credit facilities, if the cost of credit was affordable. Affordability with regard to micro-credit has two dimensions for the people. One was the rate of interest payable credit purveyed. Two, the method used for valuation of the collateral offered by the people, which we have discussed earlier. Thus, promotion of micro-credit again emerged as an important policy instrument in agriculture. An important point raised by villagers was the indifference and lack of appropriate education of the members of the Council of Aldermen, which deprived the villages of numerous opportunities to benefit from long-term concessional loans and grants provided by various international and local organisations. This can be rectified without much institutional hick-ups. Many were of the opinion that there were several opportunities for business development at the local level, where only limited investment was needed to operate and jobs could be created for more people.

(iv) ***Protection against natural calamities:*** Interventions for making inputs available and affordable, and ensuring access to water and land must be supplemented by protection against the tyranny of nature. Natural calamity is a major headache for the farming community; hail and drought visit them with regularity. While the rehabilitation of the hail-dispelling station is considered extremely important, people hoped that crop insurance could offer the much-needed protection against natural calamities, which threaten crops almost every year. In essence, people sought what has come to be called, "social risk management approach" to tackle the problem of co-variant risks of natural calamities (risks of crop failure resulting from natural calamities are co-variant risks). It is well known that general insurance companies are usually averse to cover co-variant risks nevertheless based on experience in other countries, crop insurance can be tried as part of some form of micro-insurance.[14] The experience of providing social risk management[15] in several developing countries has important lessons to offer for the RA.

(v) ***Creation of markets opportunities and price incentives for agricultural produce:*** Many of the regions in Armenia grow good quality fruits. For reasons mentioned earlier and for the fact that the farmers have no means of creating "value-addition" results in farming getting poor return. Three interventions could be suggested. First, an export oriented package. Since, export of fruits was suggested as an option for giving fair returns to farmers, setting up of either state-assisted or partly state-owned processing companies with own transport and up-to-date packaging facilities would help fruit exports. State assistance could be institutionalised for private individuals exporting fruit including waiver/reduction in custom duties and taxes, to increase exports. Second, storing facilities. It was important to establish accessible sales points and storing facilities in order to facilitate realisation of fair price for the agricultural produce. With government's assistance, agricultural produce storing factories could be created for community's use on pay-as-you-use basis, which will also help to create new jobs. Third, a state policy for the sale of agricultural products and fixing a minimal threshold price for purchase of agricultural produce by non-farmers would be necessary. Such a policy would enjoin that where the market price for any product falls below the threshold price set by the state, Government of RA would step in and buy the products,[16] offering real chances for the growers to sell their products on the market etc., at a fair price". [The agricultural goods to be procured by the state can

14. See for concepts see MICROINSURANCE, No. 6, March 2005. *insurance@microfinance.lu*
15. See for instance Robert Holzmann and Steen Jorgenson (n.d.). "Social Risk Management: A New Conceptual Framework for Social Protection and Beyond", *Social Protection Discussion* Paper No. 0006 Washington D.C.: The World Bank.
16. Called "procurement and minimum support price for agricultural produce" in development literature.

then be used for creation of economic and social overheads under food for work programme, which will have the twin effect of directly attacking poverty while at once creating the much need infrastructure.] These two measures, taken one with the other, will tackle, at least in part, the problems of exploitative intermediation. Many countries in Asia have harvested considerable success from similar schemes.

(vi) ***To improve cattle breed:*** Livestock wealth was part of the farmers' assets. But the cattle owned by the people were not of high breed. It was recommended to build production units and entities, establish collective farming and cattle breeding business, to improve the quality of livestock. Many villagers engaged in livestock were prepared to breed cows in crib-equipped stables for which state assistance is also required.

Social Welfare Reforms

The recommendations coming from the people on reforms of Armenia's social welfare sector have been on institutional issues, design and content of the scheme. These are not in particular order of priorities but form an integral package.

(i) ***Democratise selection of beneficiaries and introduce social audit:*** There are two issues involved here: one is of targeting and the other is of a mechanism to administer the targeting. Villagers across the *Marzes* wanted some objective criteria for identifying the beneficiaries. This would make the process more transparent and the public servants more accountable. Second, the villagers thought that the present mechanism for selection of beneficiaries is unsatisfactory, leading to various kinds of unfairness and arbitrariness. The government should create a Board of Trustees in the community which would decide who would get the welfare benefits and how much. Involving the village head in approving the list of families qualifying for allowances was favoured because he had tacit knowledge of the real socio-economic status of the families in the relative village. What in effect the people recommended was instituting "social audit" of the selection and targeting of beneficiaries for social welfare schemes. Concepts like Citizens' Report Cards and Public Accounting lie in the domain of social audit. Several countries like Nepal and Moldova have already begun the process.[17]

(ii) ***Information is power:*** Increasing the awareness amongst the people about the quantity, costs involved, legal provisions, methods of selection of beneficiaries and timeliness of disbursement of welfare allowances was suggested by several communities. A well-informed public is often the first step towards a transparent government and an essential element in weeding out corruption. An informed citizenry is vital for a functioning democracy

17. See for relevant concepts George Clark (1999). *Social Auditing—Feedback Control for Organisations www.caledonia.org.uk/social2.htm* and Alana Albee (1999). *Assessing Impact: Some Current and Key Issues, www.caledonia.org.uk/pia.htm*

and in containing corruption and hold the state and its instrumentalities accountable to the governed.[18]

Towards that end, the Government of RA could make right to information a basic right of the citizen of RA. Information for the purposes of the right to information could include but not restricted to any material/data in any form in records, documents, memos, emails, opinions, advices, press releases, circulars, orders, log books, contracts, reports, samples, models and data material held in any form, electronic included, relating to any private body which can be accessed by a public authority under any law for the time being in force. And the right of the citizen will be to request access to such information and the corresponding duty of the government to meet the request except information relating to the security of the country. Such a move would reflect the attitudinal change in perception of the government and the public towards the government and meet the demands of a dynamic world seeking public accountability. India has taken the step of making right to information a right of its citizens by an Act of the Parliament.[19]

It may be added that giving people access to information has a critical flip side. It opens a two-way traffic lane. An informed citizenry provides feedback to the government and corrects errors in database. If, for example, people have information on living standard indicators of the villages in the database of the corresponding social security agencies and the information is incorrect, they would bring to the notice of the government errors, both of commissions and omissions, discussed in Section 10 earlier.

(iii) ***Expand the range of service providers:*** Till now, the welfare scheme/programmes were administered by the state agencies. There are inefficiencies, which could be weeded out by a change of staff of the social services entities so that they are more responsive to peoples' needs and at once weed out any vested interest that might have grown. Where this is not possible (and even otherwise) the Government of RA could "outsource" the delivery of welfare programmes to reputed international organisations like GTZ, World Vision and other similar organisations, and create an enabling environment where they could expand the coverage for their social assistance programmes to include as many community as possible in their list of development areas. This will cut cost and increase both the efficiency and the responsiveness of the system. Expanding the range of welfare service providers will also help fight corruption and reduce wastage of resources.

Expansion of the range of service providers may also improve the quantum of pensions, grants and amounts of allowances, including support to construct houses, all of which are high on the agenda of the vulnerable groups.

---

18. "The real *swaraj* (meaning independence) will come not by the acquisition of authority by a few but by the acquisition of capability by all to resist authority when abused" Mahatma Gandhi.
19. See the Right to Information Act and one of the many commentaries in "Informed citizenry vital for democracy", *The New Indian Express*, Trivandrum, India, December 5, 2006: 7.

Annexure A-10.1

The Steps and Stages in People's Participation in PRSP Revision

Consultation Step

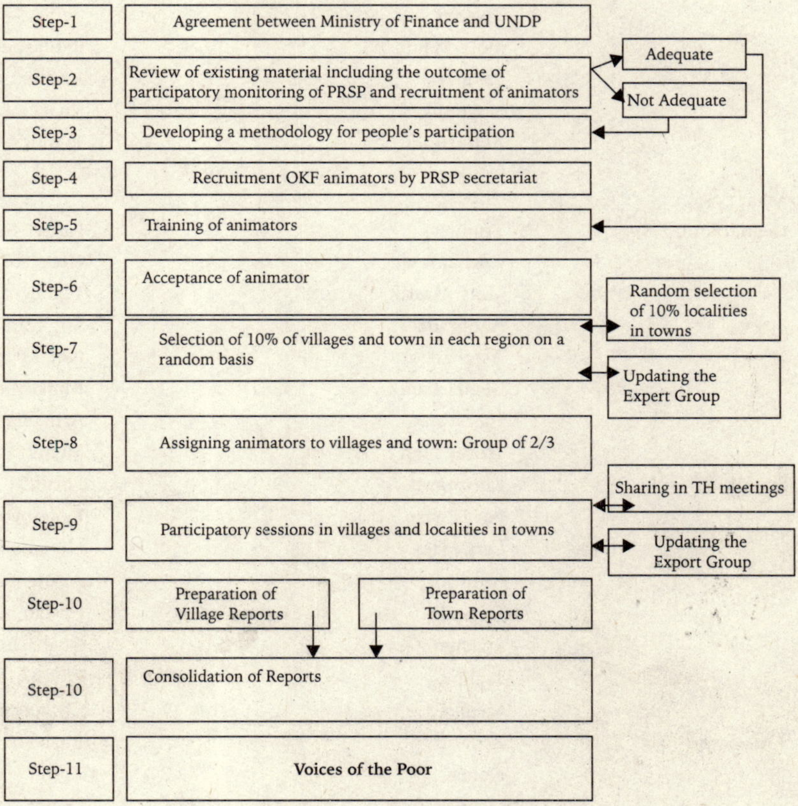

Annexure A-10.2

List of Villages and Communities Selected for Participatory Sessions

Marz (region)	*Community*	*Marz (region)*	*Community*
Shirak (7)	Berdashens	Tavush (6)	Chinar
	Tavshut		Berd
	Mets Mantash		Berdashen
	Sarapat		Azatamut
	Hoghmik		Khashtarak
	Akhurik		Taghut
	Sarakap	Ararat (6)	Verin
Artashat			
Gegharkunik (8)	Ttujur		Paruyr Sevak
	Geghamasar		Urcadzor
	Mets Masrik		Yeghegnavan
	Aghpradzor		Mrgavan
	Astghadzor		Nor Kyurin
	Gegharkunik	Lori (7)	Khnkoyan
	Hajravank		Armanis
	Tsovagyugh		Mghart
Syunik (8)	Khoznavar		Lorut
	Bardzravan		Fioletovo
	Lernadzor		Noramus
	Nyuvadi		Arjut
	Torunik	Kotayk (6)	Fantan
	Srashen		Geghashen
	Tsghuk		Zovuni
	Meghri		Charencavan
Aragatsotn (7)	Zovasar		Buzhakan
	Derek		Arzni
	Ohanavan	Armavir (6)	Doghs
	Nor Amanos		Metsamor
	Nerkin Sasnashen		Nalbandyan
	Gyalto		Koghbavan
	Tsaghkashen		Yeghegnut
Vayots Dzor (5)	Vernashen		Baghramyan
	Artavan	Yerevan (2)	Nor Nork
	Zaritap		Davitashen
	Rind		
	Hermon		

11

The Voice of the People

Enhanced Citizen Participation in Electoral Processes Through Participatory Learning and Action in Armenia

Be the change you want to see in the world

—Mahatma Gandhi

Introduction

In Spring 2007 within the framework of the "Enhanced Citizen Participation in Electoral Processes" project, the United Nations Development Programme (UNDP) initiated activities aimed at promoting citizen participation in Armenia's electoral processes. Participatory discussions on election related topics were organised and conducted with representatives of various communities from all regions of Armenia and the city of Yerevan. The discussions were held in two rounds.

First round discussions were held prior to Armenia's May 12 parliamentary elections, April-May 2007 in 44 communities of Armenia—four communities in each region and Yerevan city. More than 1100 participants attended the first round discussions. The second round of discussions were held after the May 12 parliamentary elections (July-August 2007) in half of the communities covered by the first round—22 communities (2 communities in each region and Yerevan city). More than 500 persons participated in the discussions of the follow-up round.

Goals and Objectives

The discussions were aimed at assessing Armenia's previous elections, formulating issues of concern, and creating suggestions for improving electoral processes.

The participatory discussions were also aimed at promoting more active and informed participation of community members in electoral processes. Therefore, during the discussions the participants were provided with detailed information on voting procedures.

An additional goal of the follow-up round was to measure the extent to which expectations and projections made before the May 12 parliamentary elections had come true.

Description of Participatory Discussions

Methodology

Activities were carried out according to participatory assessment methodology or the so-called Participatory Learning and Action (PLA) programme.[1]

The strength of this methodology is that people know their own situation best of all. They present the data and information based on their knowledge and personal experience. They analyse their situation themselves; they identify the problems and suggest solutions to these problems. In this case the facilitators of the meetings appear as "animators" and assist the participants to present their experience, knowledge and evolve discussions on these.

A number of methods were used during the participatory assessment to present information, including:

- scoring and ranking;
- force field analysis;
- historical transect;
- matrixes;
- participatory SWOL (Strengths, Weaknesses, Opportunities, Lessons) analysis;
- interviews;
- role play.

It should be noted that these methods are flexible both in theory and practice. Therefore, the animators were encouraged to "improvise" and apply these methods in each community or individual group with certain modifications depending on the composition of groups, timeframe of discussions, and any other specific considerations.

Process

Back in Spring 2006, within the framework of the initiative on Poverty Reduction Strategy Paper revision and Millennium Development Goals localisation, UNDP organised a 10-day training course on participatory assessment or Participatory Learning and Action (PLA) methods for a specially recruited group of animators. The trainees were selected on a competitive basis. After the training course, the group of animators, under the Poverty Reduction Strategy Paper Review, carried out "The Voices of the Poor" study in communities from Armenia's regions and Yerevan.

Since the community-based discussions on election-related issues were to be conducted using the same methodology, in February 2007 another round of training was held for the same group of animators to teach them how to

1. The earlier version of this methodology was called Participatory Rural Assessment (PRA).

apply the methodology to election-related discussions. Before the discussions, the project staff and the animators' team leader developed a detailed guide on how to organise and implement the work in the communities and how to structure reports to finalise the session outcomes. This was then given to the animators.

At the training and during all discussions it was firmly stressed that the discussions were not a part of political and pre-electoral processes, the organisers of the project and the animators did not represent any political forces, and the results of the discussions would only be used to promote the voices and concerns of the communities to the stakeholders and encourage active, informed citizen participation in electoral processes.

The participants of the meetings were selected through both random and purposive sampling. Particularly in Yerevan, participants were selected exclusively by purposive sampling and represented socially vulnerable groups, such as single elderly people, disabled persons, refugees, persons receiving family allowance, etc.

In rural areas the discussions were attended by representatives of diverse groups of community members, including school teachers, housewives, farmers, youth groups, village mayor's office employees etc. The age of the participants was 18-90 years.

In rural communities the meetings were held in the community school, club or village mayor's office as proposed by the head of the community or the participants of the meeting. Only in one village the meeting was held in the open air since no administrative building was available. In a number of cases, separate interviews were held in the village streets and fields. In Yerevan, the meetings were held in the community centres of "Mission Armenia" NGO and were attended by the beneficiaries of these centres.

The outcomes of participatory sessions were shared at the community levels and upon approval of community members were later summarised in separate reports. It should be mentioned that these reports reflected both the data and information provided by the participants and the personal observations of the animators based on separate interviews, during which participants provided information that they were unwilling to share in the group.

The discussions were carried out by eight groups of animators during the first round and by seven groups of animators during the second round.

Selection of Communities

A major concern over the general state of Armenia's democratic reforms, and citizen participation in particular, is the widespread skepticism and apathy of the general population and their so-called "voicelessness", which is especially common among the socially vulnerable groups. Therefore, selection of communities was made with the consideration of the following:

a. Since the project was implemented from the perspective of social vulnerability, it was decided to emphasise rural communities. Discussions were conducted in 40 villages, comprising some five per cent of Armenia's rural communities;[2]
b. To ensure a representative picture, four communities from Yerevan with a considerable proportion of socially vulnerable population were also included in the project;
c. For the follow-up round of discussions, two communities out of four were identified by random sampling, a total of 22 communities.[3]

Criteria for Selection of Rural Communities

The following primary factors were prioritised in the selection of villages to reflect social vulnerability of the population and communication restrictions:[4]

- percentage proportion of women in the actual composition of the village population;
- proportion of households receiving poverty family allowances;
- proportion of families with three and more children;
- proportion of single pensioners;
- proportion of the unemployed;
- access to central and local (regional) newspapers;
- access to a limited number (less than 3) of TV channels;
- proximity to the regional centre.[5]

Villages were selected as follows: in the first phase, villages with the highest indicators for the above-mentioned factors were selected within each region;[6] in the second phase, villages with the largest total number of the highest indicators were selected. In the final selection of villages, the population size was also taken into account; an equal proportion of villages with less than 1,000 residents and with more than 1,000 residents was maintained.

Criteria for Selection of Yerevan Communities

To select the Yerevan communities, the project used the database of communities with a relatively high number of residents receiving 'Household

2. See Annexure A-11.1 for the list of the selected communities.
3. See Annexure A-11.2 for the list of communities of the follow-up round of discussions.
4. These vulnerability criteria were based on "Vulnerability Assessment Survey" conducted by UNDP in 2005.
5. See Annexure A-11.3 for the profile of the selected rural communities by the mentioned characteristics.
6. These indicators on the communities were taken from Armenia's regional communities database developed by UNDP in 2006.

Poverty Allowance' provided by Armenia's Ministry of Labour and Social Affairs. In these communities purposive sampling of session participants was conducted using the database of 'Mission Armenia' NGO's beneficiaries for each community centre.[7]

Limitations

The following factors affected the course of the discussions:

a) Timing—the first round of discussions was held in April-May 2007, i.e., at the peak of the election campaign. This fact had certain limiting influence on the course of the discussions as in a number of cases a rather politicised and at times tense atmosphere prevailed in the communities. Some discussions would turn into more of a personal exchange of opinions. Moreover, some participants were overcautious and reluctant to present their genuine opinions. This required mediation skills from the animators to maintain neutral discussions. At times heads of communities were also reluctant to assist with organising the meetings. In such cases animators and the project staff would clearly explain to the Local Self-Governance Bodies and community members that the meetings were not a part of the election campaign and the political processes of the period, and that the representatives of the project are not members of any political force. During each meeting it was specially stressed that the goal of the discussions was to bring the voices of society to the attention of the authorities and stakeholders as well as to strengthen links between the authorities and society.

b) "Controllers"—In a few cases one or two persons attempted to control discussions by suppressing expression of complaints and hindering the development of political discussions. In such cases the animators "diplomatically" interrupted these participants, asking them to leave and then conducted separate interviews with them.

The Scope of the Issues Discussed

During the first round of discussions, people's approaches to and opinions about Armenia's electoral processes were mainly discussed, particularly their motives for participating, factors influencing negatively and positively on their voting and choice of candidates, sources of information on electoral processes and candidates, and how to improve electoral processes. During discussions, participants voiced their opinions based on their past experience and made projections on the upcoming parliamentary elections.

The results of both rounds and their comparative analysis are summarised and presented in this report.

7. Persons who reside in a community where a respective community centre is located, belong to socially vulnerable groups, and avail themselves of free lunches provided by a community centre, are considered beneficiaries of these centres.

Scope of Issues Discussed during the First Round of Discussions

Evaluation of Electoral Processes from Past Experience:

(a) Did people participate in past elections?
- If yes—what were their motives?
- If no—what were the reasons?

(b) Why is it important to participate in elections?

(c) What was "good" and what was "not so good" about past elections?

(d) What were the main shortcomings of the last elections?

(e) What can be done to remedy the situation and improve electoral processes?

The Coming Parliamentary Elections

(a) Are you going to participate in the elections?
- If yes—what are your motives?
- If no—what are the reasons?

(b) What sources of information on parties and candidates are available? How do people make their choice? What sources of information on electoral procedures and processes exist?

Provision of Information on Electoral Procedures—Role Play

During the follow-up round, a similar range of issues was discussed, especially emphasising the experience of the May 12 parliamentary elections. Additionally, based on the fresh experience of the recent elections, participants re-evaluated their predictions for the May 12 parliamentary elections and comments made during the previous round.

Scope of Issues Discussed during Follow-up Round of Discussions

1. Participation in elections
   (a) Did participants of the meeting participate in the election?
   (b) What were the reasons/motives for participating?
   (c) What were the reasons for not participating?
   (d) Why is participation in elections important?
   (e) Do they feel that their expectations were met?
2. Assessment of the election process
   (a) What was "good" about the election? What did you like about the last election?
   (b) What was "not so good" about the election? What were the things that you did not like most?
   (c) What could be done to improve things you did not like or were "not so good"?
3. Information available about the political parties/candidates? What information did you have about the candidates and political parties?
4. Assessment of electoral/voting procedures
   (a) Are you happy about the electoral/voting procedures? What did you like about the electoral procedures?
   (b) List the things you did not like about the electoral procedures
5. Assessment of candidates and political parties

The Results of Participatory Assessment

Electoral Participation

During the meetings of both rounds, participants mentioned whether they had participated in previous elections and the 2007 parliamentary election. Ninety (90) per cent of the participants noted that they participated in the elections. This indicator is much higher than the predictions made by the participants in the first round in the same communities. Moreover, it is higher than the official voter turnout (59.4 per cent). This can be explained by the fact that usually such events, be they social, political or cultural, are attractive for small community members.

On the whole the participants of all the discussions mentioned that voter turnout was high in their community (in the villages 70-90 per cent participation was frequently noted). During the first round of meetings, the same level of participation was predicted for the upcoming parliamentary elections. According to the participants, predictions for the turnout of the May 12 parliamentary elections in the respective communities had come true in 45 per cent of cases; in 32 per cent the turnout exceeded predicitons; in 9 per cent of cases the average level of participation predicted came true; and only in 14 per cent of cases voter turnout in the Parliamentary elections had been lower than predicted.[8]

Motives for Participation in Elections

One of the topics discussed during both rounds was motives for participation. During the follow-up round of discussions, the participants were requested to rank motives previously and presently identified by them.

The motives for participation identified by the participants of both rounds can be typically broken down into the following groups:

- expectations of and hopes for positive change in village, family, and country;
- sense of civic duty and the desire to participate in electoral processes and exercise their right to shape authorities;
- desire to value their own 'voice' and protect it from fraudulent use;
- social, cultural factors and personal interest.[9]

Expectations of and Hopes for Positive Change

As already noted, the first round of participatory assessment was conducted during the peak of the parliamentary election campaign. Perhaps this accounts for the fact that during this round, the participants often used phrases typical of pre-election campaign texts and posters to mark their motives for participation:

8. It should be noted that there is no official data on voter turnout per communities, and the participants compared the estimated voter turnout in their communities with the projections made prior to the May 12 parliamentary elections.
9. See Annexure A-11.4 for a detailed list of motives identified by participants, according to region.

"To contribute to the establishment of the state"; "To have the people's life and lifestyle and conditions improved, and to have poverty eradicated"; etc. It should be noted that the listing of such general motives prevailed during the first round of discussions, and the participants often found it difficult to be more specific. During the follow-up round of discussions, the participants formulated their expectations and hopes in a more specific and reasoned way, with the expectation of positive changes prevailing. People perceived positive changes at the level of their village first, and then at the level of their family, and then their country/state.

> The reason I voted for the ruling party is that they're solving the problems of our village.
>
> —*Lernamerdz village, Armavir Region*

Expectations and Hopes Identified During Both Rounds and Prioritised During the Follow-up Round

General Expectations:
- Improved life;
- Changes and improved social situation;
- Positive changes during electoral processes, including expectation of improvements;
- Achievement of justice;
- Improved country and state;
- A better lifestyle for our children and grandchildren in the future.

Specific Expextations:
- Laws that work so that people are not 'robbed';
- Equal rights and responsibilities;
- Hopes that newly elected officials will be helpful for residents;
- Opportunity to solve problems of the village;
- Raised pensions;
- Improved social conditions of the needy, especially single elderly persons and the disabled;
- Money (bank deposits) being returned.

A Sense of Civic Duty and the Desire to Participate in Electoral Processes and Exercise the Right to Shape Authorities

As a motive for voting, 'a sense of civic duty' or 'carrying out our responsibility' was mentioned very often during discussions. It is noteworthy that this motive was mentioned and prioritised by participants most often during the first round of discussions, but during the follow-up round of community meetings this motive was ranked among the top three motives for participation in just over a half of cases.

One recurrent feature emerging from discussions was the feeling of being ignored, which is best reflected in a comment of one of the participants of a meeting in Urtzalanj village:

> We will perform our duty—we will vote—but no one will remember us after the elections!
>
> —*Urtzalanj village, Ararat Region*

The Desire to Value their Own 'Voice' and Protect it from Fraudulent Use

In 32 per cent of follow-up round meetings, 'exercise of the right to vote and prevention of electoral fraud through the exercise of this right' were mentioned most frequently as motives for participation.

> **Motives for Participation Identified During Both Rounds and Prioritised During the Follow-up Round**
>
> - Exercise my right to shape authorities;
> - Protect our rights;
> - "My voice matters";
> - Prevent electoral fraud;
> - Desire to form a fair and democratic state;
> - Desire to have decent authorities;
> - Prevent manipulation of vote by others;
> - Vote for the person of my choice;
> - Vote for my party;
> - Desire to have a worthy representative in the National Assembly.

During the follow-up round, in three communities the concept of "my voice matters" was further expanded into the following motive for electoral participation: "The community must voice their opinion and this opinion should be reckoned with".

Social, Cultural Factors and Personal Interest

It should be noted that representatives of rural communities often emphasised that the elections, in addition to wedding parties and mourning ceremonies, were an occasion to socialise with one another. According to them:

> Life is boring in the village. Elections break the monotony. On that day we feel we are a part of a whole.
>
> —*Zedea village, Vayotz Dzor Region*

In several villages it was noted that the election was followed by happy 'dining and wining'.

When discussing the motives for electoral participation, the participants also emphasised the fact that in smaller villages people are more "law-abiding" and "traditionalist" and vote more because it is a "state affair" and a long-standing custom rather than the realisation of their civic activism.

Another reason for participation, especially in small villages, is the fact that majority of people from the surrounding area, including leaders of villages, relatives and neighbours go to vote, thus inducing others to vote.

Therefore, in many cases people go to elections because of this "environmental inducement", especially as in smaller villages it is almost impossible not to vote and go unnoticed.

During meetings some participants openly noted that they participated with the expectation of electoral bribes, and in several cases they were disappointed because they received nothing or too little.

Motives for Participation Identified During both Rounds and Prioritised During the Follow-up Round

Social Motive:

- "We participate in the election because that day differs from all the other grey days"

Personal Interest:

- To receive an electoral bribe
- Expectation that the candidate of my choice will help my family
- The request or demand of friends and relatives
- To have somebody look favourably upon them

Reasons for Non-Participation

The reasons for non-participation identified by the participants of the discussions can be typically broken down into the following groups:

- Technical reasons: people had not replaced their Soviet passport, had not applied for a new passport, or were out of the country; place of residence was different from place of registration—it was difficult to visit the latter on the election day.
- People are disappointed and frustrated and do not believe anything will change; their voice will not count.
- Illness-related: bedridden or disabled; difficult for them to move.
- Do not participate in political processes due to religious beliefs.
- Do not vote as a protest against injustice, corruption and intimidation.[10]

Of these five motives, technical reasons and lack of trust were noted most frequently. This was confirmed during the follow-up round of discussions when participants prioritised reasons for non-participation—disappointment and distrust were identified as important in 100 per cent of communities and technical reasons in 89 per cent of communities.

In smaller villages, participants mentioned with greater emphasis that they feel completely neglected. In a number of small communities, the participants welcomed animators with surprise, saying: "we are not even on the map—how on earth did you find us?"

10. See Annexure A-11.5 for a detailed list of reasons for non-participation by region.

The indifference of the elected representatives towards the community was mentioned as another important factor that discouraged voting. According to the participants, the candidates mostly remember them from elections to elections, and completely forget about them in between.

> The candidate is being appointed from the top anyway; he just comes here to be elected and then goes away again. Wouldn't it be better to use all that money they spend for some worthy cause?
>
> —*Lernamerdz village, Armavir Region*

This opinion was often shared by people who had voted simply to do a favour for somebody—the village mayor, a relative or a friend.

Another reason given in the village of Khachardzan, Tavush region, for not voting is also noteworthy: "We do not vote since we do not want to offend any candidate. In other words, we do not want to be bad guys." According to the villagers, this kind of reasoning prevails during elections of local self-governance bodies.

In summary:

The Most Important Reasons for Non-Participation Identified During Both Rounds and Prioritised During the Follow-up Round

Technical Issues:
- No Armenian passport—have not applied for one or have not had their Soviet passport replaced
- Handicapped: illness; disability
- Registered in one community but residing in another
- Outside of Armenia/working abroad

Lack of Hope and Expectations due to Previous Experience:
- Lack of faith—loss of faith in elections and in authorities
- Lack of trust
- Disappointment
- Everything is predetermined: elections are a mere formality; whoever was to be elected has already been elected; there's no point
- Our voice will not change anything
- No real results
- Indifference towards community of previous representatives
- Feeling neglected: no one visits our village
- Promises are made and never kept

Protest, grievance:
- Electoral bribes
- Intimidation/pressure

Other:
- "It is not interesting"
- "I don't care"

Importance of Participation

During the follow-up round, having discussed the above mentioned issues of electoral participation, participants were also asked to mention why they thought active public participation was important at all.[11] This question was aimed at assessing participants' civic activism and how important they considered elections to be.

It should be noted that while there was some overlap with responses on motives for participation, the prevailing responses here related to the importance of people's participation in the stabilisation of the country and the shaping of authorities. Common answers included:

> If you want your country to have a brighter future, you must participate in the important processes taking place in that country.
>
> —*Teghenik village, Kotayk Region*
>
> To go to vote is mandatory for the establishment of a state—an elected person should be thinking of the people and not of himself/herself.
>
> —*Halavar village, Lori Region*
>
> Elections are an important tool for creating faith in new authorities.
>
> —*Sassounik village, Aragatsotn Region*
>
> Elections are time when we the people are treated as humans.
>
> —*Achajur village, Tavush Region*
>
> Democratic elections are the basis of a democratic state.
>
> —*Halavar village, Lori Region*

Almost one-third of participants considered participation important due to their expectation of positive change and the solution of their problems.

> Our hope is that people's conditions can be improved, agricultural issues can be solved, and jobs can be created through elections, even though the situation is getting worse.
>
> —*Norashen village, Guegharkunik Region*
>
> We want to see people elected who will assist vulnerable groups—pensioners, mothers with three or more children, and single elderly persons.
>
> —*Ajapnyak community, Yerevan city*

Although the majority of participants were positive about participating in elections, at two meetings the participants claimed that elections in Armenia are 'useless' and 'pointless'.

> Elections are needed in this country only for international recognition—to tell the Council of Europe, 'See, we are holding elections'.
>
> —*Lernamerdz vilage, Armavir Region*
>
> Who said it's important? The elections will be held even without us!
>
> —*Karahunj village, Syunik Region*

11. See Annexure A-11.6 for details.

The Electoral Process

Factors Influencing Electoral Processes and Determining Choices

During discussions, participants pointed out several positive and negative factors and features that influenced their decision-making in the election process.[12] During the follow-up round, participants revisited the issue and, based on the recent experience of the May 12 parliamentary elections, completed the list of factors identified during the first round.

Positive Characteristics

The assessment showed that participants considered a candidate's personality more important than that candidate's specific policies. A list of features that positively affected choice of candidates is presented below. It was identified by residents of Urtzalanj village, Ararat region, but is typical for the majority of communities.

Positive Characteristics Determining Choice of Individual Candidates

- Decent, educated and knowledgeable person
- 'Benevolent'
- Person of both word and deed
- Puts public interests higher than his/her personal interests
- Socialises with the community and understands the villagers' pain and grief
- Respectable background
- Takes concrete action on behalf of the people
- Keep his/her promise
- Does not vote for MPs absent from the national assembly sessions
- Active in parliament
- Has authority in parliament

—Urtzalanj village, Ararat Region

During these discussions the animators asked additional questions to find out how participants formed their opinion about candidates, since in many communities participants insisted they do not meet the candidates (or meet them only once or twice) before elections. Despite the numerous questions posed, no clear answers were provided by the participants in any session. Among more common answers were: "Oh, you can just feel it" and "you can tell by just watching him/her."

It should be noted that as people formed their judgments—about an individual or a party—they attached great importance to work done for them or their community by the candidate/party (or their potential ability to do that work), including direct charity, road construction, etc.

Participants most frequently noted that the following factors positively affected their choice of political party:

12. See Annexure A-11.7 for a detailed list of factors by regions.

Positive Factors Determining Choice of a Party

- The party that has an educated and intelligent leader
- The political weight of the party
- The past experience of the party
- Active participation of the party in the work of the National Assembly
- The party's campaign trial

During a number of discussions, participants (especially women) attached importance to the social issues raised by the party leaders and candidates during the election campaign, the suggestions of the candidates on how to solve these issues, and the capacity of the candidates to solve these problems.

In seven cases, people mentioned that they did not trust the parties' campaigns and policies of individual candidates since they were mostly alike and unrealistic.

> They all make promises, but we know who can deliver and to what extent.
>
> —*Halavar village, Lori Region*

It should be mentioned that predictability of the authorities also influenced participants' choices. This is reflected in a comment made by a participant during discussions in Khachardzan village, Tavush region: "I'd rather be eaten by the wolf I saw" ("Better one-eyed that stone behind").

Negative Characteristics

The majority of participants mentioned 'being elected and forgetting the community' as the most significant factor negatively determining their choice of parties and candidates. In this regard, they also mentioned that elected MPs mostly behave in such a way, and in some cases do not visit the community at all—even during the election campaign; however, these candidates are still elected. In such cases the participants mentioned that they try to avoid electing the same 'bad' MP, cherishing hopes at every new election that the new MP will be better.

Other negative factors mentioned by the participants are the "dirty" criticism of a candidate by other candidates and a previously elected candidate's non-attendance at parliament.

In summary:

Negative Characteristics Determining the Choice of Candidates/Parties

- Broken promises
- Gaining the people's vote but then forgetting about them
- MPs turning their backs on the regions
- Not knowing the candidate
- Financial incentives and offers of electoral bribes
- Candidates who do not attend National Assembly sessions after election
- Bad attitude towards other candidates/parties
- Fail to compete in a civilised manner
- Make too many unrealistic promises

Although participants had clear ideas about factors that positively and negatively determine their choice of candidate/party, it was unclear how they actually assess these factors. It was also unclear whether they ultimately made their choice based on these factors or the directions given by community leaders or other persons enjoying informal authority—a factor that participants mentioned during individual interviews.

Sources of Information on Candidates and Electoral Processes

One goal of the discussions was to identify the main sources of information on candidates and electoral procedures. In this regard, television, electoral headquarters and "talks in the village centre", as well as information leaflets or campaigns were mentioned as the main sources of information.

In particular, residents of smaller villages and communities located far from the regional centre and Yerevan, especially those with access to a limited number of TV channels, complained about the obvious lack of information.

Participants also complained that due to their community's distance from the regional centre, there had been few visits from candidates/parties, and therefore they could not avail themselves of these sources of information. This neglect, even in the pre-election period, had caused strong grievances in several communities.

The table below shows data on the main sources and types of information as stated in Dprevank village, Aragatsotn Region—this is typical for the majority of communities:

Source of Information		*Type of Information*	
Candidates	*Parties*	*Candidates*	*Parties*
Television	Television	Policies	Campaign trails
Neighbours and friends in the community	Brochures	Biography/personality	Party history
Factsheets, booklets	Neighbours and friends Candidate's visit	Achievements	Capacity/ability Who represents the party

Evaluation of Elections

During the first round of discussions, participants were asked to evaluate past elections held in their community and, based on those evaluations, make predictions about the upcoming parliamentary elections in May. On the whole, the prevailing opinion during this round was that elections in their communities go on relatively well and fairly but that results are tampered with at the centre. Most participants expected the upcoming parliamentary elections to be better organised with greater participation from voters.

During the follow-up round of discussions held after the parliamentary elections, participants assessed the positive and negative aspects of the elections and compared these with their predictions.[13] Generally, an overwhelming majority of participants stated that the elections were much better organised.

The level of information provided and transparency on election day were also evaluated positively.

Positive Aspects of the 12 May, 2007 Parliamentary Elections According to Participants of the Follow-up Round of Discussions

General Comments

- The elections passed peacefully without conflicts
- There was no electoral fraud in the village
- Electoral fraud was relatively reduced
- Overall, the elections were fair
- There was an abundance of information available
- The presence of mass media on the election day
- The active participation of the people
- There was no intimidation or forced voting
- The election campaign was very well organised
- Transparency was at a high level
- "Dining and wining" was organised after the elections
- There was less direct pressure on people

Material and Tangible Benefits

- Inclusion of a number of rural infrastructure policies (roads, water mains, etc.) in government campaigns
- The road to the village was repaired for the election day
- The school building of the village underwent capital repair
- A drinking water supply system was built in the village
- Unprecedented benevolent funds distributed in the pre-election period
- Charitable work
- The candidate replaced the sewerage system of the whole apartment block
- Fences were erected around garbage bins

Procedures and Organisational Issues

- The election process was very well organised
- Showing the counting of ballots on TV was useful in terms of ensuring transparency
- Introduction of envelopes that ensured a secret ballot
- Furnishing of the polling station
- Training and certification of members of electoral commissions
- Voter lists were posted in a timely manner
- Reminders were delivered to the voters in a timely manner
- Residents were aware of electoral procedures
- Counting of votes was open—it was even televised
- Presence of observers from the beginning to end
- Work was well organised—issues raised by people were solved in advance
- People were informed about electoral procedures in advance
- Reminders helped since they somehow urged the villagers to go and vote.

Community members' main complaints about the elections related to the lack of provisions in electoral legislation to ensure votes for the sick and disabled. Another group of complaints was related to disappointment and neglect. A

13. See Annexure A-11.8 for a detailed list of evaluations of the May Parliamentary elections.

different issue that was raised and assessed negatively was the vast number of parties participating in the elections, which according to the participants considerably hampers the process of making a decision and casting a vote.

The Negative Aspects of the 12 May 2007 Parliamentary Elections According to the Participants of the Follow-up Round of Discussions

Procedures and Organisational Issues

- No mobile ballot boxes in communities
- Inaccuracies in voter lists
- Inadequate technical resources
- Poor condition of polling station steps which made it especially difficult for the elderly and disabled
- The polling station was very inappropriate
- Use of envelopes
- Queues
- The check-mark (V) had a restricting influence and caused several invalid ballot papers
- No provision enabling the ballot box to be taken to 'shepherds, the bedridden and disabled', thus they were not able to vote
- No provisions for those who were sick to cast a vote

Lack of Faith and Disappointment

- Yes, we do go and vote but there is no faith in the system
- Candidates mainly quarrelled for their post
- They solved no problems while serving as an MP
- The social problems of the village remain unsolved
- No improvements were made after the elections
- The elections were a mere formality
- There was no trust towards the parliament
- The village is small and has no serious role in the elections
- The one who had the most money was elected
- I do not believe in elections with bribes
- The candidates often make false promises

Neglect

- They forget about us after the elections
- Once they are elected, they forget where we live and the problems of out village
- After being elected, they haven't helped us with anything for five years
- Not all the candidates with a majority vote visited the community
- They remember the people neither before nor after the election

Abundance of Parties

- Parties were numerous—many were unknown
- Parties were too many—the list was too long and confusing for voting

Tension

- The residents of the village were subjected to threats and intimidation
- As a result of the elections, one part of the village opposed the other part
- The pre-election period generated social frustration

Issues Related to the Pre-Election Period

- The election campaign was organised poorly
- Lack of information
- Few visits of candidates and parties to the village
- Candidates offended one another during the election campaign

Post-election Developments

- They spent large amounts of money during elections and raised prices in the post-election period

Participation of Women and Youth

One specific topic addressed through discussions was 'participation of women and youth in electoral processes'. In several cases, separate meetings were held with women and young adults.

Participation of Women

The issue of women's participation in electoral processes was considered from the perspective of women as candidates and women as voters.

There were two attitudes towards women's participation in decision-making:

- In two-thirds of cases, participants welcomed women's entry into politics, considering it an opportunity for women to play a significant role in the solution of social issues.
- In other cases, participants objected to women's entry into political life, thinking a woman's place is in her family and that she should primarily care about her family.

As for women's participation in elections as voters, the majority of participants agreed that women are independent in making decisions and should actively participate in elections.

It should be mentioned that these opinions were shared by women and men alike, and no essential gender differences were observed.

Participation of Youth

A general concern raised by participants was that the country's youth is continuing to leave the country. During both rounds of discussions, participants noted that the majority of the community's young adults had left the village and many had even left the country.

Separate and joint discussions with young adults revealed that the majority of young people have low civic motivation. Although they participate in elections, they are mostly guided by the "for a friend's or relative's sake" principle and do not believe that public activism will make a difference. Consequently, they do not assume an active role in electoral processes.

In the majority of communities, participants stressed that young adults are 'indifferent' and explained this situation by the lack of job opportunities and the fact that they do not see their future as being in the village or country.

Suggestions

During meetings in both rounds, participants were asked to make suggestions about how to improve Armenia's electoral processes. It should be mentioned that the suggestions made during the first round were rather few and were primarily related to the following:

- Create the opportunity for people to vote at their place of residence (which may differ from their registered home).[14]
- Provide opportunities for the disabled and sick to vote at home.
- Create mechanisms to ensure regular meetings of elected representatives with their constituency.

During follow-up round meetings, participants came up with a long list of suggestions.[15] Below are suggestions from that round, grouped by beneficiaries:

Re: Voters

Voters should:

- Make informed decisions and vote for knowledgeable MPs who know the pain of the people
- Make decisions independently and not be influenced by electoral bribes
- Vote for "clean" and honest people
- Be aware that their future depends on elections
- Young voters should be brought up to realise the true value of their vote
- Never sell their vote

Re: Authorities

Suggestions Related to Electoral Processes and the National Assembly:

- Remove MP immunity
- 'Businessmen' should not have seats in the national assembly—only competent people who understand law and politics should have seats there
- Strict requirements should be developed for candidate registration so that no undeserving and illiterate person may have a seat in parliament
- Only one member of a family should have the right to be an MP
- Cut the salaries of MPs absent from national assembly sessions as there had been occasions when only 7 per cent of MPs were present in the session hall
- Political competition to be more civilised (at times very vulgar expressions were heard on TV)
- Reduce the number of parties via the Constitution
- The same candidates should be re-elected since, as the people say, "they have already had their fill and can now afford to think of the people rather than their pockets"
- To have a mobile ballot box to be taken to sick people and shepherds in the fields
- To extend voting hours by at least two hours so that those who in the fields or tending cattle in pastures can have sufficient time to vote
- To make MPs report on their activities on TV once a month
- To organise regular meetings with MPs

contd...

14. The procedure for residing in one place but registering in a different voter list in another community is in place (see Electoral Code, Article 10, Provision 3). This gap indicates the need for additional public awareness activities.
15. See Annexure A-11.9 for a detailed list of suggestions, by community and by region.

contd...

- More free time to be allocated to radio and TV broadcasts on the election campaign and elections.

Those elected:

- The elected must work in good conscience and keep their promises
- As a priority, candidates should understand the problems of village life and help to solve these
- Laws should be passed only after consultations with the relevant people/ beneficiaries

General suggestions:

- Respect the opinion of the people
- Ensure rule of law and implementation of "everyone is equal before the law"
- Eradicate corruption
- Support (rural) communities
- Provide loans
- Solve social issues in villages
- Provide more resources to the villages
- Give due attention to villages, especially those in mountainous and border areas
- Ensure enactment of laws and benefits for the disabled and pensioners—with a general change of attitude towards them
- Improve the economic situation of the people in order to reduce electoral bribes and electoral fraud
- Sums provided to MPs from the national budget should be reduced
- Ensure laws are enforced
- Instead of having so many MPs, use those resources to support socially vulnerable families

Annex A-11.1

List of the Participatory Assessment Communities
First Round: Pre-Election Period

Region	*Community*
Armavir	Araks
	Jrarat
	Lernagog
	Lernamerdz
Gegharkunik	Dzoravank
	Norashen
	Tsaghkunk
	Tsakkar
Syunik	Aravus
	Karahunj
	Shaki
	Vorotan
Tavush	Achajur
	Itsakar
	Movsesgegh
	Khachardzan
Aragatsotn	Dprevank
	Sasunik
	Hnaberd
	Melikgyugh
Vayots Dzor	Zedea
	Gnishik/Mozrov
	Vernashen
	Artabuynk
Shirak	Ani Avan
	Jajur
	Pokr Mantash
	Lernut
Ararat	Arevabuyr
	Getapnya
	Berdik
	Urtsalanj
Lori	Lernapat
	Sarahart
	Halavar
	Dzoragyugh
Kotayk	Arinj
	Marmarik
	Teghenik
	Artavaz-Pyunik
Yerevan	Ajapnyak
	Zeytun
	Shengavit
	Avan

Annex A-11.2

List of the Participatory Assessment Communities Follow-up Round: Post-Election Period

Region	*Community*
Armavir	Lernagog
	Lernamerdz
Gegharkunik	Norashen
	Tsaghkunk
Syunik	Aravus
	Karahunj
Tavush	Achajur
	Itsakar
Aragatsotn	Dprevank
	Sasunik
Vayots Dzor	Zedea
	Vernashen
Shirak	Jajur
	Lernut
Ararat	Getapnya
	Urtsalanj
Lori	Sarahart
	Halavar
Kotayk	Teghenik
	Artavaz-Pyunik
Yerevan	Ajapnyak
	Shengavit

Annex A-11.3

Profile of the Selected Rural Communities[16]

Region/ Community	Total Present Population (Persons)	Proportion of Females in Total Present Population (%)	Number of Total Present Households	Proportion of Households Receiving Family Allowance in Total Present Households (%)	Proportion of Refugees in Total Present Population (%)	Proportion of Disabled People in Total Present Population (%)	Proportion of Pensioners in Total Present Population (%)
1	2	3	4	5	6	7	8
Armavir							
Araks (Armavir)	1690	46.0	320	6.6	0.0	0.7	15.3
Lernagog	2164	52.2	550	20.4	3.7	3.3	5.3
Lernamerdz	480	47.5	189	3.7	0.4	2.1	12.1
Jrarat	3007	51.9	680	6.8	0.0	1.0	10.4
Aragatsotn							
Dprevank	110	32.7	314	1.0	100.0	1.8	47.3
Hnaberd	2041	49.3	50	58.0	0.0	0.4	11.4
Melikgyugh	1139	48.6	40	187.5	0.0	2.2	14.9
Verin sasunik	187	43.9	173	5.8	0.5	2.1	20.9
Ararart							
Arevabuyr	1090	46.4	182	22.0	1.7	1.5	10.1
Berdik	1010	50.2	256	6.3	0.0	2.3	8.4
Getapnya	1271	50.8	420	0.0	0.0	2.0	13.4

contd...

16. *Source:* RoA Community Databases created by UNDP in 2006

...contd...

1	2	3	4	5	6	7	8
Urtsalanj	217	53.9	60	25.0	0.0	5.1	1.4
Gegharkunik							
Tsakkar	2156	59.6	904	16.2	0.0	3.4	4.2
Tsaghkunk	1082	50.8	316	7.3	0.2	1.8	32.2
Dzoravank	226	62.8	72	26.4	50.9	3.5	35.4
Norashen	441	55.3	107	11.2	0.0	1.6	15.4
Lori							
Lernapat	2619	57.4	627	41.1	0.0	5.9	13.6
Halavar	126	52.4	83	7.2	3.2	12.7	28.6
Dzoragyugh	417	57.1	141	19.9	0.0	1.2	30.0
Sarahart	1533	53.6	401	56.9	0.0	1.2	13.2
Kotayk							
Arinj	5592	53.0	1600	8.5	0.8	5.9	15.8
Artavaz	1087	54.3	337	21.4	52.3	4.2	27.3
Teghenik	647	51.2	219	5.0	1.2	0.0	13.9
Marmarik	860	56.4	243	21.8	0.0	1.2	13.0
Shirak							
Ani avan	412	69.4	134	28.4	0.0	0.7	15.0
Lernut	150	54.7	38	23.7	8.0	2.0	17.3
Jajur	1074	49.8	244	32.8	0.0	1.5	17.7

contd...

...contd...

1	2	3	4	5	6	7	8
Pokr Mantash	2000	62.0	600	0.0	0.0	9.5	21.1
Vayots Dzor							
Artabuynk	1067	51.4	523	16.3	0.7	10.5	15.0
Gnishik	205	47.3	65	4.6	3.4	2.9	8.8
Zedea	197	55.3	46	37.0	100.0	4.1	8.6
Vernashen	1316	51.5	458	22.1	0.8	10.4	14.9
Tavush							
Achajur	3901	58.1	1161	23.7	0.7	8.8	19.5
Itsakar	330	51.2	113	65.5	0.0	5.2	26.4
Khachardzan	385	51.4	103	15.5	75.3	1.0	20.5
Movsesgegh	2389	52.9	210	59.5	0.0	4.0	40.3
Syunik							
Aravus	204	49.5	41	26.8	7.4	18.6	25.0
Shaki	1382	60.0	402	9.5	8.2	2.9	11.4
Vorotan/Goris/	177	87.0	81	43.2	24.9	8.5	19.2
Karahunj	1348	46.7	322	31.1	0.4	5.9	15.9

contd...

...contd...

Region/ Community	Proportion of Households having Three or more Children (Aged 0-16) in Total Present Households (%)	Proportion of Females in Total Present Population (%)	Proportion of People with University Education in Present Total Population (%)	How Frequently the Daily Press of the Republic is brought to the Community. (1-Every day, 2-Several times a Week, 3-Once a Week, 4-Several times a Month, 5-Not more than once a Month, 6-Not Brought)	How Frequently the Daily Press of the Region is brought to the Community. (1-Every day, 2-Several times a week, 3-Once a Week, 4-Several times a Month, 5-Not more than Once a Month, 6-Not Brought)	How many Television Channels the Community Population can Watch	Community Distance from Capital City (Km)	Community Distance from Regional Centre (Km)
1	9	10	11	12	13	14	15	16
Armavir								
Araks (Armavir)	11.5	27.0	3.2	2	6	20	50	8
Lernagog	1.2	43.2	13	4	4	20	75	25
Lernamerdz	5.8	6.3	5	6	6	2	35	35
Jrarat	0.6	11.8	17	2	5	21	40	40
Aragatsotn								
Dprevank	2.7	42.7	2	6	6	16	45	22
Hnaberd	7.1	0.0	8	4	3	3	79	60
Melikgyugh	20.2	54.4	42	6	6	2	80	50
Verin sasunik	3.7	38.5	15	2	1	20	15	5

contd...

...contd...

1	9	10	11	12	13	14	15	16
Ararart								
Arevabuyr	3.0	1.7	10		3	25	12	14
Berdik	2.6	1.4	30	2	3	15	35	7
Getapnya	3.1	37.0	2.3	2	1	12	0	33
Urtsalanj	5.1	27.6	8	6	6	2	100	70
Gegharkunik								
Tsakkar	16.9	25.5	7	1	2	8	107	30
Tsaghkunk	3.7	27.7	15	6	5	6	73	43
Dzoravank	4.4	13.3	3	6	5	2	140	130
Norashen	2.0	5.2	10	5	5	7	82	23
Lori								
Lernapat	1.2	3.9	7	2	3	2	110	15
Halavar	0.8	16.7	9	6	6	1	120	22
Dzoragyugh	2.2	24.0	4	2	2	3	150	33
Sarahart	2.2	1.7	2.9	2	2	5	107	29
Kotayk								
Arinj	2.1	8.0	8	3	5	25	3	45
Artavaz	8.4	18.4	10	4	4	2	69	24
Teghenik	2.0	12.4	20	6	6	25	37	26

contd...

...contd...

1	9	10	11	12	13	14	15	16
Marmarik	3.3	5.2	4	3	3	2	60	17
Shirak								
Ani avan		22.3	20	3	3	3	107	45
Lernut	8.0	17.3	15	4	4	1	150	20
Jajur	2.6	4.7	15	5	5	8	150	15
Pokr Mantash	7.4	40.5	6.2	3	3	10	110	47
Vayots Dzor								
Artabuynk	2.5	15.6	5	2	5	1	136	18
Gnishik	6.3	11.7	5	3	5	2	135	20
Zedea	11.2	8.1	2	4	5	3	139	20
Vernashen	2.8	17.2	47	1	5	5	124	4
Tavush								
Achajur	4.9	1.2	15	2	3	5	160	20
Itsakar	5.8	0.0	2	5	5	4	217	77
Khachardzan	7.0	0.0	3	3	4	2	129	30
Movsesgegh	0.8	2.7	20	6	3	1	225	85
Syunik								
Aravus	3.4	0.0	3.6	4	4	2	268	87
Shaki	4.1	11.3	27	1	3	7	204	98
Vorotan /Goris/	6.8	14.1	5	6	3	2	261	50
Karahunj	9.6	1.7	7	3	3	6	250	61

Annex A-11.4

Motives and Reasons for Voting Identified by Participants of First Round and Follow-up Round Discussions by Community and Region

Region/ Community	*Findings of First Round (Pre-election) Discussions*	*Additions made during Follow-up Round (Post-election) Discussions*
	Aragatsotn Region	
Dprevank	We believe that: • life will improve, and more attention will be paid to our village • the newly elected officials will pay great attention to our family with a refugee status • our demands will be met	We hope life will improve (1)[17]
	We listen, hoping that they will help us	We expect our money (bank deposits) back (2)
	We hope that what we have lost will somehow be compensated for	We hope there will be changes—that our social situation will improve (3)
	To improve people's lives, lifestyle and conditions, and to eradicate poverty	
	To perform my civic duty	
	We go to vote because we must go—without any expectations that problems will be solved	
	I trust there will be fair elections	
Sassunik	For the positive changes that occur during the electoral process, including expectation of improvements (1)	The community must voice their opinion—it must be taken into account
	Electoral bribe (2)	
	The request and demand of friends and relatives (2)	
	Expectation of improvement in social status (3)	
	The PR programmes and policies of candidates/parties (3)	
	Elections revive the community	
	Ararat Region	
Urtzalanj	We will perform our duty—we will vote—but no one remembers us (1)	We had expectations (2)
	We participate in elections because that day is different from all the other grey days	To elect the candidate we like
	Civic duty (3)	To see how elections are held
		For political change

contd...

17. The top three most frequently mentioned answers are ranked and indicated with numbers in brackets.

...contd...

Lernagog	To shape decent authorities (3)	We hope our situation will improve (1)
	To perform our civic duty	To vote for the person of my choice (2)
	Elections are a [public] holiday	
	Armavir Region	
	Expectation of reforms, i.e., positive change (1)	Forced participation
	Expectation of improvements in social situation (2)	
	To exercise my right to vote (3)	
	Sense of civic duty (3)	
	So that justice can triumph	
	My vote counts	
	To shape lawmaking authorities	
Lerna-merdz	It is our duty to participate (2)	By voting for the ruling party, we create the opportunity for them to solve the village's problems (1)
	To achieve justice (3)	I participated to be given money but I was not given any
	To see Armenia developed	
	To have a good parliament	
	Not to have my voice wasted/lost	
	To achieve peace	
	Guegharkunik Region	
Norashen	To perform our civic duty (1)	So that the situation improves (2)
	To shape a decent government (3)	So that no undeserving candidates get seats in the NA
	To exercise the right to vote	
	The need to support a certain candidate or party and enjoy their trust	
	To improve the country	
	To be involved in building the country	
	To have a decent representative in the national assembly	
	We hope life will get better	

contd...

...contd...

Tsagh-kunk	To improve the country (2)	To vote for my party (1)
	To perform our civic duty (3)	To support my acquaintances/relatives
	Great expectations from the newly elected national assembly	
	To shape the national assembly	
	Lori Region	
Halavar	To perform our civic duty	To replace the authorities (1)
	Hoping to head towards better days	So that candidates will somehow be useful to residents (2)
	The wish to build a 'correct' state due to their voting	Expecting that all have equal rights and responsibilities (3)
	For the improvement of the people's situation (especially for drinking water and the construction of a water reservoir)	To improve Armenia's life
	Expecting poverty reduction—that people will live in roofed housing	
	To have a good leader	
Sarahart	Hoping to head towards better days (1)	To be better-off in life in the future (3)
	To have a good leader (2)	So that the community has its own viewpoint and voices that opinion, demanding that it be reckoned with
	Sense of civic duty	The desire to eliminate inequality
	To improve people's situation	
	To reduce poverty	
	The desire to build a 'correct' state via voting	
	Kotayk Region	
Teghenik	To assist with the development of the country (1)	To vote for my party (3)
	Sense of civic duty (2)	We just do it
	To be in control of your 'voice'	

contd...

...contd...

Artavazd-Pyunik	To improve the country (1)	
	Sense of civic duty (2)	
	To have a decent candidate in the National Assembly (3)	
	The need to support a certain candidate or party and enjoy their trust	
	To gain trust	
	They hope it will be better	
	Tradition	
	Shirak Region	
Lernut	Expecting that their elected candidate will help their family (1)	At the request of a relative or friend (3)
	To perform their civic duty (2)	To exercise my right to freedom and prevent my vote from being given to someone else
	Expecting to see a free homeland and the burden of the people lifted	
	Hoping to head towards better days	
	Belief that there will be good changes made	
	To improve people's situation	
	With the hope that the situation of Armenia will improve, leading to improvements in the village and living conditions	
	To reduce extreme poverty so that people can live in good conditions	
Jajur	To protect our rights (1)	To perform our obligation—our civic duty (2)
	To change the future lifestyle of our children and grandchildren and to live better-off (3)	
	To vote fairly and impartially	

contd...

...contd...

	Syunik Region	
Aravus	The sense of civic duty (3)	Expectation to see positive changes (1)
	Expectation of improvement of the country	To prevent electoral fraud (2)
	Expectation of establishing a strong and just country	To vote for our candidate
	Expectation of good life	
	The desire to have a decent representative	
	The desire to have a decent parliament	
	For improvements in the village	
	So that someone else does not steal my vote	
Karahunj	To achieve justice (1)	
	It is a civic duty (2)	
	For the improvement of the state (3)	
	To be in control of my vote	
	For conscience's sake	
	Vayotz Dzor Region	
Zedea	Patriotism	So that their vote is not lost, and so that they vote for the people of their choice (1)
	Hope for a better future	Exercise of one's right to vote (2)
	Sense of civic duty	For someone's sake (relative/ friend/neighbour/village mayor) (3)
	Electoral bribe	To meet one another
	Because it is clear who to vote for	We just do it
	With the expectation of fair elections	
	Under pressure	
	"Out of spite" (to counter intimidation)	
Vernashen	For a bribe (2)	To prevent electoral fraud; so that their voice is not wasted (1)
	Connections (friends/relatives) (3)	Sense of civic duty
	Pressure, intimidation	By virtue of office/job
	Expectations for the future	Hoping the authorities will be replaced
	Personal interests	

contd...

...contd...

	Tavush Region	
Itsakar	Sense of civic duty (1)	Everyone went to vote, so I went too
	Exercise of the right to shape authorities (2)	To cross out everyone's name
	Desire to shape a just social country (3)	Not to have a Kharabaghi Armenian
	Desire to entrust the steering wheel of authority to competent people	
	Desire to establish a genuine democratic system in the country	
Achajur	Sense of civic duty (1)	To receive an electoral bribe (1)
	Being aware of the value of their vote; to have better authorities (3)	To win somebody's favour (2)
	Out of mere curiosity	
	To somehow influence the future of the state	
	Yerevan City	
Ajapnyak community	To improve the country's situation and create positive change	So that pensions will be raised (1)
	To perform their civic duty	To improve the social conditions of the needy—especially single elderly persons and disabled persons (2)
	So that societal programmes/projects will be initiated	For the laws to work; so that we are not 'robbed' (3)
	To have a worthy leader	So that the age structure of pensions will be reviewed and the pension age lowered
	To have a wealthy state	So that conditions in temporary accommodation 'dormitories' are improved
Shengavit community	With the hope of pensions being raised (2)	To use our vote so it is not manipulated (1)
	For a better future	Sense of civic duty
	To establish rule of law (3)	With good expectations
	To improve living conditions	

Annex A-11.5

Reasons for Not Voting Identified by Participants of First Round and Follow-up Round Discussions by Community and Region

Region/ Community	*Findings of First Round (Pre-election) Discussions*	*Additions Made during Follow-up Round (Post-election) Discussions*
	Aragatsotn Region	
Dprevank	They are frustrated/disappointed as nothing changes and their hopes are never realised	We have no expectation of change (1)
	Nothing has changed since the last elections despite promises made by candidates	There are no real results (2)
	Lack of trust towards government and MPs	No Armenian passport (3)
	My voice will not change anything	
Sassounik	Lack of faith (1)	Indifference (2)
	Lack of trust (3)	
	Lack of orientation	
	Disappointment: "Whoever we elect, the opposite happens"	
	Ararat Region	
Urtzalanj	Distrust (1)	False promises (3)
	The ex-MP was indifferent towards us after election (2)	Having no passport
	They do not expect elections to change anything	
	Social problems hinder—people have become indifferent	
	They do not believe in any of the numerous parties	
Getapnya	Distrust: nothing is going to change anyway (1)	Not being able to vote (2)
	Uninteresting (3)	Absent from the community
	Religious reasons: members of Jehovah's Witnesses	
	Armavir Region	
Lernagog	Lack of faith (1)	Disappointment (3)
	Everything is pre-determined: elections are a mere formality (2)	
	Ignoring the importance of their own vote	

contd...

...contd...

Lernamerdz	Everything is determined from "the top" (1)	Absent from the community (3)
	Being neglected: no one visits our village (2)	
	The indifference of the authorities	
	Disbelief that things will improve	
	Guegharkunik Region	
Norashen	Lack of faith (2)	Absent from the community due to working abroad (1)
	Illness, physical disability (3)	
	Distrust and indifference	
Tsaghkunk	Lack of trust and faith	Indifference (1)
	Have not applied for and do not have Armenian passport	Absent from the community (2)
	They have not had their Soviet passport replaced	Physical disability of elderly persons (3)
	Lori Region	
Halavar	Do not believe in the authorities and the promises made (1)	Our vote will not change anything (2)
	They do not trust	Elections are a formality (3)
	They consider the promises made to be false and unrealistic	Absent from the community
		Young adults are away from the community
Sarahart	Absent from the community due to work abroad (1)	
	Disbelief in the authorities (2)	
	They do not trust and do not believe in the promises made (3)	
	Unrealistic things are being said	
	Lack of jobs	
	Kotayk Region	
Teghenik	Technical reasons: illness, disability (1)	Absent from the community (2)
	Mistrust and lack of faith	Disappointment (3)
	Insufficient realisation of the importance of voting	
Artavazd-Pyunik	Have no passport and have not applied for one (1)	Absent from the country (2)
	They have not had their Soviet passport replaced (3)	

contd...

...contd...

	Shirak Region	
Lernut	Lack of trust and faith (3)	No previous results (1)
	I do not want to vote as no one will keep their promises	Absent from Armenia (2)
	Lack of prospects: poor villagers will be left buried under the burden of their worries and pains	
	Lack of jobs	
	Loss of faith	
Jajur	Lack of faith (1)	Elections are a mere formality (2)
	They think nothing will change (3)	Lack of civic duty
	People's indifference	
	Syunik Region	
Aravus	Lack of faith in elections (1)	Absent from the country (2)
Karahunj	Lack of faith	Absent from the country (1)
	Elections are a mere formality (2)	Those at "the top" decide everything anyway (3)
		Despair
		Previous promises were not kept
		It doesn't matter who will be elected
	Vayotz Dzor Region	
Zedea	Disappointment (1)	
	Electoral bribes (2)	
	Pressure (3)	
	Disorientation	
	Out of spite (to countering intimidation)	
Vernashen	Absent from the community (1)	
	Disappointment (2)	
	Disorientation (3)	
	Pressure	

contd...

...contd...

	Tavush Region	
Itsakar	Loss of faith in the authorities (1)	It doesn't matter whether we vote or not (3)
	Absent from place of registration (2)	Negative experience of previous elections
	Distrust in the electoral policies and campaigns presented by candidates and parties	
	Busy with agricultural work (in fields)	
	Uncertainty	
	Absolute illiteracy	
	Difficult weather conditions	
Achajur	"My voice won't decide anything anyway" (2)	Absent from the community due to working abroad (1)
	Arrogant position of some candidates: "I have already won"	Agricultural work (in fields) (3)
	Unable to make decision because of there being too many parties	
	Yerevan City	
Ajapnyak community	Constant disregard of voters (2)	Lack of prospects (1)
	Disappointment (3)	Lack of faith
	Lacking registration at place of residence	
	Candidates telling lies	
Shengavit community	They do not keep the promises they make (2)	Distrust and lack of faith—the one who was to be elected has already been elected—there's no use (1)
	There are no prospects (3)	Illness
	Lacking passport	

Annex A-11.6

Why Participation is Important (Reasons Identified by Participants of Follow-up Round Discussions by Region and Community)

Region/ Community	*Reasons and Substantiations*
	Aragatsotn Region
Dprevank	So that others do not use our vote
	To be able to protect our rights
	To create change for the better
	To have authorities replaced—so that candidates who actually care about the people come to power
	For the Armenian people to be well-provided for
Sassounik	[Elections] create an opportunity to shape new authorities
	[Elections] are an important tool to generate faith in new authorities
	To practise their constitutional rights
	[Elections] ensure stabilisation of the country
	Ararat Region
Urtzalanj	The participants had no comments on this issue
Getapnya	To prevent someone else from voting for me
	For "somebody's sake"
	To improve the next elections
	Armavir Region
Lernagog	To be recognised internationally
Lernamerdz	To have leaders who care about the people
	To make the people's voice heard
	To restore justice
	It's a 'matter of honour'
	Guegharkunik Region
Norashen	To improve the situation of the people, solve agricultural issues and create jobs (however, it gets increasingly worse in practice)
Tsaghkunk	To support a party
	To have your preferred MP in the National Assembly
	To shape good authorities

contd...

...contd...

	Lori Region
Halavar	To control your own vote
	To achieve justice
	To replace authorities so that Armenian intellectuals with Armenian mentality can come to power
	To amend laws so that they favour the people
	So that decent candidates are elected and human rights are not violated
	Voting is indispensable for the establishment of the state, but the elected person must care not about himself/herself but about the people
	It is a civic duty
	To shape the country's authorities
	So that reforms are made
	So that people can live comfortably and be better-off
	So that Armenia will have a higher position in the international 'arena'
	Democratic elections are the basis for a democratic state
Sarahart	To be better-off
	To ensure the importance of voting
	The people are the state
	Kotayk Region
Teghenik	To facilitate the improvement of the country
	To support a party
	To have good authorities
Artavazd-Pyunik	To have good leaders
	To have a good army
	To shape good authorities that pass good laws
	Shirak Region
Lernut	For changes to occur; for jobs to be created
	So that the country improves
	[Elections] bring a lively change to 'the routine'
	To prevent someone else from voting for me. Community members should have the same right to vote as residents of Yerevan
	To have a professional parliament, Prime Minister and President, so that laws passed by the parliament are actually implemented
Jajur	So that our voice is not wasted/lost
	To prevent someone else from voting for us
	To protect our rights

contd...

...contd...

	Vayotz Dzor Region
Zedea	To exercise the right to vote
	To vote for a preferred candidate or party
	With the prospect of solving social issues
	To have fair elections
Vernashen	So that the country becomes a [proper] country and the state becomes a [proper] state
	To prevent fraud
	To establish a voting culture
	Tavush Region
Itsakar	For the members of the Electoral Commission (because they get a salary)
	Elections do not matter; elections are false
	So that my voice is not lost and grabbed by someone else
Achajur	To prevent electoral fraud
	[Elections] are the only case when we the people are treated as humans
	To be in control of you own 'voice'
	Yerevan City
Ajapnyak community	To perform our civic duty
	To have a normal leader who will improve living conditions
	So that the law works
	To elect candidates who will assist vulnerable groups: pensioners, mothers having three or more children, and single elderly persons
	To have (state-owned) shops with affordable prices for the lower classes
	To have the issues of bank deposits regulated and the money returned
Shengavit community	To exercise our right to vote
	To improve the current situation
	To see our hopes realised (but this does not happen)
	So that some change occurs
	To have new jobs created for youth

Annex A-11.7

Factors Positively and Negatively Influencing Elections and Voters' Choices, by Region

Armavir Region	
Positive	*Negative*
The accomplishments of the candidates in the past	Bribery/Corruption
The record of candidates	Not keeping their promises
Inspiration of confidence	Clinging to their positions
Faith in the party or individual	Atmosphere of fear
Candidates' honesty; keeping his/her promise	Taking into account personalities rather than platforms
Candidate's integrity	
Candidate's informal authority	
Protecting people's interests	
Appearing as a defender of the country's independence	
Being intelligent	
Caring about the people	
Being an authority	
Guegharkunik Region	
The accomplishments of the candidates in the past	Bribery/Corruption
The record of candidates	Indifference of state officials to needs of the majority of people
Inspiration of confidence	Promises and projects not coming true
Trust towards a party or individual	Disgrace of political and state figures
Moral features of party leaders and candidates	Too much criticism of political and state figures
Ideas parties hold and advocate for	Attempts to boycott elections
Social projects presented by candidates	Ignoring smaller communities
Community development projects presented by candidates	Information vacuum
Experience in public administration	Rejection of healthy criticism
Being a good person	Caring only about themselves
Protecting interests of people	Cynicism
Not making false promises	
	Being unfamiliar with the activities of a candidate

contd...

...contd...

The will to eliminate monopoly	Making false promises
Ability of candidate or party to promote the development of the community	Turning up [in the community] only during the election campaign
Close links with people both prior to and after elections	Not working—not even being seen in the parliament
Being educated	
Aware of people's concerns	
Doesn't fall asleep in parliament	
Aware of rural residents' pain and concerns	
Ability to take people's voice to parliament	
Syunik Region	
Candidates' projects	Being a liar
Candidates' moral features	Being corrupt
Being loyal to national values	Not keeping their promises
Previous experience of protecting rights of people	Improper behaviour
Speaking the truth	Not turning up [in the community] after elections
Being a 'respectable person': looks, height, habits	Not dealing with the concerns of the village
Caring about rural residents	Not caring about the future generation
Understanding agriculture	Having a flattering tongue
Being independent from authorities and not being corrupt	
Being one of us	
Not engaging in business	
Being engaged in charity	
Past experience of project development in parliament	
The positive accomplishments of the candidate	
The informal authority of the people around the candidate	
Party's or candidate's record	
Possibilities to meet with a candidate regularly/frequently	
Position and weight of a candidate or party	
Work done for the village in the past	

contd...

...contd...

Being familiar with the village	
Successful and active election campaign	
Tavush Region	
Candidates making few but realistic promises	The fact that electoral commissions are not honest and biased and prone to corruption
Competent and experienced political figures and statesmen	Giving and taking bribes
Regular meetings of candidates with the voters of the community	An atmosphere of fear; works to the principle of "we can't be beaten"
Tactful behaviour of candidates and parties	Disinformation
Campaigns with provisions on tax privileges for border area regions	Rejection of sound critique
Campaigns with provisions on regulation of the Nagorno-Karabakh conflict	Protectionism
The experience of charitable activities	Political advertisements broadcast on TV too frequently
Honesty and patriotism of candidates	Too frequently organised public meetings
Election campaign that promises to provide job opportunities	Uncertainty
Support to counter emigration from the village	Subordinates public interests to private interests
Willingness to prefer public interests and the interests of the people over their personal interests	Disseminating political gossip
Realistic policies to alleviate the problems of border area regions	Pursuing solely party interests
Programmes to reinforce security in the border area regions	The unequal conditions for election campaign
Willingness to transport disabled voters to the polling stations	Improper behaviour of candidates and party representatives
Realistic election campaigns	Candidates and party representatives lacking professional background/education
Policy aimed at resolution of the Nagorno-Karabakh conflict	Political demagogy
The candidate to be interested in the village	Advocacy for utopian ideas
The candidate to prioritise national interests	Financial dependence on someone
Candidate or a party leader who is a popular person with good qualities	Information vacuum

contd...

...contd...

Candidate who makes investments for the community, including road construction, school renovation and improvement of the cultural sector and living conditions	Political defamation
Authorities that actively promote international recognition of the Genocide of Armenians	Priority of personal or clan interests
A candidate willing to restore "from sea to sea" Armenia	Absolute lying and not keeping promises—even denying having made them
Candidate who appears to be based on his/her deeds not promises	Excessive criticism of current authorities
	Makes promises but does not keep them/deceives
Aragatsotn Region	
The accomplishments of a person or a party	Promises that are not kept
Being concerned with problems of the village	Not caring about the village at all
Being a devoted and patriotic person	Not responding to applications
Personal connections (neighbours, relatives)	Not listening to people's voices
Position of the informal authorities of the village	Housing issues promised 20 years ago unsolved to this day
Promises and campaigns/policies	Being unemployed in the past
Long-standing activities	Leaving one party and joining another
Caring about people	Turning up only during the election campaign
Political experience	Not keeping their promises
Being an honest, educated and decent person	Looking at elections for their own sake: "they think only of themselves—to get elected and that's it"
Not offending others	Being corrupt
Respecting their word and being true to their word	Doing nothing but discrediting the authorities
Ability to change social situation of people	Remembering the village only during the election period
Caring about people	Making financial promises and distributing electoral bribes
Ability to regulate the issue of supplying gas to the community	Displaying a bad attitude towards other candidates
Candidate enjoys people's confidence	Leaving people alone in a difficult situation, not standing by people

contd...

...contd...

Good political background	Lavish, unrealistic promises
Understands people's pain and concerns	Considers elections to be a mere formality
Good attitude towards people, assisting them	
Vayotz Dzor Region	
Being recognised for their deeds	Bribery
A person who really deals with the problems of community members	Indifference towards village
Candidate to keep his/her promises made during the election campaign	Elected at previous elections but did not turn up even once
The record	Lack of opportunity to approach MP/party
Proper election campaign	Identical election campaigns/policies
A just person	Uncultured, lacks 'respectable' appearance
Someone who is known	Lack of feedback
Education, vision and intellect	Not being a local resident
Attitude towards people	
	Cannot present his/her thoughts properly
Commitment to village and his/her deeds	Similarity of election campaigns/policies
Patriotism	Promises that are not kept
The candidate to be active in law-making in the national assembly	Promises made that candidates know are impossible to keep
To be an upright person	Having no connection with the village
The laws he/she makes to be just and benevolent	Having no contact with people
	Being afraid of straightforward words and debate
Shirak Region	
Clever, educated, competent and active	Distributing electoral bribes
Popular person	Pressurise voters
Healthy, with appropriate looks for a leader	Hatred/disregard of candidates/parties towards each other, especially displayed on TV: "they discredit one another using street slang"
Has a national ideology	Promise "mountains" before elections but when elected forget everything
Patriotism	Is a bribe-taker, cares only about himself/herself
Political record	Lack of faith in them
Work experience	We see them only during the election period: they hold people in contempt

contd...

...contd...

Understanding the villagers' pain and concerns	They want to become an MP for themselves not for the people
Caring about people, respecting their people	They are liars
Thinking about the community	We do not know them
Enjoys confidence of the people	They remember the villages only on election day
Works well—is active in the national assembly sessions hall	Indifference towards community's concerns and problems: they remember about the existence of the village only at election time
Family connection	The political behaviour of the candidate/ party leader—always critical of present authorities and other candidates
Refuses bribes and combats corruption	They are striving for a position in authorities for their own business and for personal interests
Active and punctual, with a good political background	Offering electoral bribes, causing a negative attitude towards a candidate or party and altering people's positions
Understands people's pain and concerns	
Persistent in keeping his/her promises	
Lori Region	
They make promises and keep them	They make promises but fail to keep them
They are loyal to their ideas	They remember us only during the elections
They are trustworthy	They offer bribes
They are honest, intelligent and educated	They gossip rather than act
They are popular and they care about people	They think of their personal business and pockets
They have a sense of responsibility	They are 'mudslinging'
They are politically experienced	They fear losing their post
They are patriotic and follow universal ideas	They are fraudulent
Relatives (in Local Self-Governance elections)	They do not keep their promises
One of us—understands the people	They are bribe-takers/corrupt
They are already experienced in politics	"His one hand does not know what the other hand is doing"
They have already "had their fill"	They are weak in the political area
They are patriotic	They do not inspire confidence

contd...

...contd...

Their word carries weight	Electoral bribes
Their words and deeds correspond with each other	They "sell themselves" for a position
They raise villagers' issues in the national assembly	Fear of losing their position and money
Keep promises made to people	Lack of knowledge about the candidate's personality
Care about community	Financial promises and electoral bribes
Honest and educated	They promise positions to people who run the election campaign for them
Enjoys people's trust	They do not compete in a civilised manner
Is able to make proper laws for people, especially laws to reduce the land tax and the property tax	Getting the people's votes and forgetting about them
Makes investments for the community	Turn their back on the regions
Gives new life/breath to the village	Do not responsibly attend national assembly sessions after being elected
Has his/her policy, team, programmes and word	Too many unrealistic promises
Keeps promises made to people	Extreme polarisation in all economic sectors of Armenia
Cares about the community	
Sincere	
Good political background	
Sees to daily concerns	
Loves and cares for the people	
Makes commitments before people	
Considers residents' opinions	
Ararat Region	
Lives with the concerns of the villagers	Uneducated and contemptible
Frequent contact with people	Makes false promises
Able to get the people's voice to relevant levels of government	Disrespectful attitude towards the people
Adequate knowledge	A "toy" who can be manipulated
Not a "toy" in others' hands—is able, after being elected, to stand his/her ground and not be dictated to	Arrogant attitude towards villagers
Persists in solving the issues he/she raises	Abuses his/her position
Goes to national assembly to work, not to protect his/her possessions	Makes abundant promises

contd...

...contd.

Clean background	Distributes electoral bribes
A good person	
	Illiterate and disreputable criminal
Holds active meetings with people and the community to understand people's pain and concerns	
	Selfish
Clear campaign/policies	Someone who can be bought
Presents the people's voice at the National Assembly and supports them	A creep
Persistent in keeping his/her promises	
In a position to make investments in the community	
Creates jobs	
Subordinates his/her personal interests to those of the community	
Civilised and educated	
Benevolent	
Unblemished personal history	
Word and deed coincide	
Clearly understands of his/her mission	
Socialises with the community	
True to his/her word and deeds; does not make unnecessary promises	
Sets public interests higher than his/her personal ones	
A moral person	
Confident in his/her own strength	
The party's ideology and the people representing that party—no contemptible person or criminal should be in a proper party	
Actions in previous term of office	
Yerevan City	
Past record	Makes too many promises
Life experience/biography	Praise themselves too much and talk too much
Work experience	Slanders other candidates
Origin and family of the candidate	Posters too large
Moral outlook	No past actions

contd...

...contd...

Previous work done	Negative activities in the past
Patriotism	Giving bribes
Educated	Making unsubstantiated and pointless promises
Presents ideology	Bribe-givers (money, potatoes)
Benevolent	Makes false promises
Well known (personally)	Gambling in casinos
Honest, does not make false promises	Have made millions through dishonest means
Knowledgeable and educated candidate	Billionaires
Speaks well using facts (although we are not sure of that)	Those who grab what they can and are dishonest
People-orientated	Failing to keep the promises made
Strong conscience	No correspondence between words and deeds
Proves and substantiates their promises	Those who only care for themselves
Has had positive actions	Dishonesty via bribe-taking
He/she cares about the people	Destructive behaviour
Does not distribute bribes	Taking bribes
Creates jobs	Unreliable promises
Maintains justice	Nothing visibly good
Tackles problems of disabled persons and improves their situation	They say they have raised the pensions three times but they have only raised them by 500 drams
	We elect someone but in the end someone else appears to have been elected
	Candidates who only cares about their pocket
Kotayk Region	
Words and deeds coincide	Holds a post but fails to keep his promises
Inspires confidence by personal qualities	Revels in popularity
Represents the image of a true Armenian man with respective qualities and looks	Talking too much, defaming others
Stands out for their helpful actions for the people	Those who make unsubstantiated promises
The work achieved and their love for the nation	Politically short-sighted; emotional people
Meets with the people without bodyguards	A weak personality
Creates jobs in the village	One who can't speak well

contd...

...contd...

Encourages youth to stay in the village	One who makes false promises
Knows the villagers' pain and concerns	Electoral bribes
Takes the people's voice to the national assembly	Deceit
Maintains active contact with people after elections	Prioritising personal interests
Upright, honest—a man of his/her word	Criticising others too much
Caring for villagers' needs; understanding people's pain	Inactivity in the national assembly
A decent person or party	Abuse of immunity
Close relations with people before and after elections	Spending large sums of money
An individual with mature ideas	Unrealistic promises
Humane	Newly created parties
Patriotic	
Well-versed in the nation's history and culture	
Long standing membership in a party; familiar with activities of the national assembly	

Annex A-11.8

Suggestions and Considerations for Improvement of Elections (Follow-up Round Results by Community and Region)

Region/Community	*Suggestions and Considerations*
	Aragatsotn Region
Dprevank	"Clean" and honest persons should be elected
	The authorities should respect the opinion of the people
	The elected must work in good conscience and keep their promises
Sassounik	More resources should be provided to villages
	The issues of jobs and employment in the village should be solved
	Continue to improve voter lists
	Ararat Region
Urtzalanj	No suggestions and considerations
Getapnya	Create opportunities for those working overseas to participate in elections
	Restore elections in embassies and consulates
	Use a mobile ballot box to enable bedridden patients (not only those under in-patient treatment) to vote
	Include a special person in the electoral commission to help those vote who are unable to: the elderly persons, disabled persons, those with visual impairments, etc.
	Extend the election time at least by two more hours
	Members of electoral commissions should be locals—from the respective community
	Armavir Region
Lernagog	First of all, ensure rule of law and equality rights
	Solve the social problems of the village
Lernamerdz	The political will of "the top" is a primary condition for any improvements
	The public should become aware that their future depends on elections
	Youth should be brought up to realise the true value of their vote
	Guegharkunik Region
Norashen	Restrict the amount of promotional expenses
	Reduce the number of MPs
	Remove immunity of MPs
	To involve the sick and elderly in elections, use a mobile ballot box implementing strict control to exclude fraud
Tsaghkunk	Enable the elderly to participate in elections
	Lori Region

contd...

...contd...

Halavar	Be optimistic
	Not to give and take bribes; be just and hard-working
	The majority of the elected to be in control of their opinion
	Not to sell yourself
	Abolish corruption
Sarahart	Provide loans
	State assistance
	Jobs and employment to be created
	Kotayk Region
Teghenik	No suggestions and considerations
Artavazd-Pyunik	Businessmen should have no seats in the national assembly; competent people who understand law and politics should have seats instead
	Strict requirements should be developed for registering candidates so that no undeserving or illiterate person will have a seat in parliament
	Only one member of a family should have the right to be an MP
	Shirak Region
Lernut	Remove immunity of MPs
	Elect an intelligent parliament
	Create a paid and unpaid parliament
	Not to neglect the villages, especially those in remote and border areas
	To vote for knowledgeable MPs who know the pain of the people
	For voters to refuse bribes without hesitation
	People to make independent decisions and not be deceived by electoral bribes
	Eliminate injustice by joint efforts
	People to protect their rights
	Syunik Region
Aravus	Constitutionally reduce the number of parties
	The psychology of the nation should be changed
Karahunj	In the first place, candidates should understand the problems of the village and help to solve them
	Vayotz Dzor Region
Zedea	The same people to be re-elected, since, as the people say, "they have already had their fill and can afford to think of the people rather than of their pockets"
	They should pass laws after visiting villages in the border area
Vernashen	The number of parties should be reduced

contd...

...contd...

	The government should think of raising the living standards of the people
	To develop 'election culture'
	Tavush Region
Itsakar	Ensure access to broadcasts of the Public Television of Armenia in the villages
	To have a mobile ballot box to be taken to sick people and shepherds in the fields
	To extend the time to at least 10:00 pm so that those who go to the forest and those who take their cattle to the forest get sufficient time
Achajur	To make MPs report on their activities on TV once a month
	To organise meetings with the MPs on a regular basis
	Ensure enactment of laws and free of charge treatment for disabled persons and pensioners; attitude towards them should be changed
	Consider the voice of the public in such a way as to improve the situation of the people
	More free time to be allocated to radio and TV broadcasts for election campaign and elections
	To make enactment of laws stricter
	Develop a civil society
	Representatives of the criminal world should not to come to power
	Yerevan City
Ajapnyak community	Consider the voices of the people, especially of the aged
	Eliminate bribery
	Make laws stricter
	Eliminate age discrimination
	A revolution should be carried out
	MPs to report on their activities on TV once a month
	To organise meetings with the MPs
	Ensure enactment of laws
	Create civil society
Shengavit community	Improve the economic situation of the people, which will lead to reduction of electoral bribes and electoral fraud
	Actions need to be taken to raise the awareness of the people: if they realise the consequences of having MPs elected by bribes they will not do that
	Organising and holding elections should comply with European standards (which is not the case currently)

12

A Note on Concluding Remarks and Brief Policy Conclusions

Introduction

The literature on participation is burgeoning and replete with theoretical models, critical evaluation and valuable sharing of experience. And the literature also demonstrates that there are many questions regarding participation that agitate great minds. Indeed participatory development revolves around the fundamental questions about who participate, how they participate, when they participate, for whom do they participate, where and why they do so. And there is also the need to know what ultimately determines participation, that is, what is the motivation that drives the people to participate in different aspects of human endeavour. This book has provided clues to some of these critical questions and issues based on real life experiences in different places. While each chapter, barring Chapter 11, has its own conclusions and draws its own policy implications, in this chapter, especially broad cross cutting issues will be summarised.

The Learnings

The picture of participation that emerges from the analyses of the book is that people participate for a wide range of reasons, some for gains and rights that legitimately belong to them and some out of the higher human motives of sharing what "they (people) know" and we do not know. People participate in the hope that their participation can improve their lives, at least in the long run. The motivation for participation is spread over a wide spectrum, from altruistic to material gain, but none which is base or contemptible.

Participation takes various forms from information sharing (as in Chapters 5 and 6) to planning at the ground level as in Chapter 7. What kind of participation[1] actually materialises depends on the conditions obtaining at the ground level, on the nature of the event and on the way the facilitators of the processes harness the energy of the community members. Without going into

1. See Pimbert, M. and J. Pretty (1994) "Parks, People and Professionals: Putting "Participation" into Protected Area Management", *Discussion Paper No.* 57. Geneva: UNRISD, for kinds of participation.

the polemics of the meaning of various kinds of participation and at times classification of different forms of participation, it is clear that the kind of participation evident in different participatory exercises were also a function of the objectives of the respective participatory exercise. If the exercise related, for example, to conflict resolution in sharing natural resources, as in case of the Bharatpur Bird Sanctuary, India, discussed in Chapter 9, the community did not engage in interactive participation but in participation by information giving, whereas in the participatory poverty assessment, discussed in Chapter 7, a variety of interactive participation could be seen. Judged in that perspective, it seems inappropriate to place the different forms of participation in any form of "ladder" of importance or quality as is sometimes done.[2] The appropriateness of the kind of participation should always be judged against the backdrop of the nature and output expected, of the participatory sessions.

As to the questions of quality and decisiveness of participation are concerned, it varied across situations and issues. The percentage of non-active and non-decisive participants also varied. However in both cases, the reasons were not clearly apparent. The general impression one gets is that the men and women become active or passive participants depending on the subject matter under discussion. On the issue of locating the sources of conflict in natural resource allocation, as in Chapter 9, the men were more active and decisive as the livelihoods involved namely hauling *rickshaws*, agriculture and rearing bovine wealth, were mainly dominated by men, whereas when it came to issues of food security, as in Chapters 5 and 6, women were the more decisive and active participation. But in policy reviews, as in Chapters 10 and 11 there were no clear-cut dividing lines between men and women as active or decisive participants and vice versa; it varied from locations to locations. Many participants often felt that they did not have sufficient time to spare for participatory sessions for different reasons. Judged in that perspective, lack of time for the community members partake the nature of a barrier to participation.

The participation that was seen as forthcoming in the different exercises documented in the book was not born out of an autonomous process; all of it was the outcome of facilitated processes. Indeed the exercises demonstrate the critical fact that the first step in the development process (read social mobilisation) is organising the people. All major participatory processes that have left an indelible mark on the development scenario of Asia, ranging from the Grameen experiment in Bangladesh to grassroots planning in Kerala to SEWA in Gujarat have, by and large, been facilitated processes. That these

2. For example see J.P. de Campos Guimarães (2008). "Participatory Approaches to Rural Development and Rural Poverty Alleviation", *mimeograph*, ISS, The Hague, paper prepared for UNESCAP.

processes as facilitated processes provide strong evidence of the need, on the one part, to have local level animators and extension workers who would work with the communities to bring out the latent strength of communities and galvanise people into action and on the other part, to have champions, women and men, who have the vision and energy, to provide motivation and direction to people to embark on avenues that lead to increasing justice and prosperity. There is, thus, a need to create policy environment and development architecture that promotes the making of development operators over the whole spectrum from village-level animators to champions and allow them to flourish, once they arrive at the scene. Dr. Mohammad Yunus and Srimati Illa Bhatt are not mere accidents in the evolution of development paradigms of our times, but are the outcomes of the distinct antecedents in the history of their nations and the environment in which they attempted to achieve the greatest good of the greatest number.

While champions on the higher end of the spectrum of development actors cannot be created, the need to create the cutting edge level development actors like the local-level animators and extension workers, can not be over-emphasised. There has to be an infrastructure for developing local-level animators and extension workers, comprising of capacity development, system of appropriate incentives and rewards, as also institutional support. The success of the exercise indicated in the participatory exercises discussed in Chapters 10 and 11 can be attributed to the role that UNDP, Armenia played in training a cadre of animators and supporting them throughout the process. As is apparent that developing such cadres has a snowballing effect and remain a valuable resource for a considerable period of time; those animators developed for review of the PRSP Process (Chapter 10), were redeployed for the exercise of elections discussed in Chapter 11. The scheme in India of extension workers (in agriculture, horticulture and animal husbandry), including their respective prescribed incentive systems, require rehauling.

The motives behind participation and extent of true participation have also come out in bold relief in the book. Participation has also been forthcoming to inform policy makers on political and development policy-making. The experiences of Chapters 10 and 11 reveal that people are willing to give generously of their time and energy to improve policy-making and governance. Parties to a conflict repeatedly participate in participatory session to resolve conflicts where their livelihood is involved as in the case of Ghana Keolodeo Bird Sanctuary, Bharatpur, India discussed in Chapter 9. People participated in review of the PRSP and in electoral reforms in an emerging democracy, where the State was proactive in seeking public opinion through a genuinely participatory process, conducted under the aegis of the UNDP, Yerevan. Participation in these exercises, with no apparent material gain, brings into sharp focus that people participate in policy review and improvements in political processes when they have faith that their voices will be herd. This has serious policy implications. Once the Government steps in to seek people's voices, there should be in place an institutional mechanism for channelling such voices into policy-making. Lack of institutional mechanism hinders the flow of valuable data that can aid informed decision-making, notwithstanding the liberty available to powers that be to agree or decline the analysis provided by the people. Time and again it has been proved that people know if their voices have been listened to; listening *per se* is important; acting on them even more. Thus, while the facilitators must have the right attitude and exhibit the right behaviour, attitudes and behaviour of the powers that be need also to change and the attitudes and behaviour of the people must be managed to generate optimal results.

Similarly, participation has also been motivated by the concern for solving local problems such as the one seen in the participatory poverty assessment in Chapter 7, though the personal benefits may have been a motivation (even if weak) among participants, knowing as they did that the process will lead to local level planning that may bring them benefits, at least under the plethora of Government schemes in operation or that their views will have a bearing on decisions made at the relevant decisions makers with different levels of government and development agencies. The beneficiary status of the participants was not deliberately ascertained based on the principle of "Optimal Ignorance" and to prevent raising undue expectations that may not be ultimately fulfilled. Be that as it may, the exercise provides evidence that solving local problems for communal welfare is indeed a motivation for participation. As in case of participation for policy review discussed earlier, voices of the people must be hard as well when they have been sought in solving local problems.

Micro-elements are also important features in participation. It was found that the age of the participant, income of the households, ownership of land, occupational patterns, extent of landholding and political association are the factors that have bearing on participatory exercises discussed in this book. Younger people, especially among men, the relatively well-off and the combined group of men and women, have exhibited lower levels of interest in participating in almost all the participatory processes. The absence of younger males and preponderance of elderly people in the participatory processes, have implications in the sense that important perspectives do not always get reflected. There could be several good reasons for this, including the fact that younger men are hard pressed for time, breadwinners as they often are, while workplace and obligations within the households, do not always allow the younger women to be a part of the participatory processes as intensively as one would have wished to. There is also auto-elimination in some cases of the non-poor. While people belonging to higher levels of income do not always participate in participatory exercises, as they view such events as the affairs of poor, people belonging to higher income groups being often more powerful, facilitators also attempt to keep them away for separate participatory session.[3] Otherwise, the poor and disadvantaged people could be swamped by the elite groups or may not want to disclose facts fairly and fully as there could be a conflict, covert or otherwise, of interest. Similar could be the case for lower levels of participation of people who have better housing, belong to occupations that are deemed more prestigious and own large landholdings.

Some Concluding Remarks

For enlisting the participation at the meaningful level the following are needed as necessary, but not sufficient conditions:

(i) Awareness among the beneficiaries, current and potential, or participants of the fact that their opinions matter and their voices are important, both in development administration and in governance, at micro- as well as macro-levels, is critical.

(ii) There is the need to have a policy environment and development architecture promoting the making of development operators over the whole spectrum from village-level animators to champions and allow them to flourish.

(iii) True decentralisation of development administration, at least in the long run, and willingness on the part of those at the higher echelons of power to pay heed to needs, logic and views from the "bottom of the pyramid", in the interregnum where decentralisation can not be achieved in the short run.

(iv) Strengthening capacities of rural development administration in managing the participatory process for meaningful outcomes. Managing participatory process requires skilled or formally trained facilitators with the right attitudes and behaviour. It is not the happy hunting grounds of the charlatans and the quacks. Additionally there is a need to develop skills of facilitators (read local-level animators and extension workers) to manage the attitudes and behaviour of the participants, (call them beneficiaries of public or what you may), so that their implicit knowledge can be elicited.

(v) Development of institutional mechanisms for feeding the voices and views and will of the people into the relevant decision-making.

Readers will find many other interesting strands of thought and relevant questions to probe from the different chapters. But they will be left convinced

3. The non-poor and powerful people have been variously described in the development literature on participation such as gate-keepers, dominant and elite, the general consensus being that participatory session with them should be held separately, wherever possible.

of the power of the participatory methods and tools, and of the fact that these tools and methods can be extremely efficient in different contexts and different purposes. Development practitioners and administrators, students, scholars and researchers will find in these pages the many pitfalls to avoid and the rich leeway to make for, in carrying out participatory exercises and in interpreting the results.